Cognitive-Behavioral Therapy with Families

Cognitive-Behavioral Therapy with Families

Edited by

Norman Epstein, Ph.D.
Stephen E. Schlesinger, Ph.D.
Windy Dryden, Ph.D.

Brunner/Mazel, *Publishers* • New York

Library of Congress Cataloging-in-Publication Data

Cognitive-behavioral therapy with families/edited by Norman
   Epstein, Stephen E. Schlesinger, Windy Dryden.
      p.   cm.
      Includes bibliographies and index.
      ISBN 0-87630-503-6
      1. Family psychotherapy. 2. Cognitive therapy. I. Epstein,
   Norman. II. Schlesinger, Stephen E. III. Dryden, Windy.
   [DNLM: 1. Behavior Therapy—methods. 2. Cognition. 3. Family
   Therapy—methods.   WM 430.5.F2 C676]
   RC488.5.C63 1988   616.89'156—dc19   87-36809
   DNLM/DLC   CIP
   for Library of Congress

Published by
BRUNNER/MAZEL, INC.
19 Union Square
New York, New York 10003

10   9   8   7   6   5   4   3   2   1

For Carolyn, Marilyn, and Louise

Contents

Preface . . . .   *ix*

Contributors . . . .   *xi*

SECTION I
THEORY AND METHODS

1. Concepts and Methods of Cognitive-Behavioral Family
   Treatment   5
   Norman Epstein, Stephen E. Schlesinger, and Windy Dryden

2. Cognitive-Behavioral and Systems Models of Family Therapy:
   How Compatible Are They?   49
   Leigh A. Leslie

SECTION II
TREATMENTS FOR SPECIFIC FAMILY PROBLEMS

3. Cognitive-Behavioral Assessment and Treatment of
   Child Abuse   87
   Teru L. Morton, Craig T. Twentyman, and Sandra T. Azar

4. Cognitive-Behavioral Treatment of Physical Aggression in
   Marriage   118
   Ileana Arias and K. Daniel O'Leary

5. Cognitive-Behavioral Treatment of Remarried Families   151
   Leigh A. Leslie and Norman Epstein

6. A Cognitive-Behavioral Approach to the Treatment of Conduct
   Disorder Children and Adolescents 183
       Ray DiGiuseppe

7. Problems in Families of Older Adults 215
       Sara H. Qualls

8. Cognitive-Behavioral Approaches to Family Treatment of
   Addictions 254
       Stephen E. Schlesinger

9. Treating Depression and Suicidal Wishes Within the Family
   Context 292
       Richard C. Bedrosian

10. Cognitive-Behavioral Treatment of Adult Sexual Dysfunctions
    from a Family Perspective 325
        Susan R. Walen and Richard Perlmutter

11. Cognitive-Behavioral Family Therapy: Summary and
    Future Directions 361
        Norman Epstein, Stephen E. Schlesinger, and Windy Dryden

Name Index 367

Subject Index 375

Preface

This book focuses on an emerging approach to family therapy, the application of cognitive–behavioral principles to the understanding and treatment of family problems. Whereas these principles have been used widely in the treatment of individual difficulties and somewhat less broadly in the treatment of marital dysfunction, it is only recently that they have been applied in the treatment of families.

This book is intended primarily for the practicing clinician. Whereas it is not intended to serve as a treatment manual, each chapter describes the flow of cognitive–behavioral therapy and how the therapist thinks about the process of treatment.

In the first section of the book, Chapter 1 introduces the concepts of cognitive–behavioral family treatment, including basic assessment and treatment methods. Chapter 2 compares the cognitive–behavioral with systems approaches, the predominant paradigm in family therapy.

The second section of the book focuses on specific cognitive–behavioral treatment approaches with particular types of family problems. Although we did not try to be comprehensive in the selection of chapter topics, we tried to cover a range of problems family therapists are likely to see in everyday practice.

Each chapter in Section II focuses on a distinct family problem and is organized to present the following information:

1. A cognitive–behavioral view of the family problem.
2. Assessment of the problem.
3. Clinical techniques and strategies in its treatment.
4. Techniques used in joining with the family.
5. Special clinical issues in the family treatment of the problem.

Case examples are used to illustrate the principles and techniques as they are discussed. Each author discusses common clinical decisions to be anticipated in the treatment of special problems. Authors are clinicians whose contributions draw on their extensive clinical experience. Our goal is to provide readers with clinically relevant material that will convey the essence of cognitive–behavioral family treatment. We present this book to you in the belief that we meet this goal.

N.E.
S.E.S.
W.D.

Contributors

ILEANA ARIAS, Ph.D.
  Assistant Professor, Department of Psychology, University of Georgia, Athens, GA

SANDRA T. AZAR, Ph.D.
  Assistant Professor, Department of Psychology, Clark University, Worcester, MA

RICHARD C. BEDROSIAN, Ph.D.
  Director, Bedrosian Associates, Westborough and Leominster, MA

RAY DiGIUSEPPE, Ph.D.
  Director of Research and Training, Institute for Rational-Emotive Therapy, New York, NY; and Associate Professor, Department of Psychology, St. John's University, Jamaica, NY

WINDY DRYDEN, Ph.D.
  Senior Lecturer in Psychology, Goldsmiths' College, University of London, New Cross, London, England

NORMAN EPSTEIN, Ph.D.
  Associate Professor, Department of Family and Community Development, University of Maryland, College Park, MD

LEIGH A. LESLIE, Ph.D.
  Assistant Professor, Department of Family and Community Development, University of Maryland, College Park, MD

TERU L. MORTON, Ph.D.
Research Associate, Institute of Public Policy Studies, Vanderbilt University, Nashville, TN

K. DANIEL O'LEARY, Ph.D.
Professor, Department of Psychology, State University of New York at Stony Brook, Stony Brook, NY

RICHARD PERLMUTTER, M.D.
Director of Adult Outpatient Department, Sheppard and Enoch Pratt Hospital, Baltimore, MD

SARA H. QUALLS, Ph.D.
Assistant Professor, Department of Psychology, University of Colorado at Colorado Springs, Colorado Springs, CO

STEPHEN E. SCHLESINGER, Ph.D.
Clinical Psychologist, Veterans Administration Hospital, Hines, IL; and Assistant Professor, Department of Psychiatry, Loyola University School of Medicine, Maywood, IL

CRAIG T. TWENTYMAN, Ph.D.
Professor, Department of Psychology, University of Hawaii, Honolulu, HI

SUSAN R. WALEN, Ph.D.
Associate Professor, Towson State University, Towson, MD

Cognitive-Behavioral Therapy with Families

SECTION I

THEORY AND METHODS

1

Concepts and Methods of Cognitive–Behavioral Family Treatment

Norman Epstein, Stephen E. Schlesinger, and Windy Dryden

It is a basic premise of this book that in their complex interactions with one another the members of a family in most instances actively interpret and evaluate each other's behaviors, and that their emotional and behavioral responses to one another are influenced by these interpretations and evaluations. These cognitive mediation principles have their roots in the theory and practice of individual cognitive therapies (e.g., Beck, 1976; Ellis, 1962) which were subsequently applied to the treatment of marital dysfunction (Baucom & Lester, 1982; Dryden, 1985; Ellis, 1976; Epstein, 1982; Schlesinger & Epstein, 1986; Walen, DiGiuseppe, & Wessler, 1980). This book describes the extrapolation of these principles and techniques to the treatment of family dysfunction, outlining the increasing complexity of cognitions and behavioral interactions to be considered as the therapist moves from a focus on the individual to the couple to the family.

Although research has demonstrated that behaviorally oriented interventions have been successful with couples and families presenting with a wide range of problems (e.g., Falloon, Boyd, & McGill, 1984; Gordon & Davidson, 1981; Jacobson & Margolin, 1979), the important role of cognitive factors in determining relationship distress and in mediating behavior change increasingly has been recognized. Barton and Alexander (1981) proposed that family members' behaviors toward each other will change only if their views of themselves and each other change. Jacobson and Margolin (1979) stressed that establishment of a collaborative attitude in distressed spouses often is a prerequisite for efforts toward positive behavior change. In addition, a number of studies have indicated that, relative to nondistressed spouses, distressed spouses tend to discount positive acts by their partners, attributing these to unstable, transitory causes, but they attribute negative acts to spouse traits that are seen as unlikely to change (Baucom, Bell, & Duhe, 1982; Fincham, 1985; Fincham & O'Leary, 1983; Holtzworth-Munroe & Jacobson, 1985).

The use of global terms such as "distress" to describe the subjective states of family members tends to mask the variety of emotions that people in dysfunctional relationships experience. These can include one or more of a number of unpleasant emotions, such as anger, depression, anxiety, and jealousy. These varied emotions are likely to be linked to a variety of interpretations and evaluations the family members make of each other and the nature of their relationships.

Beck (1976) noted how particular emotions tend to be associated with particular perceptions that the individual has regarding life events, often in relation to other people. Depression tends to be associated with the perception that one has lost something significant from one's personal domain, anxiety with threats to one's well-being, and anger with the view that another person has inflicted (especially intentionally) pain, deprivation, or a diminution of one's self-esteem. In applying this formulation to the concept of distress in family relationships, we suggest that the particular combination of emotions that each family member feels regarding each other member is determined by the specific content of his or her perceptions of the nature and meaning of the interactions between the self and other person. Although there is ample evidence that spouses who are identified as distressed by their high scores on global self-report measures such as the Dyadic Adjustment Scale (Spanier, 1976) or by their presence in marital therapy exchange high frequencies of aversive behaviors, the experienced aversive quality of these exchanges is quite idiosyncratic. In fact, some clients remark that their most upsetting family interactions involve seemingly "trivial" events; yet further inquiry commonly uncovers very disturbing meanings that the family members have attached to these events, often regarding themes of lack of love, disrespect, and malicious intentions.

The particular content of an individual's perception of his or her interactions with other family members affects not only the quality and intensity of emotional distress, but also the individual's behavioral responses toward the other parties. Fincham, Beach, and Nelson (1987) found that the more that spouses view their partners' negative behaviors as blameworthy and due to negative intent and selfishness, the more upset they become and the stronger are their impulses to respond punitively. Fincham et al. note that the resulting emotional distress and punitive acts then can create an escalating chain reaction of negative interactions between the partners.

In the absence of longitudinal studies that would trace the development of distress in family relationships, it is not possible to determine from existing correlational studies whether family members' negative perceptions of one another cause dysfunctional behavioral interactions or whether the negative attributions and other cognitions develop in response to a history of distressing experiences with one's intimates. Fincham et al. (1987) also note that it may be that attributions are shaped initially by actual patterns of family interaction but that the cognitions then maintain or exacerbate these dysfunctional interactions. It is common for distressed family members selectively to notice behaviors that are consistent with the negative views they have of each other, just as depressed individuals attend selectively to negative life events (Beck, 1976; Beck, Rush, Shaw, & Emery, 1979; Epstein, 1985a). Consequently, although it will be important in the development of preventive efforts to understand the causal links between family members' negative cognitions and behavioral interactions, the fact that these become intertwined components of family relationships suggests that therapeutic interventions aimed at both internal cognitive events and external behavioral exchanges will modify dysfunctional interactions.

It should be noted that in contrast to Beck's model, the rational–emotive therapy (RET; Ellis, 1962) cognitive mediation view differentiates between perception or interpretation of an event and an evaluation of that perception or interpretation (Wessler & Wessler, 1980). In RET it is assumed that it is not what one perceives the facts to be in a situation but rather the degree to which one evaluates the events as positive or negative that determines one's emotional response. For example, an individual may perceive (accurately or inaccurately) criticism from his or her spouse. This person will become upset if being criticized by the spouse is evaluated in a negative rather than a positive or neutral manner. Ellis (1962) emphasized the association between extreme or irrational evaluations (e.g., "It is awful if . . .") and emotional upset. In this view, people become very upset and behave in a dysfunctional manner only when they view events as catastrophic or intolerable; otherwise their negative affect is moderated by more realistic evaluations of the unpleasant but tolerable effects of most aversive life events. Dryden (1985) noted the RET distinction between marital *dissatisfaction,* which results when an individual does not get enough of what he or she wants from the relationship, and marital *disturbance,* which consists of dysfunctional emotions (e.g., anger, depression) and behaviors (e.g., verbal attacks) when a person will not accept or tolerate the dissatisfactions.

In contrast, Beck's model (cf. Beck et al., 1979) proposes that much emotional upset and dysfunctional behavior is due directly to misperceptions and misinterpretations of events. Although a situation in fact may be positive, neutral, or mildly negative, an individual may distort his or her perception of reality and perceive the situation as negative (e.g., a depressed person may remember unpleasant daily events with a spouse selectively and ignore pleasant ones, thereby concluding "My marriage has *no* pleasure in it"). This distorted perception serves as the person's reality, and it elicits emotions and behavior comparable to those which one commonly sees among people who are experiencing such events in reality. One need not perceive an event as catastrophic or intolerable in order to find it distressing or unsatisfying, as do many people whose marital and family relationships are marked by conflict and alienation (Epstein, 1986b). Of course, if an individual also evaluates an event as catastrophic or intolerable, this is likely to increase negative affect as well.

Thus in this chapter we present a cognitive mediational model that draws most heavily on the work of Beck and his colleagues, but we also include the RET distinction between perception (or interpretation) and evaluation. Dysfunctional responses may follow from distorted perceptions and/or extreme evaluations of events. In this chapter we use the terms perception and interpretation on the one hand and evaluation on the other hand to denote the contributions to family problems of these two kinds of cognitive variables.

COGNITIVE MEDIATION IN THEORIES OF FAMILY DYSFUNCTION

The idea that family members' interpretations and evaluations of each other influence their emotional and behavioral responses to one another is a component of a wide variety of theoretical approaches to treating family problems, even though the ways of conceptualizing the nature of these cognitions and the means of modifying them differ from one orientation to another. In Barton and Alexander's (1981) *functional family therapy,* it is assumed that members of disturbed families tend to attribute their problems to negative traits (e.g., laziness, mental illness) in other members. Such views impede therapeutic change by suggesting the inevitability of the status quo, as do attributions regarding one's own inability to change. These "person" attributions are often inaccurate conceptualizations of factors influencing family problems, but they are applied routinely nevertheless and influence how family members behave toward one another. Barton and Alexander argue that these inaccurate and incomplete views of their own and others' thoughts, feelings, and behaviors leave family members with a limited sense of control over their life together. Thus any advantages of the sense of predictability that "person" or trait attributions offer the individual (Baucom, 1987) tend to be outweighed by their ineffectiveness in helping family members understand and influence their interactions.

The functional family therapist's goal is to provide the family members with new information that will impel them to new emotional and behavioral reactions in order to maintain cognitive consistency. The therapist repeatedly provides alternative attributional explanations that make the members question their views of themselves, each other, and their problems. This especially involves "relabeling," in which the therapist substitutes a more palatable explanation for the negative meanings family members attach to each other's behavior (e.g., a family member who is perceived as "controlling" could be relabeled as "very concerned and overresponsible"). It is assumed to be less important that the new labels be accurate than that they force a broader view of interactions, elicit more positive emotional responses among family members, and suggest greater potential for specific behavioral changes. Barton and Alexander (1981) propose that attributional shifts are necessary to change behaviors among family members, but also that in turn these cognitive changes are unlikely to persist unless therapists induce subsequent behavior changes that are consistent with the more positive attributions.

Similarly, in *structural family therapy* (Aponte & VanDeusen, 1981; Minuchin, 1974) and in *strategic family therapy* (e.g., Haley, 1976), it is assumed that when family members' behaviors are relabeled and thereby given new meanings, the nature of family interaction patterns changes to accommodate the new meanings. In these approaches, it is not as important that the new meanings reflect reality or that they promote insight as it is that they produce more functional interactions among family members. Thus the focus of these techniques is on process rather than on content.

In *psychodynamic* approaches to conceptualization and treatment of family dysfunction, on the other hand, insight into the meanings of behaviors is an end in itself, rather than a means to behavior change. Content is the primary focus for the therapist's attention. For example, the concept of projective identification (Greenspan & Mannino, 1974) posits that family members' perceptions of one another are biased and distorted by characteristics they project upon each other, based on denied, threatening aspects of the self and internalized representations of significant others formed in early (especially parental) relationships.

Sager's (1976) concept of the "marital contract" suggests that individuals enter a marital or other intimate relationship with a set of conscious and unconscious expectations regarding the costs and benefits to be exchanged by the involved parties. These expectations are derived from experiences in the family of origin, from basic personality traits and needs, and from exposure to a variety of other representations of relationships (e.g., in the mass media). Relationship distress (anger, depression) arises when the actual family interaction patterns violate the unstated expectations. Family members' emotional upset and negative behaviors toward those who do not meet their expectations are equivalent to those that one might expect if there had been a violation of an explicit agreement to conduct the relationship in a particular manner. Treatment, then, focuses either on an examination and alteration of unrealistic expectations individual partners may hold or on dysfunctional aspects of interactions between partners.

Cognitive–behavioral approaches to family treatment share with functional, structural, strategic, and psychodynamic orientations the assumption that meanings have an impact on family members' behaviors. There are important differences, however, between these and cognitive–behavioral approaches in terms of how cognitive processes are conceptualized and modified in treatment. These contrasts involve the explanations each approach offers of how family distress and disturbed interactions develop, the role of insight and reality testing in producing change, the focus of treatment on current or historical material, the determinants of perceptions that family members have of one another, the targets for treatment, and the role of the therapist. Table 1 outlines comparisons among the approaches in each of these areas.

COGNITIVE MEDIATION MODEL OF INDIVIDUAL FUNCTIONING

The cognitive mediation model applied to individuals posits that one's emotions and actions are mediated by specific cognitions. Understanding these cognitions makes it possible to identify factors that trigger and maintain the dysfunctional emotional and behavioral patterns which clients bring to treatment. For example, Beck et al. (1979) and Burns (1980) explored the cognitive roots of depression; Beck and Emery (1985) provided a cognitive

Table 1. Comparisons among Therapeutic Approaches

	Approach			
	Cognitive–Behavioral	Functional Family Therapy	Structural/Strategic	Psychodynamic
The role of meaning	Meanings have impact on behavior.	Meanings have impact on behavior.	Meanings have impact on behavior.	Meanings have impact on behavior.
Sources of problems	Problems arise from family members' distorted perceptions of each other and from dysfunctional behaviors among members.	Problems are distressing behaviors that serve legitimate interpersonal functions inefficiently.	Problems reflect the inadequacy of family interaction patterns in coping with stressors.	Problems reflect distorted perceptions based on individuals' internal processes.
Determinants of perceptions that family members have of one another	Perceptions and interactions have reciprocal impact. Perceptions are distorted by faulty processing of information *inputs*.	The pattern and structure of behavioral interactions are the main influences on perceptions.	The pattern and structure of behavioral interactions are the main influences on perceptions.	Perceptions influence the nature of interactions. Perceptions are distorted due to *projection* of personal characteristics onto other people.
Role of insight and reality testing	Insight and reality testing are necessary for effective change.	Insight and reality testing are not necessary for effective change.	Insight and reality testing are not necessary for effective change.	Insight and reality testing are necessary for effective change.
Temporal perspective	Therapy focuses primarily on the present.	Therapy focuses primarily on the present.	Therapy focuses exclusively on the present.	Therapy focuses primarily on the past.

(continued)

Table 1. *(continued)*

| | Approach | | | |
	Cognitive–Behavioral	Functional Family Therapy	Structural/Strategic	Psychodynamic
Focus of treatment	The synergistic relationship between cognitions and behaviors requires that both be targets of treatment.	Treatment focuses on altering the repetitive patterns of interaction that maintain symptoms. Altering meanings is a technique for achieving shifts in interaction patterns.	Treatment focuses on altering the repetitive patterns of interaction that maintain symptoms. Altering meanings is a technique for achieving shifts in interaction patterns.	Treatment focuses on uncovering individual unconscious material that impedes family functioning.
Role of the therapist	The therapist functions as a consultant as clients generate and either accept or reject new cognitions based on rational evaluation of evidence.	The therapist provides new meanings and prescribes behavioral changes.	The therapist provides new meanings and prescribes behavioral changes.	The therapist provides meaning for current events by interpreting parallels between them and unconscious (particularly historical) elements in individuals' lives.

perspective on anxiety disorders and phobias; Burns (1985) described the role of cognition in the establishment of intimate relationships; and Marlatt and Gordon (1985) emphasized cognitive factors in relation to addictive disorders. Others have discussed cognitive perspectives on loneliness (Young, 1981), agoraphobia (Coleman, 1981), and sexual dysfunction (Fox & Emery, 1981).

Figure 1–1 illustrates the basic cognitive model of individual functioning. This model posits that life events activate an individual's *schemata,* which are the longstanding and relatively stable basic assumptions that he or she holds about the way the world works and his or her place in it. Once triggered, these schemata shape the content of the individual's stream-of-consciousness thinking, which is comprised of *automatic thoughts.* The occurrence of automatic thoughts is often outside of a person's conscious control (e.g., frequently they appear as if by reflex and seem to have a life of their own). Often a person is not fully aware of them, particularly because frequently they appear in "shorthand" form rather than as fully articulated logical expressions. Although they involve untested inferences, they seem plausible, even though they may not be *accurate* representations of life events. For example, when a wife does not ask her husband's opinion before purchasing an item for their house, he may have the automatic thought "She doesn't care what I like." Although this interpretation *might* be accurate and is one of several plausible alternative explanations, the man assumes it *is* true. A person will tend to continue to believe automatic thoughts and reexperience them unless they are purposely challenged. In the absence of such systematic challenging, disconfirming life experiences likely will have minimal impact on the automatic thoughts.

One of the authors (SES) uses an analogy to illustrate the automatic thought phenomenon for clients. It goes something like this: "Imagine you have a small tape recorder in your mind. The recorder has an endless loop tape on it with a variety of messages about you and/or the events in your

LIFE EVENTS $\xrightarrow{\text{activate}}$ SCHEMATA $\xrightarrow{\text{shape}}$ AUTOMATIC THOUGHTS
(attributions)
(expectancies)
+
EMOTIONAL STATES
+
BEHAVIORS

Figure 1–1. Cognitive mediation model of individual functioning.

life. Every so often the tape recorder switches on, for reasons we cannot always explain. When it does, out comes a message. As we begin to consider what that message might be, we may find it difficult to identify it clearly. It is as if the volume on the imaginary recorder is still turned down. However, even though you may not be conscious of the message when the recorder starts, you are likely to be sensitive to it, and, just as likely, you accept it without question as if it were true, and you react accordingly."

Whereas the content of an automatic thought stems from its associated underlying schema, its logical form can be shaped by systematic *cognitive distortions*. These are errors in logical thinking which distort rational conclusions from either internal or external sources of data. This process changes an individual's perception of his or her immediate reality, and this changed perception then can become the object of further distortions. In our previous example of the man who jumped to the conclusion that his wife's failure to consult him indicated her lack of interest in his preference, this interpretation became his "reality." This potentially inaccurate inference then could lead to further distortion, such as "She *never* cares what I like."

Beck et al. (1979) described a number of common cognitive distortions. For example, *arbitrary inference* involves drawing a conclusion without adequate justification (i.e., jumping to conclusions), *personalization* is the unsupported perception that an event reflects upon oneself, *dichotomous thinking* paints the world as black or white, *selective attention* involves attending to one aspect of an event to the exclusion of others, and *emotional reasoning* equates subjective affective data with fact. Others include *overgeneralization, magnification,* and *minimization.*

The next step in the cognitive model of individual functioning involves *affective responses* and *behaviors*. Automatic thoughts, whether accurate or not, elicit emotions and behaviors that are consistent with them. These emotions and behaviors themselves are stimuli that can serve as the life events that trigger another cycle of cognitive processing.

One client's experience can be analyzed using this model. When Fran went to a party (life event), her belief that she must be accepted by others in order to be worthwhile (schema) triggered thoughts such as "I'm going to act like a jerk. I always act like a jerk around other people and no one likes me" (automatic thoughts with cognitive distortion of overgeneralization). She became increasingly anxious as the party progressed (emotional reaction) and gradually stopped participating in conversations (behavioral response). She interpreted her anxiety symptoms and withdrawal as evidence that she was truly "acting like a jerk" (further cognitive processing of her own emotional response) and thus exacerbated her anxiety.

The escalation in such an episode results from the cyclical nature of feedback loops. As the cycle continues, the emotional reaction builds and behavioral responses can be amplified. For example, Fran's anxiety became more prominent and her withdrawal more severe as her negative cognitions, emotions, and behaviors reciprocally intensified each other.

COGNITIVE MEDIATION MODEL OF DYADIC RELATIONSHIPS

A cognitive mediation model can be applied to dyadic relationships as well. It posits that cognitive processes influence 1) partners' views of each other generally, 2) the specific interpretations each makes of the other's behavior, and 3) their emotional and behavioral responses toward each other.

Social exchange theory (Thibaut & Kelley, 1959) describes how couples engage in a reciprocal exchange of reinforcing behaviors. The level of satisfaction of each member of a relationship is based on his or her ratio of positive to negative experiences with the partner. The cognitive mediation model adds to this conceptualization by stressing the subjectivity of those experiences.

Figure 1-2 depicts how cognitive processes mediate behavioral exchanges between spouses. The solid arrows in the figure depict behavioral exchanges between partners and the dotted arrows indicate internal processes within each partner. As Schlesinger and Epstein (1986) noted,

Interpersonally, each spouse's emotional and behavioral responses simultaneously *result from* his or her own cognitive appraisals of the

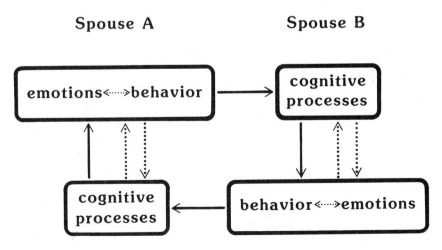

Figure 1-2. Cognitive mediation model of dyadic relationships.

partner's responses and, in turn, *serve as* stimuli that will be appraised by the partner. Intrapersonally, each partner's emotions, behaviors, and cognitions interact. A person appraises his or her own emotions and behaviors as well as those of a partner; in this process cognitions, emotions and behaviors can be altered independently of any interaction with the partner. (p. 138)

Partners' interpretations and evaluations of each other can be modified considerably by these internal feedback loops (broken arrows in Figure 1–2). What may originate as a minor distortion of the partner's behavior can become a major misperception as it undergoes sequential transformations in those loops. For example, when John does not respond when Judy addresses him (event), Judy perceives this as his being inconsiderate (automatic thought) and feels irritated (emotional response). Judy then notices that she is not as irritated as she was in the past (perception of own internal state) and thinks "I don't even react much to him any more. I must not love him as much. How terrible!" (another automatic thought, which includes an extreme negative evaluation). She then feels depressed (another emotional response). At this point she observes her "low" feelings (a further perception of her own internal state) and thinks "My feelings for him are dead. Maybe we should get divorced" (yet more automatic thoughts and major unsubstantiated conclusions) and withdraws from John (another behavior).

COGNITIVE MEDIATION MODEL OF FAMILY RELATIONSHIPS

The cognitive model as it applies to marital relationships can be expanded to understand family relationships. When other people are added to a dyadic relationship, the number of sources of external events increases as does the number of types of resulting cognitions. For each family member, there are at least three sources of external events: 1) each other family member's behaviors toward him or her, 2) the combined effects of several members' behaviors toward him or her (e.g., Mom accepts Tommy's choice of friends but Dad criticizes his buddies), and 3) observations that the individual makes about relationships among other family members (e.g., Jane notices that her brother and two sisters spend a lot of time together in leisure activities).

At least four types of cognitions may occur as family members appraise each other: 1) cognitions that each member has about himself or herself (as discussed earlier in the individual model), 2) cognitions that each has about the self in relation to each other family member (e.g., Jerry sees his talkative father as approachable and his quiet sister as unapproachable), 3) cognitions that each member has about relationships among subgroups of other family members (e.g., Jane interprets her observation that her siblings spend a lot of time together to mean that their relationship is "special"), and 4) cognitions that each has about the self in relation to a subgroup of other family members (e.g., Jane concludes that the close relationship her brother and two sisters have excludes her).

Family members have two types of behavioral response options available to them. They can respond to one other family member, and they can respond to subgroups of other family members. When the sources of stimuli, the types of cognitions, and the behavioral response options available to family members are all considered, it is evident that the number of possible points for the development of family dysfunction increases exponentially as the number of members increases.

ASSESSMENT OF FAMILY PROBLEMS

Although in clinical practice one does not conceptualize and assess cognitive and behavioral factors in family dysfunction separately, we present them separately here for the sake of clarity. We outline the relevant cognitive and behavioral factors that typically are targets in the assessment, and we describe methods of assessing each of these.

Cognitive Factors in Assessment

Three major types of cognitive factors are routinely considered in the assessment of family dysfunction. *Beliefs* each member has about the nature of relationships and individual functioning as a family member are analogous to the schemata in the basic cognitive model described earlier. *Attributions* family members make about the causes of the family's problems and *expectancies* they have about the likelihood that certain events will occur in the future under certain circumstances constitute the major types of automatic thoughts that are relevant in family interaction.

Beliefs about relationships serve as standards against which an individual evaluates the quality of family life. Among the important categories of beliefs are those concerning appropriate reciprocal roles (e.g., regarding distribution of authority and power among parents and their children) and qualities of good family interaction (e.g., regarding appropriate methods and levels of emotional expression). As these standards become more rigid or extreme, the probability increases that they will result in distress (Epstein & Eidelson, 1981).

For example, in one single-parent family, the mother believed that a parent–child relationship should be characterized primarily by an egalitarian friendship. A corollary of this belief was her belief that a person who punishes a child is a "bad" parent. She adhered to these beliefs in their extreme forms, choosing not to discipline her children at all. This approach periodically led to a building of the mother's frustration with her unruly children and subsequent incidents of child abuse. The abusive incidents made her feel guilty and reinforced her negative beliefs about punishment.

Beliefs can originate from a number of sources. Sometimes they are based on experiences in one's family of origin or other past relationships. On the one hand, an individual may emulate the relationships he or she found desirable in his or her own family, former romantic relationships, or friendships. Thus a person whose parents seemed inseparable and very happy may develop a belief that in a good relationship the partners should share in all of each other's interests and activities. On the other hand, an individual may set up standards to avoid what were perceived as *undesirable* aspects of past relationships. For example, a person who experienced turbulent arguments in a past relationship may develop a belief that a good relationship is free of any conflict. Other beliefs may be based on popular representations of family life in movies, books, songs, and other media. Still others may stem from attempts to emulate the relationships of others one admires.

When *expectancies* are accurate, they help family members predict likely outcomes of their interactions (Baucom, 1987). Such predictions are based in part on past experiences with other family members. Accurate predictions allow members to choose among available response options in order to maximize the chance for positive outcomes from their interactions with each other. In contrast, distorted expectancies can produce inappropriate responses. For example, the person who inaccurately expects a relative to "attack" him or her may choose a "preemptive strike" and thereby elicit an aggressive exchange where one would not have occurred otherwise. One possible outcome of such inappropriate responses is to create self-fulfilling prophecies.

Based on the beliefs a person holds about relationships in general and expectancies developed about particular relationships, the individual enters each interaction with family members with a set of preconceived notions about what ought to happen and what will "in fact" occur. There are several possible consequences of holding these sets of beliefs and expectancies. First, the individual uses them as a guide to behavior toward the other family members. Second, any discrepancy between a belief and an expectancy can be a source of distress for the individual. Third, these beliefs and expectancies can produce selective attention to salient aspects of family interaction. For example, the individual who believes that good family relationships require open and frequent communication among family members but who expects to meet resistance in this area from his relatives may focus on instances in which communication breaks down and may fail to notice instances of good communication.

Causal attributions are the inferences family members make regarding the determinants of their positive and negative interactions. They can serve several functions. Attributions help one understand one's intimates, predict events in one's relationships, and control outcomes in those relationships. In addition, by attributing positive outcomes to oneself and negative outcomes to other sources, one can bolster one's self-esteem (Baucom, 1987).

Studies of marital relationships (Baucom et al., 1982; Fincham & O'Leary, 1983; Holtzworth-Munroe & Jacobson, 1985) indicate that in comparison to nondistressed spouses, members of distressed marriages attribute negative partner behaviors to global, stable characteristics (i.e., traits) of the other person. In addition, distressed couples are more likely to attribute such behaviors to negative intent and lack of love on the part of their partners (Fincham, 1985; Pretzer, Fleming, & Epstein, 1983). In contrast, distressed spouses tend to discount their partners' positive behaviors by attributing them to specific, unstable causes. Taken together, these findings suggest that attributions may bias family members' perceptions of and emotional responses to one another.

Attributing relatives' behaviors to global, stable characteristics creates potential problems. For example, such attributions contribute to dichotomous thinking (i.e., the tendency to see a relative as all good or all bad) and may lead to hopelessness by portraying the causes of problems as unlikely to change. Attributions concerning a relative's negative intent or lack of love also can be problematic when they elicit anger or depression.

Not only can attributional biases exacerbate distress in family relationships, but they also can impede progress in treatment. By convincing family members that the relationship is unlikely to change, they create a sense that no therapeutic effort will be efficacious (Doherty, 1981). Also, when attributions contribute to anger, they can lead to withdrawal or attack, neither of which is compatible with conflict resolution.

Methods of Cognitive Assessment

Although some standardized measures have been developed for assessing cognitions in marital relationships, to date there is none in widespread use for assessing family relationships. Among the instruments for evaluating couples, Eidelson and Epstein's (1982) Relationship Belief Inventory (RBI) assesses potentially unrealistic beliefs that spouses hold about intimate relationships, and there have been several scales developed to assess biased attributions (e.g., Baucom, Sayers, & Duhe, 1985; Fincham & O'Leary, 1983; Pretzer et al., 1983).

In the absence of formal instruments for assessing families, the clinician must rely on informal assessment by means of the clinical interview and observations of beliefs, expectancies, and attributions spontaneously reported by family members during their interactions with one another. Interviews are by no means an inferior source of useful clinical data. Indeed, they offer the clinician more flexibility and range in gathering the cognitions that affect family functioning.

The interviewer can probe for family members' automatic thoughts (expectancies and attributions) by adapting the techniques described by Beck et al. (1979) for use in individual cognitive therapy. When a member reports an upsetting experience with a relative, the interviewer can inquire about the specific behavioral interaction that took place, as well as the accompanying mood state(s) and a detailed verbatim account of the attendant stream-of-consciousness thinking. Similarly, when the therapist notices a shift in mood or behavior during family therapy sessions, he or she can stop the proceedings and inquire about relevant associated cognitions. Finally, in the course of their interactions with relatives in the therapy sessions, family members may reveal their automatic thoughts without prompting by the therapist. Therapists must attend to such spontaneous statements because they can reflect the nature of family members' attributions and expectancies.

Inquiries by the interviewer in these areas take several forms. One might probe for attributions by asking questions such as "What do you think caused what just happened?" or "Why do you think he acted that way?" Expectancies might be investigated with questions such as "What do you think might happen if you did X?" or "Thinking back to what happened yesterday at home, how did you choose to do Y instead of Z?"

Beliefs can be identified through two major strategies. First, the interviewer can look for repetitive themes among a collection of a family member's automatic thoughts. Second, the interviewer can follow a line of questioning which probes the implications of successively elicited automatic thoughts. For example, after the first automatic thought is reported, the interviewer asks "If that were so, what would that mean?," and so on with each thought that follows until the content reflects a basic, broad assumption about family functioning.

Behavioral Factors in Assessment

A cognitive–behavioral approach to family problems is based on a premise that distress among family members stems not only from extreme or distorted appraisals of each other, but also from actual dysfunctional behavioral exchanges among the parties. The behavioral components of relationship dysfunction of interest within a cognitive–behavioral framework are those that traditionally have been the foci of behavioral marital and family therapists (Birchler & Spinks, 1980; Epstein & Williams, 1981; Falloon et al., 1984; Jacobson & Margolin, 1979; Liberman, Wheeler, deVisser, Kuehnel, & Kuehnel, 1980; O'Leary & Turkewitz, 1978; Patterson, 1975, 1976a; Stuart, 1980; Weiss, Hops, & Patterson, 1973). These include both behavioral deficits and excesses that impede family members' abilities to function as a unit for solving problems and meeting each other's needs.

Deficits in communication, assertiveness, problem-solving, and negotiation skills limit the extent to which family members can exchange information about their preferences, and these also are likely to impair the family's ability to resolve conflicts constructively. Excesses of aversive behaviors (e.g., criticism, threats, physical aggression) commonly occur at high rates in distressed family interactions, creating a "coercive system" (Patterson, 1976a) that often escalates and tends to block conflict resolution (Raush, Barry, Hertel, & Swain, 1974). Behavioral approaches to family treatment use a variety of procedures, based on learning theory, to build interpersonal skills and decrease the frequency of aversive exchanges among family members. The following is a description of the major behavioral excesses and deficits that have become foci of family assessment and intervention.

Communication skill deficits. The common complaint "we can't communicate" can represent a variety of problems in family interaction. Some family members use this statement to describe a history of actual misunderstandings that occur when they attempt to communicate with one another. In other words, the message that one person intends to send is not the message another family member receives. Gottman, Notarius, Gonso, and Markman (1976) described how such discrepancies between intent and impact can be caused by faulty expression of a message (e.g., failure to use accurate descriptions of emotions) or by factors that impede the recipient's ability to listen (e.g., formulating one's response to the other person rather than focusing on the details of what he or she is saying). Similarly, Falloon et al. (1984) identified communication deficits such as poverty of content, lack of specificity, contradictory verbal and nonverbal messages, and overgeneralized statements (e.g., "You always . . .") that detract from accurate exchange of information among family members.

It is important to assess whether an individual's failure to exhibit a particular communication behavior results from a skill deficit or a decision not to perform a behavior that exists in his or her repertoire. Failure to use a skill in interactions with one's family members (when one may choose to use it in relationships with people outside the family) may be due to cognitive factors described earlier. For example, an individual may choose not to express his or her feelings to other family members, based on a belief that loving kin should be able to read each other's minds about feelings and needs. Similarly, one may be inhibited from expressing ideas by an expectancy that such communication will be met with harsh reactions from other family members.

Excesses in communication and aversive behavior exchange. The phrase "We can't communicate" often means that family members understand each other's messages but do not like what they see and hear. Some excesses in communication such as intrusiveness (e.g., interrupting), invalidating another person's expression of thoughts or feelings (e.g., stating that the individual does not know what he or she is talking about), providing too much or redundant information, excessive questioning of another family member, and quibbling about details (Falloon et al., 1984; Thomas, 1977) not only block clear communication but also can alienate family members from one another.

The excessive discussion of negatives and the exchange of aversive behaviors such as criticism, threats, and physical violence tend to escalate family conflict (Falloon et al., 1984; Raush et al., 1974). Family members often reciprocate attempts to control each other's behavior through aversive means (Patterson, 1976a, 1976b). Not only do such exchanges block problem solving, but they also are likely to encourage distress (e.g., anger, depression) among family members. Behavioral approaches to the treatment of family problems commonly include the identification and modification of specific negative behaviors exchanged by family members. Because the escalation of aversiveness tends to result from reciprocal exchanges, the assessment of negatives includes attention to sequences rather than simple frequencies. For example, it is important to know not only that a father criticizes his son, but also that the son usually criticizes the father in return and the mother then tends to criticize the father for being too harsh.

Deficits in assertiveness skills. Assertiveness skills include the abilities to make requests of other family members, to refuse others' requests, and even to give and receive positives such as compliments. In contrast to submissive or inhibited behavior, assertion involves clear, direct expression of one's thoughts, feelings, and preferences. However, although assertion and aggression both involve expressiveness, assertion differs from aggression in terms of the former's lack of coerciveness (Epstein, 1981). Whereas an aggressive family member tends to use aversiveness (e.g., threats, criticism) to induce compliance from others, the assertive individual expresses preferences but is willing to take "no" as an answer.

Although increases in assertive communication have been associated with increases in marital satisfaction (Epstein, DeGiovanni, & Jayne-Lazarus, 1978; Epstein & Jackson, 1978), clinicians have stressed that enthusiasm for training in direct, open communication should be tempered by concern for potential negative effects of uncensored expression. Even when a family member's expressiveness is assertive rather than aggressive, the total sharing of certain sensitive information (e.g., regarding one's previous romantic relationships, fantasies of living without the stresses of raising one's children) may not be in the best interest of the involved parties. Similarly, one might choose not to assert a right or preference at a particular time when another family member's needs seem greater than one's own. Stuart (1980) reviewed research evidence indicating that uncontrolled expression can increase distress in close relationships, and he proposes the use of "measured honesty" in self-disclosure. Assertiveness deficits commonly cited in the literature involve verbal content (e.g., failure to make direct expressions of preference and "I" statements), paralinguistic variables (e.g., low voice volume, speech dysfluencies), and nonverbal behaviors (e.g., infrequent eye contact, lack of facial expressiveness). Evidence for the validity of particular paralinguistic and nonverbal behavioral indices of unassertiveness varies, but there is widespread support in the clinical literature for the idea that more than verbal content must be considered in assessing deficits in assertiveness skills (Epstein, 1981).

As is true with communication skills in general, deficits in assertive behavior may be due to cognitively mediated inhibition or to undeveloped skills.

Cognitive factors that can inhibit assertion include belief systems in which assertion is undesirable (e.g., "It is selfish to make requests of others") and negative expectancies (e.g., "If I am assertive with my father, he will punish me"). When family members exhibit assertiveness deficits, it is important to assess whether such cognitive factors play a role and whether relevant cognitions are accurate or distorted. When negative expectancies are accurate, treatment targets may then include the sequences of family interaction in which members provide negative consequences for another's assertive behavior.

Problem-solving and conflict resolution deficits. Family members face a variety of problems in their daily life together that range from the mundane to issues that threaten the integrity of the family unit. Whether a problem has been generated within the family or by forces outside it, solutions must be identified, decisions made, and resources mobilized. On the one hand, a lack of active problem solving can result in chronic conflict and distress. On the other hand, when the family fails to devise and implement effective strategies for coping with the disequilibrium caused by major stressors, a crisis can develop that may cause permanent damage to family members and their relationships with one another (McCubbin & Patterson, 1983).

Some families are resourceful in dealing with severe stresses, such as a schizophrenic member, whereas others exhibit significant problem-solving deficits (Falloon et al., 1984). Such deficits can involve the basic communication skills described earlier (e.g., expressive and listening skills), but others result from inadequate generation of solutions and coping strategies. Good basic communication skills tend to be prerequisites for problem solving, because they create a positive atmosphere in family relationships and foster accurate exchange of information. However, problem solving also involves identification of feasible solutions and the enactment of a specific plan to implement them (Epstein, 1985b; Falloon et al., 1984; Jacobson & Margolin, 1979). Stuart (1980) noted that not only must families have the ability to gather and exchange information about the nature of their problems and about potential solutions, but they also must have flexible yet clearly defined lines of authority for decision making. For example, if a family takes a fairly democratic approach to decision making by encouraging suggestions of potential solutions from all members, both children and adults, this allows them to draw upon the creativity and expertise of each individual. At times children may make significant contributions to solving a family problem by devising a feasible solution that appeals to the rest of the family. However, it still is important that the family have an established hierarchy of authority, usually with the parents comprising an "executive subsystem," as proposed by structural family therapists (e.g., Minuchin, 1974). Absence of such a hierarchy can produce confusion and conflict at times when the family must take organized action.

Stuart (1980) also describes how families who lack trust and tolerance for open expression of disagreement are likely to be inhibited, and therefore ineffective, in their problem-solving efforts. These factors appear to involve cognitive processes that inhibit behavioral problem-solving skills.

The specific behavioral components of problem solving that may be deficient in a particular family include 1) discussion about the nature of the problem, leading to consensus about its operational definition, 2) the generation of alternative solutions, without evaluation that could inhibit creativity, 3) systematic evaluation of the pros and cons of each potential solution, 4) selection by consensus of the solution, or combination of solutions, that seems most desirable and feasible, 5) the planning of specific steps each family member will carry out to implement the solution, and 6) evaluation of the results (Falloon et al., 1984; Stuart, 1980). Assessment of possible deficits in family problem solving should include attention to all these components, because difficulties with any of them would be likely to disrupt the entire process.

Deficits in negotiation skills. Family problem-solving efforts often necessitate some bargaining and compromise when there is a lack of consensus about the best solution to a problem. Even when family members have been able to communicate clearly and have generated a creative set of alternative solutions, they may have different preferences among the potential solutions. Unless disagreements are controlled, they can escalate into major conflicts that block problem solving.

Stuart (1980) stresses that conflict containment calls for adoption of a "win–win" orientation in which family members search for solutions that maximize mutual gain. Negotiation discussions also should focus on specific *issues* rather than on criticism of the *people* involved. Thus negotiation skills include substituting positive statements for criticism (e.g., regarding the solutions proposed by other family members) and proposing equitable solutions. The foregoing emphasis on equity in negotiation need not conflict with the goal of maintaining status and power differentials between parents and children, because equity can exist without equality (i.e, all parties can "win" without having to accrue identical gains).

Some family members may have negotiation skills in their behavioral repertoires, and may use them in other settings such as work but fail to apply them at home. When possible it is useful to obtain information about the manner in which family members negotiate with others outside the family, because this information can have important implications for the focus of treatment. A general lack of negotiation skills suggests that specific training should be pursued, but evidence of individuals' selective application of their skills indicates that factors blocking their use in the family should be explored and modified. On the one hand, it just never occurs to some people to use certain skills in their daily family life. On the other hand, other people make a choice not to negotiate because of a variety of cognitive factors, such as the expectancy "If I back down at all from my position, my kids will take full advantage of me" or the general belief that "Parents shouldn't have to negotiate with children." Thus family negotiation often will be facilitated by attention to members' cognitions about the process as well as by practice of constructive skills.

Methods of Behavioral Assessment

The behavioral component of family assessment focuses on the objective recording of discrete acts exchanged by family members. In general, a behavioral analysis of a presenting problem (e.g., an "out-of-control" child) includes specification of the behaviors associated with such a label (e.g., the child has tantrums, including yelling and throwing objects) and the behaviors of other family members that serve as antecedent stimuli and consequences for the problem behavior. Based on the assumption that the frequency with which a behavior occurs is influenced by environmental events, behavioral family assessment looks for ways in which other family members provide stimuli that elicit another's problematic behavior and reinforce it. In the example of the child's tantrums, systematic observation of family interactions may reveal that the tantrums occur mostly when the parents pay attention to the child's infant sibling, and that they result in the parents' spending time with their troublesome offspring. Knowledge of such contingencies helps the therapist plan interventions that are likely to decrease problematic behaviors by means of changes in environmental stimuli.

Such a "functional analysis" calls for the systematic observation and recording of concrete instances of behavior exhibited by family members. The therapist may be able to collect some of these data in the office by observing the family interacting either in an open-ended manner during therapy sessions or in structured tasks such as reaching a joint decision about how to spend some leisure time (Falloon et al., 1984). Additional data can be obtained from systematic interviews with family members, in which questions are asked regarding frequencies of particular behaviors exhibited by each person in the family and the associated behaviors of other members.

Another important source of information is logs of behavior recorded while the family is at home. Because therapists rarely have the luxury of collecting data in clients' homes, they often train family members to monitor and record their own behaviors. Such recordings tend to be structured logs rather than open-ended "journals." For example, if parents came into therapy complaining that their 10-year-old child "plays us one against the other," the therapist would help them translate this problem into discrete, observable behaviors (e.g., if one parent refuses the child's request, she goes to the other parent and makes the same request). The parents would be asked to keep logs of such specific acts as well as their specific responses to those behaviors.

Behavioral family therapists tend to take a more linear view of causality regarding family interactions than do most systems theory advocates (Goldenberg & Goldenberg, 1985), focusing on how one person's behavior is controlled by another's provision of reinforcement for it. However, behavioral approaches increasingly have attended to processes of mutual influence in family relationships. For example, Falloon et al. (1984) conduct a detailed functional analysis of any family member's problematic behavior, seeking data to determine not only what contingencies in the family increase and decrease it, but also how the problem handicaps the functioning of the family unit, and what positive and negative consequences would occur in the family interaction pattern if the behavior were ignored, reduced, or removed.

Falloon et al. assume that problem behaviors simultaneously serve positive and negative functions in a family, and their assessment of contingencies is intended to help them anticipate whether the removal of a behavior labeled as problematic also will prove to be aversive in some way to one or more family members. For example, in a family where a 20-year-old woman was unable to live independently of her parents because of her phobia of sharp objects, all members of the family identified advantages that would accrue if the fear response could be reduced. Furthermore, analysis of family interactions revealed that the problem was reinforced by the considerable amount of attention paid to it. However, the mother reported that she would miss her daughter's company very much if the daughter's problem improved enough for her to lead an independent life. The mother would be left alone with her alcoholic husband, who tended to blame their daughter for his drinking.

Thus removal of the problem would cause other problems for the family, and it is not surprising that more constructive behaviors on the daughter's part were not reinforced in the family. Based on this assessment, Falloon et al.'s treatment plan for the family included alcohol treatment for the father, exclusion of the daughter from the couple's discussions of their marital problems, family conversations not dealing with the daughter's fears, independent activities by the daughter, and family sessions to facilitate these plans.

In addition to performing a functional analysis of the complex reinforcement contingencies family members provide for one another, the therapist conducting a behavioral assessment commonly samples specific skills of individual family members and of the family as a group. Of interest are the communication, assertiveness, problem-solving, and negotiation skills described earlier. Although valuable information can be gained from asking family members to describe their own and each other's typical behaviors, these sources of data may be susceptible to bias. As noted earlier, members of distressed families often attend selectively to negative behaviors and may discount positive acts by other members. Because of the difficulty family members may have in being "participant–observers" of specific behaviors in their own interactions, it is important for the therapist to obtain firsthand observations whenever possible of family members attempting to use particular skills.

When relatively naturalistic samples of behavior are desired, the therapist or a trained coder can visit the home and use a behavioral coding system to record frequencies and sequences of responses among family members (Falloon et al., 1984). Similarly, Christensen (1979) describes how tape recorders placed in the home can be used to collect even random samples of family interaction, which can be coded at a later time.

However, when the assessment is intended to determine the extent to which family members possess specific skills, such as problem-solving skills that include particular behavioral components (e.g., brainstorming), often it is best to ask family members to work on solving a problem in the therapist's office and to evaluate the adequacy of their responses. Asking them to devise joint solutions both to a hypothetical problem provided by the therapist and to one of their own real problems may reveal whether they have some basic problem-solving skills but have special difficulty applying them with emotionally laden topics. Problem-solving skills can be rated objectively with coding systems such as that of Robin, Kent, O'Leary, Foster, and Prinz (1977).

Such structured tasks also can be used to test expressive, listening, assertiveness, and negotiation skills. For example, the therapist can set up role-play situations in which an adolescent makes requests of his or her parents and the parents' task is to refuse the requests as effectively as possible. The parents' responses then can be rated in terms of assertiveness criteria (e.g., Epstein, 1981).

A hallmark of behavioral assessment is that it is intimately tied to intervention. The purpose of identifying specific problematic behaviors and skill deficits is to define the components of families' presenting problems that can be modified by means of established treatment procedures. Assessment also is an ongoing process, as the therapist periodically checks for desired changes in targeted behaviors and revises the treatment procedures as needed if the intended impact has not occurred.

TREATMENT OF FAMILY PROBLEMS

Given the variety of cognitive and behavioral factors that can contribute to family problems, cognitive–behavioral family therapists tend to draw on a range of intervention techniques. Some of these approaches are predominantly behavioral in focus, whereas others involve cognitive restructuring. This distinction is not always a sharp one, because some interventions (e.g., communication training, problem-solving training) include both behavioral and cognitive components. It also is common for a therapist to use a behavioral intervention with the intent of producing cognitive change, or a cognitive intervention designed to induce behavior change. Although there have been debates about whether cognitive or behavioral changes are prerequisites for each other, it is possible that the causal process can operate in either direction. At present there have been no research studies completed that investigate the optimal sequencing of cognitive and behavioral interventions with clients, so the burden still falls on the therapist's clinical judgment.

We now describe the major cognitive and behavioral intervention techniques most commonly used in cognitive–behavioral treatment of families. Their separation into cognitive and behavioral categories is only for the sake of organized presentation, because in practice they are likely to be mixed and combined, depending on the therapist's assessment of each family's particular deficits and strengths. It is important to note that the interventions described here do not comprise a standard treatment "package." A cognitive–behavioral therapist who is working with a specific type of presenting problem may use some of these procedures but not others, and the choice of interventions is likely to vary from case to case even with the same basic type of problem. In the second section of this book, authors of each chapter describe their applications of cognitive–behavioral principles and procedures with specific family problems.

Cognitive Restructuring Procedures

Based on the premise that some dysfunctional emotional and behavioral responses family members have to each other are mediated by extreme or distorted cognitive processes, cognitive restructuring procedures have a goal of helping clients test the validity of their thoughts about family interactions. As in individual cognitive–behavioral therapy, it is important to help each family member become an astute observer of his or her own interpretations and evaluations of family events and to develop each individual's skills in collecting data bearing on the validity of these cognitions. Early in therapy, it is common for the therapist to present didactic materials ("minilectures," written handouts) to teach clients about this way of conceptualizing and treating family problems. For example, therapists frequently describe how interpretations and evaluations of interpersonal events influence one's responses to them, and they often describe the nature of automatic thoughts and broad underlying beliefs. Such presentations provide clients with both a preliminary education about the foci and procedures of this type of therapy and a rationale for participation in this treatment for their particular problems.

Whether testing the validity of family members' attributions, expectancies, or basic beliefs about their relationships, cognitive–behavioral therapists tend to use a Socratic, collaborative approach in working with their clients. It is assumed that cognitive change is more likely to occur when the individual "discovers" inaccuracies in his or her own thought processes rather than having a therapist argue that an automatic thought or underlying belief is distorted. Consequently, the basic message that the therapist gives the clients is "Let's take a close look together at your thoughts about the events in your family and see which ones are accurate and which are not." This process can be described as similar to the work of a team of scientists who are testing the family members' hypotheses about the nature of their family life.

Not only does this collaborative approach help reduce clients' resistance to examination of their very personal subjective experiences, but it also aids in the development of their own cognitive restructuring skills. An important goal of cognitive–behavioral therapy is to teach clients specific skills that they can apply on their own in the future to prevent or reduce family conflict. Consequently, the therapist tends to give them as much practice as possible in applying the skills without directing them to view events and cognitions in a particular way. For example, rather than suggesting how a person must have interpreted another family member's behavior, the therapist asks a series of fairly open-ended questions (e.g., "When she did that, what was the first thing that came into your mind?" "If that were so, what would that mean?" "What do you imagine that might lead to?").

Thus a cognitive–behavioral approach to family treatment is didactic, often Socratic, oriented toward skill training, and focused on reality testing of the thought processes that influence family interactions. These principles are similar to those used in individual therapy, but their application with family systems involves a number of additional concepts and procedures.

First, the ongoing interpersonal feedback loops we described earlier provide each family member continuous "data" that can actually strengthen a distorted cognition. For example, a person who expects that disagreeing with other family members is highly likely to elicit their hostility may be inhibited from expressing himself or herself but finally may become so frustrated that he or she voices an opinion in a sarcastic manner. This behavior then elicits the hostile reactions that the person feared, thereby strengthening the expectancy. Similarly, family members may hold the same unrealistic beliefs and "validate" each other's thinking through consensus. For example, if both parents believe that their children should be "protected" from exposure to the unpleasant aspects of life, when one parent has been diagnosed as terminally ill and is considering telling the children about it, feedback from the other parent may strengthen his or her resolve not to share such stressful information.

To counteract the feedback loops that reinforce dysfunctional thinking, it is most helpful to work conjointly with the family members who affect and are affected by a presenting problem. The therapist then can "track" the ongoing interactions and identify the sources of feedback that may strengthen a member's negative expectancy, attribution, or belief. This allows interventions whereby the therapist helps the individual examine how he or she actually produced a self-fulfilling prophecy by eliciting negative responses from other family members. It also provides a setting in which the therapist can guide the whole family in examining the validity and consequences of particular beliefs that they share about family life.

Conjoint treatment often provides a "laboratory" in which family members can provide each other with information that will challenge distorted thinking. Using a Socratic approach, the therapist can encourage each family member to seek information from the others that may be consistent or inconsistent with a particular cognition. For example, when parents set a curfew for their adolescent son he may interpret this to mean that they have no confidence in him. The parents may be able to describe many other ways in which they have demonstrated their confidence in him but also state clearly that they consider it their right and responsibility as parents to set certain limits for their children.

Methods for modifying distorted automatic thoughts. Family members' automatic thoughts about each other, themselves, and their interactions are tested for their validity by means of two major methods: logical analysis and the collection of relevant data. In logical analysis, the therapist poses the basic question "Does this way of thinking make sense?," particularly to challenge arbitrary inferences involved in clients' negative attributions and expectancies. For example, when a wife laughs about the clothes her husband selects to wear to a social event and his automatic thoughts include the attribution "She thinks I'm stupid," the therapist can ask him to consider whether his inference about her view of him is a logical one. An extension of this approach is to coach the person in searching for possible alternative explanations for an event. In this example, the husband would be asked what else his wife's laughter might have represented. Although the client is encouraged to conduct the logical analysis as much as possible on his or her own, the therapist can introduce additional ideas when the client is having difficulty.

The "decatastrophizing" of extreme negative expectancies also involves logical analysis. For example, if the therapist elicits a wife's fantasies of the worst possible outcome of her career and uncovers the expectancy "If I assert myself about my career goals, my husband will leave me," the logic of this inference can be examined. The wife may be able to distinguish between logical predictions (e.g., that the couple will have some disagreements and even some arguments) and those that seem improbable (that her husband would end their marriage over this issue). Of course, logical analysis must be conducted in the context of actual available data bearing on attributions and expectancies. In this example, there may be evidence that the husband would be likely to leave his wife if she exceeded certain limits in pursuing her own goals.

There are several sources of data for testing the validity of family members' thoughts. First, the therapist can ask a family member to describe past experiences that provide information about his or her current automatic thoughts. A father who thinks "My son won't love and respect me if I don't buy him the things he wants" may be able to recount past incidents when he refused his son's requests, tolerated his son's temporary rebuff, and subsequently received expressions of caring from his son. Such memories can weaken a person's belief in an automatic thought. A second source of data involves logs or diaries family members are instructed to keep regarding their interactions at home. Over time, the records of patterns and variations in family members' responses to one another serve as data that can contradict or support particular attributions and expectancies. Negative trait attributions (e.g., "She's a selfish child") can be challenged by evidence that the labeled member in fact acts in selfish ways at times but is generous and giving at other times.

As described earlier, conjoint sessions can be an important source of data for testing the validity of automatic thoughts. Family members can give an individual direct feedback challenging an inference which that person made about the others' intentions, attitudes, or feelings. Also, the therapist can "stop the action," interrupting an interaction sequence and guiding the family in examining whether the sequence unfolded as they initially perceived it. For example, as one family entered the therapy room, the parents announced about their teenage daughter "Wait until you see Susan in action today! She's looking for a fight." Then, as Susan entered the room last, her brother teased her and her sister commented about her "sour look." When Susan subsequently slammed the door and kicked her sister's foot, the whole family yelled at her, and her mother said to the therapist "See what I mean?"

The therapist announced that he thought it was important for the family to take a close look at how the fight developed. When he asked each member about his or her perception, all but Susan had the memory that she had started the trouble by slamming the door and kicking her sister. The therapist then replayed the videotape of the family's entrance into the room (he was fortunate in having started the recorder before they entered) and asked the family members what they saw. Initially some only saw Susan's negative behavior, but others then pointed out how their sarcastic comments and teasing seemed to elicit Susan's responses. This led to a discussion of how family members often overlook their contributions to each other's negative actions, and how each person might be able to decrease negative exchanges by changing his or her own behavior. The data provided in this session counteracted family members' tendencies to attribute a trait of "bitchiness" to Susan, and it began to shift them toward seeing mutual causality in the sequences of their interactions.

"Behavioral experiments" are another important source of data for testing automatic thoughts. Instead of relying on naturally occurring past or present events for evidence, the therapist and family can devise plans for one or more members to behave in particular ways and then observe the outcome. For example, if parents label their daughter "irresponsible" and expect that she will not do her chores around the house if allowed to schedule her own weekend time, family members may agree together to set up an experiment. The daughter may agree in writing to complete a list of chores by her own schedule during the weekend, and the parents may agree to remove their restrictions on their daughter's time for socializing with her friends. The parents and daughter are instructed to monitor the outcome of the experiment and report about it to the therapist at the next session. The data may indicate that the daughter is able to combine chores and socializing and can act in a responsible manner. However, if she did not do her chores, it is important for the therapist to help the family identify where the plan broke down and to devise a revised experiment with different conditions. For example, the daughter may be expected to present her preplanned schedule for the weekend chores and social time before the agreement is signed. It is crucial that the family not conclude from the daughter's initial failure that she does have a trait of "irresponsibility." The therapist should help them set up further behavioral experiments to demonstrate that her behavior is situation-specific and can be influenced by what other family members do. Behavioral experiments can be conducted both in therapy sessions and at home.

Methods for modifying basic beliefs. Because an individual's basic beliefs about personal and family functioning usually are longstanding and part of his or her basic worldview, it is likely to take considerable evidence to modify these assumptions. Furthermore, as described earlier, a person's unrealistic beliefs may be reinforced by feedback and consensus within the family. Nevertheless, cognitive theory (e.g., Beck et al., 1979) suggests that these assumptions are the basis from which dysfunctional automatic thoughts, emotional responses, and behaviors are derived, and that individuals will remain vulnerable to future intra- and interpersonal problems if these "schemata" are not modified in therapy. Recent research evidence (e.g., Rush & Weissenburger, 1986) indicates that people who recovered from depression but whose basic assumptions had not been modified were more likely to relapse. Although parallel work has not yet been conducted with family problems, cognitive–behavioral family therapists have considered the modification of extreme, unrealistic, or irrational beliefs to be a major focus of treatment.

Evidence for the validity of a belief can be examined with many of the same methods used in testing automatic thoughts: logical analysis, review of past and current experiences that are consistent or inconsistent with the belief, and use of behavioral experiments to determine the conditions under which the belief holds true. In addition, the family can gather information from observation of how other families function. Some of the common myths about close relationships portrayed in the media can be counteracted with carefully chosen bibliotherapy. For example, couples who are experiencing problems in their sexual relationships can benefit from works such as those by Barbach (1976) and Zilbergeld (1978), which provide accurate information about the range of normal sexual functioning and dispel anxiety-eliciting myths about "good" sexual performance. Similarly, there are popular books on topics such as divorce (e.g., Gardner, 1977) and stepfamilies (e.g., Berman, 1980) that can challenge unrealistic beliefs.

Another important method of modifying dysfunctional beliefs that is similar to procedures used in individual cognitive therapy (Beck et al., 1979) is collaboration with the family in listing and evaluating the advantages and disadvantages of believing and acting upon a particular belief. It is most helpful for the therapist and family to "brainstorm" all possible advantages and disadvantages they can think of for the belief, and to list these in writing. The therapist should stress to the family that there certainly are advantages even with a belief that is a cause of family problems, and that it is these advantages that have motivated them to live by it. Once the family has identified the most compelling advantages and disadvantages of a belief, they can be guided in "rewriting" it so that it is more realistic and has fewer disadvantages (Epstein, 1986a).

For example, if parents share the belief "In order to be good parents, we must do everything we can to spare our children any pain in life," it may become clear to them that one disadvantage to this "rule" is that efforts to live by it exhaust them, and that another is that their children develop low frustration tolerance. Respecting the basic value the parents place on being caring parents, the therapist may guide them toward revising their belief. Rather than constructing the revised belief *for* the parents, the therapist asks them questions that stimulate *them* to consider alternatives; for example, "How could you reword this belief in a way that maintains the value you place on helping your children get the good things in life but also helps them learn to get these things for themselves?" The problematic belief might be revised to "In order to provide good care for our children and best prepare them for life, we will give them guidance in avoiding unnecessary painful experiences, but also allow them to experience some pain and frustration that will develop their personal judgment and ability to tolerate stress."

Once a modified belief has been constructed, the therapist can help the family members devise behavioral experiments to examine the consequences of living according to the new standard. Particularly when logical analysis and gathering of data regarding the old belief have not been successful in changing it, firsthand experiences with positive outcomes of the new belief often can provide a powerful impetus to cognitive change.

Self-instructional training. Another form of cognitive restructuring that can help family members change their dysfunctional responses to one another focuses on training them to give themselves covert instructions for controlling their reactions. This approach is based on work with stress inoculation, the development of self-control in impulsive children, and the training of anger control (e.g., Deschner, 1984; Meichenbaum, 1977; Neidig & Friedman, 1984; Novaco, 1975). Epstein (1982) described the use of self-instructional training to control aversive exchanges between spouses, and these procedures seem to have utility in helping parents and children disrupt escalating spirals of aversive behavior as well. The basic procedure is to devise simple statements each individual can repeat to himself or herself when anticipating or experiencing a stressful interaction with other family members. These statements can be used to reduce unpleasant emotions (e.g., "Just stay calm," "You can reduce your tension and anger by relaxing your muscles and breathing slowly.") and to guide behavior (e.g., "Don't answer him back so fast. First listen to what he has to say, acknowledge his opinion, and then slowly state your point of view."). Each family member should select wordings that seem natural and comfortable, and then he or she should rehearse these repeatedly, first overtly and then covertly, until they are "second nature." It is advisable for clients to practice self-instruction first in a "safe" environment, before attempting to use it during actual family conflicts.

Behavioral Interventions

The behavioral interventions used by cognitive–behavioral therapists are most commonly those used in behavioral family therapy: communication training, assertiveness training, problem-solving training, and behavior-exchange procedures. Clinical decisions regarding when and to what degree each of these interventions is used with a particular family are based on a detailed assessment of the family's behavioral deficits and excesses, as described earlier.

All of these behavioral interventions use some similar behavior modification procedures: instructions, modeling, behavior rehearsal, and feedback (both corrective feedback and reinforcement for adequate performance) (Epstein, 1985b; Jacobson, 1981). Instructions include any didactic descriptions of the specific behaviors that the therapist intends to help the family increase, as well as those behaviors that appear to be problematic and will be targeted for elimination (or at least a decrease in frequency or intensity). Instructions also include a description of the procedures (such as behavior rehearsal) that the family members will be asked to use in order to modify their behavioral interactions. The format of the instructions may be a written handout, verbal description by the therapist, a standardized taped presentation, or a combination of these. Bibliotherapy, such as Gottman et al.'s (1976) self-help communication guide for couples, can serve as an ongoing source of instructions as therapy proceeds.

Modeling of examples of desired behaviors is a common method of guiding family members' attempts to modify their interactions. Although specific behaviors such as communication skills can be modeled with standardized videotapes, it is more common for therapists to demonstrate the behaviors during sessions. This allows the therapist to model variations in particular behaviors that are most relevant for changing a specific problematic family interaction pattern. The therapist also can interrupt the family interaction when he or she notices a dysfunctional behavior and can model alternative behaviors that they can try.

Behavior rehearsal is the heart of all the behavior change efforts, because it is assumed that family members will master new skills and substitute them for their old interaction patterns only through repeated practice. Consequently, the therapist asks them to practice both in sessions and at home. Home practice not only provides additional opportunities for rehearsal of new behaviors, but it is expected to facilitate the generalization of the behavior changes from the therapy office to the home. When assigning home practice, it is important that the therapist select tasks with which the family already has demonstrated competence during the therapy session, so that they are likely to have a successful experience at home. This often involves having clients practice small behavioral changes or components of more complex new behaviors. For example, problem solving includes a number of behaviors, but a therapist may have the family practice only the problem definition component and become adept at it before moving on to practicing the brainstorming of solutions.

As the family experiments with new ways of behaving toward one another, it is important for the therapist to provide them with feedback about the adequacy of their efforts. On the one hand, one may provide specific information and suggestions about how the family members could perform more effectively, and on the other hand, one can give them verbal reinforcement for a job well done. It is important that the therapist give very specific, concrete feedback about behavior rehearsals, and that he or she give positive feedback for even small improvements, so that families will be encouraged as they engage in the difficult work of changing ingrained behavior patterns.

Communication training. The specific aspects of communication targeted for treatment by a cognitive–behavioral therapist will depend on the particular behavioral deficits and excesses identified during an assessment of a family's interaction pattern. The most common foci of communication training are the ability to express both positive and negative messages clearly and the ability to listen to another person's message (thereby receiving information accurately). Expressive and listening skills are considered prerequisites for later training in family problem solving, particularly when the communication of positive feelings replaces some of the aversive exchanges in the family and creates a supportive atmosphere for resolving conflicts (Epstein, 1985b; Falloon et al., 1984; Jacobson & Margolin, 1979).

Training in expressive and listening skills has been applied with a wide variety of family problems, and with cases ranging in severity from families seeking enrichment experiences (L'Abate & McHenry, 1983) to those with a schizophrenic member (Falloon et al., 1984). By means of instruction, modeling, behavior rehearsal, and feedback, family members are taught specific guidelines for expressing messages to each other and for "active listening." In active listening, the person receiving a message not only attempts to understand the expresser's subjective experience but also reflects that understanding back to the expresser, in the manner of a therapist using empathic listening and paraphrasing. Although there are standard procedures and guidelines for the training of expressive and listening skills, most notably those of Guerney's (1977) Relationship Enhancement program, the therapist tailors interventions to the needs of each family. For example, some family members may need a considerable amount of feedback and rehearsal to overcome their tendency to jump from one topic to another when trying to send a message, or their tendency to give suggestions and opinions when listening to another member expressing feelings. Falloon et al. (1984) describe strategies they use to modify a variety of specific communication problems such as unclear communication, invalidating others' ideas, intrusiveness, and threats.

Assertion training. Assertion training can be considered a specialized form of communication training that focuses on how family members attempt to influence each other by making and refusing requests, as well as how they express thoughts and feelings to one another (Epstein, 1985b). Training in these skills often is integrated into a general communication training program (e.g., Falloon et al., 1984; Jacobson & Margolin, 1979; Stuart, 1980), but it also can be presented as a separate training "module" (Epstein et al., 1978) when a behavioral assessment identifies specific assertiveness deficits in a family.

Assertion training typically includes didactic presentations describing differences among assertion, direct aggression, passive aggression, and submission, discussions of when it may be most appropriate to be assertive and when not, instructions and modeling of specific verbal and nonverbal components of assertion, and repeated behavior rehearsal with performance feedback from the therapist (Epstein, 1981). The major goals of assertion training are to develop family members' abilities to make requests of one another in a direct but nonthreatening manner, to refuse another's request directly without being aggressive, to express negative opinions and feelings without attacking other members, and to express positive messages such as compliments clearly. Training exercises often focus on specific behaviors such as phrasing requests in the form of "I" statements, increasing eye contact when talking with other family members, and persisting in stating one's position even in the face of resistance (e.g., firmly repeating one's refusal of another's request when that person keeps stating new reasons why one should comply). During assertion training, it is stressed repeatedly to families that assertiveness is not coercive, and that the assertive individual may be more likely than an aggressive or submissive person to achieve his or her goals but should be prepared to accept others' noncompliance as well.

Training in problem solving. The goal of problem solving is for family members to devise and implement specific solutions to problems for which no clear solution initially exists. Problems a family may face can include relatively minor issues such as how to spend a leisure day together, as well as more substantial difficulties such as how parents can control a child with severe behavior problems or how alienated spouses can create some mutually satisfying experiences together in the midst of a hectic work and family life. Although expressive and listening skills are necessary if family members are to communicate during problem-solving sessions, it is considered important that the family approach the exercise as a cognitive, task-oriented process, with minimal expression of emotions (Epstein, 1985b).

Through the use of instructions, modeling, rehearsal, and feedback, family members are coached in collaborative efforts which are focused on a sequence of steps: 1) defining the problem in concrete behavioral terms; 2) "brain-storming" a list of possible solutions (being creative and nonjudgmental about the solutions at this stage); 3) evaluating the desirability and feasibility of each proposed solution (its costs and benefits for the family members, individually and collectively); 4) selecting a solution (which may be a combination of some of those from the initial list); 5) constructing a concrete plan for implementation of the solution, which specifies the behavior required of each family member; and 6) evaluating the success of the plan. Selection of a solution often involves negotiation among family members who have different preferred solutions, and the success of this process is likely to depend on whether the family previously had established a collaborative atmosphere and is able to communicate in a clear, nonaggressive manner (Epstein, 1985b; Jacobson & Margolin, 1979). Clinical procedures for marital and family problem solving have been detailed by authors such as Falloon et al. (1984), Jacobson and Margolin (1979), and Stuart (1980).

Behavior exchange procedures. The use of behavior exchange contracts to resolve marital conflicts is based on theoretical and empirical evidence that marital satisfaction is related to the ratios of positive and negative behaviors exchanged by spouses. Stuart (1980) emphasizes training couples to negotiate exchanges in a "two-winner" context, rather than the "win–lose" orientation that typifies many distressed relationships. Construction of a behavioral contract consists of each partner specifying behaviors he or she desires from the other party and a formal agreement (usually written) that each person will provide some of the desired behaviors. There has been a shift away from *quid pro quo* contingency contracts, which often falter when the spouses "stand on ceremony," refusing to give until they get (Jacobson, 1981). Whereas in quid pro quo contracts each person's reinforcement consists of the positive acts the other person agreed to perform, in "good faith" contracts the reinforcements each spouse receives are independent of the other person's performance. Many therapists have shifted to the use of even less formal behavior exchange agreements in which spouses list desired behaviors and state a broad agreement to increase these, with no reinforcement contingencies specified (O'Leary & Turkewitz, 1978).

Behavioral contracts are a common component of behavioral family therapy with adolescents and younger children. Goldenberg and Goldenberg (1985) note that although there has been an emphasis on training parents to modify their children's behavior (e.g., Berkowitz & Graziano, 1972; Patterson, 1975, 1976b), behavioral parent training actually changes the entire family interactive system; that is, the parents' behaviors toward the child are changed as much as the child's toward the parents.

Interventions with child behavior problems are based on a concept of reciprocity in which the parents attempt to control the child's behavior by coercive means (threats, punishment) and the child responds to the negative parental behavior with more negative behavior (Patterson & Reid, 1970). To change this pattern, parents are taught behavioral principles such as "time-out" from positive reinforcement, consistent use of reinforcement to produce effective reinforcement schedules, and use of contracting. In contingency contracting, a formal written agreement is devised whereby the child or adolescent earns points for performing specific behaviors desired by the parents. Behavioral goals must be feasible for the child to achieve them and thereby collect the agreed-upon rewards for amassing certain point totals. Contracting usually is used in combination with other family interventions such as communication training.

LIMITATIONS AND CONTRAINDICATIONS

The research which will determine the limits of application of cognitive–behavioral principles and techniques to family treatment has yet to be done. Thus, although a discussion of such limitations essentially is an empirical matter, the consideration which follows reflects the clinical experiences of the authors. Similar discussions in ensuing chapters reflect the experiences of their contributors.

The principles and techniques in this introduction seem applicable to most families seeking treatment. Our experiences suggest, however, a few general exceptions which may limit their effectiveness.

A low level of intellectual functioning is the first exception. Cognitive–behavioral techniques require families to learn a number of skills and to build a repertoire of responses which together redirect crucial aspects of family functioning. Limited intellectual capacity in families may impede the learning process that characterizes these approaches and may reduce the techniques' effectiveness. However, the concreteness with which the skill training components are construed may extend rather than truncate the range of families to which they are applicable.

Limited ability for abstract thought may interfere with a family's ability to grasp and apply techniques whose effectiveness relies on accurate recognition of cues to trigger their application. Difficulty thinking abstractly may impede this crucial process and limit the effectiveness of these treatment techniques, whether the difficulty is related to low intellectual capacity or to rigid thought processes among intellectually endowed individuals. Once again, however, the concreteness with which they can be introduced to families may in fact increase the number of families for whom they are appropriate. Generally, family members grasp cognitive–behavioral concepts quite well, and concepts are widely applicable, as is illustrated by the diverse contributions to Section II of this book.

Families with young members may present limitations to application of cognitive–behavioral techniques. Most cognitively oriented treatment with children seems to focus on those school-aged and older (Meichenbaum, 1977). Because their logical capacities are not well-formulated until children reach the age of 7 or 8 and because they have had fewer life experiences within which to formulate concepts, techniques of disputing concepts are usually not applied before this age, and those for disputing irrational beliefs before age 11 or 12 (Ellis & Bernard, 1983), although clinically it seems that children as young as 5 or 6 years old can learn and apply some cognitive interventions (DiGiuseppe & Bernard, 1983).

Young members of families may be inappropriate participants in some of the higher-order cognitive treatment discussed previously. For other techniques, especially those that do not require them to logically manipulate thoughts (DiGiuseppe & Bernard, 1983), they may fit in very well. Especially in families in which trauma has been prominent (e.g., abusive behaviors and addictions), children seem, in the words of one 6-year-old, to "learn a lot real quickly—a lot more than my friends"—about family functioning.

Families characterized by little good will and intractable blaming are also exceptions. As has been noted throughout the chapter, a cognitive–behavioral approach to treatment is based on collaboration between the therapist and family, and among family members. Interventions are explicit (the therapist generally provides a rationale for each technique), straightforward, and require the clients' cooperation. Although particular techniques (e.g., challenging attributions that involve inaccurate blame, challenging extreme beliefs such as the belief that one must punish those who have done hurtful things) often can be used to reduce blame, some families are entrenched in blaming an identified patient. Others cling strongly to the belief that to collaborate with other family members is to remain vulnerable to harm, and such individuals may demand unilateral change by the other family members. Progress in cognitive–behavioral treatment may be blocked by intractable blaming and an absence of good will among family members. Such families also may be poor candidates for any form of family therapy, including strategic approaches that capitalize on a family's resistance. At present we lack research data that may identify the relative efficacy of different treatments with families whose members lack a collaborative orientation to therapy.

OTHER CLINICAL ISSUES

There are some other concerns that clinicians may have about the applicability of cognitive–behavioral procedures with particular aspects of family problems. The following descriptions are based on our clinical experiences in dealing with these issues.

Is cognitive–behavioral family therapy appropriate for dealing with crisis situations? The full course of cognitive–behavioral assessment and treatment can be time-consuming. However, this need not preclude the application of this approach with family crises such as child abuse, spouse abuse, suicidality, substance abuse, and other situations that pose serious immediate threats to the welfare of family members. In fact, the structured and fairly directive nature of cognitive–behavioral interventions can prove to be advantageous when a therapist faces a need to stabilize disorganized family interactions. These procedures have their roots in the treatment of problems such as depression, anxiety, and stress, and thus they have been designed to produce change quickly. In the chapters that comprise Section II of this book, authors describe specific strategies they use to deal with acute danger. When the therapist is faced with a family crisis, resolution of the crisis precedes a shift of attention to the modification of more chronic and less dangerous cognitive and behavioral problems.

Do cognitive–behavioral techniques consider emotions in family treatment? Some may claim that, by their nature, these approaches exclude emotions in their treatment strategies. This clearly is *not* the case. Emotions are important factors in treatment, and they are not excluded. Emotions are integrally involved in dysfunctional family functioning and crucial to eventual improvement in such functioning. From the cognitive–behavioral perspective, emotions are both mediators of and mediated by cognitive processes and are tightly woven into the fabric of family life. As such, they may become important cues to be used by family members in reformulating family interactions.

In some cases family members may conclude from a therapist's presentation of cognitive–behavioral principles that emotions are not welcome in treatment. We urge therapists to do whatever they can to avoid this inappropriate conclusion; nevertheless, some family members may develop the expectation that expression of emotions is taboo in treatment. As a result, they may come to believe that the therapist will not be the appropriate one for them. Others may conclude that emotions are not welcome in treatment and will find this consistent with their reluctance to talk about their feelings generally. To the extent that family members believe that their emotions have no place in treatment, therapy will be impeded. Therapists should be alert to these misperceptions and correct them when they arise.

In this introduction we have presented an overview of cognitive–behavioral techniques of family therapy. Quite consciously, we have restricted our discussions to general principles. Contributions in the latter portion of the book address the specifics of cognitive–behavioral principles as they are applied to the understanding and treatment of various clinical syndromes. Each follows a specific outline so that readers can compare particular applications of generic principles to various family problems.

Chapter 2 completes the first section of the book. Dr. Leslie reviews the points of comparison between cognitive–behavioral and systems approaches and addresses the concern about whether they can be integrated in the treatment of families.

REFERENCES

Aponte, H.J., & VanDeusen, J.M. (1981). Structural family therapy. In A.S. Gurman & D.P. Kniskern (Eds.), *Handbook of family therapy* (pp. 310–360). New York: Brunner/Mazel.

Barbach, L. (1976). *For yourself: The fulfillment of female sexuality.* New York: Signet.

Barton, C., & Alexander, J.F. (1981). Functional family therapy. In A.S. Gurman & D.P. Kniskern (Eds.), *Handbook of family therapy* (pp. 403–443). New York: Brunner/Mazel.

Baucom, D.H. (1987). Attributions in distressed relations: How can we explain them? In S. Duck & D. Perlman (Eds.), *Heterosexual relations, marriage and divorce* (pp. 177–206). London: Sage.

Baucom, D.H., Bell, W.G., & Duhe, A.D. (1982). *The measurement of couples' attributions of positive and negative dyadic interactions.* Paper presented at the annual meeting of the Association for the Advancement of Behavior Therapy, Los Angeles.

Baucom, D.H., & Lester, G. (1982). *The utility of cognitive restructuring as a supplement to behavioral marital therapy.* Paper presented at the annual meeting of the Association for the Advancement of Behavior Therapy, Los Angeles.

Baucom, D.H., Sayers, S.L., & Duhe, A. (1985). *Assessing couples' attributions for marital events.* Unpublished manuscript, University of North Carolina at Chapel Hill.

Beck, A.T. (1976). *Cognitive therapy and the emotional disorders.* New York: International Universities Press.

Beck, A.T., & Emery, G. (1985). *Anxiety disorders and phobias: A cognitive perspective.* New York: Basic Books.

Beck, A.T., Rush, A.J., Shaw, B.F., & Emery, G. (1979). *Cognitive therapy of depression.* New York: Guilford Press.

Berkowitz, B.P., & Graziano, A.M. (1972). Training parents as behavior therapists: A review. *Behavior Research and Therapy, 10,* 297–317.

Berman, C. (1980). *Making it as a stepparent.* New York: Bantam.

Birchler, G.R., & Spinks, S.H. (1980). Behavioral-systems marital and family therapy: Integration and clinical application. *American Journal of Family Therapy, 8*(2), 6–28.

Burns, D. (1980). *Feeling good.* New York: New American Library.

Burns, D. (1985). *Intimate connections.* New York: William Morrow.

Christensen, A. (1979). Naturalistic observation of families: A system for random audio recordings in the home. *Behavior Therapy, 10,* 418–422.

Coleman, R.E. (1981). Cognitive–behavioral treatment of agoraphobia. In G. Emery, S.D. Hollon, & R.C. Bedrosian (Eds.), *New directions in cognitive therapy: A casebook* (pp. 101–119). New York: Guilford Press.

Deschner, J.P. (1984). *The hitting habit: Anger control for battering couples.* New York: Free Press.

DiGiuseppe, R., & Bernard, M.E. (1983). Principles of assessment and methods of treatment with children. In A. Ellis & M.E. Bernard (Eds.), *Rational-emotive approaches to the problems of childhood* (pp. 45–88). New York: Springer.

Doherty, W.J. (1981). Cognitive processes in intimate conflict: I. Extending attribution theory. *American Journal of Family Therapy, 9*(1), 3–13.

Dryden, W. (1985). Marital therapy: The rational-emotive approach. In W. Dryden (Ed.), *Marital therapy in Britain: Vol. 1. Context and therapeutic approaches* (pp. 195–221). London: Harper and Row.

Eidelson, R.J., & Epstein, N. (1982). Cognitions and relationship maladjustment: Development of a measure of dysfunctional relationship beliefs. *Journal of Consulting and Clinical Psychology, 50,* 715–720.

Ellis, A. (1962). *Reason and emotion in psychotherapy.* New York: Lyle Stuart.

Ellis, A. (1976). Techniques of handling anger in marriage. *Journal of Marriage and Family Counseling, 2,* 305–316.

Ellis, A., & Bernard, M.E. (1983). An overview of rational-emotive approaches to the problems of childhood. In A. Ellis & M.E. Bernard (Eds.), *Rational-emotive approaches to the problems of childhood* (pp. 3–43). New York: Springer.

Epstein, N. (1981). Assertiveness training in marital treatment. In G.P. Sholevar (Ed.), *The handbook of marriage and marital therapy* (pp. 287–302). New York: Spectrum.

Epstein, N. (1982). Cognitive therapy with couples. *American Journal of Family Therapy, 10*(1), 5–16.

Epstein, N. (1985a). Depression and marital dysfunction: Cognitive and behavioral linkages. *International Journal of Mental Health, 13*(3–4), 86–104.

Epstein, N. (1985b). Structured approaches to couples' adjustment. In L. L'Abate

& M. Milan (Eds.), *Handbook of social skills training and research* (pp. 477–505). New York: Wiley.

Epstein, N. (1986a). Assessment and modification of dysfunctional belief systems in marital therapy. *British Journal of Cognitive Psychotherapy, 4,* 1–9.

Epstein, N. (1986b). Cognitive marital therapy: Multi-level assessment and intervention. *Journal of Rational-Emotive Therapy, 4*(1), 68–81.

Epstein, N., DeGiovanni, I.S., & Jayne-Lazarus, C. (1978). Assertion training for couples. *Journal of Behavior Therapy and Experimental Psychiatry, 9,* 146–156.

Epstein, N., & Eidelson, R.J. (1981). Unrealistic beliefs of clinical couples: Their relationship to expectations, goals and satisfaction. *American Journal of Family Therapy, 9*(4), 13–22.

Epstein, N., & Jackson, E. (1978). An outcome study of short-term communication training with married couples. *Journal of Consulting and Clinical Psychology, 46,* 207–212.

Epstein, N., & Williams, A.M. (1981). Behavioral approaches to the treatment of marital discord. In G.P. Sholevar (Ed.), *The handbook of marriage and family therapy* (pp. 219–286). New York: Spectrum.

Falloon, I.R.H., Boyd, J.L., & McGill, C.W. (1984). *Family care of schizophrenia: A problem-solving approach to the treatment of mental illness.* New York: Guilford Press.

Fincham, F. (1985). Attribution processes in distressed and nondistressed couples: 2. Responsibility for marital problems. *Journal of Abnormal Psychology, 94*(2), 183–190.

Fincham, F., Beach, S.R.H., & Nelson, G. (1987). Attribution processes in distressed and nondistressed couples: 3. Causal and responsibility attributions for spouse behaviors. *Cognitive Therapy and Research, 11,* 71–86.

Fincham, F., & O'Leary, K.D. (1983). Causal inferences for spouse behavior in maritally distressed and nondistressed couples. *Journal of Social and Clinical Psychology, 1,* 42–57.

Fox, S., & Emery, G. (1981). Cognitive therapy of sexual dysfunctions: A case study. In G. Emery, S.D. Hollon, & R.C. Bedrosian (Eds.), *New directions in cognitive therapy: A casebook* (pp. 160–180). New York: Guilford Press.

Gardner, R.A. (1977). *The parents' book about divorce.* New York: Bantam.

Goldenberg, I., & Goldenberg, H. (1985). *Family therapy: An overview* (2nd ed.). Monterey, CA: Brooks/Cole.

Gordon, S.B., & Davidson, N. (1981). Behavioral parent training. In A.S. Gurman & D.P. Kniskern (Eds.), *Handbook of family therapy* (pp. 517–555). New York: Brunner/Mazel.

Gottman, J., Notarius, C., Gonso, J., & Markman, H. (1976). *A couple's guide to communication.* Champaign, IL: Research Press.

Greenspan, S.I., & Mannino, F.V. (1974). A model for brief interventions with couples based on projective identification. *American Journal of Psychiatry, 131,* 1103–1106.

Guerney, B.G., Jr. (1977). *Relationship enhancement.* San Francisco: Jossey-Bass.

Haley, J. (1976). *Problem-solving therapy.* San Francisco: Jossey-Bass.

Holtzworth-Munroe, A., & Jacobson, N.S. (1985). Causal attributions of married couples: When do they search for causes? What do they conclude when they do? *Journal of Personality and Social Psychology, 48*(6), 1398–1412.

Jacobson, N.S. (1981). *Behavioral marital therapy.* In A.S. Gurman & D.P. Kniskern (Eds.), *Handbook of family therapy* (pp. 556–591). New York: Brunner/Mazel.

Jacobson, N.S., & Margolin, G. (1979). *Marital therapy: Strategies based on social learning and behavior exchange principles.* New York: Brunner/Mazel.

L'Abate, L., & McHenry, S. (1983). *Handbook of marital interactions.* New York: Grune & Stratton.

Liberman, R.P., Wheeler, E. G., deVisser, L.A.J.M., Kuehnel, J., & Kuehnel, T. (1980). *Handbook of marital therapy.* New York: Plenum.

Marlatt, G.A., & Gordon, J.R. (1985). *Relapse prevention: Maintenance strategies in the treatment of addictive behaviors.* New York: Guilford Press.

McCubbin, H.I., & Patterson, J.M. (1983). Family transitions: Adaptation to stress. In H.I. McCubbin & C.R. Figley (Eds.), *Stress and the family: Vol 1. Coping with normative transitions* (pp. 5–25). New York: Brunner/Mazel.

Meichenbaum, D. (1977). *Cognitive-behavior modification: An integrative approach.* New York: Plenum.

Minuchin, S. (1974). *Families and family therapy.* Cambridge, MA: Harvard University Press.

Neidig, P.H., & Friedman, D.H. (1984). *Spouse abuse: A treatment program for couples.* Champaign, IL: Research Press.

Novaco, R. (1975). *Anger control: The development and evaluation of an experimental treatment.* Lexington, MA: Heath.

O'Leary, K.D., & Turkewitz, H. (1978). Marital therapy from a behavioral perspective. In T.J. Paolino & B.S. McCrady (Eds.), *Marriage and marital therapy: Psychoanalytic, behavioral and systems theory perspectives* (pp. 240–297). New York: Brunner/Mazel.

Patterson, G.R. (1975). *Families: Applications of social learning to family life* (rev. ed.). Champaign, IL: Research Press.

Patterson, G.R. (1976a). The aggressive child: Victim and architect of a coercive system. In L.A. Hamerlynck, L.C. Handy, & E.J. Mash (Eds.), *Behavior modification and families: Vol. 1. Theory and research* (pp. 267–316). New York: Brunner/Mazel.

Patterson, G.R. (1976b). *Living with children: New methods for parents and teachers* (rev. ed.). Champaign, IL: Research Press.

Patterson, G.R., & Reid, J.B. (1970). Reciprocity and coercion: Two facets of social systems. In C. Neuringer & J. Michael (Eds.), *Behavior modification in clinical psychology* (pp. 133–177). New York: Appleton-Century-Crofts.

Pretzer, J.L., Fleming, B., & Epstein, N. (1983). *Cognitive factors in marital interaction: The role of specific attributions.* Paper presented at the World Congress on Behavior Therapy, Washington, DC.

Raush, H.L., Barry, W.A., Hertel, R.K., & Swain, M.A. (1974). *Communication, conflict and marriage.* San Francisco: Jossey-Bass.

Robin, A.L., Kent, R., O'Leary, K.D., Foster, S., & Prinz, R. (1977). An approach to teaching parents and adolescents problem-solving communication skills: A preliminary report. *Behavior Therapy, 8,* 639–643.

Rush, A.J., & Weissenburger, J. (1986). Do thinking patterns predict depressive symptoms? *Cognitive Therapy and Research, 10,* 225–236.

Sager, C.J. (1976). *Marriage contracts and couple therapy.* New York: Brunner/ Mazel.

Schlesinger, S.E., & Epstein, N. (1986). Cognitive-behavioral techniques in marital therapy. In P. Keller & L. Ritt (Eds.), *Innovations in clinical practice: A source book* (Vol. 5, pp. 137–155). Sarasota, FL: Professional Resource Exchange.

Spanier, G.B. (1976). Measuring dyadic adjustment: New scales for assessing the quality of marriage and similar dyads. *Journal of Marriage and the Family, 38,* 15–28.

Stuart, R.B. (1980). *Helping couples change: A social learning approach to marital therapy.* New York: Guilford Press.

Thibaut, J.W., & Kelley, H.H. (1959). *The social psychology of groups.* New York: Wiley.

Thomas, E.J. (1977). *Marital communication and decision making: Analysis, assessment and change.* New York: Free Press.

Walen, S.R., DiGiuseppe, R.A., & Wessler, R.L. (1980). *A practitioner's guide to rational-emotive therapy.* New York: Oxford University Press.

Weiss, R.L., Hops, H., & Patterson, G.R. (1973). A framework for conceptualizing marital conflict, a technology for altering it, some data for evaluating it. In L.A. Hamerlynk, L.C. Handy, & E.J. Mash (Eds.), *Behavior change: Methodology, concepts and practice.* Champaign, IL: Research Press.

Wessler, R.A., & Wessler, R.L. (1980). *The principles and practice of rational-emotive therapy.* San Francisco: Jossey-Bass.

Young, J.F. (1981). Cognitive therapy and loneliness. In G. Emery, S.D. Hollon, & R.C. Bedrosian (Eds.), *New directions in cognitive therapy: A casebook* (pp. 139–159). New York: Guilford Press.

Zilbergeld, B. (1978). *Male sexuality: A guide to sexual fulfillment.* New York: Bantam.

2

Cognitive–Behavioral and Systems Models of Family Therapy: How Compatible Are They?

Leigh A. Leslie

A growing trend in psychotherapy has been to focus on the family as an integral part of the intervention process. The family has been used in conceptualizing the etiology of a problem, as a focus for direct intervention, and as an ally of the therapist for maintaining individual changes (Kendall, 1985). Within this family shift in psychotherapy, "systems" models of family therapy have enjoyed extraordinary growth and increasing popularity in recent years. Systems models refer broadly to those models of family therapy which have been largely influenced by, or based in part on, the concepts of von Bertalanffy's (e.g., 1950, 1968) general systems theory. As the domain of cognitive–behavioral therapy has expanded to include work with couples, and now families, researchers have begun either to offer integrative models of systems and cognitive–behavioral therapy (Birchler, 1983) or to address the potential utility of such efforts (Turkewitz, 1984). For the most part, these works have focused on a specific model of systems therapy and have considered the pragmatics of utilizing both cognitive–behavioral techniques and "systems" techniques in conducting couple or family therapy. As Lebow (1987) pointed out, however, the first principle guiding any integrative approach should be that there is internal consistency in the theoretical foundations of the models. Given clinicians' continuing efforts to enhance their effectiveness, and the

Sincere thanks are expressed to Dr. W. Edward Craighead and Dr. Ned Gaylin for their helpful comments on an earlier draft of this chapter.

suggestions of clinical researchers that these two modes of therapy both complement and overlap one another, it seems important to examine further the extent to which cognitive–behavioral and systems approaches to family therapy are *both* theoretically and pragmatically compatible. Such an undertaking should provide therapists with the knowledge necessary to determine the appropriateness of an integrative approach utilizing techniques from these two models of therapy.

The question of compatibility between these two approaches to family therapy is more complicated than it may initially appear. Unlike cognitive–behavioral therapy, numerous models of family therapy have evolved from a systems framework. In reality, the question of compatibility is most appropriately addressed in a two-tiered fashion. First, it must be asked whether these approaches are *theoretically* compatible; that is, is there common ground in the underlying theoretical frameworks of these approaches to family therapy? Such a question allows us to speculate on possible areas of overlap or integration without having to compare cognitive–behavioral therapy with numerous, and often distinct, systems models of therapy. The second area of inquiry concerns the compatibility of the primary *methods of intervention* growing out of the theoretical assumptions of each model. This chapter is organized in the following way to address these two questions. First, the theoretical foundations of systems models of family therapy are examined. Second, specific models of family therapy which have evolved, in part, out of general systems thinking are considered, focusing particularly on the treatment techniques and strategies common to each model. Finally, utilizing the review of cognitive–behavioral therapy in Chapter 1, the question of the theoretical and practical compatibility of cognitive–behavioral and systems approaches to family therapy is addressed.

SYSTEMS THEORY

It is important to understand that systems theory is not a sociological or psychological theory, but a domain-free scientific theory for the "analysis of objects of reality" (Blauberg, Sadovsky, & Yudin, 1977, p. 43). A system can be defined as "a complex of elements or components directly or indirectly related in a causal network such that each component is related to at least some other parts in a more or less stable way within a particular period of time" (Buckley, 1967, p. 41). Many individuals have contributed to the development of systems thinking, but none has been as pivotal or influential as von Bertalanffy. His work on general systems theory has been translated and integrated broadly into both the physical and social sciences. The basic tenet of this theory is that an organism cannot be viewed as a compilation of elements, but instead must be seen as an organized entity composed of interdependent parts and possessing "wholeness" (von Bertalanffy, in Blauberg et al., 1977). Thus the nature or character of a system is not merely a summation of the components but is a function of the emergent relational qualities among the components (Ackerman, 1984). With this emphasis on wholeness, the movement of each component of a system is thought to influence the whole, and movement of any component is explained, in part, by movement in related parts of the system. It follows logically, then, that attributions of causation in systems thinking are multidirectional or circular as opposed to linear. One cannot explain behavior simply by looking at what precedes or what follows it. Instead, the focus is the multidirectional flow of influence between the behavior and interactional field in which it is located.

Application of these ideas to the family suggests that families are more than "the sum of the members" and that the focus of analysis should be the family entity itself. The traditional focus on the functioning of one element, or in this case one family member, becomes secondary to an understanding of the connections or relationships among family members and the overall organization of the system. At minimum, this suggests that an individual's behavior cannot be understood outside the familial context in which it occurs, and that the appropriate focus is the pattern of interaction within the family. In the fullest sense, this idea suggests that the functioning of a family member is determined, in part, by the person's position in the family (Blauberg et al., 1977). For example, the Smith family with two children does not merely add a new member when a baby is born, but the family becomes a distinctively different entity with the onset of the changes in interaction and relationships which accompany the birth. Similarly, the hostile outbursts of the 2-year-old are not explained merely by an individual concept such as jealousy, or by a linear dyadic explanation which states that the toddler's behavior is a reaction to the loss of attention from the mother, who has been devoting a great deal of time to the new baby. Instead, a systems perspective would suggest that changes in the overall organization and functioning of the family after the birth of the child be examined. Perhaps the family has reorganized around the infant in a way that leaves the toddler with no role in the family; mother is the primary caretaker for the infant, father has become primarily responsible for the older children, and the older son has been designated "mom's helper" around the house and with the baby.

In this scenario the 2-year-old's behavior is viewed as a signal to the family that their reorganization is inadequate or incomplete to meet the needs of the family. It may be that the family is not accustomed to finding roles for that many people, or that boundaries around specific subsystems have not been established clearly; but whatever the resolution to their incomplete reorganization, the interaction pattern of the entire family must be addressed. One may ask at this point whether a "systemic" focus on the whole precludes an individual or dyadic analysis. This question will be dealt with in greater detail later in the chapter. For now, it can be stated that individual or dyadic analysis may certainly be a component of a larger system focus, but would not typically occur independently of the more comprehensive analysis.

The implications of a systems perspective for how we think about and work with families are far reaching. Although a thorough review of the systems model is far beyond the scope of this chapter, the following four critical concepts or principles emanating from general systems theory are considered: 1) purpose/goal, 2) hierarchical organization/structure, 3) boundaries, and 4) feedback/control mechanisms. The implications of these concepts for understanding family behavior are examined.

Purpose/Goal

A basic assumption of systems theory is that living systems are purposive and their activities are goal directed. Von Bertalanffy (1968) referred to a final state or equilibrium which all systems strive to attain. Though in an abstract form this argument is teleological—systems work to exist and because they exist they continue to work—attempts have been made to enhance the utility of the concept. Kantor and Lehr (1975) refer to "targets" or ends to which family behavior is directed. They identify families' primary targets as obtaining affection, power, or meaning. They suggest that the behavior of family members, individually or collectively, can be seen as designed to achieve one of these ends with one another or with those outside the family. On the other hand, Becvar and Becvar (1982) suggest that goals cannot be delineated this clearly for all families, and that goals are instead "inferential and definitional like systems themselves" (p. 21). Furthermore, they suggest that the "identification" of goals is based on their utility to the observer; they may not be openly recognized by family members. That is, if an observer sees a family crisis develop every time one of the young adult children attempts to move outside the family home (e.g., leaves for college, rents an apartment, takes a job in another city), the observer might conclude that the goal of this family is to stay bonded together, perhaps as a protection from the outside world. Although a family crisis might be oriented toward this goal, it is possible that family members might not acknowledge or even be aware of the function the crisis serves.

Whether one maintains that overt common goals exist for all families, or that goals are idiosyncratic and inferential, the primary implication of this concept is that any behavior or pattern of behaviors is assumed to be serving, or to have served, some purpose within the family's set of goals.

Feedback

Systems are thought to be constantly in flux as they simultaneously pursue goals and respond to outside forces. Homeostasis refers to the state in which a stable balance is achieved between the need for change and the need to control change in order to maintain the integrity of the system. The regulatory mechanism by which a system maintains homeostasis and monitors its attempts to achieve certain goals is referred to as feedback. Feedback consists of the flow of information concerning how well the system is achieving its desired state and changes made in the system's behavior in response to this information (Broderick & Smith, 1979). The source of the information may be either internal or external to the system, and the information itself may take several forms, such as verbal or nonverbal communication, goods, services, and energy. Whatever the source and form of the information, the basic concept is that the system must take in the information (input), evaluate it relative to the goal, and respond in some way (output). *Positive feedback* occurs when there is an amplification of the original input. For example, a young child pouts (input) and is spanked by a parent (output). This in turn leads to more pouting and yet another spanking (i.e., the response is increasing the pouting). *Negative feedback,* on the other hand, has a dampening effect, or decreases the original input. In the previous example, if the spanking was followed by appropriate behavior by the child, the sequence would be labeled negative feedback. As illustrated by the example, the terms "positive" and "negative" are nonevaluative and simply imply a continuation/acceleration or decrease/termination of the behavior (Broderick & Smith, 1979).

At this point the reader with a cognitive–behavioral orientation may surmise that the concept of feedback is just a relabeling of the social learning paradigm in which a behavior is maintained or terminated by its consequences. Although some systems writers (e.g., Anderson & Carter, 1984) do conceptualize the feedback process in a manner compatible with a social learning model, this is not the predominant perspective among systems theorists. Systems theorists are concerned with feedback as it relates to change in a family. By and large, the accepted viewpoint is that negative feedback serves to maintain homeostasis in a system by returning behavior to the predeviation level. Positive feedback, on the other hand, unbalances the system's homeostatic state and promotes continued deviation and change (Becvar & Becvar, 1982; Watzlawick, Beavin, & Jackson, 1967). In this conceptualization the input is being evaluated by some standard or pattern that was in existence prior to the input's occurrence, and a response is made to bring the input closer to the preexistent standard. This differs from a reinforcement/punishment analysis in that the type of feedback is not determined by an increase or decrease in the behavior but by how it changes relative to the standard. That is, the input, or behavior, may be either increased or decreased in each type of feedback. For example, a teenage daughter is expected to be in by 11:00 P.M. on weekends; however, one Friday night she does not come in until 1:30 A.M. In response, her parents "ground" her, and from then on she is always home on time. This would be considered negative feedback, because it returned the functioning of the family to the predeviation level (i.e., daughter returning home by 11:00 P.M.). However, if the daughter's response had been to run away from home, the feedback cycle would be a positive, deviation-amplifying one because the behavior was moving further away from the standard and the family could become destabilized. In this way positive feedback leads to change in the system in that the family's response may have to change to bring the behavior back in line with the standard (e.g., a one-to-one mother–daughter talk versus grounding), or the standard may have to change to incorporate the new behavior (e.g., daughter's curfew is changed to midnight). It is important to note that movement toward change may be functional in that it may represent the family's adapting to new needs within the system. In the previous example, the entire feedback process was adaptive in helping the family respond to new needs arising from the developmental stage of the daughter.

Boundaries

All systems have boundaries which distinguish them from their surroundings, as well as boundaries between the various units or components within the system (e.g., individuals, dyads). Boundaries control the flow of energy, information, and people between the system and the environment and within the system itself. Boundaries vary in their permeability, or the level of exchange (flow) they allow with the environment. A system which has a high level of exchange with its surroundings is referred to as open, whereas a closed system is one whose boundaries are not easily crossed. In reality, no system is fully open or closed because a totally open system in which the exchange between the system and the environment is not constricted in any way would not exist as a separate entity but would be part of the surrounding environment. On the other hand, a totally closed system would have none of the necessary exchange of essential resources with the environment and would die. Thus systems exist along a continuum in terms of the flexibility or the rigidity of their boundaries. A family's placement on this continuum is important in understanding issues of access and connection, both within the family and with the outside world. Logically, the more interconnected the family members, the more impact the change in one family member will have on others in the family.

Hierarchical Organization/Structure

The organization or structure of a system refers to the way in which the parts (individuals and subsystems) of the system are arranged, specifically, the organization that has evolved as a system pursues its goals. A family system may have several tasks or goals it wants to accomplish (e.g., harmony among family members, financial security, and socialization of the children), and those tasks often are the responsibility of smaller groupings (subsystems) within the family. These groupings may follow a normatively defined pattern (e.g., mother and father are the parental subsystem responsible for the socialization of the children), or a family may organize itself in more idiosyncratic ways to achieve particular goals (e.g., the oldest child is responsible for maintaining harmony in the family by interrupting arguments or tension among family members). It should be noted that "responsibility" for goals, or functional organization, is not always a logical, overt process acknowledged by family members. In the previous example, it is quite likely, from a systems perspective, that neither the oldest child nor the other family members acknowledge or accept that he or she is responsible for family harmony. However, this conclusion is reached by observing the child intervene whenever there is tension among family members.

Not only does the organization influence how effectively the family can function as a unit in achieving its goals, but it also has important implications for the flow of affection, information, and power in the family. For example, a family in which the father typically communicates with the children through the mother will be more likely to have a difficult time adjusting to the mother's absence due to illness than will a family in which the children have always communicated directly with the father.

Undoubtedly, the four concepts presented here are highly interrelated. It is easy to see, for example, how a family's organization or structure will affect its goal achievement or, conversely, how the goals a family sets will affect the way it structures itself. Although the link between general systems theory and the development of specific models of family therapy is not direct, the concepts just presented are all incorporated, in varying degrees, into the models of therapy typically referred to as "systems" models of therapy.

SYSTEMIC MODELS OF FAMILY THERAPY

Recent decades have witnessed the development of numerous models of family therapy which utilize general systems theory to explain family functioning. The application of systemic concepts and principles has resulted, however, in varied approaches to therapy. Differences among approaches are based not so much on varying interpretations of family functioning from a systems perspective as on the characteristics of families which each model emphasizes in conceptualizations and interventions. Various typologies have been offered for organizing systemic models of family therapy. Whereas some emphasize the "paradigmatic" differences in the models (Ritterman, 1977), Levant (1983) offers a schema which highlights the relationship between the models. He proposes that family therapy models emphasize aspects of family process, structure, or history, with the various models becoming both more comprehensive and inferential as one progresses along this continuum.* That is, process models focus on what is presently occurring in the therapy room (present focused, limited to current interaction), whereas historical models, at the other end of the continuum, typically focus on multigenerational patterns of interaction and emotional connection in the family over time.

A comprehensive review of all systemic approaches to family therapy is not possible here, but two models have been selected for examination as a sample of the larger group of systemic models of therapy. The two models chosen are *structural* family therapy, developed by Minuchin; and *interactional* (sometimes referred to as *communications*) family therapy, which grew out of

---

* Although Bowen theory and therapy do propose concepts similar to those found in general systems theory, and has, at times, been critiqued as a systems model of family therapy, this perspective does not align itself with general systems theory and does not utilize or acknowledge the theory as critical in the formulation of this therapeutic approach.

the work of Jackson, Watzlawick, Weakland, and others, at the Mental Research Institute (MRI) in Palo Alto, California.

Structural Family Therapy

Structural family therapy was developed by Salvador Minuchin and his colleagues, first at the Wiltwyck School for Boys, and later at the Philadelphia Child Guidance Center. The primary focus of this approach is the structure or organization the family has developed in its efforts to carry out the basic functions of supporting, nurturing, and socializing family members. To carry out their numerous functions, families delegate responsibilities or tasks to subsystems, or smaller groupings within the family. This delegation of functions to subsystems can be implicit or explicit, and family members typically belong to more than one subsystem simultaneously (e.g., female adult is part of the marital subsystem and the parental subsystem). Two subsystem characteristics, *boundaries* and *alignment,* are particularly important to structural therapists.

Boundaries. Minuchin (1974) defined subsystem boundaries as the "rules defining who participates and how" (p. 53). It is thought to be critical that family members have a clear understanding of who belongs to various subsystems and how these subsystems can be accessed. Minuchin pointed out that the membership of a subsystem is not nearly as important as the clarity of its boundaries. A nonnormative arrangement, such as the parental subsystem being comprised of a parent and child, can operate effectively (and, in fact, is often a necessity in single-parent families) as long as family members understand who belongs in the subsystem.

From a structural perspective, the problems that are typically faced by families are a result, in part, of boundaries that are excessively blurred or unclear (enmeshment) or excessively rigid (disengagement). *Enmeshment* is characterized either by subsystem boundaries that can be easily intruded upon by other family members or by a heightened emphasis on family membership that promotes some sacrifice of autonomy and suggests a "functioning as one" mentality. An example of the former would be a school-age child consistently being able to distract or interrupt his or her parents as they discuss or argue about issues in their marital relationship. The latter is illustrated by a young adult who cannot successfully move out of the parents' home and who shares all aspects of his or her life with the parents. *Disengagement,* on the other hand, is characterized either by an inability to alter or cross subsystem boundaries when necessary or by a lack of involvement among family members; that is, the emphasis on autonomy to the exclusion of support and intimacy. For example, a family in which a junior high student's plummeting grades go unattended and a family in which an adolescent is free to make major decisions (e.g., curfew, college) with no input from parents both typify families at the disengaged end of the continuum.

Alignment. In contrast to the concept of boundary, alignment refers to the way family members join together or oppose each other as they carry out their activities (Aponte, 1976). Boundaries address how a family is organized, while alignment has to do with the emotional or psychological connections among family members. Aponte and VanDeusen (1981) offer an example of a family structure in which the term "boundary" describes the mother as sole disciplinarian, whereas the term "alignment" refers to how supportive or unsupportive the father is of her in that role. Although in all families one is likely to see special bonds between particular family members, certain alignments typically are thought to be dysfunctional for families. *Triangulation* (Minuchin, Rosman, & Baker, 1978) results when two family members seek to make the same third person their ally against one another and the third person is caught in the middle, siding sometimes with one and sometimes with the other. An example would be the biological mother in a remarried family whose new husband encourages her to handle her children in a different way and whose children complain to her that her new husband is pushy and insensitive. *Coalitions* (Minuchin et al., 1978) are formed by two or more family members joining together against another. When a coalition becomes inflexible and a dominant pattern in the family, it is referred to as a *stable coalition*. A *detouring coalition* is a particular type of stable coalition in which coalition members hold a third person responsible for any trouble they are having and thus decrease the stress in their own relationship.

Therapeutic approach. From a structural perspective, these characteristics are thought to determine the development of interaction patterns (referred to as transaction patterns by Minuchin) which regulate behavior in a family. The goal of therapy, then, is to change the underlying family structure so that problematic interaction patterns can be exchanged for more functional ways of relating to one another. Minuchin (1974) presents a three-tiered therapeutic approach.

The first task of the therapist is to observe interaction patterns and boundaries as they are revealed in the therapy session. Toward this end, spatial relationships within the therapy room (e.g., where family members sit in relation to one another) are considered a valuable index of structural relationships. In addition, several techniques are used to enable the therapist to see family members' typical patterns of dealing with one another. These include prescribing in-session tasks which are expected to reveal organization features of the system and inducing enactment of established patterns in the session. A typical task assignment might be to have one parent control the behavior of a fidgety 7-year-old. The expectation is that as the parent and child begin to interact, the family will play out their typical patterns and the therapist will gain insight into parameters such as hierarchies, power, and support in the family. It should be noted that task assignment can be used as a technique for promoting change in the family structure in addition to revealing family structure, as described here. Enactment inducement may take the form of the therapist siding with one family member against another or bringing up for discussion a topic which is thought to be conflictual. These techniques, when used in this preliminary stage of therapy, are designed to reveal interaction patterns which the therapist can observe firsthand and use to develop hypotheses concerning the family structure. The interested reader is referred to Aponte and VanDeusen (1981) for a concise but more thorough discussion of techniques common to structural family therapy.

Second, the therapist further refines hypotheses and goals for therapy by "probing the family structure" or "joining with the family" (Aponte & VanDeusen, 1981; Minuchin, 1974). It is important to note that in the structural approach the therapeutic goals are developed by the therapist based on a structural assessment of the family and may not directly address the specific problem for which the family sought treatment. It is thought to be unnecessary, and sometimes counterproductive, for structural therapists to discuss their goals with the family. The assumption is that the planned restructuring which is based on these goals will free the family from the pattern of interaction that has been dysfunctional. The emphasis in joining with the family, or becoming involved in their normal interaction, is to test for areas of flexibility or possible change in the system. The therapist does this through adopting the family's style of communication and interaction and then observing what happens as he or she begins to vary the pattern. By affiliating with the family and probing its established pattern, the therapist can experience the family as a "quasi" insider and get a better sense of how parameters such as family rules and alignments can be changed.

Finally, the restructuring phase of therapy consists of the therapist's attempts to dismantle, reinforce, or reorganize old structures and build new structures as needed. Again, the variety of techniques that are useful here can be grouped into three categories: 1) systems recomposition, 2) symptom focusing, and 3) structural modification (Aponte & VanDeusen, 1981). An example of *system recomposition* would be adding the youngest daughter in the family to an already established close female sibling subsystem so that she can benefit from her older sisters' knowledge of how to negotiate with parents, each other, and the outside world. This might be done by finding a common interest among the daughters or getting each of the older sisters to agree to take a certain day as her day to spend time talking with the younger sister about what is happening in her life (e.g., school, parents, boys).

An approach to *symptom focusing* would be relabeling a symptom in such a way that it has new meaning for the family or allows members to see the situation differently. For example, the therapist can focus on the concern and devotion of a mother who likes to know exactly where her adolescent children will be each evening instead of accepting the family's label of her as "nosey" or "a worrier." Another symptom-focusing technique is symptom exaggeration, in which the symptom is repeated to such an extent that the function it had been serving in the family is diminished. If, for example, a school-age boy regularly exhibits temper tantrums at home, the therapist might state that it is very important for the parents to know how unhappy the boy is. The therapist could prescribe that, at the least, the boy get angry, and preferably have a tantrum, every day to make sure his parents understand his displeasure. By so doing, the therapist blocks the function the tantrum had been serving. It becomes a compliant behavior rather than something the boy can do to upset, attract, or engage his parents.

Finally, *structural modification* techniques include emphasizing differences among family members to dispel the need for detouring coalitions (i.e., if differences are viewed as natural, no one has to be "blamed" for them), and blocking established interaction patterns to encourage (or force) family members to find new ways to interact with one another. An example would be for the therapist to encourage parents to prevent their 7-year-old from interrupting them when they are discussing a problem either in session or at home.

Interactional Family Therapy

As with systems therapies in general, there is no one interactional model of family therapy. Rather, the various approaches which have been influenced by the early work of Gregory Bateson and his colleagues and developed by therapists associated with the Mental Research Institute tend to be referred to as "interactional" (Bodin, 1981). Although distinctive in some ways, these approaches can be addressed as an entity given the high degree of similarity in their basic assumptions and therapeutic techniques. Most significantly, interactional therapies are problem focused. Assuming that problems are a function of ongoing behavior and interaction patterns, it is the contention of interactional therapists that one need only observe and address present behavior in any intervention. The etiology of a problem is not relevant for its resolution. The emphasis of therapy, then, is on identifying and interrupting the pattern of interaction maintaining the problem.

Theoretical assumptions. In assessing family interaction patterns, several assumptions are primary for interactional family therapists. First, drawing heavily from Jackson and his colleagues' early work on communication theory, it is believed that all communication has two levels, "report" and "command" (Lederer & Jackson, 1968) or "content" and "relationship" (Watzlawick et al., 1967). That is, when an individual communicates he or she not only sends a specific message but also communicates something about the relationship between sender and receiver which frames the interpretation of the message. For example, a mother may tell a child "you're a mess" as she straightens up after the child. The "report" or "content" level of communication is the verbalized message, but it is the associated behavior that provides the clue about how to interpret the statement. The "command" or "relationship" level of communication is that the mother will be there to pick up after and take care of the child or, more specifically, that no change in the child's behavior is really needed.

Second, in understanding individuals' interpretations of their communication and interaction patterns it is imperative to identify how they "punctuate" the interaction. That is, if influence is multidirectional and circular, as a systems perspective proposes, participants in any interaction are simultaneously and sequentially influencing each other. Rarely, however, do the participants view their own interaction from such a perspective. Instead, they tend to define for themselves when a certain interaction started, how it started, and who started it. Conflict typically results when participants "punctuate" their interaction differently. For example, although a wife is "certain" the husband started the argument by coming home and being quiet and sullen, the husband "knows" the fight began when the wife nagged him and kept asking about his day.

A third assumption of interactional approaches is that all families have rules and metarules concerning the nature of their relationships with one another and with the outside world. These rules help families coordinate their activities and find a balance between internal (family) and external (environment) demands. In a healthy family these rules will fluctuate as needed, based on feedback, to keep the desired balance intact. It should be noted that rules can be implicit or explicit beliefs which family members hold, individually or in common, such as "It is not good to show your anger," or "We must present a united front." They may, however, be implicit properties of the family unit which guide members' interaction but which none of the individual members are fully aware of. More will be said about the nature of "properties of the family" in the "Theoretical Compatibility" section of the chapter.

Therapeutic approach. As might be expected given the theoretical premise of interactional therapy, assumptions about dysfunction in a family have to do with the family's interaction patterns. As Watzlawick, Weakland, and Fisch (1974) explain, problems in families often become exacerbated by the family's reliance on solutions that are not effective, even after their inadequacy has become evident. For example, although the parents have been grounding their teenage daughter regularly for her refusal to obey her curfew, she continues to break curfew. The parents nonetheless continue to use grounding to attempt to change the daughter's behavior in spite of its ineffectiveness. Reliance on an inadequate solution can take three forms: 1) ignoring a problem when action needs to be taken, 2) overreacting (i.e., taking more action than is necessary or setting unrealistic expectations), and 3) taking action at the wrong level.

This third form of inadequate solution deserves special attention because it is perhaps both the most unique contribution made by the interactionalists and the aspect of therapy for which they are best known. It is the contention of interactionalists that families often implicitly establish metarules, or rules about their rules for interaction, which prohibit them from truly examining the nature of the problem and making needed changes. Members of a couple who implicitly believe that conflict is bad for a relationship can attempt to decrease the tension in their relationship by "being honest with each other." Although this approach may keep them from breaking the metarule, it will not, in all likelihood, resolve the tension in their relationship. A move toward honesty and openness may, on the surface, seem desirable; it is a new rule to guide the interaction. However, if their metarule is still intact and dictates that they cannot really say anything that may be conflictual or highlight their differences, such changes or new rules may only frustrate them further. What is needed in such a situation is not merely to change the way they interact with one another and attempt to solve their problems, but to change the metarules that guide their interaction. This kind of change is referred to as a second-order change, or one that changes the basic premise behind the system's pattern of interaction rather than making changes only in the particular problematic patterns themselves. In the preceding example, a second-order change would consist of the couple no longer seeing conflict as harmful or avoiding it. From a cognitive–behavioral model the validity of this belief would be challenged directly with the therapist having family members explicitly examine the rule underlying their behavior. An interactional therapist, however, would be more likely to initiate such a change indirectly because of the paradoxical nature of the metarule. In other words, if a couple's interaction is structured to avoid conflict, they would break the metarule by discussing the metarule, that is, discussing conflict. Thus the interactional therapist would attempt to make the rule ineffective or irrelevant without having the couple address it directly. Paradoxical techniques used by interactional therapists for addressing second-order change are discussed shortly.

Finally, therapy from an interactionalist perspective is symptom-focused in that therapy is structured around the problem presented by the family. At the same time, however, there is an assumption that change extends beyond the symptom. In the beginning sessions the therapist seeks a clear statement of the problem, inquires into how the family has been and is addressing the problem, and provides a clear statement of goals for therapy. Believing that a problem is maintained, in part, by the way a family is attempting to solve it, the therapist needs to know the specific types of solutions that have been tried. This both communicates to the family that the therapist knows they sincerely have been trying to change and informs the therapist of the family's rules about change.

Although interactionalists focus on the family's presenting problem and develop clear, concise goals, their methods of inducing change are, by and large, counterintuitive or "inconsistent with dictates of common sense" (Bodin, 1981, p. 300). Given the emphasis on second-order change, it is rarely thought to be sufficient to alter the behavioral patterns maintaining a problem. In addition, the family's metarules, which block them from effective problem resolution, must be addressed. This is not to say that the therapist would avoid straightforward skill training or task assignment which offers a family new ways of interacting. Some therapists associated with MRI, such as Virginia Satir, have made a communication skill emphasis the basis of their work. However, as Bodin (1981) points out, the preferred method for most interactionalists is not to teach such skills using social learning principles, but to allow clients to discover naturally the behaviors that are effective as they follow the therapists' counterintuitive directives. Believing that it is often metarules which keep a family from finding a workable solution, being counterintuitive or paradoxical is seen as a valuable tool for interfering with the established pattern of interaction in the family. This is thought to be a more effective strategy than addressing metarules directly for two reasons. First, because metarules are thought to be a family property, individual family members are frequently unaware of the metarules that guide their interaction. Second, families often resist the change they desire because of their need to maintain an established order. It may be helpful here to remember the concept of homeostasis and families' need to maintain a balance between change and constancy. Thus any noticeable change will be met with a pull toward constancy. For example, although having a young child stop his or her noncompliant behavior is truly desired by the family, this change will not occur in isolation. It will, by necessity, alter other patterns of behavior in the family (e.g., the parent–child relationship may improve, the negative behavior of another child may come to the parents' attention, or the parents may not need to spend as much of their time together focusing on the child). These associated changes may not be as desirable to the family, and the family may "slip" back into the old pattern that, although not completely satisfactory, did balance a host of family needs. A counterintuitive approach to intervention is designed to make the family's typical methods of maintaining balance—countering and controlling behavior, or keeping members in line with the rules and metarules—inoperative.

Common counterintuitive and paradoxical techniques utilized by interactional therapists include the following. First, interactional therapists might request that family members observe behavior in its natural setting. The intent, however, is not to establish a baseline but to challenge perceptions held by family members (e.g., "Our daughter *always* comes home late") and prevent self-fulfilling prophecies from being established. Also common to this model of therapy is "advertising," or making explicit the pattern or characteristics that the family has been trying to avoid or ignore (Bodin, 1981). This strategy requires that the therapist be direct about what he or she has observed in watching the family interact. Other techniques include relabeling and symptom prescription, both of which are used paradoxically to allow change to occur in the problem behavior. By prescribing that a husband continue to be withdrawn and sullen so that the wife and children can more closely study how these moods develop, the therapist negates the function these withdrawn periods serve in maintaining family balance. If family members have tended to respond with great care and concern to these periods, sullenness which is prescribed will not be as worthy of family concern or worry. If, on the other hand, these quiet periods have been accompanied by frustration and anger from other family members, it is not likely that they will be as upset about an individual "following the doctor's orders." Regardless of what the specific type of interaction has been (and the specific reaction, whether care or anger, really is unimportant), the critical point is that the behavioral sequence no longer serves that same function in the family and family members are free to find new ways of interacting with one another.

A COMPARISON OF SYSTEMS AND COGNITIVE–BEHAVIORAL APPROACHES TO FAMILY THERAPY

The task of comparing systems and cognitive–behavioral models of family therapy and examining the question of their possible integration must be addressed on both a theoretical and an applied level. As discussed previously, existing models for integrating these approaches (e.g., Birchler & Spinks, 1980) focused on the pragmatics of therapeutic intervention. However, a relatively neglected question is whether systems and cognitive–behavioral models have compatible theoretical foundations. In other words, can a therapist "think" from both a systems perspective and a cognitive–behavioral perspective without any paradigmatic conflict? If so, the issue of integrating therapeutic methods is not problematic. If, however, the theoretical foundations present different ways of "seeing" the family, the limits this places on therapeutic compatibility must be addressed.

I begin by examining similarities and differences in the basic tenets of general systems and social learning theory. The implications of these theoretical tenets for the compatibility of therapeutic models, including techniques and procedures, are then considered. Finally, I review previous attempts at integration and offer an evaluation of the theoretical and pragmatic compatibility of systems and cognitive–behavioral approaches to family therapy.

Theoretical Compatibility of Systems and Cognitive–Behavioral Models

Cognitive–behavioral therapy has grown out of a social learning paradigm which is based on a unity-of-science, or mechanistic, worldview. Such a worldview maintains that one set of principles or laws of nature controls all phenomena and that highly complex phenomena can be understood by "reducing" them to their basic elements (Lerner, 1976; Overton & Reese,

1973). Traditionally, the basic analytic unit in a social learning perspective
has been the S–O–R model, which maintains that behaviors (R) are a function
of the presence of certain stimuli (S) being processed by the individual (O).
Utilizing the terminology of Epstein, Schlesinger, and Dryden in Chapter 1,
this model can be described as life events (S) activating cognitive schemata
(O) which shape thoughts, emotional states, and behaviors (R). Bandura
(1977) questioned the accuracy of labeling the social learning model as
mechanistic, maintaining that the cognitive processing capabilities of individuals
cannot be reduced to a unidirectional, reflexive property. Bandura suggested
that humans' capacity for symbolic thought gives them the unique ability
for self-regulation and self-direction (motivation). That is, humans can both
observe and evaluate the impact of their behavior on personal and environmental factors and adapt their behavior accordingly. Thus human cognitive
processing and adaptation does not follow the unidirectional S–O–R model
often associated with a social learning framework. Bandura suggested that a
more appropriate representation of a social learning analysis of human behavior
is provided by the concept of "reciprocal determinism," which proposes that
personal factors (O), environmental factors (S), and behavior (R) are interdependent. This corresponds with the circular model of family functioning
proposed in chapter 1 in which a continuous feedback cycle operates in
families. In that model, the behaviors and emotions of family member A
serve as stimuli to trigger certain cognitive processes and subsequent behavior
in family member B. This in turn activates B's behavior or emotion, which
then serves as a stimulus to family member A; and so on.

It is true that social learning theory, as elaborated by Bandura (1977,
1978) and applied to families in Chapter 1, breaks with traditional reinforcement theories of behavior in that the emphasis on cognitive evaluation
and self-regulation does not lend itself to a unidirectional, automatic, stimulus–response model of behavior. It is important to note, however, that
although reciprocal determinism is not unidirectional, it is still reductionistic
in that the same principle is thought to account for human behavior at all
levels of social complexity. Bandura maintains that reciprocal determinism is
the "basic principle for analyzing psychosocial phenomena at varying levels
of complexity, ranging from intrapersonal development, to interpersonal behavior, to the interactive functioning of organizational and societal systems"
(1978, p. 356). Therefore, when considering family interaction, the same
analytic unit used to explain individual functioning is adapted to explain
family functioning. The result is that in trying to explain family behavior,
a social learning model would encourage the observer to "reduce" interaction

to the interdependent and multidirectional S–O–R connections among family members. The model is now quantitatively, but not qualitatively, different.

In direct opposition to a mechanistic model, systems theory is based on an organismic worldview which maintains that at each level of organization or complexity new characteristics "emerge" for all natural phenomena (Lerner, 1976; Overton & Reese, 1973). That is, more complex phenomena are qualitatively different from simple, lower-level phenomena. The operation of an organism at one level cannot be explained totally by the principles which guide an organism at a lower level because organisms are more than the sum of their parts. Thus the family is thought of as a distinct unit with characteristics or properties that are unique to this level of organization, and it cannot be understood fully by looking only at family members individually. This does not imply, however, that an understanding of individuals' functioning is irrelevant for understanding family functioning. A belief in emergent properties does not negate the validity or utility of principles guiding behavior at other levels of complexity. Instead it suggests that principles which explain individual functioning are themselves insufficient to fully explain family functioning. Systems-oriented family therapists would acknowledge the benefit of having (some would say necessity of having) a thorough understanding of the principles guiding individual and dyadic behavior, but would maintain that, in addition, one must understand what is unique about the family as a unit. These unique properties are ascertained by observing the entire family. Examples of emergent qualities of the family discussed in this chapter which have no counterpart from a social learning perspective are the family's homeostatic process, its boundaries, and its structure.

From a social learning perspective one might respond to the concept of emergent properties of the family in two ways. First, one could reason that what is emergent about the family is the interaction which occurs among members; that is, the relationship is the emergent quality. In this case the obvious social learning counterpart is the principle that individuals serve as stimuli for one another. Second, one might argue that these emergent properties are simply patterns of interaction that exist because of shared beliefs among family members. Support for such an explanation might be construed from systems theorists themselves. For example, Minuchin (1974) refers to boundaries as rules and Reiss (1981) proposes that families develop joint explanatory systems or paradigms for interpreting reality. Nonetheless, neither of these explanations would be totally embraced by systems theorists because they reduce or explain family behavior, ultimately, in terms of individual beliefs. Reiss maintains, for example, that families' joint explanatory systems or perceptual frames "are rarely explicit or conscious in the experience of any family. . . . They are manifest, more typically, in a mixture of fleeting experiences of the family and its enduring patterns of action" (1981, p. 1).

Further, systems theorists would maintain that families may engage in patterns of interaction (e.g., channeling all negative communication through a particular family member) which are counter to their *individual* beliefs. Two examples—one family and one nonfamily—may illustrate this point more clearly. A therapist observes a child becoming involved in the parents' heated arguments and interrupting the parental conflict, yet family members may be unaware of this feature of their interaction and maintain—and believe—that the child is not needed to help moderate family conflict or stress. A systems theorist would view this highly permeable boundary between child and parent as something which characterizes the group as a unit and which cannot be explained fully by looking at individual characteristics. A second example of an emergent property is the behavior of a large group or "mob." Social psychologists have long been interested in the phenomena of "group behavior" which cannot be explained by the characteristics of the individual members. That is, a mob or group will sometimes behave in ways that none of the members would on their own. From a systems perspective this would be considered an emergent property of groups.

It would appear then that the general overall stances of systems theory and social learning theory toward family functioning are quite different. One sees the family in a reductionist light, whereas the other claims that the family has unique emergent properties. In spite of this major difference, these two theoretical perspectives do not take totally different approaches to explaining family behavior. Several similar concepts can be found in the two models.

First, a systems perspective on family functioning suggests that the family must be considered as an entity composed of interacting parts. To understand behavior in a family, one must look at the relationship qualities and interactions among the members as well as the characteristics of the family as a unit. Similarly, a cognitive–behavioral perspective focuses on the interaction among family members with a particular emphasis on the interrelated nature of family members' expectancies, beliefs, and attributions. Although a social learning model does not conceptualize the family as having "emergent" properties, both models share an emphasis on multidirectional, reciprocal influence and the necessity of looking at behavior in that context. Given this focus on the reciprocal nature of influence, both models acknowledge the arbitrary nature of defining or "punctuating" interactional sequences. For example, Bandura (1978) illustrates how the same event (cognition or behavior) can be seen as either stimulus or response, depending on how one defines or where one limits the interaction. Furthermore, both theoretical perspectives focus on the role of cognitive factors in guiding behavior. The cognitive–behavioral model focuses on the expectancies that individuals have about how interactions will proceed and what their relationships will provide for them. These expectancies serve both as a standard by which current behavior or relationship functioning is evaluated and as a guide used in decision making about future behavior. From a systems perspective, these expectancies exist at an individual level; in addition, the family as a unit has goals or purposes which also serve as evaluation standards. Similarly, in both theoretical orientations a feedback process is associated with the monitoring of expectations or goals. Epstein, Schlesinger, and Dryden outlined in Chapter 1 the intrapersonal and interpersonal feedback loops thought to be operative from a cognitive perspective. Although a systems perspective emphasizes the cybernetic features of feedback for the family as a unit, both approaches conceptualize a process by which incoming information or perceptions are interpreted or evaluated relative to some standard and a behavioral option is selected based on the evaluation.

In conclusion, then, a social learning analysis of family functioning and a systems analysis of family functioning seem to share several explanatory principles. It could be argued that a social learning perspective is inherently included in the systems framework in that the cognitive operations of each family member, as well as the interplay between these cognitions, is simply one of the most basic levels of relatedness and interaction incorporated within the systems framework. That is, both individuals and dyads are subsystems in the larger family system, and principles which explain functioning at these levels can be incorporated into a "systems" perspective. However, if one is to remain theoretically pure, such a mental exercise ignores the conflictual nature of the fundamental scientific paradigm underlying the two perspectives.

The question then arises of whether theoretical compatibility should guide any attempts to integrate models of therapy. If one argues that the way we think about a family guides our interventions, then the paramount issue is *theoretical* compatibility instead of *procedural* compatibility. Given, however, that various clinicians have maintained the compatibility of the two models of therapy derived from these theories, a closer examination of how theoretical premise guides therapeutic conceptualization and strategy is in order.

Therapeutic Compatibility of Systems and Cognitive–Behavioral Models

In addressing the question of the compatibility of systems and cognitive–behavioral models of family therapy we are faced with both similar explanatory concepts and incompatible paradigmatic assumptions. The implication of this theoretical dilemma on the practice of therapy can perhaps be best understood by focusing on the therapeutic approach to change as conceptualized and constrained by each theoretical perspective. Given that the goal of all psychotherapy is some type of perceptual and/or behavioral change, it would seem that the most important criterion in determining the compatibility of modes of therapy would be how they address this primary issue of change. Although various systems therapists have written about the nature of change in family functioning, I focus here on the writing of Watzlawick and his colleagues. I have chosen these theorists as a starting point for the discussion of change for two related reasons. First, the mode of therapy emanating from their work (i.e., interactional or "communications" therapy) is typically utilized in attempts to integrate systems and cognitive–behavioral therapy (e.g., Birchler, 1983; Margolin, 1981). Second, this perspective on change allows for the most overlap with a cognitive–behavioral approach to change, as its utilization in previous integrative efforts would suggest. Other systems theorists focus much more on the emergent properties of family, and to carry the question of compatibility past the theoretical level would not be as fruitful as focusing on a model where applied compatibility has been suggested.

A brief example from structural therapy will illustrate this. Viewing family structure as an emergent characteristic of the family unit, Minuchin suggests that change occurs "through the process of the therapist's affiliation with the family and his restructuring of the family in a carefully planned way so as to transform dysfunctional transactional patterns" (1974, p. 91). The techniques for making such structural changes were examined previously in this chapter. The point that is relevant here is that the therapist's attention and therapeutic efforts would be aimed at the "family" level. The end point of both therapeutic approaches might be changed interaction patterns, but the disparity in how the therapists would conceptualize the problem and needed changes would seem to make this a less productive route to pursue in considering applied compatibility. Therefore, the work of the interactional theorists and therapists is used here to represent "systems" thinking. The reader should be aware, however, that some variations exist in the way other systems theorists address the issue of change.

In writing about the process of therapeutic change from a systems perspective, Watzlawick et al. (1974) maintained that problems are often exacerbated by the way a family attempts to deal with them. The goal of therapy in these cases is not merely to solve the problem for the family (first-order change) but to alter their approach to change or problem solving (second-order change). As discussed previously, three types of inadequate problem-solving or change strategies are often practiced by families. Two of these strategies, and the clinical response to them, seem similar in cognitive–behavioral and systems approaches to therapy. One type of inadequate problem-solving strategy addressed by both models of therapy is not taking action when it is needed. It is not unusual for family members to feel inadequate to tackle a particular problem or to hope unrealistically that, with time, everything will be resolved. The locus of the impediment to change in either of these situations is the individual beliefs of family members or their individual, or corporate, lack of necessary skills. In such instances, both therapeutic approaches would address the impediment so that the family can begin to take the needed action and implement change. If, for example, a couple claims that they have basically stopped talking because "we just always end up fighting," either therapeutic approach could, and cognitive–behavioral most likely would, spend some time on communication skill training, on examining the spouse's beliefs about disagreements in relationships, or on observational skills.

A second type of inadequate solution that both models would address would be overreaction, or taking action when it is not needed. Watzlawick and his colleagues discuss what they call the Utopian syndrome, in which family members have unrealistic expectations about any number of issues concerning their life together and are distraught when reality does not mirror their ideas. Again, the locus of the impediment to appropriate change is at the individual level. The direct counterpart in cognitive–behavioral therapy is referred to as "catastrophizing" or "irrational beliefs," and it emphasizes the impact of an individual's perceptions and expectations on how he or she defines a problem. In such instances, the aim of both therapeutic approaches is to challenge the cognitions that are maintaining the problem and modify the reciprocal behavior patterns which have developed as a result of these beliefs.

Consider a situation in which the parents of a 12-year-old boy are distraught because they see him as "disobedient" and "rebellious." It seems the boy does not always complete his chores such as making his bed and taking out the trash. The parents report that the boy is doing well in school, but they see him as directly challenging their authority by running out of the house to play before his chores are done. The son has become increasingly frustrated, maintaining he just "forgets sometimes." In such a case a cognitive–behavioral therapist might utilize procedures aimed at cognitive restructuring, inquiring into the parents' behavioral expectations for a 12-year-old boy or challenging their attributions for his behavior. A systems therapist, on the other hand, is more likely to be indirect, reframing the situation as the family having the "typical" problems and frustrations of early adolescence. As this example typifies, reframing is a method of changing cognitions in which the therapist provides the new perspective, as opposed to soliciting it from the clients. This is an important distinction between cognitive–behavioral therapy and systems therapy. Although the goal of these two modes may be cognitive change, a basic difference exists in their method of choice.

Cognitive–behavioral therapists are more concerned than systems therapists with identifying family members' actual cognitions. The emphasis would be on drawing out the expectations or beliefs concretely and then inviting clients to examine them. Systems therapists, on the other hand, would be more concerned with identifying beliefs, or a perspective on the situation, which would allow the family to change. The idea here is that, though understanding exactly what a person's current cognitions are may be helpful, all that is really needed is the knowledge that the cognitions are blocking change. Thus offering a new perspective may suffice if it enables the family members to deal effectively with the problem. Interestingly, a systems therapist may utilize more structured examination of beliefs and expectations if "reframing" does not allow the family to change. Similarly, a cognitive–behavioral therapist might offer alternative cognitions to the family if attempts at more structured examination have failed.

One basic difference should be noted here. Cognitive–behavioral therapists believe it is imperative that clients gain some insight into how their cognitions influence the problem, and the therapist takes responsibility for seeing that such understanding develops. Systems therapists, on the other hand, do not maintain the necessity of intellectual understanding and are more interested in changing the interactional sequences than in furthering the family's understanding. However, due to the cognitive–behavioral therapist's belief that changes in behavior may precede insight, the sequencing of intervention strategies used by therapists in the two models may appear similar. The reason for this differing perspective on the necessity of insight is discussed later in the chapter.

It is the third conceptualization of family problem solving and change which the two models of therapy do not seem to share. Watzlawick et al. (1974) suggest that family problems are sometimes maintained or complicated when the family's attempts at resolution are directed at the wrong level. They are not merely referring to solutions that involve the wrong family members or subsystems, but to solutions that do not acknowledge that inherent in family behavior are paradoxes which do not exist at an individual level. To identify these paradoxes, one must look at the family level of analysis with its emergent characteristics. In such situations many systems therapists would use indirect, counterintuitive interventions in the belief that direct "common-sense" approaches will be rendered ineffective by the paradoxical nature of family interaction.

For example, a husband in a traditional marriage may prefer his wife to be more independent and assertive. It is becoming increasingly important to him that he not be "in charge," or the primary decision maker, but that the relationship be a genuine partnership. The paradox is that a strong, independent wife who makes her desires or demands known is not something that can be requested, because by asking for it the husband remains in charge and the wife is responding to his requests, not her desires. Interestingly, if such a request is made and she refuses to change her style, she is, in fact, being the type of partner that her husband wants (assertive, independent). In other words, the only way she can be what the husband wants is to not be what he wants. Systems therapists would suggest that intuitive, logical discussion is not the most efficient approach to unlock the couple from this paradox; instead the therapist must attempt a second-order change by moving beyond the paradox. The therapist might, for example, congratulate the wife on how assertive and independent she is being by not changing to satisfy her husband even though she knows that he wants her to change. What such an intervention would do is invalidate the definition of the problem that the husband, or perhaps couple, has developed (i.e., he wants an independent wife and she is too dependent, or she doesn't know how to be independent). Thus first-order change (i.e., resolving "the problem" either through his acceptance of her or her becoming more independent) would no longer be the issue. They must now approach their marriage from a different perspective.

The lack of a counterpart to this approach in cognitive–behavioral therapy is not surprising since this mode of intervention results from a focus on the family entity. The absence of such a theoretical concept in social learning theory prohibits this conceptualization from being considered. It is possible that a cognitive–behavioral therapist might choose to explain the preceding example as conflicting or incompatible expectations by family members. This frame or interpretation would in turn lead to a therapy mode that would include cognitive restructuring, communication training, and problem-solving training. Such a frame of the situation and therapeutic strategy would be no more or no less accurate than the systems view of the problem, but the fact that a cognitive–behavioral therapist might suggest that the situation could be reduced in this manner lends further support to the basic difference offered by these two approaches on how to think about the family. It is important to reemphasize here that a therapist from each perspective might observe the same phenomenon but conceptualize what needs to be done differently. One would focus on the individual beliefs and behavior of the partners and the reciprocal influence between them, whereas the other would focus on the paradox that exists in the larger unit without trying to reduce it to an individual phenomenon. There is, unfortunately, no evidence available for settling the argument between the perspectives that family dynamics can be understood by breaking it down to interactive cognitive and behavioral processes or that it must be seen as unique and qualitatively different from the processes of individuals or individuals in interaction. This reduction versus emergent argument exists throughout science, and it is not the purpose of this chapter to attempt to resolve it or to build a case for the superiority of either approach. As noted earlier, this comparison is intended to determine how the basic underlying theoretical difference affects the compatibility of cognitive–behavioral and systems models of therapy.

The previous discussion suggests that there is a great deal of overlap in how one might work with families from a cognitive–behavioral and a systems perspective. As long as the focus is on the interdependency of family members' cognitive processes and behaviors, the two modes of therapy could operate similarly. However, where the modes of therapy become both theoretically and pragmatically incompatible is in the focus on change at the "family" level. Seeing this organizational level as having unique emergent qualities and using non–insight-oriented paradoxical techniques separate systems conceptualizations and interventions from a cognitive–behavioral approach.

Integrative Efforts

Given this preliminary analysis of the conditions under which cognitive–behavioral and systems therapies might be compatible, it now seems appropriate to consider specific efforts that have been made toward integration. The focus in this section is how the actual process or practice of therapy might be similar or compatible, and where theoretical differences may lead to incompatible practices.

In recent years various models have been offered which utilize concepts and methods from both systems and behavioral (e.g., Stuart, 1969, 1976) and in some cases cognitive–behavioral (e.g., Margolin, 1981) models of therapy. This work has been oriented primarily toward couples. The systemic model of therapy utilized in these integrative models has logically been the interactional model because it shares an emphasis with behavioral and cognitive–behavioral therapy on identifying family goals and observing and altering interactional patterns in the family.

In her work with marital jealousy, Margolin (1981) incorporates the systems and social learning concepts of interdependency of family members and mutual and reciprocal causation with the behavioral notion of operant conditioning. She describes a process by which partners' behaviors build on one another and serve as stimuli for each other's cognitions, feelings, and behaviors, as well as reinforcement or punishment for the other's behavior. Margolin offers a model of circular influence and regulation which is analogous to the deviation-amplifying (positive) and deviation-dampening (negative) feedback cycles discussed in systems theory. In addition to the standard behavioral emphasis on skills training and restructuring reinforcement contingencies, Margolin incorporates reframing into the actual treatment in an effort to "relieve spouses' resentment" (p. 477) and help them gain a different perspective on the situation.

Similarly, Birchler (1983) and Birchler and Spinks (1980) utilized the interactional systems model of therapy in developing what they call a behavioral–systems approach to marital and family therapy. Suggesting that differences between the models are largely a function of the language or terminology used and the therapeutic techniques or procedures typically employed, they maintain that an integrated model combines the efficacy of skill-oriented behavioral therapy with the flexibility and depth of interactional therapy. Initial assessment consists of 1) formulating hypotheses concerning family dynamics such as rules, control, or feedback mechanisms (systems therapy), 2) identifying skill deficits (behavioral therapy), 3) determining how families have attempted to solve this problem in the past (systems and behavioral therapies), and 4) setting and prioritizing goals for therapy (systems and behavioral therapies). In general, a systemic way of conceptualizing family interaction is used in developing strategies for intervening, although the actual treatment is structured in a largely behavioral way (e.g., communication and problem-solving skill training, behavioral shaping).

Although not offering an integrated model of therapy, Turkewitz (1984) also suggested that conceptualizing child problems from a systems viewpoint can aid the therapist in understanding the development and maintenance of a problem. She suggests guidelines as to when a family focus can be useful in assessment and treatment programs as well as in maintaining treatment gains.

In summary, then, integrative attempts typically center on aspects of the models that highlight the interactional nature of families (interdependent, reciprocal influence) and rely on techniques that modify cognitions (e.g., reframing, cognitive restructuring) and alter interaction patterns (e.g., problem solving). That is, integrative attempts focus on the first two types of problem solving addressed by Watzlawick and his colleagues. The similarities between the two therapy models which lend themselves to integration are perhaps most clearly articulated by Birchler and Spinks, who propose that these two therapeutic approaches can be merged because both

> . . . focus on: 1) present versus historical events; 2) interactional versus intraindividual phenomena; 3) behavioral (observable) versus unobservable (unconscious or intrapsychic) events; 4) communication variables as central in formulations of distress and in the development of intervention strategies; 5) the interactional influence of stimulus–response (action–reaction) contingencies; 6) viewing target behaviors (presenting problems) as representative of broader classes of interactional patterns; 7) increasing members' cooperative problem-solving abilities; 8) directive versus nondirective therapist activities (including homework assignments between sessions); and 9) strategies for brief, versus long-term intervention. (Birchler & Spinks, 1980, p. 25)

An additional similarity not addressed by Birchler and Spinks is that both models focus on rule-guided behavior in the family. The beliefs of individual family members form the locus of these rules in the cognitive–behavioral model, and treatment is aimed at that level. The locus of these rules for systems therapists is the family's behavioral interaction pattern, and they tend to focus interventions here. Again, a focus on either beliefs or interaction patterns does not negate the utility of the other approach but tends to highlight a systematic variation in therapeutic method.

The similarities delineated, of course, refer to a constrained aspect of systems (i.e., interactional) therapy. Greater focus on the "emergent" qualities would lead, however, to some specific differences in the way therapy is conducted.

First, systems-oriented therapies often emphasize the role of metacommunications or metarules in families, whereas cognitive–behavioral therapists focus more on communication and rules. Utilizing the concepts of "report" and "command" discussed previously, it is common for cognitive–behavioral therapists to focus on the report, or actual message, in a communication, whereas systems therapists would tend to focus on the command or message about how to interpret the message. This leads cognitive–behavioral therapists to put more stock in what a client is actually saying than would systems therapists. Again, this is a difference in emphasis which would tend to lead, but not mandate, therapists working from each approach to intervene in different ways. The following case will help illustrate this point.

A therapist is seeing a mother and father and their adolescent daughter, whom they label obstinate, angry, and hard to handle. The daughter tells the therapist how she believes her parents are extremely strict and have unrealistic rules for a 17-year-old. She states that if they do not begin to give her some say in her own life and decisions, she will just take it. "They have to start letting go," she claims. Even though the daughter is making what seems to be fairly reasonable requests, she is engaging in behavior that would heighten most parents' involvement in their child's affairs (e.g., skipping school, coming home drunk). In session she amplifies her demands for less parental involvement until the parents jump in to defend themselves or become involved with her in a verbal struggle. In this scenario, a cognitive–behavioral therapist is likely to focus on the daughter's request for change in family interaction patterns and family members' beliefs about what are appropriate limits and freedoms for a young woman this age. Attention might also be given to how the parents and their daughter have attempted to communicate about this issue and where the discussion falls apart. This is not to imply that a cognitive–behavioral therapist would not address the daughter's style of behavior. However, if the therapist did so, the focus would be on the "content" or beliefs which are affecting her style of behavior (i.e., what beliefs lead the daughter to behave so provocatively?). A systems therapist, on the other hand, would most likely look beyond the content of the daughter's message and attend to the fact that such a request is being made in the face of behavior which elicits parental involvement or interference. This pattern might be pointed out to the family, perhaps asking them what the "message" really is or how to interpret these mixed signals. Alternatively, a systems therapist might use a reframe, such as, "Your daughter really wants your help in learning to be an adult or learning to separate from you, but she doesn't know how to ask for it." Therapy then would focus on how the parents would help teach the daughter independence.

A second area of therapeutic difference between the models is the role insight is thought to play in change. Cognitive–behavioral therapy emphasizes the role that family members' cognitive processes play in individual and family dysfunction. Change is focused on having the individuals understand the role their cognitions play in maintaining the situation and on altering these cognitions and associated behavior patterns. Thus understanding or insight is paramount. Systems therapists, on the other hand, do not emphasize the necessity of insight. Insight is not avoided or thought to be counterproductive; it simply is not thought to be needed in all cases for change to occur. Two primary factors contribute to systems therapists' downplaying the need for insight. First, a belief in "emergent" properties makes it possible for a therapist to intervene at the family level without being concerned about individual understanding. That is, it is thought that change can occur at the "family" level without any or all of the family members understanding what has "caused" the change. For example, in restructuring family boundaries through blocking the involvement of certain family members and facilitating the involvement of others, a structural family therapist may not be concerned that family members understand how their alliances or poor boundary definition contributed to their presenting problem. What is important is that the necessary boundaries are established through changed interaction patterns.

A second factor that leads many systems therapists to downplay insight is the "perceptual" nature of reality. Family members often define situations differently, and in ways that limit their options for change. Given that there is no one correct way of defining a situation, a systems therapist is often more concerned with providing the family with a definition of the situation which all can accept and which enhances their options for change than in clarifying or identifying specifically what is happening; that is, identifying a specific S–O–R cycle. In the scenario of the parents and the 17-year-old daughter described earlier, a therapist working from either model might help the parents see that their assumption that the daughter is challenging their control leads them to be more controlling, increasing the chances that the daughter will challenge further, and so on. However, it is just as likely that a systems therapist would *not* work toward clarifying family members' current cognitive processes, or toward increasing their understanding of the feedback cycle into which they are locked. Instead, the therapist might work to offer the family another view of reality or way of seeing the situation. In the example, the therapist gave family members a view of their situation that all could accept. It acknowledged the daughter's need for increasing autonomy and independence while giving the parents a way to stay involved and have some control in the daughter's life. Whether or not the daughter's behavior actually communicated a need for the parents to teach her how to be an adult is thought to be irrelevant if such a new frame is reasonable or possible and offers the family an alternative to their dysfunctional pattern of dealing with one another.

A final area in which cognitive–behavioral therapists and systems therapists may vary in conducting therapy is how they view and deal with resistance. The cognitive–behavioral therapist starts from the assumption that family members have beliefs or expectancies which prohibit them from working toward change. The therapist accepts that these cognitions may seem logical to the client but works to have the client examine and evaluate them. For example, a family member may claim that "I've done enough sacrificing, I'm not changing until I see some change on her part," or he may believe that being open to change is synonymous with admitting that he is to blame for a particular situation. The therapist's task, then, is to help clients examine the validity of their beliefs and assess the advantages and disadvantages of holding such beliefs. The emphasis here is on individual beliefs, with the assumption that concerns or resistance may be found in only one person. If that individual's concerns can be addressed, therapy can continue for the group.

A systems therapist would be more likely to approach resistance from a family level of analysis than an individual level of analysis. The focus would be on the homeostatic tendency in systems. It would be assumed that any significant change which altered the homeostatic balance or steady state of the system would be met by a move that counters the change or by attempts to keep the system in balance. The goal of the therapist at that point is to block or temper the pull to the previous balanced state. Given this conceptualization, resistance is seen in a positive light in that it signals that some changes are, in fact, occurring in the system or that the system is recognizing the pull toward change (Anderson & Stewart, 1983). Resistance, like change, is a normal, expected part of the therapy process. In addition, the resistant behavior of an individual is seen as a group response. That is, the individual family member may be acting in such a way to provide balance for the entire system. Thus the therapist will not simply address the concerns of the individual but will take it as a signal that the family is reacting to the actual or anticipated change. Given the homeostatic tendency in families, the belief is that if only the individual's concerns are addressed, the family may find another way to counter that change.

How the systems therapist chooses to deal with resistance will depend, in part, on his or her particular mode of therapy (e.g., structural, strategic, symbolic–experiential) and on the way the resistance is manifested. A fairly standard approach, however, is to attempt to offset its likely occurrence by having the family anticipate or actually enact resistant behavior. For example, if parents have finally been successful in decreasing a 7-year-old's temper tantrums, the therapist might tell the parents that they should expect some backsliding. The therapist might even work with the parents to identify when and how the child is most likely to test their resolve in maintaining the change. A different approach with a similar intent would be for the therapist to suggest to the child that he get mad at his parents "at least" once this week because they are used to dealing with an angry child and may not know how to handle a child who never gets angry. By using either of these approaches the systems therapist is trying to recast resistant behavior as a normal part of the change process. There are times, however, when the therapist may fail to realize the extent of the change that has occurred in a family and not anticipate the resistance. In such instances the techniques of deflecting or incorporating resistance mentioned previously may be ineffective. In such situations various techniques are available to the therapist. These include slowing down or accepting that change is happening too fast for the family, taking responsibility for the resistance or backslide ("I asked too much of you, I should have known you weren't quite ready to change"), moving to another level of processing (e.g., emotional or experiential work for intellectualizing clients), or letting clients know that no change is permanent (e.g., "You may want to try this one for a week or two and you can always go back to previous ways of interacting") (Anderson & Stewart, 1983). Again, the goal of these techniques is to allow the change process to continue while acknowledging that resistance is normal.

In summary, then, it has been suggested that integrating cognitive–behavioral and systems models of family therapy poses few applied dilemmas. Reconsideration of procedural compatibility in light of theoretical differences suggests, however, that the theoretical differences do lead, in some instances, to procedural differences in conducting therapy.

CONCLUSIONS

The intent of this chapter was to assess the compatibility of cognitive–behavioral and systems approaches to family therapy. What appears to exist is some therapeutic or procedural overlap in the face of paradigmatic differences. This situation, unfortunately, provides an ambiguous answer to the question of whether systemic and cognitive–behavioral models of therapy are compatible. Strong cases have been made by other clinicians for possible integration when a limited theoretical and procedural focus (the direct, logical techniques of interactional therapy) is taken from systems theory. It appears, however, that such an "integration" often leads on the one hand to *systemic conceptualization,* which focuses on rules, myths, and feedback or control mechanisms (e.g., Birchler & Spinks, 1980; Turkewitz, 1984), but on the other hand to *behavioral intervention*. The limited scope of these integrative efforts may result from the fact that most researchers offering integrated programs of therapy are themselves cognitive–behaviorists. Whatever the reason, the effect seems to be that, to date, integration merely serves to allow more flexibility in the assessment/conceptualization phase of cognitive–behavioral therapy. Rarely are the full implications of a systemic framework, such as seeing the emergent qualities in families or utilizing indirect paradoxical interventions, incorporated into any integrative model. When such features are included, they tend to be utilized for pragmatic reasons (i.e., what works) without a clear conceptual rationale for their use.

What seems to be the most theoretically "pure" resolution to the question of compatibility is that these two approaches to family therapy cannot truly be integrated because a therapist "thinks" about the family and change differently from each theoretical model. This, however, does not negate the compatibility of the models in certain limited circumstances, or the value the models have for one another. Cognitive–behavioral therapists have already discovered the similarities in many therapeutic techniques and the utility of borrowing concepts and techniques from systems approaches which do not violate their assumptions about family interaction and change. In the opposite direction, cognitive–behavioral therapy has much to offer systems therapy.

A systems approach to the family maintains the operation of different principles at different levels of organization. Thus individual and interactive functioning should be just as important as the emergent properties of the family system. Viewing a system as multilevel suggests intervention could also be aimed at more than one level. Unfortunately, however, systems therapists have often emphasized the uniqueness or "wholeness" of the family unit to the exclusion of individuals. It is important for systems therapists to remember that even though family properties cannot be explained by individual processes, individual processes do affect family functioning. Individual members are, in fact, subsystems in the larger family system. A cognitive–behavioral approach offers systems therapists a valuable reminder of the importance of individual properties, as well as offering therapeutic strategies for addressing these properties. Most notable, perhaps, is the fact that individuals are active information processors. Individual belief systems not only interact with family properties but can limit the changes the family and therapist seek to make. Systems therapists may further their understanding of family functioning by focusing on the cognitive schemata that each person brings to therapy as well as on family level variables (e.g., boundaries, homeostasis). Such an addition both broadens the therapist's avenues for intervention and provides the therapist with a truly "systemic" picture of the multiple levels of influence and causation in the family.

REFERENCES

Ackerman, N.J. (1984). *A theory of family systems.* New York: Gardner Press.

Anderson, C.M., & Stewart, S. (1983). *Mastering resistance.* New York: Guilford Press.

Anderson, R.E., & Carter, I. (1984). *Human behavior in the social environment: A social systems approach* (3rd ed.). New York: Aldine.

Aponte, H.J. (1976). Underorganization in the poor family. In P.J. Guerin (Ed.), *Family therapy: Theory and practice* (pp. 432–448). New York: Gardner Press.

Aponte, H.J., & VanDeusen, J.M. (1981). Structural family therapy. In A.S. Gurman & D.P. Kniskern (Eds.), *Handbook of family therapy* (pp. 310–360). New York: Brunner/Mazel.

Bandura, A. (1977). *Social learning theory.* Englewood Cliffs, NJ: Prentice-Hall.

Bandura, A. (1978). The self system in reciprocal determinism. *American Psychologist, 33,* 344–358.

Becvar, R.J., & Becvar, D.S. (1982). *Systems theory and family therapy: A primer.* Lanham, MD: University Press of America.

Bertalanffy, L. von (1950). An outline of general systems theory. *British Journal for the Philosophy of Science, 1,* 134–165.

Bertalanffy, L. von. (1968). *General systems theory.* New York: Braziller.

Birchler, G.R. (1983). Behavioral-systems marital therapy. In J.P. Vincent (Ed.), *Advances in family intervention, assessment, and theory* (Vol. 3, pp. 1–40). Greenwich, CT: JAI Press.

Birchler, G.R., & Spinks, S.H. (1980). Behavioral-systems marital and family therapy: Integration and clinical application. *American Journal of Family Therapy, 8,* 6–28.

Blauberg, I.V., Sadovsky, V.N., & Yudin, E.G. (1977). *Systems theory: Philosophical and methodological problems.* Moscow: Progress Publishers.

Bodin, A.M. (1981). The interactional view: Family therapy approaches of the Mental Research Institute. In A.S. Gurman & D.P. Kniskern (Eds.), *Handbook of family therapy* (pp. 267–309). New York: Brunner/Mazel.

Broderick, C., & Smith, J. (1979). The general systems approach to the family. In W.R. Burr, R. Hill, F.I. Nye, & I.L. Reiss (Eds.), *Contemporary theories about the family* (Vol. 2, pp. 112–129). New York: Free Press.

Buckley, W.Q. (1967). *Sociology and modern systems theory.* Englewood Cliffs, NJ: Prentice-Hall.

Kantor, D., & Lehr, W. (1975). *Inside the family.* San Francisco: Jossey-Bass.

Kendall, P.C. (1985). Cognitive–behavioral therapy for impulsive children. New York: Guilford Press.

Lebow, J.L. (1987). Developing a personal integration in family therapy: Principles for model construction and practice. *Journal of Marital and Family Therapy, 13,* 1–14.

Lederer, W.J. & Jackson, D.D. (1968). *The mirages of marriage.* New York: Norton.

Lerner, R.M. (1976). *Concepts and theories of human development.* Reading, MA: Addison-Wesley.

Levant, R. (1983). Diagnostic perspectives on the family: Process, structural, and historical contextual models. *American Journal of Family Therapy, 11,* 3–10.

Margolin, G. (1981). A behavioral-systems approach to the treatment of marital jealousy. *Clinical Psychology Review, 1,* 469–487.

Minuchin, S. (1974). *Families and family therapy.* Cambridge, MA: Harvard University Press.

Minuchin, S., Rosman, B., & Baker, L. (1978). *Psychosomatic families.* Cambridge, MA: Harvard University Press.

Overton, W.F., & Reese, H.W. (1973). Models of development: Methodological implications. In J.R. Nesselroade & H.W. Reese (Eds.), *Life-span development psychology: Methodological issues* (pp. 65–86). New York: Academic Press.

Reiss, D. (1981). *The family's construction of reality.* Cambridge, MA: Harvard University Press.

Ritterman, M.K. (1977). Paradigmatic classification of family therapy theories. *Family Process, 16,* 29–48.

Stuart, R.B. (1969). Operant interpersonal treatment for marital discord. *Journal of Consulting and Clinical Psychology, 33,* 675–682.

Stuart, R.B. (1976). An operant interpersonal program for couples. In D.H. Olson (Ed.), *Treating relationships* (pp. 119–132). Lake Mills, IA: Graphic Publishing Co.

Turkewitz, H. (1984). Family systems: Conceptualizing child problems within the family context. In A.W. Meyers & W.E. Craighead (Eds.), *Cognitive–behavioral therapy with children* (pp. 69–98). New York: Plenum.

Watzlawick, P., Beavin, J.H., & Jackson, D.D. (1967). *Pragmatics of human communication.* New York: Norton.

Watzlawick, P., Weakland, J., & Fisch, R. (1974). *Change: Principles of problem formation and problem resolution.* New York: Norton.

SECTION II

TREATMENTS FOR SPECIFIC FAMILY PROBLEMS

3

Cognitive–Behavioral Assessment and Treatment of Child Abuse

Teru L. Morton, Craig T. Twentyman, and Sandra T. Azar

Although the frequency of reported child abuse appears to have increased dramatically during the past two decades, any attempt to assess systematically whether the frequency of abusive episodes is changing must first clarify a number of definitional and methodological issues. Problems in defining what is meant by child abuse are legendary. There is inconsistency in the literature, for example, with abuse defined sometimes in terms of the *intent* of the parent and sometimes in terms of the *effect* a parental action has on the child (Parke & Collmer, 1975). Clearly, it is a difficult task to determine parental intent *post hoc* in an abusive situation. This difficulty has led state and federal agencies as well as most persons who are involved in legal matters (i.e., custody suits and criminal proceedings) to focus largely on the *effects* upon the child when establishing whether abuse has occurred. In many states, for example, statutory definitions of physical abuse to a child are stated in terms of actions on the part of a parent or caretaker that leave bruises or welts for a specified period of time (usually 48 hours or more). It should be noted, however, that statutory definitions vary from state to state.

For the purpose of this chapter, we adopt a definition of abuse which emphasizes that physical injury of a child has occurred and that some evidence is present that it was not accidental in nature. This definition distinguishes child abuse from two other forms of child maltreatment. That is, child abuse is distinguished from child *neglect,* in that the latter represents a form of maltreatment in which the child is endangered or harmed by an *omission* of appropriate parental action—withholding of necessities or proper care. It can also be distinguished from *sexual abuse,* in that the latter typically and primarily involves sexual activities with a child which may or may not also involve physical damage to the child. Although having some features of dysfunction in common, families characterized by physical abuse, sexual abuse, and neglect differ in several significant ways, including epidemiological profiles, interactional patterns, and attributional or cognitive errors—as well as in presenting problems (e.g., Bousha & Twentyman, 1984; Burgess & Conger, 1978; Jason, Williams, Burton, & Rochat, 1982; Larrance & Twentyman, 1983). The population characteristics and assessment and attendant treatment strategies for these groups are sufficiently different (Morton & Ewald, 1987) that we submit they should be conceptualized as having separate problems. In this chapter, therefore, we restrict ourselves to the problem most commonly encountered by clinicians—physical maltreatment of children.

A COGNITIVE–BEHAVIORAL VIEW OF CHILD ABUSE IN A FAMILY CONTEXT

We begin this discussion by presenting certain salient characteristics of abusive families relevant to a cognitive–behavioral approach to family therapy for child abuse. Then we focus on the sequence of cognitions and behaviors which appears to be most central to the abuse itself.

Given that most incidences of child abuse arise from attempts of parents to discipline their children (Gil, 1970), it is not surprising that abusive parents lack effective parenting skills. They are inconsistent in their disciplining or have inadequate discipline skills (Reid, Taplin, & Lorber, 1981; Smith & Hanson, 1975). Moreover, they infrequently discuss matters pertaining to discipline (Young, 1964) and have difficulty setting limits with their children. Abusive mothers are, on the average, younger and less mature (Holmes, 1978) and provide less stimulation to their infants than nonabusers (Dietrich, Starr, & Kaplan, 1980). Abusive parents interact less, and more negatively, with their children than do other parents (Burgess & Conger, 1978), and they show more active physical aggression in interactions with their children (Bousha & Twentyman, 1984).

Abusive families are also subjected to higher levels of stress than other families (Justice & Justice, 1976) and show poor ability to respond effectively to stress. Compared to nonabusive parents, abusive parents are also hyper-responsive to aversive stimuli (Bauer & Twentyman, 1985), show heightened arousal patterns (Disbrow, Doerr, & Caulfield, 1977), and are more defensive in their response to both crying and smiling infant stimuli (Frodi & Lamb, 1978). Moreover, abusive mothers are more impulsive on both cognitive and behavioral tasks than nonabusive comparison mothers (Rohrbeck & Twentyman, 1986).

When parent–child interactions are considered, the abusive parent frequently sees the interactions as more aversive than do nonabusive mothers (Plotkin, 1983) and engages in more aggressive responding (Burgess & Conger, 1978). Abusive parents are also more likely to report that their children are hyperactive and aggressive (Lynch, 1976). In short, these parents are likely to face more stressful situations and also have perceptual biases that lead them to perceive an unusual amount of aversive stress in their world. They are impulsive and irritable, and much of their irritation is child-focused.

Many abusive parents also lack the social skills and competencies that might help counteract the stresses they feel. Additionally, a large number of abusive parents have dysfunctional marital relationships (Green, Gaines, & Sandgrund, 1974; Johnson & Morse, 1968), suffer unemployment (Galdston, 1965), and are socially isolated, with few social support networks (Kempe, 1973; Light, 1973; Polansky, Chalmers, Buttenweiser, & Williams, 1979). Because social support systems are thought to serve as a buffer against stress in general and abuse in particular (Caplan, 1976), this is an important factor for therapists to consider when planning to enter into a family social system.

Abusive parents exhibit cognitive distortions that may interfere with appropriate child treatment. They lack knowledge of child development and of what can be reasonably expected of a child at different ages (Blumberg, 1974; Elmer, 1977; Pollock & Steele, 1972). In addition, there are some abusive parents who are adequately knowledgeable about child development but simply expect that *their* child will conform to their own rigidly held set of expectations. Such unrealistic expectations for a child may be disturbing to the child but may not pose a serious problem when taken alone. A far more serious threat to the child occurs when the parent believes that the child is *intentionally* misbehaving and then punishes the child in order to change his or her "attitude." For example, in our own clinical work, we have repeatedly experienced situations where parents perceive a crying infant as behaving spitefully, with the intention to annoy them.

Although we have centered our attention on parental factors, there is also some evidence that abused babies have more difficult temperaments and that abused preschool children are more likely to be overtly aggressive (Bousha & Twentyman, 1984; George & Main, 1980; Reidy, 1977). They are also more likely to have low birthweight and complications (Fontana & Bernard,

1971; Green et al., 1974), sleeping and eating disorders (Harrington, 1972), cognitive deficits (Birrell & Birrell, 1968; Hoffman-Plotkin & Twentyman, 1984), and developmental delays in language (Blager & Martin, 1976). In short, they may be "difficult" children. We hasten to note that we are not arguing for "blaming the victim" but simply pointing out that a therapist who wishes to work with a family should be cognizant of some of the child responses which may have a significant impact on parental responses such as aggression.

In considering variables that contribute to child abuse, it has proven useful to look at factors that occur immediately prior to an incident (e.g., a household argument between the parents) as well as factors such as the abusive history of the individual or even the employment history in the family. Although it is difficult to determine what deficits causally relate to child abuse, currently there exists correlational evidence suggesting that a number of factors are related to abusive episodes. These include deficits in parenting and social skills, greater sensitivity to stress and impulsivity, and cognitive distortions and misattributions. It is important to realize, however, that a number of authors (Gelles, 1973; Parke & Collmer, 1975) have found that no single variable differentiates abusive from nonabusive parents. Hence it appears that abuse is probably a multiply determined event.

The attributes of abusive family situations described in this section, demonstrated by convergent research lines, will help the therapist identify the problems commonly associated with child abuse. They become even more meaningful when viewed from our theoretical orientation, which is a combination of cognitive–behavioral and family systems approaches to therapy.

In our view, we draw attention to the abuse event itself, and the behaviors, cognitions, and affect associated with that occurrence. We have found it useful to conceptualize the sequence as occurring in a four-stage process, using the parent as "actor" or "perceiver," and involving the sequence of parent cognition–child behavior–parent cognition–parent behavior as the heuristic. Within this model, the parent is said to hold unrealistic expectations for the child (Stage 1). The child's behavior disconfirms these expectations (Stage 2), and then the parent subsequently misattributes the child's action to "spite" or some other intentional response on the part of the child (Stage 3). Finally (Stage 4), the parent overreacts and excessively punishes the child. This simple four-stage microanalysis of the abuse event itself provides a helpful heuristic for capturing the unique problems of assessing and treating abuse and reflects many of the features of abusive families. To illustrate these sequences, we present the following vignette, with recommendation that the interested reader pursue a fuller development of this model in Twentyman, Rohrbeck, and Amish (1984).

Little Johnny's mother has just had arguments with a bill collector, the landlord, and her ex-husband, who is still seeking custody of Johnny. She has also just washed and waxed the kitchen floor, is waiting for the landlord's inspection, and feels physically and emotionally taxed. She expects Johnny to know all this, to help keep the floor clean, be easy on her "frayed nerves," and be considerate at a time when she really feels that she deserves it. This is Stage 1. Johnny, who is accustomed to nagging her to give up watching television and give him a cookie, now enters from outdoors with dirty feet, beginning his tirade for a cookie (Stage 2). Mother's immediate thoughts are, "How could you hassle me like this? *I'll* teach *you* consideration" (Stage 3). Mother then grabs Johnny's arm and slaps his head, scolding him for the nagging, the dirty floor, and the general misery he has given her (Stage 4).

If Mother had thought carefully about it, she might have foreseen Johnny's behavior and might have seen her expectation as unrealistic. Then she might have taken other steps, such as discussing the situation first with Johnny, roping off the floor, counting to 10 and reminding herself that she should have expected it and that it was not Johnny's fault when he first marched into the kitchen, or sending Johnny to a neighbor's house while she relaxed her "frayed nerves." Stage 1, expecting him to know her circumstances, would not have occurred. Even if it had occurred (as it often does in family life) and therefore brought with it Stage 2 (Johnny's messy, noisy entrance), Mother's thoughts about Johnny might have been different. She could have seen him as only doing what he always does, as not knowing any better, or even as a hungry, physically active fellow. Had any of these attributions occurred, Mother probably would have decided not to discipline with physical punishment, but rather to work with him in the future on such desired behavior as wiping his feet before entering, not snacking before dinner, or taking greater responsibility for sharing household duties. Her misattribution that his behavior reflected willfully antagonistic or deliberate provocation (Stage 3) led her to her Stage 4 reaction of overly severe punishment.

There are many modes and mechanisms of aggression (Bandura, 1983). The first three stages could also, of course, lead to verbal rather than physical abuse. Where a parent is repeatedly verbally aggressive with a child, however, the effect over time is likely to be escalating intensity of parental aggression and reactive or retaliatory child behavior (which further provokes parental aggression), with escalation from verbal to physical expression highly probable.

Our focus is on the end result of physical abuse, with or without verbal abuse.

This simple four-stage model focuses considerable attention on the cognitions of the parent both before and after the child's action, drawing attention to the ways that thoughts can mediate the parent's behavioral response to the child's behavior, and suggesting different points in the sequence building toward an abusive event where interventions are possible.

Incidents like this one, when they occur in isolation, are not uncommon. If mother continued to show this pattern in her orientation to Johnny, however, abuse would probably be repeated and many of the patterns characteristic of abusive families might begin developing. Mother's lack of effective parenting skills are evident in both her cognitions and her behavior. An effective parent has the skills of an effective teacher, such as accurately assigning what the child does not know, what the child will and will not respond to, and how to effectively break down the desired larger component behavior (e.g., being considerate of others) into smaller, more teachable units (e.g., wiping feet at the door, asking the parent, "How is your day going?"). An effective teacher keeps both the child's rising competency levels and the desired behavioral goals in mind at all times and employs a broad array of teaching strategies to structure the learning environment so that the child's learning will be maximally successful and rewarding. Johnny's mother did not behave effectively in this situation. The extreme physical punishment (Stage 4) will not by itself help him become a more considerate child. Indeed, if it represents a usual disciplinary strategy, it may well help him become more aggressive and lower in skills of empathy, "consideration," and conflict resolution. Mother's unrealistic expectations of Johnny (Stage 1) and her misattribution about his behavior (Stage 3) could easily spiral toward an increasingly fixed negative view of him and a self-fulfilling prophecy. Thus if he grows older but continues to show lack of consideration or difficulty in getting what he wants without imposing on others around him, he may come to rely more and more on aggressive strategies. Mother may continue to expect (increasingly unrealistically) that "A good beating will teach him who's boss," and in her disappointment at his learning difficulties her attributions concerning him may take on increasingly negative features. Each stage, according to this model, brings the possibility of the next stage, with an abusive episode occurring at Stage 4.

This mother's cognitive distortions are evident in the unrealistic expectations of Johnny and in her misattributions of deliberately antagonistic behavior. Ineffective parenting skills are seen in her impulsive, abusive disciplinary effort.

Johnny, if not already a "difficult" child by most people's standards, could well become one in this environment. Poor child management results in greater stresses in family living, ultimately increasing sensitivities to other stresses, such as the ongoing custody dispute and problems with bill collectors in this vignette. A well-functioning social support system might have eased this mother's stress by providing such friendly assistance as babysitting, mediation of the arguments, or consolation and other emotional support. But if she lacks such a support system and also the skills required to develop one, her stresses will probably become even more overwhelming over time.

Although we have presented a basic four-stage cognitive–behavioral model— and we have seen many cases in our practices where it describes the interactional references quite accurately—it is also a model we are currently elaborating. For example, there are cases, with older children especially, where parental attributions about a child's intentions may in fact be accurate. Moreover, children develop their own cognitive and attributional systems over time; sometimes their systems contribute functionally to the family process, such that the child might, for example, act in a purposefully oppositional way to gain independence from the parent. Since in families all participants are both "actors" and "reactors," interaction sequences typically reflect reciprocal or mutual causality, and the causal agent will vary depending on where the interaction is punctuated and on who is selected as "actor." This inherent circular causality is a part of family life and requires attention by practicing therapists and consideration in future extensions of cognitive–behavioral modeling of child abuse.

Another area for elaboration concerns greater differentiation of the cognitive processes. We believe that there is a difference between having an unrealistic expectation about a child (e.g., "A 2-year-old should be able to flush the toilet"), making a misattribution about the child's action (e.g., "He deliberately left his mess to make me clean up after him"), and the catastrophizing irrational beliefs (e.g., "People will think I'm a bad parent if he does that") described by Ellis (1976). Furthermore, attributional biases can be differentiated in terms of whether the characterization is behavioral or intentional, situation-specific or stable across situations, and positive or negative. The relationships between the three cognitive variables (expectations, attributions, and beliefs) and the differentiation of the cognitive distortions involved in attributions require further exploration. The model presented here represents the most parsimonious cognitive–behavioral sequence resulting in the criterion behavior of child abuse.

To summarize to this point, child abusive parents typically have ineffective parenting skills, cognitive distortions, high levels of stress and low stress thresholds, inadequate social support systems, and often "difficult" children. The cognitive–behavioral model of the abuse episode presented here depicts the way in which parents' unrealistic expectations of their children, when disappointed, lead to misattributions about the child and excessively harsh discipline. We turn next to discussion of the assessment of such families, where the necessity of considering the larger family context becomes apparent in the breadth of the evaluation.

ASSESSMENT

Multimodal assessment for child abuse must take into consideration the relevant functioning of all family members, the interaction patterns among family members, and the larger extrafamilial context. This is a multifaceted, multimethod assessment strategy, and although standard assessment procedures (e.g., intelligence tests, personality measures) are easily incorporated, we have found no substitute for careful interviewing, review of court-sponsored investigations of the case, and observation of *in vivo* interaction of family members. We prefer an assessment strategy combining behavioral assessment methods (e.g., Kanfer & Saslow, 1969) with a cognitive assessment methodology (Meichenbaum, 1976) to ensure coverage of situational variables and the content of cognitions which interfere with successful functioning. The desired outcome of assessment is a detailed functional analysis of the high-risk, abusive situation involving cognition, behavior, and interactional sequencing, all in a context of the situational variables affecting the family's functioning and ability to change.

In this section we discuss specific, target-oriented assessment, conducted to determine therapeutic strategy. In identifying the nature of specific high-risk or abusive situations, it is important to determine who is involved, in what way, under what conditions, and with what outcome. Most typically, child abuse is directed primarily toward one child and by one parent, although there are families where abuse is employed by both parents and with all children. Contrast two cases. In the first, a "spare the rod and spoil the child" orientation is dispensed liberally on all children by both parents, and in the second, the young, stressed mother engages in an escalating conflict with her hyperactive 5-year-old son until the child cries and mother "beats the devil out of him." In the latter family the father may discover the abuse and be instrumental as a therapeutic ally in the change process.

The potent situational variables, as well as the cognitions and behaviors of the abuser and abused, must be examined thoroughly. Sometimes certain child behaviors predictably lead to abusive situations (e.g., failure to obey an instruction, unremitting crying, or causing another sibling to cry), sometimes certain parental conditions predictably lead to child abusive situations (e.g., drinking or quarreling), and a considerable literature exists suggesting that some situations (e.g., bedtime, dinner time, public places) produce higher stress and higher risk than others (cf. Dubanoski, Evans, & Higuchi, 1978).

Once the content of abuse for a particular family is established, then a microlevel analysis of the behaviors and cognitions involved may be developed. Using the four-stage cognitive–behavioral model described earlier, which focuses on inappropriate cognitions and behaviors of the parent, three assessment foci become central: parents' unrealistic expectations, parental systematic misattributions, and parents' abusive responses to a child's behavior.

Unrealistic expectations about the child are commonly based on incorrect presumptions that the child is emotionally or mentally capable of some action or reaction. Such cases include the parent expecting an infant to refrain from crying even when it is in pain, a toddler to understand complex verbal instructions, or a young child to be more empathic, nurturant, and protective of a distressed parent. Many of these unrealistic expectations may be rooted in misunderstanding of child maturational processes and of what can be legitimately expected of a child of a given age. Therefore, assessment focuses on the parents' degree of understanding about child development at the most gross level. One simple approach here is to ask parents to describe the areas in which their child is developing relatively rapidly and areas where he or she appears "slow." Alternatively, we might ask parents to describe what they are "working on" with the child (e.g., sleeping through the night, weaning, going to bed or coming home on time) to elicit this kind of information. Probes to clarify parents' views of their child's development and their own role in facilitating this development will often reveal unrealistic parental beliefs that a preoperational child should be operational, or that some behaviors which require extensive coaching and shaping should be manifest spontaneously by the child without help and feedback.

Systematic parental misattributions involve the attributing of intentional malevolence or negative personality attributes to the child, typically with the attendant implication that the parent has the moral responsibility to correct these child attributes. Most common are attributions that the child is willfully and purposely "baiting" or spiting the parent, or knowingly causing problems for the parent. Indeed, some of the most severe child abuse cases involve such attributions of devilishness or badness and the attendant self-justifications of moral righteousness on the part of the parents. These attributions may be assessed by presenting a series of vignettes to parents which involve problematic parent–child interaction sequences, and then asking parents to characterize the problem, its causes, and its possible solutions. A variation is having the parents describe actual recent events where the child was irritating and their own thoughts as the irritation mounted:

Client: Jim made Suzie cry, so I spanked him. He kept screaming, so I kept hitting him.
Therapist: You find it hard to handle Jim?
Client: Yes. He's got a mean streak in him a mile wide.
Therapist: What were you thinking when you started spanking him?
Client: He's getting on my case and trying to get me in trouble with the social workers again.
Therapist: Could he do that?
Client: Oh yes. Sometimes I even think he's trying to give me a mental breakdown.

Another variation involves asking the parent what an "ideal parent" would do in that situation. The parent just described might well have responded that an ideal parent would not have had such a child as Jim, or simply be unable to imagine what an ideal parent would do. This would be an opportunity for the therapist to begin to suggest alternative thoughts, such as "The baby is about ready for a nap" or "Jim is acting bored; maybe we can figure out a fun thing to do together." The assessment of parental abusive responses requires careful work by the clinician. What forms of physical aggressiveness are used, and to what degree are impulsivity and irritability contributing to the problem? What cognitions and perceptions occur just prior to the abuse? How conscious is the parent of his or her escalating frustration, and how much is the parent attempting to regulate his or her own aggressive impulses at the time? What behavioral sequence leads to the abusive event? What other child management or self-control strategies does that parent already have to her or his repertoire, and what alternatives may need to be developed for such situations? Information about the specific behaviors associated with abuse, and about the larger behavioral repertoire, is critical in determining the best intervention strategy for use with that parent.

In our own clinical work we usually proceed by asking the parent about situations which cause trouble and suggest that the parent and child "solve" an ongoing problem in front of the therapist. In the course of a few minutes of interacting, most children will display some positive problem-solving behaviors (e.g., making suggestions, generating alternatives, or elaborating their point of view). Typically, the parent ignores these and focuses on other child behaviors, or even verbally punishes the child's apparent attempts to be helpful. In some cases, using this method, we have seen parents become physical with their children in the session itself, which we will hasten to interrupt. The *in vivo* "problem solving" described here can be repeated, easily and naturalistically, either for purposes of assessment or to permit the therapist to coach the parents repeatedly as necessary. It is indeed our experience that the parents' willingness to change is reflected in their ability to accept feedback and try alternative approaches such as verbally praising the child.

To assess the role and nature of cognitions in relation to feelings of irritability, we usually ask the parent to describe three or four specific situations (both child and nonchild) that *currently* cause the parent to become irritable; we also ask them to rate their level of annoyance in each situation and to describe their thoughts during these situations. Taken together, these probes provide useful information to the therapist about the client's idiosyncratic views or intrusive thoughts.

We have targeted parental cognitions and behaviors for special attention in assessment and subsequent treatment, and the parent is more commonly the focus of first-order change efforts in the four-stage model we present. The third stage in this model of the child abuse sequence, however, is the child's behavior. Careful assessment of this component is necessary too. Because, as noted earlier, abused children are often more "difficult" and may be poorer at attending, learning, and responding to adults in general, a full intellectual, emotional, and physical assessment should be available. We have encountered cases where children were frequently beaten for "not listening" when one was deaf, for "not paying attention" when another had pharmacologically remediable hyperactivity, and for "crying too much" when a third was in pain from a tumor. In other situations detailed assessment of the child's behavior may help the parent become a better observer of the precise situational variables affecting the child at the time, and of the variability in the child's behavior across different situations. Such information alone may sometimes alter dysfunctional attributions about the child. In all of these families, assessment of the child's behavior and its causes and maintaining circumstances is necessary whether targeting parental change primarily or directly targeting the child's behavior initially.

In addition to careful assessment of the specific high-risk or abusive situations in a particular family, and the cognitions and behaviors involved, it is also necessary to assess the ancillary conditions that might cause and maintain the abusiveness or militate against sufficient therapeutic change. As mentioned earlier, these families often share a long history of using abuse as a child disciplinary method, and they may have had no instruction in alternative means of child rearing. Many of these families, or members of these families, are also deficient in a variety of social skills necessary for satisfactory relationships. Inability to listen well and receive another's message as it was intended, for example, restricts the information the listener has and therefore the potential for desirable changes in that person and in his or her relationships. Poor self-expression skills will prevent adequate communication of what an individual feels, thinks, and wants, and includes both positive feedback (e.g., compliments, statements of appreciation) and negative feedback (e.g., criticism, expressions of disagreement or disapproval). Skill in describing and explaining oneself and in giving evaluative feedback to others is a major ingredient of social adjustment and is of particular importance in family life where all members are involved in mutual social influence processes. A common problem in this regard is failure to communicate with efficient behavioral specificity (complaining about another's inattentiveness, for example, is not as likely to produce the desired change as requesting that he or she refrain from watching television during dinner or call if he or she will not be home for supper). These skills of listening, asserting, explaining, and requesting change in another, when combined with negotiation skills, provide an individual with the means for nonviolent conflict resolution and the development of positive intimate relationships. Individuals and families who possess only low levels of these social skills will experience difficulties in child rearing and family life. They may also lack social support and other friendship systems, as we have noted, and their marital conflicts may be caused, or exacerbated, by poor communication and social skills, which may in turn further impair their parenting skills.

In addition to these interactional variables, the individual levels of mental, social, and emotional functioning are assessed for parents and child in order to determine to what extent, if any, common correlates such as retardation, depression, psychosis or other acute disturbances, and social isolation might exist, reflecting cause, consequence, or mitigating circumstances for abusiveness. These ancillary modes and levels of functioning for the involved individuals and relationships for the family as a whole thus require detailed and extensive assessment.

CLINICAL STRATEGIES AND TECHNIQUES

For the most part, cognitive–behavioral strategies and techniques with demonstrated effectiveness with other problem populations have been adopted by therapists for use with child abusive families. The list of possible cognitive–behavioral techniques for intervening in abusive families is exceedingly long. However, four primary strategies are so common as to be nearly always employed in some form in treating one of these families.

Strategy: Facilitate family conflict resolution by decreasing perceptions of other members as adversaries with hostile intentions. Members of these families all too often perceive each other in rigidly held and negative ways—"rotten egg," "troublemaker," "uncaring," "hysterical." These negative labels reflect a perceptual bias which militates against close and careful observation of changes (even positive ones) in the offending other, and therefore obstruct celebration and rewarding of positive changes in the other. In addition, of course, negative labels can serve a self-fulfilling prophecy role, in that the "bad boy" or "bully" eventually is likely to act that way. The therapist can help "weaken" these negative attributions, challenging or questioning the implied hostile intentions and helping parents replace them with objective or more positive attributional explanations.

The technique of "positive reframing" (Haley, 1976) is a powerful tool in the therapist's armamentarium. When the hungry, crying child is described by the parent(s) as demanding, greedy, or selfish, the therapist tactfully restates this as vulnerable, in pain, and appropriately seeking assistance from a stronger, more able and compassionate parent. When the hostile parent describes the young boy's reluctance to go to bed as a malicious "power play" or "deliberate needling," it is positively reframed by the therapist as simply a reflection of the boy's admiration of adults and his desire to stay up late with them. Positive reframing usually begins within the first session and typically continues throughout the treatment, or until the target individuals have adopted the new attribution satisfactorily.

There is a fine line between positive reframing and the more usual socratic approach commonly used by most cognitive–behavioral therapists. The advantage of the socratic approach is that it rests on self-generated cognitions, so a new attribution is likely to have more face validity to the client; by the same token, this method offers a clear means by which the client can learn to identify and correct for attributional bias (which might seem to increase generalization and maintenance of treatment gains). That is, the Socratic approach seems to hold greater potential for teaching the client to "think about how he or she thinks." The advantage of the positive reframing technique is strategic. Where family members are caught in an attributional war of blaming such that acknowledging a weakened cognition in the presence of the others is seen as "giving in," the therapist's directive positive framing is used to disrupt the usual blame cycles and shift explanatory schema and cooperative alliances into qualitatively different interaction contexts.

We have found that positive reframing has particularly high comparative value in situations where the need for dramatic behavior change is relatively urgent. This is sometimes the case where a family (typically with older children) is caught in fiercely competing and mutually exclusive attributional schemes to such a degree that the interaction style is continuing overt conflict; here the therapist must establish control over the process and move quietly toward a less defensive, more cooperative problem-solving form. Indeed, it was for these kinds of overtly conflictual entanglements (both behaviorally and symbolically, or in terms of "meanings") that Haley (1976) developed this particular technique. The other kind of situation where there are clear advantages to positive reframing is where the risk and severity of abuse are high. In such cases, direct and immediate assault of an attributional error along with an immediate focus on alternative strategies for child discipline and impulse control are often called for. Positive reframing, in short, offers a rapid means of altering meanings differently to set the stage for a focus on relatively immediate behavior change; this is useful where the criterion behavior of abuse is necessarily the focus of an intensive and direct change effort. The socratic method can be more consistently used as a way to teach clients to examine and modify their own cognitions and is preferable when cognitive change is of high priority (or when immediate behavioral change is less necessary).

"Objectification" exercises (Weiss, 1980) train a client to be nonjudgmental but very observant. They require detailed description of an interaction sequence or behavioral pattern without resorting to judgments of intentionality or evaluations of goodness or badness. Where such exercises are used successfully with all family members, this technique permits the family to agree on scenarios of past events or desirable future events. Families who can converse with neutral language will solve problems more effectively.

We have found it therapeutic to make ample use of humor, role playing, and other tension-reducing, enjoyable activities. This diminishes the aversiveness and stressfulness of therapy sessions and makes the therapist and the therapy itself less threatening. In a more relaxed and pleasant setting, clients more readily drop self-justificatory cognitions and defensive behaviors and more easily adopt positive relabeling and reframing. This approach was so effective in one case that a parent, newly able to laugh at himself, brought newspaper cartoon clippings about cognitive distortions to therapy visits.

Sometimes a brief education about child maturational stages is necessary when parents are found to have unrealistic expectations of their children's potential competencies. In most cases therapists provide impromptu reminders of such behavioral concepts as "shaping" and "successive approximation," and where more education is necessary, it is commonly provided through formally conducted group sessions or through bibliotherapy. For those parents willing and able to profit from bibliotherapy, we have found *Parents Are Teachers* (Becker, 1971) and *Families: Applications of Social Learning Theory to Family Life* (Patterson, 1971) to be particularly useful.

Often we have found it useful to redirect each family member's attention to his or her own self-change rather than toward futile and frustrating attempts to change someone else. Thus an abusive mother might be encouraged to focus not on "changing the attitude" of her child but rather on monitoring her own frustration level and employing a series of anger-control mechanisms (e.g., relaxation techniques, counting to 10) to "cool off" instead of acting in a physically aggressive manner. When a family constellation permits, an orchestrated array of self-change programs can be adopted by several members at once. In one family, the abused 10-year-old worked to improve school performance and homework, as well as mastering new chores and self-help responsibilities (e.g., dishwashing, vacuuming her own room) while the abuse-prone mother worked on improving her stress management and pleasurable social contacts. The previously uninvolved father worked with the mother on marital communication, and he was given the role of monitoring and administering rewards and praise to both child and mother as they progressed in their self-change programs.

Strategy: Reduce risk of abuse by providing training in effective child-management techniques. Because abuse incidents typically occur as a result of a parent's attempt to discipline a child, parent training has become a central treatment component in virtually all child abuse regimens. These training programs were developed originally for parents of "difficult" or "behavior problem" children, and they usually consist of helping parents identify desirable and undesirable behaviors, praise more and criticize less, and be more attentive and consistent in their child management. Such parent training components have been used successfully for a wide range of child problems (e.g., Alvord, 1971; Conger, Lahey, & Smith, 1981; Denicola & Sandler, 1980; Egan, 1983; Patterson, 1976, 1982; Wolfe & Sandler, 1981). More recently, such parenting effectiveness training has been applied successfully as the treatment of choice for child abusive families (Blythe, 1983; Gambrill, 1983). This strategy involves training the parent to 1) pinpoint the child's appropriate and inappropriate behaviors; 2) provide consistent consequences for those behaviors; 3) monitor behavioral changes; 4) shape more complex behavioral clusters through successive approximation; and 5) use effective communication, and, if the child is sufficiently mature and verbal (typically age 4 or older), negotiation and behavioral contracting (Kelly, 1983).

At times it is helpful for the therapist to participate directly in a program to modify a specific child behavior as a way to bring that behavior under control with expediency and to demonstrate effective parenting. An example of the first would be bedwetting, which can often be successfully altered in a very brief period of time. An example of the second with a resistant, disbelieving parent could be a demonstration by the therapist of how easily a child can change when target behaviors are clearly identified and approached systematically, one at a time. At times, then, the therapist will assume a greater directiveness in isolating a target behavior and designing a change program for it, assisting the parent in administering it at home between sessions. Later, of course, the therapist will assume progressively less directiveness as the parents assume greater responsibilities for parenting.

Finally, it is sometimes advantageous to use behavior modification techniques to "help the child help the parent" with his or her newly acquired parenting skills. Independently training a child to provide "please and thank you" rewards facilitates acquisition and maintenance of parents' new behaviors. In using a token economy home program, it is sometimes helpful to have the child, not the parent, initiate the daily review of contracted chores and attendant consequences. Frazier and Levine (1983) provided an interesting case study where the therapists used behavioral conditioning techniques with an abused child so that the child was less offensive to the mother.

Strategy: Provide all relevant individuals with alternative means of coping with anger and frustration. Another central treatment strategy for abusive families is teaching improved self-control, particularly improved means of managing irritation, aggressive impulses, and frustration-producing cognitions. Probably the best known example of this is provided by Novaco (1978), although others (e.g., Beck, 1976; Beck, Rush, Shaw, & Emery, 1979; Bedrosian, 1982; Ellis, 1976) have also described various cognitive behavioral interventions for coping with anger and stress. All of these techniques require that the aggression-prone client pinpoint the onset of anger, identify irrational beliefs about one's self, the irritating child, or the world that "drive" the anger, and delay impulsive responding, substituting new, more realistic and tolerant cognition and dissipating anger in alternative ways.

The identification of the irrational beliefs and unrealistic expectations of abusive parents concerning their children has already been discussed as a key feature for assessment and treatment of such families. In addition, such parents may have irrational beliefs quite independent of their children that cause the buildup of anger and increase the risk of abuse. These include "catastrophizing" and "perfectionistic" beliefs (e.g., "I cannot recover the 'loss of face' when my son contradicts me in public" or "If I slip up once in my self-change program I might as well throw in the towel"). Often simply identifying the irrational belief or unrealistic expectation is enough to weaken conviction sufficiently to allow the client to consider alternative and more appropriate cognitions. In most cases identification of irrational or dysfunctional cognitions must be followed with the structuring of repeated trials over the course of therapy to ensure that the replacement of cognition has become an automatic process.

Delay of impulsive responding is approached through a variety of techniques (Azar & Twentyman, 1984; Wolfe & Sandler, 1981; Wolfe, Sandler, & Kaufman, 1981). Very commonly, clients profit from relaxation training, which orients them toward monitoring their own tension levels more closely and teaches them to intervene early in times of mounting tension to relax their muscles, "empty their minds," slow their breathing, and so on. Thought stoppage approaches are sometimes helpful; the client is trained to interrupt a predictable and destructive cognitive–affective sequence, often facilitated by abruptly switching to a distracting and interfering activity, by counting to 10, by breathing deeply and practicing relaxation techniques. In some cases we have found it possible for a client in a highly charged situation to learn to refrain from habitual conflict-enhancing and frustration-producing behavior, substituting a "loving act" followed by a self-reward.

In one case a highly frustrating situation occurred each night with the parent periodically yelling to the five-year-old son to turn off the television and get ready for bed, while the child ignored her until the shouting shifted to physically rough and sometimes abusive treatment. Here, the mother was directed to join the child 20 minutes before bedtime and interact "lovingly" (operationally defined, of course, as praising, inquiring about his day, and conversing with him about topics known to be of interest to him, or which he brought up in response to inquiry). After 20 minutes of this joint television period, she was then to rise, turn off the television, and tell the child to complete bedtime preparations and meet her in his bedroom for a bedtime story. This technique was successful in negotiating the bedtime hour peacefully, and the parent was instructed to then treat herself to a hot bath, one of her few pleasures, and some self-congratulatory thoughts about her effectiveness as a child manager. In this situation it is noted that the parent might not have *felt* loving but was able to emit sufficient self-control to *act* more lovingly (i.e., in an effective parental way), a performance for which self-reward was indeed well earned.

Sometimes it has proven useful to employ explicit desensitization techniques when family members have become highly reactive to each other. Not uncommonly a parent will improve his or her parenting behaviors, resulting in improved child functioning, but the parent will continue to be wary of the child, experiencing agitation even when thinking of that child or hearing the child's voice. In such situations modification of the affect can occur through a combination of relaxation training with covert desensitization (guided imagery involving the child in situations of increasing arousal value). *In vivo* desensitization can also be effective, as in the case where an abusive parent afraid to touch a crying infant for fear of hurting it is coached in repeated trials to approach, then touch, then pick up the baby in a sleeping state, then in an awake but not crying state, and finally in a crying state.

Many techniques encompassed by an intervention strategy for teaching family members new ways to deal with anger and conflict involve problem-solving and communication training. Where marital conflict contributes to the stresses resulting in child abuse, or when marital conflicts are themselves characterized by spousal abuse, cognitive–behavioral techniques for training these skills are recommended. Margolin (1979) described such an approach to enhance anger management and improve individual and dyadic problem solving. Treatment components in this approach include identification of cues contributing to angry exchanges for use as discriminative cues for coping responses antagonistic to anger, establishing ground rules and consequences for rule violation, designing a way to interrupt the conflict pattern (commenting on it in a neutral tone, switching the topic, or leaving the situation), eliminating the provocation through a behavior modification or environmental effort, modifying faulty thinking regarding relationship functioning, developing problem-solving skills such as defining a problem in a nonblaming way, being attentive and understanding to the other, and brainstorming specific suggestions for change.

Where children are old enough to participate in discussions (sometimes as young as 4 years), they are properly included in family problem-solving training along these lines, with negotiated behavioral contracts a useful product. Indeed, we have found that the family discussions of family problems and possible solutions required for developing a good contract, whether conducted in the office or in the home, are usually the ideal context for informal communication and problem-solving training. The resulting behavioral contracts, in turn, allow members to develop their own change programs and are helpful in developing realistic expectations for change in both the self and the other family members.

As in the other intervention strategies, it is sometimes desirable to work with children directly, desensitizing them to parents, or teaching them the skills of anger control, problem solving, and communication. On occasion this is most fruitfully conducted in child-only sessions with the therapist. We tend to prefer problem-solving practice involving the entire family, for the most part, as it affords the richest opportunity both to assess and to intervene with the myriad of problematic family interactions. Interaction in family systems operates with circular causality, with each member's participation being both in response to the behaviors of others, and in turn a cause of another's behaviors (see Chapter 2). Working with the full family permits a larger array of potential change points in that system.

Strategy: Provide means of reducing overall stresses and improve stress management. To this point, the three general strategies presented for intervening in abusive families—improving perceptions, child management effectiveness, and anger and frustration control—focus on changes integral to the cognitions, behaviors, and affect most directly related to the abuse itself. This fourth and final strategy addresses alleviation of ancillary stresses on stress-related dysfunctions which maintain an abuse-prone environment. Often this will mean specialized treatment for such concomitant problems as alcoholism or drug abuse, parental depression or migraine headaches, and children's problems associated with physical or learning disabilities. In some instances we serve as primary therapists for these treatments as well, and in many situations we might refer to other therapists. Although it would seem ideal and expedient to treat child abuse as directly and immediately as possible and to arrange for treatment of ancillary conditions after the abusive pattern has been altered, there are times when one of these conditions may be so extreme as to prohibit effective intervention with child abuse.

A rich and thorough assessment of the individual family members, their relationships with one another, and the larger social context for the family usually permits isolation of stresses which can be reduced or eliminated through cognitive–behavioral interventions. Because these family members commonly are highly stressed and have low stress thresholds, we typically provide training in general coping and stress-management skills. These skills include but are not limited to those of assertion, time management, money management, social support building, and sometimes even home safety management. More specifically targeted skills training for anger and stress management, problem solving, and communication may be employed to enhance the family members' competence in dealing with extrafamilial factors and individuals. Where caseload numbers permit, such coping skills for general life problems are often enhanced in group therapy. Group approaches, when participants are sufficiently motivated and agendas (including homework sessions) are well planned, can offer a rich source of social support and social comparison for participants as they work toward improving their coping skills and social support–building talents.

Many of the techniques taught in this approach involve the assignment of homework (e.g., reading, practice, observing, or recording), permitting continuing progress at home between sessions. Establishing adequate motivation for doing the homework and ensuring that expectations are clearly understood are thus further tasks of the therapist in this approach. While some approaches build incentives through concrete rewards or money, we have typically relied on the involvement of the client in designing the homework in collaboration with the therapist, and occasionally on the use of telephone calls to prompt and encourage homework between sessions in cases where such encouragement seems needed.

Special attention is given here to the lack of social support systems and the lack of social support–building skills found so often in abusive families. We have found that reversals of these trends have considerable value in maintaining other treatment gains and in providing a buffer against posttherapy stressors that could promote recidivism. Ongoing support groups are usually offered by social agencies in large cities, often targeted specifically to abusive parents (e.g., Parents Anonymous) or to those with other distinguishing characteristics (e.g., Alcoholics Anonymous, Al-Anon, Parents Without Partners, Parents of Learning Disabled Children). For the social isolates, these forums provide for a social exchange with peers as emergent (non–mental health professional) role models. Improving relationships with neighbors, local church- or school-sponsored groups, or extended family members is sometimes fruitful too.

Many of these families lack social support systems due to the lack of requisite social skills necessary to build and maintain such networks. In many of these families, there is little positive, cooperative exchange and a predominance of hostile, antagonistic, and combative interaction, a pattern that often extends to their extrafamilial relationships as well. Teaching these families the art of cooperative and pleasurable exchange is a time-consuming but worthwhile process. Some evidence suggests that a dysfunctional family behaves dysfunctionally only in those situations framed as competitive and is indistinguishable from well-functioning families in those situations framed as cooperative (Barton & Alexander, 1979). Helping to frame an ever increasing list of daily events as essentially noncompetitive and even cooperative is a challenging but productive approach. This usually begins in therapy sessions, where the skillful therapist may make use of humor, games, and guided interactions concerning nonthreatening, rewarding topics (e.g., a Sunday picnic at the beach), but may extend into homework assignments where family members are asked to support one another's attempts to develop new social skills and enhanced social support systems. We commonly ask families to express strong endorsement of each other's affiliations with local school-, agency-, or church-sponsored groups such as Little League, Girl Scouts, or a Bible studies class, and we encourage renewed relationships with neighbors and members of the extended family.

In summary, we have presented four clinical strategies we use in virtually all child abuse families: 1) changing perceptions of other members; 2) modifying child-management techniques of the parents; 3) changing methods for coping with anger and frustration; and 4) reducing overall stresses and improving overall stress management. There is no fixed sequence in which we recommend employing such strategies; indeed in most cases we follow these strategies simultaneously. Typically, the specific changes targeted in each of these areas are introduced and discussed early in treatment, as part of establishing a treatment contract with the family, and initial change techniques will be employed for all of these areas. Particular emphasis on any strategy or any sequencing involved is dependent on the characteristics of the particular family involved.

TECHNIQUES USED IN JOINING WITH THE FAMILY

Child abusive families are particularly defensive and resistant to entering family therapy. They are likely to hold to their negative and blaming attributions about one another tenaciously and, like other dysfunctioning families, each member may compete to get the therapist to adopt his or her own perceptual biases and misattributions. Successful "joining" with the family as a unit is therefore a serious challenge to the therapist, who strives for eventual acceptance by the family for their collective good.

Joining with the family presents different problems depending on the referral source and the presenting problem. On occasion parents will seek therapy on their own initiative, worried that their disciplinary methods might be abusive, or frightened that they cannot control their rageful reaction to their children. These cases, while relatively rare, are comparatively easy because the parent, child, and therapist usually quickly agree about the definition of the problem and the desirability of change.

More common than this is a different presenting problem—usually an aggressive, misbehaving, or otherwise "difficult" child, or alternatively an unhappy marriage, spouse abuse, or depression in one or both parents. In these cases child abuse is "discovered" by the therapist in the course of assessing or treating another problem. In these situations we will treat the presenting problem seriously, at least at face value, and work to build rapport while subtly substituting a new or additional focus on parenting difficulties. If adequate rapport has already been established, it is often relatively simple to induce clients to admit to additional problems. Refraining from pejorative labeling is obviously important, and we are careful to frame the problem as "child-management difficulties" or "having a hard time with angry feelings" rather than "child abuse."

Most child abusive families are referred by agency workers, typically accompanied by a court order to obtain treatment. In some cities the family will have already undergone an extensive social and psychological "workup," again by court order. This referral history typically results in an especially denying, defensive, and blaming family, whose members feel angry and coerced into coming to therapy. They are likely to feel that people in the "helping professions" have not in fact been operating in their best interest, and will be reluctant to work cooperatively and trustingly with the new therapist.

These motivational issues need to be addressed at the outset of therapy, because it is nonproductive in many cases for the therapist to be identified with a system that clients may have experienced as abusive. To avoid a future possibility of conflict of interest, the therapist must assert his or her unique role and responsibility and explain his or her relationships with the other court and agency professionals involved. Mandatory reporting laws, designed to protect the child's welfare, supersede usual guarantees of confidentiality, and they require the therapist to report abusive incidents. In addition, there may be continuing contact between court or agency workers, and the clinician may even be required to submit periodic reports to them. We typically describe ourselves as advocates for the "family," explain our separateness from the legal system, and explain the commitment to report abuse as protection for the family. Indeed we have often met with a family, and sometimes an attendant court worker, *during* the period when an abusive event was reported. Because each new report of abuse is extremely stressful for the family, possibly provoking further incidents, these are in fact ideal times to demonstrate advocacy for the family, and to provide support and problem-solving strategies.

The first issue in nearly all intake sessions is whether the alleged abuse in fact occurred or, more generally, whether the family has this problem. Here we have found it most helpful to remain uninvolved in the "detective work" necessary to ascertain veracity, if that is in contention with the family, and to reframe the problem instead. Thus we propose to the family that the problem is that someone in authority (e.g., a judge) thinks they have a problem. Focus can then turn with less defensiveness to how the family can solve that problem.

We typically express acknowledgment of the current stresses already impinging on the family, as well as the difficulties facing them in the immediate future (in terms of making extremely difficult changes in how they relate to each other, as well as in terms of their future involvement with the court and related agencies). Our efforts in this initial intake session focus on establishing our willingness to work with the family and to offer them support throughout this process. Such families, under siege from forces both within and outside of the family, are reflexively resistant and defensive in this circumstance; establishing adequate rapport with the family as a unit is thus a critical first step.

With resistant families we often find it is useful to refrain from dealing *immediately* with issues of abuse. Rather, our approach is to get the clients to state what their problems have been and why they are coming to therapy at the present time. In this way issues of abuse which are blatantly denied by the clients can be "reframed" into issues concerning a problem with the legal system or a state agency. In defining the client's problem this way, the therapist need not avoid an important and usually central issue which brought the clients to therapy in the first place, but the therapist also avoids getting stuck on issues of the factuality of whether abuse did or did not really occur.

In avoiding defensive posturing, the therapist seeks to join the family with a problem-solving approach. Initially this usually takes the form of "What can I do to help you solve your problems better?" This stance usually helps direct the clients to give examples of what their current problems are. If this approach is effective, the therapist has usually taken the first step in forming an alliance with the family. Sometimes, however, families begin by defining their only problem as harassment by social services and the courts. At this point the therapist should highlight the fact that they indeed may have a very large problem but also begin an exploration to determine whether the family believes that working with a therapist can have any impact on that problem. At this point some families are open enough to respond by saying that they do not believe the therapist can help. It has been our experience at these times that a useful joining technique is to continue with the problem-solving and exploratory stance, asking the family how they want to solve their problem with social services and the court then, because they have admitted that those parties continue to cause them difficulty. This approach allows the family to explore their alternatives, including not returning to therapy, as well as some of the realistic consequences of the alternatives (e.g., violation of a court order to obtain therapy often has known consequences).

SPECIAL CLINICAL ISSUES IN THE TREATMENT OF CHILD ABUSE

Mandatory Reporting of Child Abuse

Mandatory reporting laws present a particularly salient clinical issue for child abuse therapists. The clinician should be aware of the language of the law where he or she is practicing. Although these laws are usually sufficiently clear, many of the specific incidents encountered while working with a family may not have clear implications. For example, if a therapist encounters a child with severe bruises, it is clear that a report must be filed. In other instances, such as a parent reporting spankings (without leaving bruises), more thought may be required on the part of the therapist, especially if the family has been able to make some form of alliance with the therapist to work on their problems and in light of the fact that foster care placement may, singly and just by its very nature, have a long-term negative impact on the child. The characteristic tensions among commitment to the law, to the family unit, and to the individual members, particularly the abused child, give the field its peculiar flavor. A clinician must be very clear about his or her allegiances and about who the "client" is, and still obey the law, which is designed to protect the child.

Therapist Reactions of Child Abuse

Treatment of child abuse can be a highly distressing enterprise, and some of the more violent, torturous, and vindictive cases can be very moving. The tendency for novice therapists and caseworkers is to side with the child, and in a way which impedes effective case management because it increases parents' defensiveness and resistance to treatment. If indeed the client is the family and the therapeutic goal is to improve family functioning, the therapist must take special care to remain objective and refrain from imposing personal emotion-based evaluations unnecessarily upon the case. We know therapists who found child abuse so heinous and unacceptable an act that they were psychologically unable and morally unwilling to take such cases. Such selective practice is honorable and appropriate when based on self-knowledge and forethought. Contributing to the negative labeling process in the role of a therapist is antitherapeutic and should be avoided.

Use of Home Visits

Regular home visits facilitate several therapeutic aims. First, they increase access to therapy for families who often fail to keep scheduled appointments, and whose social isolation may be so severe that they have no telephone or reliable transportation. Second, they increase generalizability to the home setting of skills acquired in the office. Third, they provide a far richer source of information about the family's lifestyle than office assessment alone. The frequency of such home visitation is a matter of pragmatics and logistics, in many cases, but we recommend at least one such visit where possible. Such visits permit comparison of interaction patterns in the office to the naturalistic home setting and can also provide important assessment information, particularly with regard to the differential diagnosis and treatment planning necessary where abuse is combined with neglect (as evidenced in unsanitary or dangerous home conditions, for example).

Who Is Included in Treatment, and When?

Where possible, we find it most helpful to include all family members in all sessions. This is consistent with assessment and treatment focused on the family system. Children's participation adds a considerable amount of information about the actual interactional patterns with their parents. This is especially important in working with abusive parents because of the possibility that considerable cognitive distortion occurs on the parent's part, so that parents' reports are particularly unreliable. The therapist can also gain useful information about the specifics of an abused child's problems and can identify child changes which might have helpful impact on parent changes. Consistent with the systems perspective, it is very important that the nonabusive parent and nonabused child be included as fully as possible. Their presence ensures assessment and treatment of the problem in its larger context, and these members have roles that may be altered to modify the abusive relationship(s). Times for excluding children or other adults are largely restricted to those sessions where discussion of unsuitable content (e.g., sex or money) is planned, or when structured training with considerable educational material is expected, for which children's presence might be simply a distraction. Otherwise, we recommend the inclusion of even very young children in all sessions where possible. They may represent additional stresses in the therapy interaction, but this only heightens the realism of the interactions in terms of a sample of high-stress family life.

Presence of Excessive Physical Harm to the Abused Child

If the abuse pattern is chronic and the episodes are severe, the child is at too much risk and should be removed from the home for safety reasons. Of course, these methods are still useful even when the child has been removed from the home, if treatment plans call for treatment of parents during this period and subsequent experimental reuniting of the parent(s) and child. Where this is the case, strategies for changing parental cognitions, anger and stress management, overall stresses, and sometimes didactic parent training may be employed in preparation for return of the child to the home.

Alcoholism and Drug Abuse

Where alcoholism or drug abuse by the child abusing parent is too pronounced, the effectiveness of family therapy directed at the child abuse will be limited. As many as 50% of all abusive incidents occur in connection with drugs or alcohol. Extreme and chronic chemical dependency by child abusing parents dramatically reduces the efficacy of this and other forms of treatment. The extent of substance abuse generally, and of intoxication during abusive periods particularly, must be evaluated carefully, and plans must be made for its treatment. This may be accomplished by referring the particular individual to detoxification, residential treatment, or other outpatient substance abuse treatment programs or by incorporating substance abuse treatment into the overarching multicomponent primary treatment of the entire child abuse family.

Severe Psychopathology

Where psychopathology is too severe, this approach is also limited. Again, because it employs cognitive techniques, its application with severely cognitively disturbed individuals (e.g., psychotics) would probably be unproductive. However, many personality types are amenable to the approach described here. Similarly, the maternal depression commonly found in these families is often remediable in a concurrent treatment effort. In most cases we recommend that the therapist treating the family also treat the depression of such a parent, especially when that depression is related to parenthood or to the parent–child relationship. This provides greater assurance of treatment coordination and maximizes the impact of treatment on the entire family system. Where the therapist does not have sufficient expertise in a specialty treatment or where the logistics of the family therapy plan militate against this, of course, referral for individual treatment to another therapist is desirable.

REFERENCES

Alvord, J.R. (1971). The home token economy: A motivational system for the home. *Corrective Psychiatry and Journal of Social Therapy, 17,* 6–13.

Azar, S.T., & Twentyman, C.T. (1984, November). *An evaluation of a parent training program for child maltreatment.* Paper presented at the annual meeting of the Association for Advancement of Behavior Therapy, Philadelphia.

Bandura, A. (1983). Psychological mechanisms of aggression. In R.G. Green & E.I. Donnerstein (Eds.), *Aggression: A theoretical and empirical review* (pp. 1–40). New York: Academic Press.

Barton, C., & Alexander, J.F. (1979, August). *Delinquent and normal family interaction in competitive and cooperational conditions.* Paper presented at the annual meeting of the American Psychological Association, New York.

Bauer, W., & Twentyman, C.T. (1985). Abusing, neglectful, and comparison mother's reactions to child-related and non–child-related stressors. *Journal of Consulting and Clinical Psychology, 53*(3), 335–343.

Beck, A.T. (1976). *Cognitive therapy and the emotional disorders.* New York: International Universities Press.

Beck, A.T., Rush, A.J., Shaw, B.F., & Emery, G. (1979). *Cognitive therapy of depression.* New York: Guilford Press.

Becker, W.C. (1971). *Parents are teachers.* Champaign, IL: Research Press.

Bedrosian, R.C. (1982). Using cognitive and systems intervention in the treatment of marital violence. In J.C. Hansen & L.R. Barnhill (Eds.), *Clinical approaches to family violence* (pp. 117–138). Rockville, MD: Aspen Systems Corp.

Birrell, R.G., & Birrell, J.H. (1968). The maltreatment syndrome in children: A hospital survey. *Medical Journal of Australia, 2,* 1023–1029.

Blager, F., & Martin, H.P. (1976). Speech and language of abused children. In H.P. Martin (Ed.), *The abused child: A multidisciplinary approach to developmental issues and treatment* (pp. 83–92). Cambridge, MA: Ballinger.

Blumberg, M.L. (1974). Psychopathology of the abusing parent. *American Journal of Psychotherapy, 28,* 21–29.

Blythe, B.J. (1983). A critique of outcome evaluation in child abuse treatment. *Child Welfare, 62,* 325–335.

Bousha, D.M., & Twentyman, C.T. (1984). Abusing, neglectful and comparison mother–child interactional style: Naturalistic observations in the home setting. *Journal of Abnormal Psychology, 93,* 106–114.

Burgess, R.L., & Conger, R.D. (1978). Family interaction in abused, neglectful and normal families. *Child Development, 49,* 1163–1173.

Caplan, G. (1976). The family as a support system. In G. Caplan & M. Killilea (Eds.), *Support systems and mutual help: Multidisciplinary explorations* (pp. 19–36). New York: Grune & Stratton.

Conger, R.D., Lahey, B.B., & Smith, S.S. (1981, July). *An intervention program for child abuse: Modifying maternal depression and behavior.* Paper presented at the Family Violence Research Conference, University of New Hampshire, Durham.

Denicola, J., & Sandler, J. (1980). Training abusive parents in child management and self-control skills. *Behavior Therapy, 11,* 263–270.

Dietrich, K.N., Starr, R.H., & Kaplan, M.G. (1980). Maternal stimulation and care of abused infants. In T.M. Field, S. Goldberg, D. Stern, & A.M. Sostek (Eds.), *High risk infants and children: Adult and peer interactions* (pp. 25–41). New York: Academic Press.

Disbrow, M.A., Doerr, H., & Caulfield, C. (1977). Measuring the components of parents' potential for child abuse and neglect. *Child Abuse and Neglect, 1,* 279–296.

Dubanoski, R.A., Evans, J.M., & Higuchi, A.A. (1978). Analysis and treatment of child abuse: A set of behavioral propositions. *Child Abuse and Neglect, 2,* 153–172.

Egan, K.J. (1983). Stress management and child management with abusive parents. *Journal of Clinical Child Psychology, 3,* 292–299.

Ellis, A. (1976). Techniques of handling anger in marriage. *Journal of Marriage and Family Counseling, 2,* 305–315.

Elmer, E. (1977). *Fragile families, troubled children: The aftermath of infant trauma.* Pittsburgh: University of Pittsburgh Press.

Fontana, V.J., & Bernard, M.L. (1971). *The maltreated child.* Springfield, IL: Charles C Thomas.

Frazier, D., & Levine, E. (1983). Reattachment therapy: Intervention with the very young physically abused child. *Psychotherapy: Theory, Research and Practice, 20,* 90–100.

Frodi, A.M., & Lamb, M.E. (1978). Fathers' and mothers' responses to the faces and cries of normal and premature infants. *Developmental Psychology, 14,* 190–198.

Galdston, R. (1965). Observations on children who have been physically abused and their parents. *American Journal of Psychiatry, 122,* 440–443.

Gambrill, E.D. (1983). Behavioral intervention with child abuse and neglect. In M. Hersen, R.M. Eisler, & P.M. Miller (Eds.), *Progress in behavior modification* (Vol. 15, pp. 1–56). New York: Academic Press.

Gelles, R.J. (1973). Child abuse as psychopathology: A sociological critique and reformulation. *American Journal of Orthopsychiatry, 43,* 611–621.

George, C., & Main, M. (1980). Social interactions of young abused children: Approach, avoidance and aggression. *Child Development, 50,* 306–318.

Gil, D.G. (1970). *Violence against children: Physical child abuse in the United States.* Cambridge, MA: Harvard University Press.

Green, A.H., Gaines, R.W., & Sandgrund, A. (1974). Child abuse: Pathological syndromes of family interaction. *American Journal of Psychiatry, 31*(8), 882–886.

Haley, J. (1976). *Problem solving therapy.* San Francisco: Jossey-Bass.

Harrington, J. (1972). Violence: A clinical viewpoint. *British Medical Journal, 1,* 228–231.

Hoffman-Plotkin, D., & Twentyman, C.T. (1984). A multimodal assessment of behavioral and cognitive deficits in abused and neglected preschoolers. *Child Development, 55,* 794–802.

Holmes, M.B. (1978). *Child abuse and neglect programs: Practice and theory.* Washington, DC: U.S. Department of Health, Education, and Welfare, National Institute of Mental Health [DHEW No. (ADM) 78-344].

Jason, J., Williams, S.L., Burton, A., & Rochat, R. (1982). Epidemiological differences between sexual and physical child abuse. *Journal of the American Medical Association, 24,* 3344–3348.

Johnson, B., & Morse, H.A. (1968). Injured children and their parents. *Children, 15*(4), 147–152.

Justice, B., & Justice, R. (1976). *The abusing family.* New York: Human Sciences Press.

Kanfer, R.F., & Saslow, G. (1969). Behavioral diagnosis. In C.M. Franks (Ed.), *Behavior therapy: Appraisal and status* (pp. 417–444). New York: McGraw-Hill.

Kelly, J.A. (1983). *Treating child-abusive families: Intervention based on skills-training principles.* New York: Plenum.

Kempe, C. (1973). A practical approach to the protection of the abused child and rehabilitation of the abusing parent. *Pediatrics, 57,* 804.

Larrance, D.T., & Twentyman, C.T. (1983). Maternal attribution and child abuse. *Journal of Abnormal Psychology, 92,* 449–457.

Light, R. (1973). Abused and neglected children in America: A study of alternative policies. *Harvard Educational Review, 43,* 556–598.

Lynch, M. (1976). Risk factors in the child. A study of abused children and their siblings. In H.P. Martin (Ed.), *The abused child: A multidisciplinary approach to developmental issues and treatment* (pp. 43–56). Cambridge, MA: Ballinger.

Margolin, G. (1979). Conjoint marital therapy to enhance anger management and reduce spouse abuse. *American Journal of Family Therapy, 7,* 13–24.

Meichenbaum, D. (1976). A cognitive-behavior modification approach to assessment. In M. Hersen & A.S. Bellack (Eds.), *Behavioral assessment: A practical handbook* (pp. 143–171). New York: Pergamon.

Morton, T.L., & Ewald, L. (1987). Family based interventions for crime and delinquency. In C.J. Braukmann & E.K. Moris (Eds.), *Behavioral approaches to crime and delinquency: A handbook of applications, research, and concepts.* New York: Plenum.

Novaco, R.W. (1978). Anger and coping with stress. In J. Foreyt & D. Rathjen (Eds.), *Cognitive behavior therapy: Research and application* (pp. 135–173). New York: Plenum.

Parke, R.D., & Collmer, C.W. (1975). Child abuse: An interdisciplinary analysis. In E.M. Hetherington (Ed.), *Review of child development research* (Vol. 5, pp. 509–540). Chicago: University of Chicago Press.

Patterson, G.R. (1971). *Families: Applications of social learning theory to family life.* Champaign, IL: Research Press.

Patterson, G.R. (1976). The aggressive child: Victim and architect of a coercive system. In L.A. Hamerlynck, L.C. Handy, & E.J. Mash (Eds.), *Behavior modification and families: Theory and research* (Vol. 1, pp. 267–316). New York: Brunner/Mazel.

Patterson, G.R. (1982). *Coercive family process.* Eugene, OR: Castalia.

Plotkin, R.C. (1983). *Cognitive mediation of disciplinary situations in mothers who maltreat their children.* Unpublished doctoral dissertation, University of Rochester, Rochester, NY.

Polansky, N., Chalmers, M., Buttenweiser R., & Williams, D. (1979). The isolation of the neglectful family. *American Journal of Orthopsychiatry, 49,* 149–152.

Pollock, C., & Steele, B. (1972). A therapeutic approach to the parents. In C.H. Kempe & R.E. Helfer (Eds.), *Helping the battered child and his family* (pp. 3–21). Philadelphia: Lippincott.

Reid, J.B., Taplin, P.S., & Lorber, R. (1981). A social interactional approach to the treatment of abusive families. In R.B. Stuart (Ed.), *Violent behavior: Social learning approaches to prediction, management and treatment* (pp. 83–101). New York: Brunner/Mazel.

Reidy, T.J. (1977). The aggressive characteristics of abused and neglected children. *Journal of Clinical Psychology, 33*(4), 1140–1145.

Rohrbeck, C.A., & Twentyman, C.T. (1986). A multimodal assessment of impulsiveness in abusing, neglecting, and non-maltreating mothers and their preschool children. *Journal of Consulting and Clinical Psychology, 52*(4), 687–691.

Smith, S.M., & Hanson, R. (1975). Interpersonal relationships and child-caring practices in 214 parents of battered children. *British Journal of Psychiatry, 127,* 515–525.

Twentyman, C.T., Rohrbeck, C.A., & Amish, P.L. (1984). A cognitive-behavioral model of child abuse. In S. Saunders, A.M. Anderson, C.A. Hart, & G.M. Rubenstein, (Eds.), *Violent individuals and families: A handbook for practitioners* (pp. 87–111). Springfield, IL: Charles C Thomas.

Weiss, R.L. (1980). Strategic behavioral marital therapy: Toward a model for assessment and intervention. In J.P. Vincent (Ed.), *Advances in family intervention, assessment, and theory* (Vol. 1, pp. 229–271). Greenwich, CT: JAI Press.

Wolfe, D.A., & Sandler, J. (1981). Training abusive parents in effective child management. *Behavior Modification, 5,* 320–335.

Wolfe, D.A., Sandler, J., & Kaufman, K. (1981). A competency based training program for child abusers. *Journal of Consulting and Clinical Psychology, 49,* 633–640.

Young, L. (1964). *Wednesday's children: A study of child neglect and abuse.* New York: McGraw-Hill.

4

Cognitive–Behavioral Treatment of Physical Aggression in Marriage

Ileana Arias and
K. Daniel O'Leary

Until recently, the occurrence of physical aggression during marital conflict has been a concern primarily of sociologists. The focus of the sociological work in this area was on establishing accurate estimates of the prevalence of physical aggression in marital relationships and delineating demographic characteristics of spouses who engaged in such behavior. Fortunately, there has been increased concern among psychologists and other mental health professionals with the spouse's use of repeated physical aggression as a method of dealing with or resolving conflict (Surgeon General's Workshop on Violence and Public Health, 1985). Such physical aggression can result in physical injury to the recipient and often is labeled spouse abuse. It is considered detrimental to the mental health and safety of the recipient of the aggression and has come under the purview of emergency room physicians and all mental health personnel (O'Leary, 1985). Recently there has been increased pressure to regard spouse abuse as a criminal behavior rather than a psychopathological response or a response to low self-esteem, hostile feelings, and an inability to communicate well (Stark & Flitcraft, 1985).

A major difficulty facing any researcher or practitioner in the area of spouse abuse is the definition of "spouse abuse." There seems to be general consensus among professionals in this field that physical aggression of any kind is an

Preparation of this chapter was supported in part by NIMH Grant MH35340 to K.D. O'Leary.

inappropriate manner for resolving interpersonal differences, especially among intimately related individuals. At minimum, there are less destructive, if not more appropriate means of dealing with conflict than using physical aggression against the other. However, some forms of physical aggression are more destructive than others, at least physically. Psychologically, some individuals may experience intimidation as more destructive than most forms of physical aggression. It would seem that in defining spouse "abuse," factors such as severity of physical impact, frequency of occurrence, intent of the "abuser" (Did he or she intend to do physical harm to the partner?), and perceptions of the "abused" should be considered. However, at this point little empirical work has been conducted that addresses the issue of what constitutes "abuse," as viewed by the general public, professionals, or those who have been the recipients of physical aggression (Greenblat, 1983; Jouriles & Collins, 1986).

Physical aggression includes behaviors ranging from throwing an object at the other to using a lethal weapon, such as a knife or gun, against the other. In intimately related dyads such aggression is quite high during conflict. Prevalence studies indicate that the rate of occurrence of some form of physical aggression among married couples in the United States at some point during the length of the marriage is approximately 20–30% (Schulman, 1979; Straus, Gelles, & Steinmetz, 1980). However, incidence figures obtained with couples about to be married indicate that premarital aggression may occur in as many as 50% of the couples (O'Leary & Arias, in press, a). Furthermore, approximately 10% of married couples report the repeated occurrence of physical aggression in their marriages (Straus et al., 1980). At least 23% of couples who report the occurrence of physical aggression in their marriages state that the onset of the physical aggression, that is, the first physically aggressive episode, occurred before marriage (Dobash & Dobash, 1978). Of those who report the repeated occurrence of severe physical aggression (e.g., hitting with an object, punching, beating up, using knives and/or guns) and who attend family violence clinics, approximately 30% report that the physical aggression began prior to marriage (Rosenbaum, 1979). Finally, there is evidence from a number of studies that spouse abuse is related to observation of parental fighting (e.g., Arias, 1984; Kalmuss, 1984; Straus et al., 1980). Thus the use of physical aggression is fairly widespread among married couples, and it is transmitted from one generation to the next for a significant portion of those individuals who observe parental aggression. Finally, a substantial proportion of physically aggressive spouses appear to engage in such behavior for many years.

Two social learning models of spousal aggression have been presented elsewhere (O'Leary, 1987, a; O'Leary & Arias, in press, a). These models emphasize a multifaceted approach to spousal aggression, as have some other models such as that of Gelles and Straus (1979). In fact, there have been so many risk factors associated with spousal aggression (Straus et al., 1980) that it now seems best to develop intermediate-range theories or models of spousal aggression. More specifically, in models of spousal aggression it seems important to use only those factors which account for the majority of variance in such aggression.

Our more restricted model of spousal aggression includes six major predictors or correlates of aggression (O'Leary, 1987, a): 1) observation of parental aggression or being the target of parental aggression, 2) aggressive personality style, 3) stress, 4) alcohol use, 5) marital discord, and 6) a negative partner interchange (the precipitant). There is almost no research on cognitive variables that distinguish individuals in abusive relationships from those who are in discordant nonabusive relationships. Consequently, we do not have cognitive factors per se highlighted in our restricted model of spousal aggression. Second, to evaluate empirically the effects of cognitive variables in a model such as ours, it is necessary to have measures of these factors. Such factors are in the more expansive model of spousal aggression (O'Leary & Arias, in press, a), and we are evaluating the effects of positive attitudes toward spousal aggression, the meaning of spousal aggression to individuals in abusive and nonabusive relationships, perceived consequences of spousal aggression, and the perception of daily stressors to abusive and nonabusive individuals. However, no data have been collected on cognitive factors in combination with other family, personality, relationship, and stress variables. Therefore, none could be incorporated in our empirical evaluation of a model of spousal aggression. Nevertheless, they will be discussed throughout the chapter where we believe that cognitive variables are important in the treatment of spouse abuse.

Based on our own research and clinical experience, it seems very important to know what the client's attitudes are toward physical aggression in a marital relationship. At some point in the development of a negative marital interchange, an individual makes a choice about whether he or she will hit the partner, and we believe that this choice is in part a function of the attitude one has toward physical aggression in marriage. On the basis of research at Stony Brook (Riggs, 1986), it also appears that a cognitive variable, jealousy, characterizes college dating women who report that they engage in physical aggression with their partners. Contrary to the prediction of the experimenter, aggressive men were not different from nonaggressive men. However, clinicians often report that jealousy is a very frequent issue in abusive relationships (Neidig & Friedman, 1984).

As will be apparent in the treatment section of this chapter, cognitive interventions clearly play a major role in the treatment of spousal aggression, and there have been several reports which highlight roles that cognitive factors play in general marital therapy (Arias & Beach, 1987, a; Weiss, 1980). We next review factors that have been addressed as variables that can distinguish individuals and couples in abusive relationships from those not in such relationships. These characteristics are presented because they can help guide a clinician in planning treatment programs for individuals involved in abusive relationships. In essence, they help the clinician form an implicit model of spousal aggression.

CORRELATES AND PREDICTORS OF PHYSICAL AGGRESSION IN MARRIAGE

Research on the etiology and correlates of the use of physical aggression as a conflict resolution method originally focused on individual cognitive and behavioral factors of both the victim and the aggressor. Subsequently, more attention has been devoted to relationship or dyadic factors common among couples who experienced physical aggression during conflict.

Individual Characteristics

Aggressor characteristics. Significant sex differences in the use of physical aggression during spousal arguments have not been found consistently (cf. O'Leary, Arias, Rosenbaum, & Barling, 1986). However, the majority of studies that have investigated the correlates of *engaging* in physical aggression have examined male aggressors. It has been hypothesized that having conservative attitudes about appropriate role behavior for women (e.g., women should not have their own checkbooks; in marriage, men should make most of the important decisions) would be related to men's use of physical aggression against their spouses. Research, however, has failed to confirm this hypothesis (Neidig, Friedman, & Collins, 1984; O'Leary & Curley, 1986; Rosenbaum & O'Leary, 1981).

It is more likely that men who engage in physical aggression against their partners will be distinguished from nonaggressive men more by their personality styles than their sex-role attitudes toward women. Arias (1984) and Riggs (1986) found that men who were physically aggressive with their partners were more aggressive in general than men who did not engage in such behavior as assessed by Jackson's (1974) general measure of aggression. Additionally, men who reported engaging in physical aggression against their fiancees during the year preceding their marriages have been found to be more impulsive and defensive (or quick to take offense) than men who were not physically aggressive (O'Leary et al., 1986). Women who report engaging in physical aggression against their partners also have been found to be more predisposed toward aggression (Arias, 1984; Riggs, 1986) and toward impulsivity and defensiveness (O'Leary et al., 1986).

Although attitudes toward women have not been found to be related consistently to men's physical aggressiveness, attitudes toward physical aggression have been found to be related to aggressive behavior during dyadic conflict. Arias and Johnson (1986) surveyed 200 dating male and female subjects. Subjects were asked to report their experiences as aggressors and victims of physical aggression during an argument with their partners. Additionally, they were instructed to evaluate physically aggressive acts in hypothetical situations on the part of a wife and on the part of a husband during an argument. Men who reported engaging in physical aggression during conflict with their partners evaluated physical aggression on the part of the wife and the husband less negatively than men who reported never having engaged in physical aggression. Women who reported engaging in physical aggression against their partners evaluated physical aggression only on the part of the wife less negatively than women who had not engaged in physical aggression. Differences between physically aggressive and nonaggressive women on their evaluations of the husband's physical aggression were not found. Men's aggression against women was consistently evaluated negatively.

Low self-esteem has been found to be related to spouses' use of physical aggression during dyadic conflict (Neidig et al., 1984; Rosenbaum, Goldstein, & O'Leary, 1980; Spinetta & Rigler, 1972). In a related vein, lack of assertion has been proposed as a contributing factor to the occurrence of physical aggression in marriage. Research has failed to find a significant relationship between engaging in physical aggression and standard measures of global assertion (cf. O'Leary & Arias, in press, a). However, spouses who engage in physical aggression against their partners have been found to exhibit deficits in *spouse-specific* assertion (O'Leary & Curley, 1986; Rosenbaum & O'Leary, 1981). It should be noted that spouse-specific assertion does not distinguish between physically aggressive discordant spouses and nonaggressive discordant spouses. Thus although unassertiveness is common among physically aggressive spouses, it seems to be characteristic of unsatisfactorily married discordant spouses generally.

Among approximately 400 couples engaged to be married (O'Leary et al., 1986), spouse-specific assertion did not differentiate physically aggressive men and women from nonaggressive subjects. However, both men and women who reported engaging in physical aggression against their fiance(e)s during the year before their weddings exhibited higher levels of spouse-specific verbal *aggression*. Among this sample, engaging in physical aggression for both men and women was also related to the occurrence of stressful life events and specifically to the level of subjective negative impact (but not subjective positive impact) of life events. Thus individuals engaging in physical aggression seem to experience greater daily stress and to experience greater negative impact of these stressors. It is not clear whether the higher levels of negative impact are the result of a greater occurrence of unpleasant events or of these subjects' more negative evaluations/perceptions of the events due to cognitive distortions. The plausibility of a perceptual or cognitive component is supported by the finding that both men and women who engage in physical aggression against their partners show significantly higher levels of depression than nonaggressive individuals.

One of the most consistent characteristics of spouses who engage in physical aggression against their partners is a history of interparental physical aggression. Ulbrich and Huber (1981) found that men who, during their childhoods, were exposed to fathers who physically aggressed against their wives were more approving of husband-to-wife physical aggression than men who had not been exposed to such aggressive parental models. Further, in this investigation, women who, during their childhoods, were exposed to mothers engaging in physical aggression against their husbands were more approving of husband-to-wife physical aggression than women who had not been exposed to physically aggressive parental models. Ulbrich and Huber did not assess attitudes toward or approval of wife-to-husband physical aggression. Therefore, it is not clear on the basis of these results whether exposure to a physically aggressive same-sex parental model is related to approval of physical aggression regardless of the aggressor's gender.

Studies using the victims of male/husband aggressors as the primary informants (O'Leary & Curley, 1986; Pagelow, 1981; Rosenbaum & O'Leary, 1981) have shown that men who come from families in which the fathers were physically aggressive against their wives are more likely to engage in physical aggression against their partners. Using the aggressor's self-reports of the occurrence of physically aggressive behavior in the current relationship and in the family of origin, Kalmuss (1984) found a significant relationship between exposure to physically aggressive models and engaging in physical aggression. The probability of men engaging in physical aggression against their wives in the absence of exposure to a physically aggressive parental model was 1%; exposure to interparental physical aggression alone increased the probability to 6%. Similarly, Arias (1984) found exposure to interparental physical aggression to be a significant predictor of men's use of physical aggression even after controlling for their general tendencies to engage in aggressive behavior during interpersonal conflict.

The results for female aggressors' actual use of physical aggression against an intimate partner are more equivocal. Kalmuss (1984) found a significant relationship between exposure to interparental physical aggression and women's use of physical aggression: the probability of engaging in physical aggression against the husband in the absence of exposure to physically aggressive parental models was 2%; exposure to interparental physical aggression alone increased the probability to 8%. On the other hand, Arias (1984) did not find interparental physical aggression to be a significant correlate of physical aggression in a current intimate relationship for females about to be married. Rather, exposure to physically aggressive parental models was a significant correlate of engaging in physical aggression against individuals other than the intimate partner. When general aggressive tendencies or predispositions were controlled, interparental physical aggression did not significantly predict women's use of physical aggression against others.

Alcohol use and/or abuse has long been reported as a correlate of spousal aggression. Our reviews of the literature as well as our own research lead us to conclude that about 50% of spousal aggressive incidents involve alcohol use and about 20% of individuals in abusive relationships are alcoholic (Rosenbaum, 1979; Rosenbaum & O'Leary, 1981). Further, we know that even in couples about to be married, alcohol use is associated with partner aggression (O'Leary et al., 1986). Finally, it should also be noted that subjects with a history of light drinking excuse spousal violence more when the aggressor has been ingesting alcohol than when the aggressor has not had any alcohol (Jouriles & Collins, 1986). In brief, as has been discussed in detail elsewhere (O'Leary, 1987, a), alcohol use involves both pharmacological and psychological effects; it is pharmacologically associated with a weakening of cortical control, but it is also associated with an expectation that drinking alcohol leads to aggressive and criminal behavior.

In sum, men who are at risk for engaging in physical aggression against their partners have general aggressive, impulsive, and defensive styles. They report a high occurrence of stressful events and they experience such events as negative. They are characterized by a lack of spouse-specific assertiveness skills, low self-esteem, depression, and histories of exposure to interparental physical aggression. They have less negative attitudes toward physical aggression between spouses than men who do not engage in spousal violence and they often abuse alcohol. Women who have general aggressive, impulsive, and defensive styles and who experience high levels of negative stressors are at risk for physically aggressing against their partners. Women who lack spouse-specific assertiveness skills, have low self-esteem, and are depressed are also at risk for aggressing. Finally, women who engage in spousal aggression view hitting as less negative than those who do not hit.

Victim characteristics. As was found true of individuals who engage in physical aggression against their partners, Arias and Johnson (1986) found that men who report being victims of their partners' physical aggression evaluate both a husband's and a wife's use of physical aggression less negatively than men who are not victimized. Women who reported victimization evaluated physical aggression on the part of a wife less negatively than women who had not been victimized. Again, there were no differences between victimized and nonvictimized women on their evaluations of physical aggression on the part of a husband. As already mentioned, Rosenbaum and O'Leary (1981) found that conservative attitudes toward women and their roles (e.g., women should not have their own checkbooks; in marriage, men should make most of the important decisions) were associated with their victimization; nonvictimized, happily married women endorsed significantly more conservative attitudes than unhappily married women, either victimized or not. However, attitudes toward women did not differentiate between victimized and nonvictimized *unhappily married* women.

O'Leary et al. (1986) found that, as in the case of men who engage in physical aggression, men who are victims of their partners' physical aggression score significantly higher on trait measures of aggression, impulsivity, and defensiveness than nonvictimized men. Victimized women, similarly, were found to score higher on trait measures of aggression, impulsivity, and dominance than nonvictimized women. Both victimized men and women in this investigation reported a higher occurrence of stressful life events and a greater negative impact of life events than nonvictimized subjects.

Both men and women who report victimization appear to be significantly more aggressive with their partners specifically than nonvictimized individuals (O'Leary et al., 1986). Victimized men and women in the O'Leary et al. (1986) sample also show greater levels of depression than nonvictimized men and women.

It follows logically from social learning principles and in particular from research on modeling (Bandura, 1977) that observing a parent being victimized by the spouse would result in or be related to being victimized in adulthood in the individual's own marriage. For example, some professionals thought that as a child of a *wife*-abusing father, the individual would learn the "appropriateness" of wife abuse and so would remain in a relationship characterized by physical abuse. In fact, however, the modeling effects of interparental physical aggression do not appear to be *sex*-specific; rather they appear to be *role*-specific (Kalmuss, 1984). That is, in at least one recent study, the significant statistical relationship between exposure to interparental physical aggression and engaging in physical aggression against a current intimate partner is independent of or not affected by the gender of the physically aggressive parent or the gender of the individual. In our opinion, the "modeling of aggression" hypothesis has been given undue weight in explaining interpartner aggression. Most modeling research has involved the observation of a model and the assessment of whether the observer imitates the model shortly thereafter. There are a number of problems with the modeling of interpartner parental aggression. First, the observation of the critical behavior and the performance of the behavior may be delayed by as many as 10 or more years. It is possible that a modeling effect may operate across many years, as has been *assumed* in the case of elevated suicide rates of individuals whose parents committed suicide. However, many other factors may account for these observed concordance rates. Second, in studies of aggression in dating partners and in studies of couples about to be married, only 10–15% of the population observed their parents engage in physical aggression against one another (Arias, Samios, & O'Leary, 1987; O'Leary et al., 1986). On the other hand, at least 30–40% of the total population studied engaged in physical aggression against a partner. In brief, since many people report engaging in physical aggression against a partner but few report observing such parental aggression, modeling of parental aggression as a major construct for explaining such aggression is simply not consistent with most data.

The characteristics of individuals who report being victims of their mates' physical aggression are very similar, and in some cases exactly the same as the characteristics of individuals who engage in physical aggression (e.g., O'Leary et al., 1986). In the O'Leary et al. (1986) investigation, 36% of the men and 31% of the women reported being victims of some form of physical aggression; however, only 13% of the men and 6% of the women reported exclusive victimization, that is, they did not engage in physical aggression themselves. Hence more than half of the subjects who reported being victims of physical aggression were physically aggressive against their mates as well. It is not clear who initiated the physically aggressive episodes in these situations. Likewise, it remains to be seen whether individuals adopting both the victim and the aggressor roles did so during the same interactions or whether they adopted one role during one argument and the other during a separate conflictual interaction. Nevertheless, the similarity in characteristics of victims and aggressors may be the result of the interrelationship between these two roles. The pattern of results that has emerged for "victims" may include characteristics of individuals who are willing to engage in physical aggression during an argument with their partners. If so, individuals who initiate physical aggression may have similar psychological characteristics to individuals who will return physical aggression in kind; the common factor may be the *willingness* to engage in physical aggression or a perceived *appropriateness/legitimacy* of the use of physical aggression against an intimately related other.

Relationship Characteristics

Not surprisingly, couples in which at least one partner engages in repeated physical aggression during arguments are characterized by global relationship dissatisfaction of both the victim and the aggressor. Rosenbaum and O'Leary (1981) and O'Leary and Curley (1986) found that couples who reported the occurrence of physical aggression were significantly less satisfied and/or maritally adjusted than a comparison group of couples coming to a marital therapy clinic presenting marital discord, but not physical aggression, as the target complaint. Research has not determined whether the marital dissatisfaction of physically aggressive couples is the result or cause of the physical aggression. Clearly, the individuals who are engaging in physically aggressive behavior in their relationships eventually must experience some dissatisfaction with the relationship, if for no other reason than that the physical aggression is occurring. On the other hand, it is also conceivable that other factors, such as faulty communication patterns and deficient problem-solving skills, lead to global relationship dissatisfaction. In turn, an increase in the stressful nature of the relationship can influence the individual's sense of competence and level of depression. In combination these factors increase the probability that physical aggression will occur during arguments.

As has been found with global relationship satisfaction, both aggressors and victims report significantly lower levels of positive affect or positive feelings for their partners (Arias et al., 1987; O'Leary et al., 1986) compared to members of nonaggressive couples. Again, it is not clear whether negative affect or less positive affect of these individuals is a cause or consequence of the occurrence of physical aggression.

There is some suggestive evidence that couples who engage in physical aggression during arguments exhibit communication patterns different from those of satisfactorily married couples. Margolin, John, Gleberman, Miller, and Reynolds (1985) compared nonclinic married couples who were satisfied with their relationships, those couples who were dissatisfied but reported no incidents of physical aggression, and couples who were dissatisfied with their relationships and reported the occurrence of physical aggression. Couples who reported physical aggression showed more physiological reactivity while discussing a topic of disagreement than happy couples or unhappy, nonaggressive couples. More specifically, individuals who experienced physical aggression reported greater global body restlessness and increased heartbeats during their discussions. In addition, physiological reactivity during conflictual situations has been established as a significant correlate of marital adjustment and communication effectiveness (Gottman & Levenson, 1984).

In the Margolin et al. (1985) investigation, objective observers rated the behaviors of the spouses during their discussions. Happily married individuals were rated as displaying more positive physical behavior and less negative physical behavior than either the dissatisfied, nonaggressive couples or the dissatisfied, aggressive couples. However, the two dissatisfied groups did not differ from each other. Thus although emotional or physiological reactivity sets physically aggressive couples apart from others, overt behavior during conflictual discussions differentiates them from satisfied or adjusted couples but not from other dissatisfied couples. Inappropriate or negative physical and verbal behavior during interactions seems to be a characteristic of marital discord and not of the use of physical aggression per se.

In sum, it would appear that individuals who are under stress, lack confidence, and are generally aggressive, consequently not employing or even lacking appropriate assertion and problem-solving skills, are initially at risk for engaging in physical aggression. The probability of actually engaging in physical aggression seems to increase when such individuals experience or react with high autonomic arousal during stressful situations. High autonomic arousal may be a pervasive characteristic of the individual or may be a relatively temporary result of the concurrent high stress. In either case, high autonomic arousal interferes with higher cortical functioning (Janis, 1982; Mandler, 1982) and could prevent the individual from engaging in preexisting or newly acquired appropriate behaviors during a difficult situation. It would then seem that self-esteem and assertion and problem-solving skills would be appropriate targets for treatment. Further, as often implemented (Neidig & Friedman, 1984; Rosenbaum, 1985), it would be desirable to include cognitive–behavioral interventions to aid the individual in altering his or her autonomic responses during conflictual or generally undesirable situations. Such interventions may help clients engage in appropriate behaviors that already exist in their repertoires or that therapy is attempting to instill.

ASSESSMENT OF INDIVIDUALS AND COUPLES IN AGGRESSIVE RELATIONSHIPS

In working with couples who engage in physical aggression, there are three major areas of assessment: 1) the assessment of physical aggression, 2) the assessment of individual characteristics that have been found to be related to engaging in physical aggression, and 3) the assessment of relationship characteristics related to the occurrence of physical aggression. Assessment of the occurrence of physical aggression in therapy is restricted to self-report of the aggressor and the victim. Based on our experiences at the University Marital Therapy Clinic at Stony Brook, we recommend that couples routinely be asked directly about physical aggression occurring at the time they present for therapy or that has occurred at any point during their relationships. Approximately half the couples coming to our clinic indicated that there had been at least one episode of physical aggression at some point during their marriages and/or that some form of physical aggression was occurring at the time of intake. These couples did not contact the clinic because of the physical aggression; rather, the presenting complaint was marital dissatisfaction characterized by communication difficulties. The spouses did not offer information on physical aggression during interviews with a therapist; rather, the information was based on their responses to paper-and-pencil measures. The instrument used routinely to assess for the occurrence of physical aggression, historical or current, was the Conflict Tactics Scale (CTS; Straus, 1979).

The CTS is the most uniformly used tool for assessing physical aggression among intimately related partners. Originally the scale consisted of 14 items to be administered during telephone or face-to-face interviews. The original form was modified to an 18-item scale for self-administration. The current form assesses the occurrence of 18 behaviors that an individual might engage in during the course of an argument with another. These behaviors range from discussing an issue calmly to using lethal weapons against the other. Respondents typically are instructed to indicate how frequently they have engaged in any of the 18 behaviors presented; the seven response categories range from "never" to "more than 20 times." Individuals are sometimes asked to use the same scale for reporting how frequently their spouses have engaged in the 18 behaviors included in the CTS. The time period for which respondents are to report their own and their partners' behavior varies; individuals may be asked to report their experiences during the one-year period preceding the assessment or their experiences during the entire length of their relationships.

The CTS has been factor analyzed (Hornung, McCullough, & Sugimoto, 1981) and the following four factors have been extracted: 1) verbal reasoning (three items ranging from discussing an issue calmly to bringing in a third party to help settle the difference); 2) psychological abuse/aggression (seven items ranging from insulting the other to throwing and/or smashing objects during the argument); 3) physical aggression (five items ranging from throwing an object *at the other* to hitting or trying to hit the other with an object); and 4) life-threatening violence (three items ranging from beating up the other to using a knife or gun). Straus and his colleagues (Straus et al., 1980) identified an overall violence index (eight items of the CTS ranging from throwing an object at the other to using a knife or gun) and a severe violence index (five items ranging from kicking, biting, and striking with a fist to using weapons). Reliabilities or homogeneity coefficients as assessed by item-total correlations for the overall violence index for males and females are .87 and .88, respectively; alpha coefficients are .83 and .82 for males and females, respectively (Straus, 1979).

More recent factor analyses have been conducted with clinic subjects, subject couples in which physical aggression is a primary complaint, and in a sample of newly married couples. These factor analyses generally confirm the factors found by Hornung et al. (1981), but life-threatening violence sometimes does not emerge as a single factor, and one item, threatening to hit partner, previously included by Straus as verbal aggression, consistently has had a higher loading on the physical aggression factor (Barling, O'Leary, Jouriles, Vivian, & MacEwen, 1987).

It seems pertinent to obtain information about physical aggression from couples routinely because some couples will not volunteer such information. Individuals may feel embarrassed or afraid of the aggressor's reaction to such disclosure, or they may not see the physical aggression as a concern for therapy (cf. Ferraro & Johnson, 1984). However, it is incumbent upon the therapist to assess any ongoing physical aggression because of the potential detrimental impact on the victim and the relationship. Similarly, if the physical aggression is presented as "a thing of the past," the therapist should be careful to assess the possibility of recurrence. Undetected physical aggression, past or current, could attenuate or compromise marital treatment effectiveness. At minimum, the current occurrence of physical aggression should prompt the therapist to include a component in his or her treatment package to deal with or to help the couple deal with the aggression.

A word of caution is in order regarding assessment of physical aggression. Individuals may not present physical aggression as a target for treatment if the partners are interviewed together. Direct and unsolicited assessment of such behavior should be done individually with each spouse either during face-to-face interviews or with paper-and-pencil measures such as the CTS. If a victim of physical aggression is confronted in the presence of the aggressor, confirmatory evidence may not be forthcoming for fear of later retaliation from the aggressor. Alternatively, the victim may report physical aggression during a conjoint interview by erroneously not expecting retaliation; hence the therapist has placed the victim in a dangerous position. If both victim and aggressor report the occurrence of the physical aggression, the therapist should then continue assessment of the conditions precipitating and following the aggression with both partners present. If only the victim reports physical aggression, the therapist may discuss the issue further *with the victim* and additionally discuss options for dealing with discussions or any treatment of the physical aggression. It is rare for only the aggressor to report physical aggression; however, if this happens, there are few negative implications for the aggressor as a result of confronting the victim. A notable example of a potential negative outcome would be a case in which an aggressor's disclosure regarding violent behavior later is used as evidence against him or her in a child custody hearing, when therapist confidentiality no longer holds.

Partners agree moderately on their reports of the occurrence of physical aggression using the CTS (Jouriles & O'Leary, 1985; O'Leary & Arias, in press, b). The exact nature of the typical disagreement is not clear. Social desirability has been proposed as a possible factor. That is, given the generally unacceptable nature of engaging in physical aggression against an intimate other (Arias & Johnson, 1986; Greenblat, 1983), it was expected that the aggressor would not want to divulge such information, especially if he or she were concerned with presenting the self in a favorable light. Arias and Beach (1987) found a significant relationship between social desirability and both husbands' and wives' reports of engaging in any form of physical aggression at least once. However, among men and women who reported engaging in physical aggression, social desirability was not related to reports of the frequency or severity of aggression. Social desirability was not related to reports of victimization.

In addition to assessing physical aggression, assessment procedures should obtain information on variables that have been linked to engaging in physical aggression, such as general aggressive tendencies, stress, depression, spouse-specific assertion, self-esteem, and autonomic arousal. "Traitlike" characteristics such as aggression and impulsivity can be assessed at the outset of therapy by using instruments such as the subscales of the Personality Research Form (Jackson, 1974). Given the general stability of these characteristics, pre- to posttherapy performance on these instruments should not be selected as an outcome criterion. Rather, performance on these measures at the initiation of treatment can offer the therapist guidelines for observable behavior that could serve as treatment targets and suggest possible points of intervention.

Indices of daily stress, spouse-specific assertion, depression, and self-esteem can be obtained both before and after treatment. A convenient measure of level of depressed mood is the Beck Depression Inventory (BDI; Beck, Ward, Mendelson, Mock, & Erbaugh, 1961). The BDI consists of 21 items, each corresponding to a category of symptoms and attitudes characteristic of individuals suffering from clinical levels of depression (Beck, 1972; Bumberry, Oliver, & McClure, 1978). Its brevity and sensitivity to treatment changes additionally would allow its administration throughout therapy, for example, every two sessions, in order to assess beneficial effects of treatment.

The Spouse-Specific Assertiveness Inventory (SSAI; O'Leary & Curley, 1986) is a 29-item inventory comprised of two subscales assessing 1) individuals' tendencies and willingness to communicate pleasant and unpleasant content to their spouses in an open and honest fashion without fear of reprisals and 2) their willingness to engage in aggressive or passive–aggressive methods of communicating their needs or desires. The SSAI has high internal consistency and discriminant validity (O'Leary & Curley, 1986). Because spouse-specific assertion differentiates physically aggressive from nonaggressive spouses, albeit most likely because of the accompanying discord and dissatisfaction in the former, changes in spouse-specific assertiveness may be used as an indication of progress. The SSAI may be used to evaluate therapeutic progress in which a goal is to obtain less spouse-specific aggressiveness and more spouse-specific assertiveness. However, care must be taken to readminister the scale at points in time *after* assertion has been addressed and after the spouses have had time to practice and use spouse-specific assertiveness skills (assuming that some form of spouse-specific assertion training is included in the treatment program).

The Life Experiences Survey (LES; Sarason, Johnson, & Siegel, 1978) is a 47-item inventory assessing the occurrence of positive and negative events, such as being promoted at work or being fired. The LES has demonstrable reliability and convergent and divergent validity (Sarason et al., 1978). The major advantage of the LES is that in addition to assessing the actual occurrence of events that have been determined to be positive or negative *a priori,* the respondent is instructed to indicate his or her subjective reaction to the events that occurred. The typical set of instructions asks the individual to report on the one-year period preceding the assessment. Given the reliability of reports of stressful events on the LES, the instrument could be used before and after therapy to assess whether cognitive–behavioral interventions have been effective in changing spouses' perceptions and evaluations of the external environment, that is, their subjective ratings of impact. Decreases in subjective ratings of *a priori* negative events or decreases in the magnitude of negative subjective ratings (regardless of the *a priori* valence of the event) may be indicative of a decrease in the individual's subjective experience of stress and, relatedly, indicative of more adequate coping with whatever external negative events do occur. Administration of the LES as follow-up assessments offers information on the maintenance of the client's ability to cope adaptively and successfully with stress.

The principal instruments that we use for assessing relationship characteristics are the Marital Adjustment Test (MAT; Locke & Wallace, 1959) and the Positive Feelings Questionnaire (PFQ; O'Leary, Fincham, & Turkewitz, 1983). The MAT is a widely employed self-report measure assessing global relationship satisfaction. The questionnaire has been shown to be reliable (Kimmel & Van der Veen, 1974) and valid (O'Leary & Arias, 1983; Sears, 1977). The PFQ was designed to assess positive affect or caring for one's intimate partner. This instrument has been shown to be reliable across three weeks to six months, and it correlates with a number of other measures of marital satisfaction (O'Leary & Arias, 1983; O'Leary et al., 1983). Although there are paper-and-pencil measures of communication available (e.g., the Primary Communication Inventory, Navran, 1967; the Marital Communication Inventory, Bienvenu, 1970; the Verbal Problems Checklist, Carter & Thomas, 1973), the recommended method for assessing marital communication and problem solving is observation of couples engaging in these behaviors. Further, assessing autonomic arousal during stressful situations would be possible with this method. Regarding autonomic arousal, actual physiological measures of autonomic responses might be ideal, but it should be recognized that autonomic arousal sometimes bears little or no relation to general anger or even experimentally provoked anger (Deffenbacher, Demm, & Brandon, 1986). Further, given the expense involved, self-report measures of variables that have been found to be related to physiologically measured indices of autonomic arousal such as heartbeat and body warmth (cf. Margolin et al., 1985) can be obtained readily.

Low self-esteem has frequently been found to be a correlate of generalized aggressive behavior (cf. Feshbach, 1971), and it has often been suggested as a correlate and/or precipitant of wife abuse. The Rosenberg Self-esteem Scale (Rosenberg, 1965) was utilized in differentiating abusive men from satisfactorily married men and nonviolent maritally discordant men (Goldstein & Rosenbaum, 1985).

Formal assessment of individuals or couples who have been in abusive relationships may have to be done at a time after the initial intake if the abuse has just occurred. It has been our experience in a county family violence center in Suffolk County, New York, that many women who have just been beaten are not psychologically able to complete any psychological tests or rating instruments. Often we obtain such information after the initial visit to the center. In addition, the choice of the assessment instruments may have to be tailored to the needs and capabilities of the individual client or couple. As indicated elsewhere (O'Leary, 1987, b), systematic assessment in general and assessment in marital therapy in particular are receiving much more prominence, and we have a formal assessment battery at the University Marital Therapy Clinic at Stony Brook which includes most of the assessment instruments reviewed here. At a minimum, for any clinician assessing an abusive or potentially abusive couple, it would seem most important to include the Conflict Tactics Scale and the Marital Adjustment Test to assess marital aggression and relationship satisfaction or dissatisfaction. Further, detailed information in an intake interview should be obtained about depression, alcohol use, suicidal thoughts, and the extent to which the client(s) displays aggressive behavior in various situations. Finally, detailed information should be obtained about the thoughts and feelings that accompany anger and physical aggression. If the client is unable to give such information readily, daily logs of thoughts and feelings that accompany anger should be used (O'Leary & Wilson, 1987).

CLINICAL STRATEGIES AND TECHNIQUES

Goals

The major goal of cognitive–behavioral interventions with physically aggressive spouses is, of course, the discontinuation of physical aggression.

Cognitive–behavioral interventions attempt to decrease the probability of the occurrence of physical aggression by altering individual functioning and improving the current relationship. The major strategies of intervention are to have the physically aggressive spouse accept responsibility for engaging in physical aggression, to relabel physical aggression as illegitimate, and to replace the use of physical aggression with more appropriate or less destructive techniques for resolving conflict (Frank & Houghton, 1982; Neidig & Friedman, 1984; Rosenbaum & O'Leary, 1986). A second goal of some intervention programs for physical aggression is to enhance marital satisfaction. Although this goal has been a secondary one in most programs for individuals or couples where abuse has occurred, because a majority of women stay with or return to their partners, if the marital relationship is not improved, the likelihood of physical abuse seems high.

Therapy Context

Both group therapy for the aggressor (Rosenbaum & O'Leary, 1986) and group therapy for a couple characterized by physical abuse (Neidig & Friedman, 1984) have been used as methods of altering the attitudes of individuals or couples in abusive relationships. In addition, it would seem that marital therapy with some supplementation for especially abusive couples would be an equally viable method of intervening. The family has not generally been included in the treatment of the couples in which physical abuse has occurred, but with adolescents, particularly those who have seen physical abuse between their parents or who have been directly involved as a mediator or as a target of physical aggression, counseling often is in order. If both spouse abuse and child abuse are evident, special treatment regarding the child abuse is certainly warranted and in many states legally mandated.

The therapist must take an active and sometimes directive role in the treatment of couples in which there has been physical abuse. Couples who have been physically abusive with one another may be very argumentative in session if left unchecked, and it is of little value and in fact therapeutically detrimental if the therapy session is characterized largely by verbal attacks, complaints, criticisms, and mind reading.

In group sessions for men or for couples, a man and woman cotherapist pair is generally recommended (Neidig & Friedman, 1984; Rosenbaum, 1985). Modeling of egalitarian roles by the therapists and the showing of empathy and sensitivity by the therapists are important in producing therapeutic change. The presence of an understanding woman may help a great deal in allowing a woman client in a couples' group to feel that her needs may be addressed, and the presence of a woman to whom an abusive man may relate in the mens' groups may help the man develop better feelings toward women in general. Having a male therapist is important in order to have someone with whom the male client may identify. If the therapy is conducted in a conjoint marital context with a single therapist, special attention must be paid repeatedly to the issue of siding with one or another client. One cannot make significant progress if it is apparent that the therapist is simply a one-sided mediator or negotiator. It is unclear at present if group therapy for couples or therapy with an individual couple is more efficacious with problems of physical aggression. The context of our therapeutic approach, however, is conjoint marital therapy, which sometimes is supplemented or preceded by individual therapy for either one or both of the partners. However, whether the context of therapy is group therapy for men or couples therapy, the content of the therapy has a number of common elements, and we consider examples from both contexts.

Content of Therapy

Like many others (cf. Rosenbaum, 1985; Rosenbaum & O'Leary, 1986), we believe that issues of responsibility for stopping physical aggression and the illegitimacy of physical aggression should be addressed during the initial phases of treatment. An individual who does not take personal responsibility for stopping physical aggression will not be successful in replacing that physical aggression with prosocial behavior or indeed may not even genuinely attempt to replace it. Similarly, an individual who views physical aggression as legitimate and justifiable is unlikely to attempt to change a physically aggressive pattern of handling conflict. Cognitive restructuring techniques are typically employed to achieve these attitudinal or cognitive changes on the part of the aggressor. For example, the therapist can point out to the aggressor that he or she does not engage in physical aggression at every provocation. Therefore, the therapist may continue, the client apparently has the ability to exert some amount of control over the expression of anger and aggression. The goals of therapy then are presented as finding out under which circumstances the individual can control his or her anger, identifying factors related to those circumstances that facilitate anger control, and increasing control over anger cross-situationally by generalizing these factors. Engaging in physical aggression then is presented to the client not as a behavior resulting from lack of control but as a behavior displayed in situations where existing control has not been exerted *before* but will be exerted *now*. Detailed examples of the specific therapeutic strategies for altering attitudes about responsibility for changing one's own behavior have been outlined in therapy manuals by Neidig and Friedman (1984) and Rosenbaum (1985). As emphasized by Rosenbaum (1985) in his group therapy format for abusive men, the intervention is largely didactic in that the two major foci of treatment are attitude change and behavior change. To change attitudes about the use of physical aggression in marriage, cognitive interventions are the cornerstone of the therapist's strategies.

For treatment to have any long-range impact on the physically aggressive spouse, the illegitimacy of physical aggression must be emphasized. The therapist should take the stance explicitly that physical aggression against the other is never justified. This does not mean that frustration, anger, and other negative feelings cannot be acknowledged. However, it must be emphasized that there typically is an alternative to physical aggression in any situation. This point is critical when the physically aggressive individual is being treated conjointly rather than individually. The presence of the spouse–victim during discussions of the occurrence of physical aggression may tempt the aggressor to claim that the victim's behavior was responsible for the use of physical aggression. Victims can be provocative prior to a physically aggressive incident; however, there are ways of dealing with provocation other than by hitting. The individual's *affective* reaction to any provocation may be understandable and perhaps even legitimate. However, the crucial point to be made is that the manner in which the individual chooses to handle or express that affective reaction (i.e., physical aggression) is not legitimate. It is imperative to impress upon the client that there is always a choice and that physical aggression is not a legitimate alternative.

An additional attitudinal issue to discuss during the initial stages of therapy concerns the destructive effects of physical aggression. That is, physically aggressive spouses at times do not recognize the self-defeating nature of physical aggression. Especially for spouses who use physical aggression instrumentally (i.e., to get something they want), it often is not apparent that they are creating situations that they may not desire, such as resentment, dislike, and possible abandonment on the part of the victim. Thus therapists should point out that in addition to whatever short-term "positive" consequences result from the physical aggression, "negative" consequences result as well and can have an impact on *all* family members. The cycle of violence across generations should be discussed, as should the negative consequences of children's observing repeated instances of aggression (Rosenbaum & O'Leary, 1986; Wolfe, Zak, Wilson, & Jaffe, 1986). More specifically, information is presented about the increased probability of an individual engaging in physical aggression if he is the object of repeated beatings as a child or if he observes physical fighting of parents. On the basis of our research with children, it appears that being the target of repeated spankings or beatings is more frequently associated with behavior problems of children than is witnessing parental fighting (Jouriles, Barling, & O'Leary, 1987). After the negative consequences of engaging in physical aggression against a child or an adult has been pointed out, the clients are then told that a major goal of therapy is to help the individual learn ways of getting needs and desires met (i.e., "positive" consequences) while simultaneously avoiding negative consequences. Methods by which good outcomes are achieved and bad ones avoided are presented as preferable to methods by which negative outcomes are not avoided, such as physical aggression.

To provide the client with alternative choices, cognitive–behavioral approaches to physical aggression typically employ anger control (Novaco, 1975), stress inoculation (Meichenbaum & Turk, 1976), and behavioral marital therapy techniques such as problem-solving and communication skills training (cf. Jacobson & Margolin, 1979). Anger control and stress inoculation techniques are used to teach the client to recognize physiological and cognitive cues which for that particular client are associated with physical aggression. Upon recognition of these cues, the client is encouraged to engage in behaviors other than physical aggression and incompatible with physical violence. For example, if general body tension or muscle rigidity is a preceding and/or accompanying characteristic of engaging in physical aggression, the client would be taught relaxation techniques and instructed to engage in relaxation immediately upon becoming aware of the signal for physical aggression—in this case, tension. The stages of violence are described to the client(s) using Walker's (1979) cycle of violence paradigm and Deschner's (1984) stages of aggression. Almost all couples can relate to one or another stage or cycle of aggression model, and it is helpful to have the individual or couple become close observer(s) of their behavioral/emotional interactions.

The majority of the cues available to the client that signal the imminence of physical aggression are physiological and nonverbal as well as cognitive (e.g., self-statements such as "I believe my husband is taking advantage of me again," "I believe that my wife is sleeping with my best friend," "The reason my wife will not do x, y, or z, is because she doesn't love me"). Unrealistic expectations such as "My spouse should address all of my physical, social, and emotional needs" also lead to physiological arousal and anger. Hence targets for treatment during the initial phases of therapy are nonverbal behavior and cognitive behavior. The physiological cues typically associated with physical aggression are mostly responses indicative of high autonomic arousal. Given the usual high levels of stress experienced by physically aggressive spouses and given their intense physiological reactions during conflict, relaxation training procedures often are recommended. When relaxation is implemented, the individual is instructed to engage in relaxation exercises regularly. The regular practice of relaxation exercises reduces general feelings of tension and stress which have been linked or hypothesized to be linked to the occurrence of physical aggression. Further, regular practice of relaxation techniques gives the individual mastery over physical tension and increases the probability that the individual will use relaxation procedures successfully during conflict in order to avoid physical aggression. Relaxation, however, must be coupled with reality testing and reattribution of the spouse's thoughts, feelings, and behavior. Neidig and Friedman (1984) describe an A–B–C model of emotional arousal in which three components of emotional arousal must be addressed: antecedent events, irrational and highly charged self-talk, and consequent anger and resentment. The clients can be taught this model, and they may need special help in realizing the importance of the attributions that we have about events. They can profit from exercises in relabeling and reevaluating reasons for certain actions. Finally, it may be useful to borrow from the "Double Column Technique" in depression treatment in which one lists the advantages and disadvantages of anger. This technique is advised especially when individuals feel that frequent anger release is both necessary and mentally healthy. Unfortunately, the popular media present many depictions taken from psychiatrists and psychologists in which catharsis and "getting it out of your system" are seen as a key to emotional health (Tavris, 1982), and these attitudes may form the first line of resistance that must be addressed in the therapy sessions.

Therapy may employ techniques other than relaxation training to alter the "physically aggressive" nonverbal and cognitive stance of spouses. Specific nonverbal behaviors appear to be incompatible with engagement in physical aggression. For example, it is much more difficult to aggress physically against another when you are sitting down than when you are standing (Rosenbaum, 1985). It is less likely that an individual will strike out against another during an argument if he or she is sitting back in a seat than if he or she is sitting at the edge of the seat; physical aggression cannot occur if the conflict is discussed during a telephone conversation rather than in person; discussion of a disagreement is less likely to escalate to physical aggression if the individuals involved whisper. The therapist can find behaviors that are incompatible with physical aggression per se or with cues preempting physical aggression and set them up as *rules* to guide the physically aggressive individual's behavior during conflict. Some of these incompatible behaviors may seem "silly" or "extreme" to clients and therapists alike. However, some cases of marital physical aggression are extreme or can become extreme if the aggression is not addressed early in its cycle, and the welfare of the victim(s) is more important than the apparent silliness of the intervention.

Self-statements of the aggressor to attend to usually involve the negative interpretation or evaluation of the spouse's behavior, and maritally distressed individuals interpret messages sent by the partner as more negative than the partner intended (Schachter & O'Leary, 1985). These negative perceptions typically involve the aggressor's feelings of low self-esteem. For example, a husband may interpret his wife's announcement that she is considering finding employment outside the home as an indication that he is not a good provider. Attributing negative intent to the partner's behavior is common in distressed dyads (Fincham, Beach, & Nelson, 1987). By perceiving his wife's behavior as a deliberate insult, or as an intent to harm, the husband is likely to become highly aroused and agitated, label the arousal as anger, and face the increased probability that he will hit her. In this case, his physical aggression may not necessarily be instrumental (i.e., to punish her), but his high arousal may interfere with decision making and related cognitive functions and processes enough so that responses more appropriate than aggression are not accessible to him. Therapy can teach such a husband to recognize his pattern of perception/interpretation and his habit of responding to these cognitions rather than to the environment. Further, therapy can encourage and teach such a husband to not *evaluate* the spouse's behavior so precipitately but rather to be responsibly assertive in expressing his desires and displeasures.

Once therapy has succeeded, through cognitive restructuring, in obtaining genuine commitment from the physically aggressive spouse to replace physical aggression, and once the individual has gained some control over his or her physiological, cognitive, and behavioral reactions during conflict situations, more traditional marital therapy procedures are introduced. By addressing marital difficulties and dysfunctions, the partners' general stress levels are reduced. Additionally, aspects of couple interaction that are maladaptive and elicit high autonomic arousal can be addressed and altered, leading to a further decrease in the probability of occurrence of physical aggression.

The major relationship targets for treatment are problem-solving skills and communication skills. It is impressed upon the couple that all married individuals have problems and that a major distinction between people who are happily married and people who argue and are unhappily married is the way these common problems are approached. Couples are taught to be clear, specific, and objective in identifying their problems. Care is taken to ensure that spouses do not single each other out as responsible for the problem at hand; rather, it is stressed that because the problem has an impact on both spouses, it is a problem for both. Further, deciding who is to blame is not going to resolve the difficulty. Thus, upon identifying the problem, spouses are taught brainstorming techniques in order to generate possible solutions. The "brainstorming" aspect is emphasized for two major reasons: 1) not evaluating potential solutions until all possible solutions have been generated increases the absolute number of solutions generated; and 2) not evaluating potential solutions moment-by-moment is incompatible with tendencies that spouses present at the beginning of therapy whereby they evaluate each other's behavior moment-by-moment. As the number of potential solutions generated by the couple increases, the probability that the couple will generate at least one mutually satisfying solution similarly increases (cf. Goldfried & Davison, 1976). Additionally, if the couple engages in an activity that is incompatible with evaluating their behavior in a continuous fashion, they are discouraged from engaging in such an evaluation process. Consequently, rather than evaluating behavior immediately, which can lead to anger and physical aggression, spouses may come to suspend evaluation until a conflict has been resolved or may reject evaluation altogether.

Once spouses learn to identify problems and brainstorm solutions for those problems, therapy shifts to implementation of those solutions. During this phase, the therapist's major task is to anticipate obstacles to implementation of the agreement, point them out to the couple, and have the couple discuss how to remove those obstacles or how to handle noncompliance/failure to implement solutions if the obstacles cannot be removed. Although the solution decided upon by the couple was generated, designed, and agreed upon by both spouses, the therapist has to ensure that each individual is comfortable with the solution. If there is any hesitation, an alternative solution should be decided upon. Hesitation can mean noncompliance with the agreement, disappointment, annoyance, and/or anger consequent to the noncompliance, presenting a potential occasion for discord and physical aggression.

Throughout the problem-solving skills training, therapy addresses the spouses' communication skills. The goal of communication skills training is to lower the probability that a "discussion" of a conflict will escalate and develop into an "argument" or "fight" during which stress and arousal increase and physical aggression occurs. The major communication skills introduced are 1) reducing highly negative interchanges between spouses; 2) staying on the topic and thus increasing the probability that the issue will be resolved; 3) using "I" statements to force individuals to take responsibility for their needs, wants, and displeasure rather than accuse the other (e.g., "I would like . . ." instead of "You should . . ."); 4) clarifying and paraphrasing the partner's messages to increase feelings of empathy and understanding; and 5) providing corrective feedback to the partner so that a mutually comfortable pattern of communication is established.

Special care must be exercised when spouses in marriages where physical aggression occurs are encouraged to provide each other with corrective feedback. Typically, spouses are taught to use "I" statements to provide corrective feedback to their spouses regarding behaviors that interfere with their *own* effective participation in the problem-solving process. For example, if a spouse feels criticized when the partner requests behavior change, and thus is discouraged from complying with the request, corrective feedback in the following form is encouraged: "I feel criticized and put down when you tell me what *not* to do instead of asking me what you *would* like me to do." There is a potential for a physically aggressive spouse, who may have low self-esteem, to react negatively to this statement. It is possible for the aggressive spouse to become angry and for the probability of physical aggression to increase. Any spouse can react negatively to corrective feedback no matter how constructive and nonthreatening the presentation of the feedback. However, given the potential of severely damaging and dangerous consequences, great care must be taken when employing these techniques with couples who engage in physical aggression.

TECHNIQUES USED IN JOINING WITH THE COUPLE

It is of primary importance for the therapist to be nonjudgmental of both the aggressor and the victim. It is true that the therapist does not accept the legitimacy of the physical aggression, stressing to the aggressor that it is unacceptable and unjustified and that there are "better" ways of resolving conflict. However, it is also true that engaging in physical aggression does not render the individual less of a human being and therefore less worthy of the therapist's understanding and respect. This has to be genuinely believed by the therapist if he or she is to be of help to the couple; this has to be successfully *conveyed* to the aggressive client if he or she is going to become engaged in the therapeutic process and change. The therapist can provide an overt distinction for the client between the self and behavior—the therapist offering the rationale that the task of therapy is not to change him or her but rather to change the behavior in which he or she engages. Further, the point can be made that by changing behavior from less desirable/acceptable forms to those that are more desirable/acceptable, the aggressor's spouse will have fewer distractors to deal with (i.e., protection from and fear of physical aggression) and therefore will be able to relax and enjoy the client. Additionally, many spouses who are physically aggressive do not enjoy engaging in physical aggression because of the effects and social interpretations of such behavior. This can be acknowledged so that the client feels understood rather than despised or disapproved of.

It is also proven important to specify to the physically aggressive spouse what his or her gains are likely to be as a result of changing. It is not enough to offer the victim's welfare as *the* reason for changing, if for no other reason than because of the mutual animosity presented at the beginning of therapy. A careful analysis of the physically aggressive spouse's needs and concerns should be conducted in order to determine what will "motivate" the client to change. For example, some individuals would like to avoid appearing crazy to themselves, their spouses, their children, and the external world. For such individuals, the therapist can claim that therapy and change offer them the opportunity *not* to appear crazy and instead be viewed as the rational people that they, in fact, are but have not been able to show. Some individuals are frightened or concerned about losing control over themselves and their environments. For such individuals, physical aggression may be presented as an indication that they are not exerting control when they can and when they should; therapy and change can be presented as means for establishing appropriate control. The crucial point is for the client to perceive a personal "payoff" and to perceive the therapist as an agent who is willing to work *for* him or her.

In addition to being concerned about the reactions of the aggressor to therapy, we should regard the victim's experience as very important. The greatest risk with regard to the victim is the therapist's failure to understand why this individual is willing to stay in a relationship that puts him or her at risk for unwarranted physical punishment and in some cases at risk for death. The reasons for the victim's continuation of the relationship are varied and not well understood. Often victims do not perceive alternatives to the current aggressive situation. That is, they lack confidence and self-esteem, and they doubt that they can ever find another mate. Victims may not have other sources of financial or emotional support, such as family or friends, and may not be able to create alternatives for themselves. Victims may not have adequate skills for living on their own and supporting their children.

At times, victims are concerned about losing their children as a result of leaving their physically aggressive spouses. Often victims, especially those experiencing high levels of severe physical aggression and psychological intimidation, are afraid that their spouses will find them if they do leave and are understandably afraid of the consequences. Finally, victims may be significantly emotionally attached to their spouses. Tolerating the physical aggression may not be as distressful to the victim as losing the spouse and fulfillment of whatever needs the spouse satisfies. The therapist must be careful to convey understanding of the bind that the victimized spouse is in and that both positive and negative feelings about the aggressor are respected.

SPECIAL CLINICAL ISSUES IN THE TREATMENT OF MARITAL PHYSICAL AGGRESSION

Treatment Format

Couple therapy is not always the best way to deal with physical aggression in marriage. Individual therapy with the aggressor is frequently used to achieve cognitive change, that is, acceptance of responsibility for change in and the illegitimacy of physical aggression. Similarly, a group format is frequently used for this same purpose. Upon some cognitive change and some commitment to replacing physical aggression with nonaggressive techniques, couples therapy is introduced. If individual therapy for the aggressor is employed initially, the victim will also be engaged in individual therapy to deal with feelings of low self-esteem, anxiety, depression, and any other consequences of the physical aggression. Individual therapy with the victim offers a "safer" atmosphere for providing feedback regarding provocative behavior. In the absence of the aggressor, the therapist can begin to point out to the victim behaviors in which he or she engages that increase the probability of physical aggression. Because the aggressor is not present, the probability of the therapist "legitimizing" the physical aggression is decreased. Caution must be exercised. It is imperative that the victim is not *blamed* for the physical aggression; rather, he or she must see what factors are under his or her direct control in order to maximize safety.

Orders of Protection

Although often distasteful to both the therapist and the victim, severe and frequent physical aggression sometimes warrants or even requires obtaining legal orders of protection. The victim usually feels uncomfortable with such a move, because of fear of the aggressor's reaction (i.e., escalation in severity of physical aggression) or a sense of guilt about taking legal action against the spouse. The therapist also may be concerned about the implications for the viability of the relationship when one spouse takes legal action against the other. However, orders of protection often lead to a *reduction* in physical aggression. Anecdotal evidence suggests that aggressors will not engage in physical aggression *because of* the victims' procurement of orders of protection. Thus in severe cases of physical aggression, legal protection may be considered and discussed with the victim during individual sessions. If the victim agrees to obtain a restraining order, the therapist can present it to the aggressor as an external form of control for the physical aggression given the apparent current lack of internal control.

Community Support Services

When treating physical aggression in marriage, the therapist is advised to become acquainted with existing community resources. These include both financial and social resources. In cases of severe physical aggression, it is important to be aware of temporary shelters for both the victim and children. In addition to community sources, the therapist can discuss with the client family members and friends who could provide at least temporary shelter and financial aid. The therapist may even keep a record of specific family members or friends whom he or she can contact for the client in cases of emergencies or imminent danger.

Safety

At all times, the physical safety of the individuals involved is the primary goal. Thus whatever treatment specifications are made, it is incumbent upon the therapist to ensure that the detrimental effects on the victim(s) in the couple are minimized. Certainly some risk is always present. If detrimental or destructive effects cannot be avoided, the therapist should be confident that the effects will not be severe. At any rate, for the sake of the clients' welfare, detrimental effects should be anticipated and procedures for dealing with such impact should be outlined in advance.

Liability

The therapist must be aware of his or her liability in the event that physical aggression occurs while therapy is ongoing. Mental health professionals are not legally bound to report occurrences of physical aggression against a spouse, as they are for cases of child abuse. However, as in cases where the therapist suspects homicide or suicide is likely, the therapist bears the responsibility of the "duty to warn." If during the course of treatment the therapist becomes aware, either on the basis of the intended victim's or the aggressor's report, that a spouse is in danger of being severely attacked, the police must be notified and the victim warned if he or she is not aware of the danger (*Tarasoff versus Regents of the University of California,* 1976). Failure to carry out these moves could mean legal prosecution (Margolin, 1982; Rosenbaum, in press).

REFERENCES

Arias, I. (1984). *A social learning theory explication of the intergenerational transmission of physical aggression in intimate heterosexual relationships.* Unpublished doctoral dissertation. State University of New York, Stony Brook.

Arias, I., & Beach, S.R.H. (1987, a). The assessment of social cognition in the context of marriage. In K.D. O'Leary (Ed.), *Assessment of marital discord* (pp. 109–137). Hillsdale, NJ: Lawrence Erlbaum Associates.

Arias, I., & Beach, S.R.H. (1987, b). Validity of self-reports of marital violence. *Journal of Family Violence, 2,* 139–149.

Arias, I., & Johnson, P. (1986, November). *Evaluations of physical aggression in marriage.* Paper presented at the 20th Annual Convention of the Association for Advancement of Behavior Therapy, Chicago.

Arias, I., Samios, M., & O'Leary, K.D. (1987). Prevalence and correlates of physical aggression during courtship. *Journal of Interpersonal Violence, 2,* 82–90.

Bandura, A. (1977). *Social learning theory.* Englewood Cliffs, NJ: Prentice-Hall.

Barling, J., O'Leary, K.D., Jouriles, E.N., Vivian, D., & MacEwen, K.E. (1987). Factor similarity of the Conflict Tactics Scales across samples, spouses, and sites: Issues and implications. *Journal of Family Violence, 2,* 37–54.

Beck, A.T. (1972). *Depression: Causes and treatment.* Philadelphia: University of Pennsylvania Press.

Beck, A.T., Ward, C.H., Mendelson, M., Mock, J., & Erbaugh, J. (1961). An inventory for measuring depression. *Archives of General Psychiatry, 4,* 561–571.

Bienvenu, M.J. (1970). Measurement of marital communication. *Family Coordinator, 19,* 26–31.

Bumberry, W., Oliver, J.M., & McClure, J.N. (1978). Validation of the Beck Depression Inventory in a university population using psychiatric estimates as the criteria. *Journal of Consulting and Clinical Psychology, 46,* 150–155.

Carter, R.D., & Thomas, E.J. (1973). Modification of problematic marital communication using corrective feedback and instruction. *Behavior Therapy, 4,* 100–109.

Deffenbacher, J.L., Demm, P.M., & Brandon, A.D. (1986). High general anger: Correlates and treatment. *Behaviour Research and Therapy, 24,* 481–490.

Deschner, J.P. (1984). *The hitting habit.* New York: Free Press.

Dobash, R.E., & Dobash, R.P. (1978). Wives: The "appropriate" victims of marital violence. *Victimology, 2,* 426–442.

Ferraro, K.J., & Johnson, J.M. (1984, August). *The meanings of courtship violence.* Paper presented at the Second National Conference for Family Violence Researchers, Durham, NH.

Feshbach, S. (1971). Dynamics and morality of violence and aggression. *American Psychologist, 26,* 281–292.

Fincham, F.D., Beach, S.R.H., & Nelson, G. (1987). Attributional processes in distressed and non-distressed couples: 3. Causal and evaluative inferences for spouse behavior. *Cognitive Therapy and Research, 11,* 71–86.

Frank, P.B. & Houghton, B.D. (1982). *Confronting the batterer: A guide to creating the spouse abuse workshop.* New City, NY: Volunteer Counseling Service of Rockland County.

Gelles, R.J., & Straus, M.A. (1979). Determinants of violence in the family: Toward a theoretical integration. In W.R. Burr, R. Hill, F.I. Nye, & I.L. Reiss (Eds.), *Contemporary theories about the family* (pp. 549–581). New York: Free Press.

Goldfried, M.R., & Davison, G.C. (1976). *Clinical behavior therapy.* New York: Holt, Rinehart and Winston.

Goldstein, D., & Rosenbaum, A. (1985). An evaluation of the self-esteem of maritally violent men. *Family Relations, 34,* 425–428.

Gottman, J.M., & Levenson, R.W. (1984). Why marriages fail: Affective and physiological patterns in marital interaction. In J.C. Masters & K. Yarkin-Levin (Eds.), *Boundary areas in social and developmental psychology.* New York: Academic Press.

Greenblat, C.S. (1983). A hit is a hit is a hit . . . or is it? Approval and tolerance of the use of physical force by spouses. In D. Finkelhor, R.J. Gelles, G.T. Hotaling, & M.A. Straus (Eds.), *The dark side of families: Current family violence research.* Beverly Hills, CA: Sage Publications.

Hornung, C.A., McCullough, B.C., & Sugimoto, T. (1981). Status relationships in marriage: Risk factors in spouse abuse. *Journal of Marriage and the Family, 43,* 675–692.

Jackson, D.N. (1974). *Personality Research Form manual.* Goshen, NY: Research Psychologists Press.

Jacobson, N.S., & Margolin, G. (1979). *Marital therapy: Strategies based on social learning and behavior exchange principles.* New York: Brunner/Mazel.

Janis, I.L. (1982). Decision making under stress. In L. Goldberger & S. Breznitz (Eds.), *Handbook of stress: Theoretical and clinical aspects.* New York: Free Press.

Jouriles, E.N., Barling, J., & O'Leary, K.D. (1987). Children of battered women: Correlates of witnessing and experiencing intrafamily aggression. *Journal of Abnormal Child Psychology, 15,* 165–174.

Jouriles, E.N., & Collins, R.L. (1986). *Women's attitudes concerning the justification of relationship aggression: Effects of alcohol consumption by the assailant and the subject's drinking experience.* Unpublished manuscript. State University of New York, Stony Brook.

Jouriles, E.N., & O'Leary, K.D. (1985). Interspousal reliability of reports of marital violence. *Journal of Consulting and Clinical Psychology, 53*(3), 419–421.

Kalmuss, D. (1984). The intergenerational transmission of marital aggression. *Journal of Marriage and the Family, 46,* 11–19.

Kimmel, D., & Van der Veen, F. (1974). Factors of marital adjustment in Locke's Marital Adjustment Test. *Journal of Marriage and the Family, 36,* 57–63.

Locke, H.J., & Wallace, K.M. (1959). Short marital adjustment and prediction tests: Their reliability and validity. *Marriage and Family Living, 21,* 251–255.

Mandler, G. (1982). Stress and thought processes. In L. Goldberger & S. Breznitz (Eds.), *Handbook of stress: Theoretical and clinical aspects.* New York: Free Press.

Margolin, G. (1982). Ethical and legal considerations in marital and family therapy. *American Psychologist, 37,* 788–801.

Margolin, G., John, R., Gleberman, L., Miller, C., & Reynolds, N. (1985, August). *Abusive and non-abusive couples' affective response to conflictual discussions.* Paper presented at the 93rd Annual Convention of the American Psychological Association, Los Angeles.

Meichenbaum, D., & Turk, D.C. (1976). The cognitive-behavioral management of anxiety, anger, and pain. In P.O. Davidson (Ed.), *The behavioral management of anxiety, depression, and pain.* New York: Brunner/Mazel.

Navran, L. (1967). Communication and adjustment in marriage. *Family Process, 6,* 173–184.

Neidig, P.H., & Friedman, D.H. (1984). *Spouse abuse: A treatment program for couples.* Champaign, IL: Research Press.

Neidig, P.H., Friedman, D.H., & Collins, B.S. (1984, August). *Attitudinal characteristics of males who have engaged in spouse abuse.* Paper presented at the Second National Conference for Family Violence Researchers, Durham, NH.

Novaco, R. (1975). *Anger control: The development and evaluation of an experimental treatment.* Lexington, MA: Heath.

O'Leary, K.D. (1985). *Prevalence and correlates of spouse abuse.* Distinguished Scientist Award, Division 12, Section III, Paper presented at the American Psychological Association, Los Angeles.

O'Leary, K.D. (1987, a). Physical aggression between spouses: A social learning perspective. In V.B. Van Hasselt, R.L. Morrison, A.S. Bellack, & M. Hersen (Eds.), *Handbook of family violence* (pp. 31–56). New York: Plenum.

O'Leary, K.D. (Ed.). (1987, b). *Assessment of marital discord.* Hillsdale, NJ: Lawrence Erlbaum Associates.

O'Leary, K.D., & Arias, I. (1983). The influence of marital therapy on sexual satisfaction. *Journal of Sex and Marital Therapy, 9,* 171–181.

O'Leary, K.D., & Arias, I. (in press, a). Prevalence, correlates and development of spouse abuse. In R. DeV. Peters & R.J. McMahon (Eds.), *Marriage and families: Behavioral treatments and processes.* New York: Brunner/Mazel.

O'Leary, K.D., & Arias, I. (in press, b). Assessing agreement of reports of spouse abuse. In G.T. Hotaling (Ed.), *Proceedings of the Second National Conference for Family Violence Researchers.* Beverly Hills, CA: Sage Publications.

O'Leary, K.D., Arias, I., Rosenbaum, A., & Barling, J. (1986). *Premarital physical aggression.* Unpublished manuscript. State University of New York, Stony Brook.

O'Leary, K.D., & Curley, A.D. (1986). Assertion and family violence. *Journal of Marital and Family Therapy, 12* (3), 281–289.

O'Leary, K.D., Fincham, F.D., & Turkewitz, H. (1983). Assessment of positive feelings toward spouse. *Journal of Consulting and Clinical Psychology, 51,* 949–951.

O'Leary, K.D., & Wilson, G.T. (1987). *Behavior therapy: Application and outcome.* Englewood Cliffs, NJ: Prentice-Hall.

Pagelow, M.D. (1981). Factors affecting women's decisions to leave violent relationships. *Journal of Family Issues, 2,* 391–414.

Riggs, D.S. (1986). *Conflict resolution in dating couples: A multiple predictor approach.* Unpublished manuscript. State University of New York, Stony Brook.

Rosenbaum, A. (1979). *Wife abuse: Characteristics of the participants and etiological considerations.* Unpublished doctoral dissertation. State University of New York, Stony Brook.

Rosenbaum, A. (1985). *Marital violence workshop manual.* Unpublished manuscript, Syracuse University, Syracuse, NY.

Rosenbaum, A. (in press). Family violence. In W.J. Curran, A.L. McGarry, & S.A. Shah (Eds.), *Modern legal psychology and psychiatry.* Philadelphia: Davis.

Rosenbaum, A., Goldstein, D., & O'Leary, K.D. (1980, August). *An evaluation of the self-esteem of spouse abusive men.* Paper presented at the American Psychological Association Annual Convention, Montreal, Canada.

Rosenbaum, A., & O'Leary, K.D. (1981). Marital violence: Characteristics of abusive couples. *Journal of Consulting and Clinical Psychology, 49,* 63–71.

Rosenbaum, A., & O'Leary, K.D. (1986). The treatment of marital violence. In N.S. Jacobson & A.S. Gurman (Eds.), *Clinical handbook of marital therapy* (pp. 385–405). New York: Guilford Press.

Rosenberg, M. (1965). *Society and the adolescent self-image.* Princeton, NJ: Princeton University Press.

Sarason, I.G., Johnson, J.H., & Siegel, J.M. (1978). Assessing the impact of life changes: Development of the Life Experiences Survey. *Journal of Consulting and Clinical Psychology, 46,* 932–946.

Schachter, J., & O'Leary, K.D. (1985). Affective intent and impact in marital communication. *American Journal of Family Therapy, 13*(4), 17–23.

Schulman, M.A. (1979). A survey of spousal violence against women in Kentucky. Washington, DC: U.S. Government Printing Office, Study No. 792701.

Sears, R.R. (1977). Sources of life satisfactions of the Terman gifted men. *American Psychologist, 32,* 119–128.

Spinetta, J.J., & Rigler, D. (1972). The child-abusing parent: A psychological review. *Psychological Bulletin, 77*(4), 296–304.

Stark, E., & Flitcraft, A.H. (1985). Working paper on spouse abuse. Surgeon General's Workshop on Violence and Public Health. Leesburg, VA.

Straus, M.A. (1979). Measuring intrafamily conflict and violence: The Conflict Tactics (CT) Scales. *Journal of Marriage and the Family, 41,* 75–86.

Straus, M.A., Gelles, R.J., & Steinmetz, S.K. (1980). *Behind closed doors: Violence in the American family.* New York: Anchor Books.

Surgeon General's Workshop on Violence and Public Health: Source Book. (1985). Leesburg, VA.

Tarasoff versus Regents of the University of California. 17 Cal. 3d 425, 131 Cal. Rptr. 14, 551 P.2d 334. (1976).

Tavris, C. (1982). *Anger: The misunderstood emotion.* New York: Simon and Schuster.

Ulbrich, P., & Huber, J. (1981). Observing parental violence: Distribution and effects. *Journal of Marriage and the Family, 43,* 623–631.

Walker, L. (1979). *The battered woman.* New York: Harper and Row.

Weiss, R.L. (1980). Strategic behavioral marital therapy: Toward a model for assessment and intervention. In J.P. Vincent (Ed.), *Advances in family intervention, assessment, and theory* (Vol. 1, pp. 229–271). Greenwich, CT: JAI Press.

Wolfe, D.A., Zak, L., Wilson, S., & Jaffe, P. (1986). Child witnesses to violence between parents: Critical issues in behavioral and social adjustment. *Journal of Abnormal Child Psychology, 14,* 15–21.

5

Cognitive–Behavioral Treatment of Remarried Families

Leigh A. Leslie and Norman Epstein

An increasing number of individuals in our society live in a remarried or blended family at some point in their lives, either as a child or as a spouse/ parent. At present, about 26% of the marriages in the United States include at least one partner who has been married previously (Hacker, 1983), and approximately 25% of children in this country are being raised in a remarried family (Glick, 1984; Visher & Visher, 1985). No official statistics are available for Britain, but Burgoyne (1983) reports that between 7 and 10% of British children under age 16 are living in remarried family arrangements.

Although the divorce rate has stabilized in the United States, if current rates hold it can be expected that about one of every two to three marriages will end in divorce (Hacker, 1983). Given that approximately 83% of all divorced men and 75% of all divorced women remarry (Cherlin, 1981), it appears that the remarried family will be a very common family structure for years to come. Thus clinicians can expect and should be prepared to work with increasing numbers of remarried families.

Remarried families face a host of problems and issues typical of all families. However, unlike other families, they also face many problems which are in large part a function of this particular family structure. It is important to understand the unique strains inherent in this type of family and the particular demands it places on therapists. This chapter describes common sources of stress and dysfunction in remarried families and applies a cognitive–behavioral approach to understanding and treating these problems.

COMMON SOURCES OF STRESS FOR REMARRIED FAMILIES

In approaching therapy with remarried families, clinicians should be aware of several general areas of stress commonly experienced by these families. It is important to note, in considering these areas of stress, that they have been identified primarily in the clinical literature, based on the observations of therapists and others who have worked with these families. At this point, there have been few systematic empirical investigations into the problems facing remarried families.

First, the issues of *role definition and appropriate role behavior* often are problematic as new families are formed through remarriage (Kent, 1980; Pasley & Ihinger-Tallman, 1982). In our society today, no clear set of norms exists for how individuals should behave in the new roles (e.g., stepparent, stepchild) created by this union, although research findings have suggested that roles in remarried families tend to be given negative stereotypes when compared with roles in intact nuclear families (Bryan, Coleman, Ganong, & Bryan, 1986). Visher and Visher (1985) noted the persistence of negative stereotypes such as "wicked stepmother." Furthermore, there is no societal consensus about whether a stepparent or stepchild is supposed to "replace" a biological counterpart (parent, child) in any manner. The lack of clear role expectations for the individuals in remarried families led Cherlin (1978) to label remarriage as an "incomplete institution."

The absence of fixed roles for remarried families would appear to provide family members with an excellent opportunity for creative decision-making concerning how they would like their family to be organized. However, members of remarried families commonly have incorporated into their belief systems societal myths about how their families "should" be. Perhaps the most pervasive of these myths is that a remarried family should operate just like a first-marriage family (Visher & Visher, 1978). Johnson (1980) notes that although the traditional first-marriage "intact nuclear family" is now only one of several common family forms, people tend to see it as the "normal" form. With no clear guidelines for understanding the special qualities of a remarried family, most individuals resort to the roles and guidelines they operated by in their first families. Thus the stepfather in a new family may take as his model the role of "father" and assume that it is his responsibility to be the disciplinarian in the home, both to his biological children and to his stepchildren. However, Hetherington, Cox, and Cox (1982) found that the most effective approach for a stepfather was to develop warm, communicative relationships with his stepchildren and to be supportive of the custodial mother's rules and discipline practices, rather than trying to become the disciplinarian.

Similarly, although it might be considered normal for a child to feel comfortable with both natural parents in a nuclear family, it is not likely that a child will quickly feel the same level of comfort with a parent's new spouse as he or she feels with the natural parent. Anderson and White (1986) found that children in remarried families did not have as high a level of positive involvement with their stepfathers as children in intact nuclear families had with their fathers. Bray and Berger (1986) found that after six months of marriage both custodial mothers and stepfathers reported less cohesiveness, less satisfaction with emotional bonding, and more child behavior problems in their families than did parents in intact nuclear families. Consequently, believing that a child should view a new stepparent as his or her "new mommy" or "new daddy" and that the remarried family now constitutes a "complete" unit is likely to lead the natural parent and the stepparent to feel disappointed and to place pressure on the child.

Not only are these changing roles problematic for adults and children in the remarried family, but grandparents also may be affected. Sager, Brown, Crohn, Engel, Rodstein, and Walker (1983) note that following the end of a marriage (either through divorce or the death of a spouse) the children's grandparents often become more deeply involved with them, providing childcare and other forms of support. However, when a remarriage subsequently takes place, two changes occur that can be sources of family stress. First, although the grandparents and grandchildren had developed stronger bonds during the single-parent family stage, the grandparents' role may become a more peripheral one as the natural parent and stepparent become the primary parenting team. Second, remarriage adds a set of stepgrandparents (two sets if both divorced natural parents remarry), whose roles with the children are perhaps even more ambiguous than those of stepparents. Thus the structure of the extended remarried family can be very complex, and its members are faced with defining and coordinating many roles.

A second problem common to many remarried families is the issue of *loyalty conflicts and questions about family membership* (Visher & Visher, 1985). Unlike the nuclear family where traditional boundaries fairly well establish who is "inside" and who is "outside" the family, the boundaries in a remarried family are not easily drawn and may vary in the minds of different family members (Clingempeel, 1981; Sager et al., 1983). Loyalty conflicts and membership issues can take many forms. Children may perceive themselves as disloyal to their noncustodial biological parent if they enjoy their stepparent. Parents, particularly noncustodial ones, may feel guilty if they are living in a new remarried family with their partner's children. It is not unusual for a noncustodial parent, usually the man, to spend more time with his wife's children who live with him than with his own children. Such an arrangement can lead not only to guilt on the father's part, but resentment and anger on the part of his biological children. Still other loyalty issues may arise when children from two different households are brought together to form "one family." At least initially it is likely that family members, especially children, will not view this as one family but rather as two families living under one roof. Statements such as "You're not my brother" or "Don't talk to *my* mother that way" may be heard frequently during this time. Moreover, Anderson and White (1986) found that, even after two years, children in remarried families were not equally involved with both adults, but spent a greater amount of time with their natural parent.

Closely related to the problem of loyalty conflicts is the problem of *competition*. This too can take many forms, such as a struggle between natural children and stepchildren for the attention of a parent, or a struggle between natural parents for the favor and loyalty of a child. Clingempeel's (1981) finding that remarriages in which both of the partners have children from previous marriages tend to be less satisfying and are characterized by more negative interaction than remarried families where only the wife has children is consistent with the idea that there is greater opportunity for conflict and tension when children from two biological families are brought together in one household. Regardless of whether it is stepsiblings competing for the attention of a parent or natural parents competing for the at-tention of a child, such arrangements often leave family members feeling trapped in the middle of an uncomfortable interpersonal situation.

Still other problems surface in remarried families in regard to *parenting and discipline* (Cherlin, 1981; Visher & Visher, 1978). Several factors seem to make this a sensitive area for most of these families. First, the two adults in this new family did not develop their parenting style together, but rather in different households. Thus although they may be compatible as spouses, they have not had the opportunity that natural parents have had to develop collaborative roles as "co-parents" while their children were growing up. They are suddenly expected, by themselves and others, to work as a team even though they have had no practice. This situation can be exacerbated by the fact that during courtship each partner may have left the parenting or disciplining issues to the natural parent. However, once they are a "family" most couples assume that this is no longer acceptable and that each of them has a say in parenting all of the children in the house.

This situation may be complicated further if the two adults are at different developmental stages as parents; for example, if one has raised children through adolescence while the other has only parented a preschool child or perhaps never been a parent. Remarried partners often agree *in theory* about the rules and parenting style for their family, but unlike families with two natural parents, they can, and often do, resort to claiming "She's my child, I'll handle it" when parenting disagreements occur. The ages of the children in the family and their willingness to accept a new "parent" can significantly affect the prominence of this issue in a particular family. For example, we have seen conflict develop between stepparents and natural parents when older children and adolescents challenged the stepparent's "right" to impose rules different from those the natural parent had used with them for years.

Other difficult issues faced by families formed through remarriage involve having to cope with the *physical arrangement* of family members living in more than one household and potentially having to adjust to different standards and patterns of appropriate behavior in the different settings. When children divide their time between the homes of their custodial and noncustodial parents, this demands flexibility on the children's part to accommodate to any differences in the expectations held for them in the two homes. The differences may exist in factors such as the degree of autonomy given to a child, curfew and bedtime restrictions, participation in family decision making, and the degree to which a child is allowed to express negative feelings toward an adult. Parents also may find it difficult to accept the different standards in their children's other home, particularly if parenting conflicts were problematic in the first marriage.

People in remarried families also may feel "out of sync" in terms of normal family development. As noted earlier, remarried families often involve a combination of families at different developmental stages, which may cause some confusion or may demand readjustment from the family members (Visher & Visher, 1985). For example, in a family that includes both adolescents and preschool children, the adolescents are likely to be moving toward autonomy and heavy involvement in peer relationships, whereas young children's lives are centered in family activities. The remarried parents' efforts to promote family cohesiveness (especially in the early stages of this family's formation) may meet the needs of the young children quite well but may elicit anger and acting-out behavior from the adolescents.

Finances often are a highly problematic and sensitive area in remarried families. Adults' incomes may be split between supporting the family with whom they are living and contributing to the support of another family (most often, a man paying child support). The sharing of money or other resources not only can place fiscal strain on a family, but it also certainly can elicit or exacerbate whatever jealousy and conflicts about family loyalty exist, or increase any existing competition for attention.

Finally, there are special _sexuality issues_ that can arise in a remarried family. "Loosened sexual boundaries" may exist between stepparents and stepchildren on the one hand, and between stepsiblings on the other hand (Sager et al., 1983; Visher & Visher, 1979) because they are not related biologically. Problems can arise that range from pleasurable or distressing fantasy to actual sexual relationships. As Sager et al. note, even in the absence of sexual behavior, sexuality issues can be problematic, as when a stepparent copes with sexual attraction toward a stepchild by minimizing _any_ type of interaction with the child.

Because the large majority of remarried families today are formed following divorce rather than the death of a spouse, we focused our examples on the problems faced by this group. This is not intended to suggest that the issues reviewed may not exist when remarriage follows a death. In fact, most of the stresses experienced by remarried families are generic, whether the unit was formed between divorced or widowed individuals. Of course, some differences do exist. With a widowed parent, issues such as children living in two households and income being divided to support two families will not serve as triggers for questions of loyalty or competition. Also, children will not be caught in the middle of arguments between former spouses.

However, children in remarried families formed after the death of a spouse still may feel torn by conflicts of loyalty between stepparents and deceased natural parents. On the one hand, a child may believe that it is an act of disloyalty to the deceased parent to do things with the stepparent that used to be done with the natural parent. On the other hand, the stepparent and/ or surviving natural parent may apply pressure to the child to make the new unit a "complete" family, thereby blocking the child's natural period of mourning for the lost parent. This pressure also does not allow the step-parent–stepchild relationship to develop gradually over time. Thus when working with remarried families, therapists need to be attentive to the varied sources of stress reviewed here, regardless of whether remarriage followed divorce or death of a spouse.

A COGNITIVE–BEHAVIORAL MODEL OF DYSFUNCTION IN REMARRIED FAMILIES

Both cognitive and behavioral aspects of family interaction are likely to affect the extent to which any of the areas we discussed become problems for a family. We turn now to the major cognitive and behavioral factors that can influence the level of conflict and distress in a remarried family.

Cognitive Factors Affecting Stress in Remarried Families

Three major types of cognitive phenomena can be problematic for members of remarried families: basic beliefs about family life, attributions about causes of problems among family members, and expectations family members hold about each other's likely future behavior. Although all of these phenomena can contribute to dysfunction in *any* family (see Chapter 1), there are some specific themes to the content of beliefs, attributions, and expectancies relevant to problems of remarried families.

Unrealistic and incompatible beliefs. As noted earlier, many individuals approach their relationships with members of their remarried family with *unrealistic beliefs or assumptions* about the nature of those relationships. For example, if an adult enters a remarried family with the belief that "all family members should love each other," issues of loyalty and the meaning of family membership may become crucial. With such a cognitive set, normal adjustment issues that arise in the course of trying to establish a new family unit, such as competition, will be viewed as transgressions of the expected code of family love and loyalty.

People commonly do not evaluate the validity of such beliefs, and they tend to conclude that the distress they experience when the realities of remarried family life do not meet their standards is due to failings of the family (as a group, or any individual member) rather than to limitations of their beliefs.

Visher and Visher (1985) described typical unrealistic beliefs held about the nature of remarried family life: stepparents can be accepted in parental roles by their stepchildren if they just work hard enough at it; love, harmony, and a sense of closeness will appear instantly among family members; and the new family unit will be similar in structure but better than the former nuclear families.

In addition to this common set of beliefs, idiosyncratic beliefs that family members hold about the nature of remarried family relationships may pose problems. For example, the competition a stepparent engages in directly or indirectly with a noncustodial biological parent (alive or deceased) for a child's affection or loyalty often is generated by beliefs such as "If she cares about her [biological] father, then she must not care about me"; that is, those relationships are mutually exclusive, or there is a finite amount of caring a person has available to distribute to others. Many remarried individuals assume that their new relationship will be better than their previous one (Sager et al., 1983) and believe that their interactions with their new partner should be especially free of conflict. However, given the complexity of remarried family life, this standard most likely will be violated repeatedly.

Finally, beliefs about individual performance standards may affect family members' responses to remarried family life. Spouses' abilities to cope with basic disagreements can be impeded by a belief that there is a right way to do something and a wrong way (Ellis, 1962, 1977), and that one person must "win" in order for the right way to prevail. Such a belief certainly is not specific to people's thinking about remarriage, but as we noted earlier, remarried spouses commonly developed their approaches to family issues such as child rearing in separate families and have had little opportunity to form joint philosophies. Consequently, their tendencies to see their own views as "right" and the other person's views as "wrong" easily can be intensified.

Furthermore, a biological parent's distress about his or her difficulty in distributing time, money, and other resources "adequately" among family members living in two households may be exacerbated by a belief that one must meet all one's responsibilities perfectly in order to be a worthwhile family member or person. Again, perfectionistic beliefs have been implicated in a wide range of intrapersonal and interpersonal problems (Ellis, 1962, 1977), but the multiple roles of the remarried adult would seem to make him or her especially vulnerable to the effects of such thinking. For example, trying to be both a perfect parent *and* a perfect stepparent is likely to increase an adult's sense of inadequacy and feelings of stress.

Finally, although prevention of sexuality problems in remarried families may depend on the establishment of clear boundaries and standards for appropriate behavior, some problems may develop when family members hold unrealistically negative views of what constitutes "normal" versus "abnormal" responses to people with whom one lives. As noted earlier, a stepparent might withdraw from a child when he or she has sexual fantasies about the child, because he or she believes that such fantasies are "sick" and will lead to abusive behavior.

This review of unrealistic beliefs that may contribute to problems in the functioning of remarried families is intended only as an illustration of the types of beliefs a therapist working with these families may uncover. By no means is this list intended to be comprehensive, and it is important to note that with any specific family problem described here there may be beliefs operating other than those that we identified. The main point is that members of remarried families bring with them, based on their own past experiences and popular societal views, beliefs about their new families that may be unrealistic and may result in distress and family conflict.

Not only may an individual hold beliefs that are in themselves unrealistic, but he or she also may struggle with *incompatibilities* within his or her belief system. For example, a woman who lives with her husband and his children may want to be "like a mother" to the kids, but she also may think that it is inappropriate for her to be responsible for disciplining his children. Although a person may recognize his or her own ambivalence in a situation such as this, both of the incompatible beliefs may be strongly held and difficult to change.

Regardless of whether each family member holds unrealistic beliefs about remarried family life, conflict may occur when there is incompatibility among members' beliefs. In remarried families, members' experiences and related beliefs about family life have evolved in other family units. The new family unit is then faced with integrating or altering the various beliefs of both adults and children. For example, it is common for a husband and wife or a parent and child to differ in what they believe is an appropriate division of an adult's time between the marital dyad and the parent–child dyad. It also is important to remember that in the single-parent family which preceded the remarriage the parent (usually the mother) may have been much more accessible to the child, with none of her time and energy allocated to her new role of wife. Consequently, the child may believe that such an arrangement is appropriate and expect that it will continue even when the parent's new partner is added to the interaction. In contrast, the parent may believe that it is more appropriate to divide time between the child and the new partner. Later in this chapter we describe procedures for modifying remarried family members' basic beliefs.

Dysfunctional attributions. Although members of all families make inferences about the causes of one another's behavior, the types of inferences or attributions that can be made are more extensive in a remarried family. The structure of a remarried family and its extended family system increase the number and *combinations* of causes to which problematic behaviors may be attributed. For example, an adolescent daughter's negative behavior might be attributed to a cause within the family (e.g., "She challenges our authority as parents"), a cause outside the new family unit (e.g., "Your daughter would be fine if your ex-wife would leave her alone"), or to an *interaction* between factors within and outside the family (e.g., "Your ex-wife caters to your rebellious daughter").

Given the wide variety of attributions that remarried family members can make, the particular attributions chosen by each person can lead to a range of functional or dysfunctional emotional and behavioral responses to each interaction with the other family members. For example, whereas attributions of problems to global, stable causes (i.e., traits) can elicit a sense of hopelessness in family members regarding the potential for change (see Chapter 1), attributions of blame for problems tend to fuel anger and conflict, and attributions that infer low levels of respect and caring by other family members can elicit anger and sadness (Fincham, 1985; Pretzer, Fleming, & Epstein, 1983).

Inaccurate expectancies. Closely related to the attributions one makes for another's behavior are the expectancies or predictions one makes about how that person will behave in the future. If, for example, a child believes that her mother feels closer to her new husband than to the child, the child may expect that there is a high probability that in any disagreement the mother will side with her husband against the child. Such expectancies affect how family members interact with one another, and unfortunately they may produce negative self-fulfilling prophecies. In the preceding example, if the child's negative expectancy leads her to criticize her mother and stepfather, she may increase their tendency to form the type of alliance she had predicted. Thus expectancies can play an important role in creating "positive feedback loops" (in the systems theory sense) that amplify destructive family interactions.

Behavioral Factors Affecting Stress in Remarried Families

The effectiveness with which a remarried family copes with the various stressors they face is likely to depend not only on their cognitive appraisals but also on the specific ways in which family members behave with one another and with others outside the family unit. Deficits in communication, problem-solving, and negotiation skills can impede the family's ability to resolve their problems.

Communication problems. A gradual building of family cohesion is likely to be difficult if family members lack skills for sharing their thoughts and feelings with one another. Sager et al. (1983) note that members of remarried families often do not take each other's perspective into account and therefore do not realize the extent to which their conflicts are caused by differences in what they expect or want from their relationships. The accurate exchange of information about relationship expectations is needed if family members are to understand and best meet each other's needs. Without accurate communication about expectations, the potential for misattributions about other family members' intentions and motivations may be increased.

Problem-solving deficits. Because there are no clear guidelines for operating a remarried family, each family is faced with devising its own solutions to the complexities of combining two families, such as loyalty conflicts, incompatible parenting strategies, and the disruption caused by having children "shuttle" between two homes. Their attempts at problem solving may be hampered by their reliance on solutions that may have worked in a previous family but do not apply in the current family, or by their general ineffectiveness at generating creative solutions to problems. Furthermore, if the family has not yet developed cohesiveness, their teamwork in searching for solutions that are both effective and satisfying for all members will be impeded.

Negotiation deficits. Closely linked to problem-solving skills are the family members' abilities to negotiate with one another. Remarried family life calls for many compromises, and it is important that the family members be willing and able to sort through alternative solutions to a problem and reach a joint decision that is equitable for all parties. One's willingness to negotiate certainly is influenced by cognitive factors such as one's investment in being "right," but working toward a compromise also includes the ability to devise new solutions that simultaneously maximize gains and minimize costs for all family members. Many families are not practiced at using the analytic and bargaining skills involved in effective negotiation.

The Interaction of Cognitive and Behavioral Factors in Family Dysfunction

Our model of remarried family dysfunction takes into account the interaction of the various cognitive and behavioral factors we described. In this model, family members and the other significant people with whom they interact (e.g., noncustodial parents, grandparents, school officials) approach the remarriage with sets of beliefs about the way such a family "should" be. Many of these beliefs are unrealistic, and often the beliefs of various parties are incompatible. These beliefs constitute what Beck and his colleagues (e.g., Beck, Rush, Shaw, & Emery, 1979) label "schemata." These schemata are fairly stable over time and may be relatively dormant except when activated by family interactions that are relevant to their particular themes, such as family love, cohesiveness, or loyalty.

When family interactions do not meet the standards set in individuals' schemata, family members become upset, perhaps angry, anxious, or depressed. When they make inferences about *why* the schemata were violated, their attributions often involve a perception that other family members and related persons are uncaring, disrespectful, and malicious in their intentions. Their attributions also commonly involve the assigning of blame for negative family interaction to individuals within and/or outside the family.

Lacking effective communication to clarify misunderstandings, as well as good problem-solving and negotiation skills to resolve differences and devise creative solutions to problems, family members resort to dysfunctional interaction styles such as withdrawal and aversive control (e.g., verbal attack) to cope with their disappointments and conflicts. When family members see another member respond in this manner, they interpret the behavior in the context of their own schemata and attributional processes, often leading to further dysfunctional behavior on their parts. Each party tends to elicit negative behaviors in the others which are self-fulfilling prophecies, confirming their original negative attributions about the other people and further violating the person's beliefs about the nature of good remarried family relationships.

CLINICAL ASSESSMENT WITH REMARRIED FAMILIES

Considering the unique situations faced by remarried families and the ample opportunity for the operation of dysfunctional cognitions and behavioral interaction patterns, the assessment phase of therapy is crucial for the cognitive–behavioral family therapist. At present, no standardized cognitive–behavioral assessment measures exist which have been designed specifically for work with remarried families. In general, however, assessment of remarried families should be designed in such a manner that 1) the distress or problems that are influenced by the remarried family's structure can be distinguished from those that are common to all families, 2) the contributions of both cognitive distortions and behavioral deficits can be assessed, and 3) the family can begin to learn the cognitive–behavioral model during the assessment phase.

The key initial element in assessment is identifying the contribution of this particular family structure to the presenting complaints. Two cautions should be noted here. First, it is common for remarried families to enter therapy maintaining that although they are having problems (e.g., marital, parenting), the fact that they are remarried actually has nothing to do with the presenting complaints. Given that some individuals hold a belief in the similarity of remarried and first-married families, it is not surprising that they want to minimize the contribution of this family structure to their current problems or are truly unaware that their particular family arrangement plays a role in the problems. In fact, we have found that clients typically present generic complaints, such as a disobedient child, and may even fail to tell a therapist that they are a remarried family until he or she inquires about their history.

In such instances when the family makes no connection between their presenting problems and their family structure, it seems most helpful to the family for the therapist simply to "normalize" the stresses of remarriage with statements such as "most people find that parenting is a very different proposition in a remarried family; how has it been for you?" or "Remarriage almost always presents some unique situations for people to deal with." These general context-setting statements do not force the family to acknowledge the role of their family structure before they are ready to do so, and thereby they prevent a therapeutic impasse. Visher and Visher (1985) stress that it is often a great relief to clients to learn that their family can be different from the traditional intact nuclear family but still be healthy, and that it takes time to develop family cohesion, caring, and trust.

The second caution is against erring in the *opposite* direction: overattributing family problems to the state of remarriage. It is easy for the therapist, as well as the family, to be lulled into thinking that all problems in remarried families are a function of this family structure. In reality, these families experience many problems which are common to all types of families. Thus it is critical to distinguish whether the distress is due to a "typical" family problem or has arisen or become amplified by the remarried family structure.

For example, adolescent acting-out behavior is not specific to a particular family type, but the problems of adolescence (e.g., the development of autonomy) may be intensified if the family is struggling with an undefined, ambiguous role for the new stepfather.

We suggest that assessment with remarried families be characterized as a decision tree (see Figure 5–1), which distinguishes between problems experienced by *any* family and those that are either unique to remarried families or take on a different dimension in the context of the remarried family.

The focus of this chapter is the remarriage branch of the decision tree and the dysfunctional cognitive and behavioral factors that contribute to the development or maintenance of problems in these families. In actual practice, therapists usually need to address both branches when working with remarried families. Consequently, many treatment strategies that are generally relevant for a variety of family problems will be applicable with remarried families. However, these problems also will have a dimension or focus not common in other families, and the clinician may need to take the responsibility for identifying the contribution of remarried family issues to a family's presenting problems.

In the absence of standard measures for assessing remarried families, the two major sources of data are the clinical interview and observation of the family's interaction patterns in the office.

Interviewing the Remarried Family

Interview procedures for determining the contribution of a remarried family structure to a family's presenting problem tend to be straightforward. First, when seeing any family that has been formed through a remarriage it is important to find out how long the couple has been married or living together.

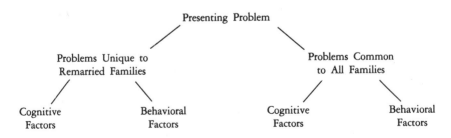

Figure 5–1. Decision tree for assessment of remarried families.

Although couples may assume that the adaptation to this new family occurs quickly, clinical experience suggests that when there are children present in a remarriage, the adjustment period typically takes two years (Visher & Visher, 1979). Therefore, although after 18 months of marriage members of a family may say "We've worked out all of our differences," it would be wise to continue to consider that issues concerning adjustment to the new family may still be relevant for some, if not all, family members.

In addition to ascertaining the duration of the marriage, the therapist can ask questions directly concerning the contribution of remarried family issues to the presenting problem. For example, one may pose the question of how family life and, in particular, the presenting problem would be different if "it were still just you and your mom," or if "you two were the natural parents of these children." Responses to such questions can reveal not only how family members view the role of remarried family issues in their current problems, but they also can provide the therapist insight into family members' attributions about the causes of the problems.

As valuable as the family's views about the role of the remarried family structure in their presenting problems may be, it is important for the therapist to consider that their reports may be influenced by cognitive biases (e.g., unrealistic beliefs and distorted attributions). Also, family members may censor their responses to the therapist's questions about family life when particular other members are present (e.g., a child may be inhibited in the presence of a stepparent). Consequently, to determine whether one really is dealing with a problem caused by aspects of the remarriage, it is important to conduct a cognitive–behavioral *functional analysis* of the presenting problem(s), inquiring about details concerning the antecedent events and consequences associated with the occurrence of the problem.

One may conduct a family interview for the purpose of completing a functional analysis first by verifying with members of the family that a presenting problem such as a child's disobedience seems to occur not continuously but only at certain times. The interviewer then can ask them to recall as much detail about the conditions existing when the problem occurred, especially with recent incidents that are more likely to be remembered accurately. Relevant details include the time of day, the location, who was present, what interactions occurred before the onset of the problematic behavior, what each person remembers thinking about each other at the time, and what interactions occurred after the onset of the problem.

When conducting this type of interview, it is important that the clinician pursue enough detail to remove as much ambiguity as possible from his or her mind concerning the sequence of behaviors and cognitions in which the presenting problem was embedded.

Similarly, one must probe consistently for the family members' relevant cognitions in the situation. For example, if a stepfather reports, "When she [the stepdaughter] told me that she didn't want to discuss her poor school grades, I thought, 'She's not going to get away with this!,' " the therapist might ask, "What were you thinking she wouldn't get away with?" His reponse may reveal a perception that the stepdaughter does not accept his authority. What the clinician listens for is any evidence of cognitive themes involving remarried family issues such as loyalty, lack of family cohesiveness, and lack of "appropriate" love between stepparents and stepchildren.

A note of caution is in order here. During assessment, as well as throughout therapy, a therapist must be aware of a family's possible hypersensitivity to issues of alliance. Given the realignment and integration of families and family members that accompany remarriage, individuals often are highly reactive to perceived favoritism on the part of other family members. It is possible that this reactivity may generalize to aspects of the therapist's behavior (e.g., "You are paying more attention to what my stepfather wants than to what my mother wants").

Another issue that may arise during the assessment period is the extent to which the therapist needs to gather information about the spouses' previous marriages. Our experience has been that remarried spouses are typically not hesitant to describe previous family situations that they believe influence their current family life or affect their own reactions. In fact, we believe that they often overattribute responsibility for present problems to prior marital and family experiences.

Once it has been established that elements of the problem arise from the remarried family structure, the second task of assessment is to identify the cognitions (beliefs, attributions, and expectancies) and behavioral deficits which contribute to the problem(s). The following are some general guidelines for gathering information about cognitive and behavioral factors by means of the clinical interview.

Interview assessment of cognitions. Attributions can be assessed by asking family members about their hypotheses regarding the causes of upsetting events in their daily interactions. The therapist also can utilize information from ongoing interactions in sessions by interrupting family members when they become upset with one another and probing for the upsetting attributions they are making about their interactions right at that moment. Expectancies can be identified in a similar manner, by asking family members to report what they expected others to say and do in past situations, and how those predictions seemed to influence their subsequent actions. Again, the "here-and-now" setting of the therapy session can be used to identify expectancies as well. For example, when a child fails to comment when his father tells him that he should have been at home helping his stepmother with chores, the therapist could ask the child why he decided not to respond to his father. The child may give an answer such as "I knew he'd jump on me if I said I wanted to play with my friends." Whether or not the child's prediction is accurate, it provides some initial information about the contingencies he believes operate in the family.

There are two major approaches to assessing belief systems. First, the therapist can listen for repetitive themes in the perceptions or "automatic thoughts" family members report about their interactions (see Chapter 1 for a detailed description of this process). However, although it may be tempting for the therapist to deduce the specific nature of a common theme in a client's statements, there is no substitute for asking the client what he or she thinks is the basic assumption about family life that underlies his or her perceptions. The therapist can aid a client in identifying a basic belief by asking a series of questions in response to a reported thought, of the form "If that is true, then what would that mean?" or "What would the implications of that be?" (Again, the reader is referred to Chapter 1 for a description of these procedures.)

A second approach for identifying underlying beliefs is to ask family members directly about their attitudes and beliefs about issues that tend to be stressful for remarried families. For example, "What were your expectations of your husband going into this marriage? How did you want him to act with the children?" Questions can be asked of all family members regarding issues such as family structure and organization (e.g., "How did you figure that decisions would be made about the way you would spend your leisure time together?"). Other questions can tap beliefs about family roles and rules (e.g., "When one or more of the children need disciplining, how do you think that should get done?"). Unrealistic beliefs may be revealed by statements such as "I am the mother in this house, and you must treat me like it," but the therapist needs to make an additional inquiry of the speaker (e.g., "How do you want them to treat you?") in order to specify what standards are included in the belief.

When strong beliefs are voiced, it is important to clarify whether they are held by other members of the family, and if not, to identify any conflicting beliefs on the others' parts. Many beliefs concerning family rules and structure are not, in and of themselves, unrealistic; however, if they are not shared by other family members, rules may not be enforced and conflicts are likely to arise.

It is important to assess what beliefs members of a remarried family hold about loyalty to the new family unit, the original family, or particular family members. Children may distance themselves from a new stepparent for fear of being disloyal to the noncustodial parent, whereas the custodial parent may push vigorously for the child to accept this "new mommy" or "new daddy." Although various types of loyalty expectations may coexist, the most typical unrealistic belief about loyalty to be raised in therapy tends to be the custodial parent's desire for the children to accept the new spouse and for the family to be a cohesive unit. The loyalty beliefs of children may have to be broached by the therapist, because children are less likely to be open and direct in therapy, or even aware of the beliefs that influence their actions. Questions such as "How would your daddy feel if you and Jim [stepfather] became good friends?" or "What do you do (think) when Jim corrects what you do?" may assist the therapist in getting a picture of the child's view of loyalty and family boundaries.

Interview assessment of behavioral deficits. First, it should be determined whether each adult has the parenting skills appropriate for the ages of the children in the family. Given the mix of developmental stages in many remarried families, it is not atypical to find a new spouse who has never had children or who has children different in age from his or her stepchildren. Parenting problems may arise simply as a function of lack of experience or skill in dealing with children of a certain age. Such assessments can be made by asking adults about their beliefs concerning appropriate behavior for children of different ages, their specific previous experiences with children, and some examples of the methods and outcomes of their current efforts to guide the children in their new family.

All the adults and children in the family can be polled about their patterns of communication, problem solving, and negotiation. The inquiry can begin with questions addressed to the group as a whole, such as "When you are all faced with coming to a decision about something that involves your family, how do you do it? What happens?" As noted in our earlier description of the functional analysis, it is important to ask whatever additional questions may be necessary to obtain a clear operational definition of the behaviors the family members are trying to describe. Broad statements such as "We decide it together" do not provide the specific information needed to evaluate whether there are behavioral deficits in need of modification.

Finally, the family's time management ability should be assessed. A reality of remarried family life is that it is more hectic and often more chaotic than life in first marriages, because of family members' involvement in more than one household. Consequently, the family frequently is faced with conflicting, or at least demanding, schedules. The family members' descriptions of typical sequences of events that occur when they need to handle time and scheduling problems can elucidate the degree to which they have the abilities to be flexible and manage their time effectively.

Behavioral Observation Procedures

Since the accuracy of self-reports is limited, it is valuable to make systematic observations of the family's actual interaction patterns whenever possible. This can be done both by observing unstructured interactions during therapy sessions and by giving the family a specific task and observing the sequence of events that occurs as they perform it. In the latter procedure, the therapist may state, "In order for me to get a firsthand idea of how you solve problems together, I would like you to spend several minutes talking among yourselves about a solution to a specific problem. You already mentioned that there has been some disagreement among you regarding [some problem the family identified]. What I would like to do is listen while you discuss what could be done to solve this problem. I won't get involved at all in your discussion." Whenever possible, it is desirable to record or videotape such interactions for later review. Although it is likely that the therapist will notice some important aspects of the family interaction during the live interaction, it is our experience that many of the "fine points" become clear only during a review in which sections of the tape can be replayed several times if necessary. This kind of analysis is helpful in identifying circular processes in the family interaction that can impede effective communication and problem solving. For example, at first glance it may seem that every time a child offers a suggestion the stepmother interrupts her. A second viewing of a videotape may reveal that just as the child begins each statement she hesitates briefly and glances at her stepmother, a nonverbal cue that may "invite" interruption. This type of process easily can become circular, and its modification may be best approached by attending to the behavior of each party that tends to maintain it.

Although it may be a luxury in clinical practice, it can be highly revealing for the therapist to observe family interaction during a home visit. Not only does this procedure reduce the degree to which samples of interaction are biased by the context of the therapy room, but it also gives the therapist an opportunity to observe some of the special aspects of daily remarried family life, such as unexpected calls or visits from a noncustodial parent. One also can note the physical arrangements in the home that might contribute to problems (e.g., the fact that two stepsiblings who had their own rooms in their previous families now share a room). However, the evaluation of such observational data must take into account the likelihood that the therapist's presence in the home influences the family's interactions.

CLINICAL STRATEGIES AND TECHNIQUES

The major strategies in a cognitive–behavioral approach to therapy with remarried families are 1) to modify dysfunctional beliefs, attributions, and expectancies that impede a family's adjustment to the new family structure and 2) to improve the family's communication, problem-solving, and negotiation skills to the extent necessary for them to deal with the stresses of remarried family life effectively. The following are specific techniques that can be used to pursue these strategies. In general, these techniques are standard cognitive–behavioral interventions that are used with a variety of families and family problems, but we will describe how the *content* of these interventions is tailored to deal with issues specific to remarried families.

Structuring the Therapy Session with Remarried Families

One of the major issues most remarried families wrestle with is defining the boundaries of the family. Therefore, the initial therapeutic question—"Who should be included in therapy?"—becomes more critical in work with remarried families than with other types of families. The therapist's decision about which family members are to be included in the assessment and treatment sessions makes a statement to the family about the nature of their family structure even before their own beliefs about the structure are examined thoroughly. As the therapist begins to clarify perceived boundaries by including or excluding particular people from sessions, guidelines for making such decisions are often helpful. First, although grandparents often play roles in remarried family problems, we include them in our sessions only when they live in the home. Our reason for this, which we explain to the family, is that it is important for the remarried family unit to develop its identity, with boundaries that allow inclusion of others such as grandparents but which also set appropriate limits to such inclusion. We suggest that the best way for the family to deal with issues involving grandparents frequently is to plan changes during therapy sessions and then carry these out with the grandparents outside the therapy office.

Second, we believe that the decision to invite a noncustodial parent to a session should be based on a discussion with the family about the reasons for doing so. When family problems (e.g., children's loyalty conflicts) appear to be due to difficulties in the way that custodial and noncustodial parents coordinate their roles, it often is useful to have them meet and define or negotiate those roles. However, if the therapist believes that one parent's request that the other be included reflects that person's desire to maintain a personal relationship with the former partner or to address "unfinished business," such a meeting should be discouraged. An explanation should be given concerning the importance of maintaining clear boundaries. In addition, the therapist may uncover a parent's belief (e.g., "I can't talk to my former wife without my therapist present") that itself needs modification so that parental conflicts can be resolved between the parents, without involving children and other parties inappropriately.

Finally, we ask remarried couples initially to bring along all children who spend time in their home, including noncustodial children who visit. This guideline serves several purposes. First, it communicates to children who may be doubtful of their family standing that they are considered a part of the new family unit. Second, this procedure allows interventions with the stepsibling subsystem. It also helps the family improve their ability to adjust repeatedly to the entrance and exit of those family members which occurs with visitation and joint custody. It should be noted that the decision to include all children, at least initially, may make the adults' beliefs about who belongs in the family more overt. Questions from spouses about whether each other's children who do not live in the house should be included provide an excellent opportunity for the therapist to pursue beliefs about family membership.

In general, we find that it is easier to begin therapy with a larger group of family members, and then work with a subset of the family, than to do the opposite. This is especially the case because members of remarried families who join an ongoing therapy may be sensitive to the possibility that alliances will have developed among family members and between the therapist and certain family members.

As may be clear in the preceding discussion, it is common for a therapist working with a remarried family to spend more time than he or she might with other families explicitly discussing family roles. It is most helpful to encourage all family members to exchange their ideas about how the family "should" be, with the therapist describing current knowledge about issues that may arise in remarried families.

Modifying Dysfunctional Cognitions

Modifying unrealistic beliefs. When one or more family members have a particular unrealistic belief, one common technique involves *logical analysis* of that belief. For example, when a child's loyalty conflict seems to be fueled by a stepparent's belief that "If the child loves her noncustodial parent, then she cannot care about me at the same time," the therapist can guide the stepparent in examining whether this reasoning is logical. For example, the therapist can ask whether the parent can care for his or her own children *and* stepchildren simultaneously. When the parent (typically) gives a response such as "Of course I can!" the therapist can question whether this principle can be generalized so that the children also can care for noncustodial parents and stepparents simultaneously. If a parent concludes that this is not possible, the therapist might challenge him or her (in a noncritical Socratic manner) to explain why the principle would not apply to children in general, or to these children in particular. When a logical analysis is not sufficient for modifying the parent's belief, the therapist may need to help the parent test the belief more directly, using the techniques described later.

A second technique for testing the validity of a family member's belief about family life is to collaborate with the individual in *examining the evidence* that supports or refutes the belief. In the foregoing example, one would gather evidence relevant to whether a child has a finite amount of caring and whether the child's relationships with a biological parent and a stepparent must be mutually exclusive. Evidence can include the stepparent's memories of past incidents that were consistent or inconsistent with the belief (e.g., the child returned from a visit with the noncustodial parent and asked the stepparent to play a card game with him). Additional evidence can be gathered from observation of other remarried families, from popular books describing remarried family life (e.g., Berman, 1981), and from discussions with members of other remarried families. When family members do not know other remarried families, it often is useful to help them find a remarried family support group in the community.

Because a remarried family consists of individuals with histories in different families, it is important to discuss historical material that may have shaped members' beliefs about family life. For example, a stepparent's belief that the family must be free of overt conflict between adults and children may be based on his or her experiences with destructive handling of conflict in a first marriage rather than on current experiences with stepchildren. If remarried family members are somewhat defensive about competition and loyalty issues, they may have some discomfort discussing such historical material. The therapist can communicate to them that the topic need not be taboo by talking about it openly with them and noting how past experiences can make people uneasy about new situations. When it appears that a family member's unrealistic belief has been based on past experiences, the therapist can guide the family in exploring how current circumstances in their family differ from those in the person's past. When the present family dynamics *do* seem similar to those of the past, the therapist and family then can engage in problem solving to devise new ways of coping with the problem (e.g., more effective ways for resolving parent–child disagreements about the children's friends).

It also often is helpful to guide the family in *weighing the advantages and disadvantages* of an individual's unrealistic belief. The therapist stresses that a person usually has some fairly convincing reasons for adhering to a particular way of viewing family life, and that he or she will be unlikely to change that belief unless it is clear that its disadvantages outweigh its advantages. The therapist and family then collaborate to compile separate lists of the advantages and disadvantages of viewing the world in terms of the particular belief. For example, an advantage of believing that members of a remarried family should feel instant love for one another is an expectation that the turmoil one experienced during a prior divorce finally will end. In contrast, disadvantages of that belief include the inevitable disappointment, perceived rejection, and hurt that result when the expected closeness does not materialize.

Simply comparing the advantages and disadvantages of a belief will not necessarily decrease an individual's adherence to it, but the process often increases all the family members' understandings of the basic assumptions influencing that person's behavior, and it can increase the individual's openness to *constructing a revised belief.* The therapist can coach the individual and other family members in "rewriting" the belief so that it still includes attractive advantages but has fewer disadvantages. In the preceding example, the belief about instant family love might be revised to "In our new family, we will make a concerted effort to be sensitive to each other's stresses and needs. However, we will take the needed time to get to know each other, and will not expect our feelings for one another to match those of family members who have grown up together. In remarried families, the pains of adjustment often cause some tensions. More loving feelings may develop, but this takes time and cannot be forced." This belief not only sets up a different standard, but it also suggests how family members can try to behave toward one another.

Behavioral experiments can be devised and conducted by the family to test the validity of an old belief or the viability of a revised belief. For example, the therapist might suggest that the custodial parent and stepparent test their belief that a noncustodial parent must change the late bedtime he or she sets for the child in order for the child to accept the earlier bedtime rule set by the custodial parent and stepparent. The experiment could involve their explaining to the child that adults sometimes differ about what they want children to do, but that it is not the child's responsibility to decide on one way of doing things. They can explain to the child that what is important is for the child to respect his or her parents' wishes in either home. They then can describe the rules in *their* own home in detail and the (reasonable) consequences they will impose if those rules are not followed. Rather than debating with the child, they are to note that there are different rules in different situations, and to enforce their rules consistently. Often they will discover from such an experiment that the struggle about rules ends fairly quickly, particularly because the child was removed from the parental conflict and because there are consistent and reasonable consequences imposed.

When there is a problem of incompatible beliefs among family members, rather than unrealistic beliefs on the part of any individual, the therapist still can use the foregoing techniques to help the family evaluate the validity, advantages, and disadvantages of each belief. However, the most appropriate intervention frequently is guiding them in negotiating a compromise set of standards. Guidelines for negotiation can be found in Chapter 1. Family members' positions frequently become polarized during conflict, so it is important to help them move from an all-or-nothing view to a search for compromises.

Finally, the therapist should keep in mind that whenever one works conjointly with a family on the evaluation and modification of basic beliefs, it is likely that any competition or loyalty dynamics will be "played out" in the session. For example, during a discussion of a stepparent's particular belief, a child initially may voice agreement with the stepparent but shift her support to a disagreeing natural parent when the latter expresses disapproval. This presents a choice point for the therapist, and one's clinical judgment should be one's guide. If the current "process" is an excellent example of a central dynamic the therapist has discussed earlier with the family and seems to be tied to a problematic unrealistic belief, the therapist might choose to shift the family's attention to the other topic explicitly, stressing that they can return to the original topic later. An alternative would be to stop the interaction long enough to describe the process and propose discussing it later. Videotape replay facilities will make the latter option much more feasible.

Modifying faulty attributions. When the therapist determines that family members are attributing problems in their interactions inaccurately to traits (e.g., "She's a 'bad seed' "), malicious intent (e.g., "He disobeys me because he wants to get me upset"), and other negative factors (e.g., "He wants to visit his [noncustodial] father because he cares more about him than about me"), several techniques are useful for modifying these attributions. The therapist can coach the individual and other family members in listing possible *alternative explanations* (different attributions) for the observed interaction problem. It also is useful for the therapist to introduce a "reframe," or alternative attribution, for a problem when the family has not thought of one. We find, however, that many family members are more likely to accept the validity of alternative attributions that they have generated on their own. In general, we begin such a discussion with a remark such as "Well, that certainly is one possible cause of the problem, but it is important not to jump to conclusions, in case there are other causes that need our attention. What else might explain the behavior you have seen?"

A second technique involves *examining the evidence* for the validity of an attribution, as well as the evidence for alternative attributions. The procedures are similar to those described earlier for testing evidence relevant to beliefs; for example, examining a series of past incidents to determine whether someone indeed has a particular trait or whether the person's behavior is situation-specific.

Behavioral experiments also are useful for testing the validity of an attribution. For example, if a parent makes the attribution that "my new spouse doesn't help me control my children because he has no interest in doing so" and the therapist has good reason to believe that this inference is inaccurate, the parent might be asked to "conduct an experiment to test that idea." In this case, an experiment could involve asking the spouse to take responsibility for overseeing a specific chore the children have been assigned. The doubting parent is asked to monitor the outcome of the experiment and to ask the spouse about his or her feelings about performing the task. Of course, the person whose attribution is being tested may be skeptical about the new data, saying, "He only cooperated because you made us set up that experiment" (another negative attribution). The therapist then has the task of challenging the new attribution with procedures such as those we described.

Correcting inaccurate expectancies. When family members make inaccurate predictions about each other's behaviors, the techniques for modifying these are similar to those used with unrealistic beliefs and faulty attributions: *logical analysis* (e.g., "Is it logical that, because your former wife blocked your efforts to discipline the kids, now your new wife is certain to do the same?"), *collecting evidence* from past and current incidents, and *behavioral experiments.* Testing the validity of expectancies in remarried families often involves exploration of historical material from the former family lives of the various family members.

Conjoint family therapy sessions are a rich source of data for identifying inaccurate attributions and expectancies, and an excellent forum for modifying them as they occur during family interactions in the session. As the therapist monitors the ongoing process of the interaction, he or she should look for shifts in which one family member responds negatively (emotion or behavior) to another member. For example, if the therapist notices that a child becomes upset when her biological mother and stepfather are talking about going away alone for the weekend, the therapist might ask the child what thoughts upset her. The child might reveal thoughts indicating that she perceives that her mother is abandoning her for the new spouse.

Monitoring of interaction sequences also gives the therapist opportunities to draw the family's attention to patterns by which their behaviors toward one another produce self-fulfilling prophecies. For example, a therapist might point out that a stepmother who attributes a trait of "selfishness" to her spouse elicits what looks like selfish behavior from him when she repeatedly attacks him verbally and he spends a considerable time justifying his behavior by describing his feelings and needs.

Of course, family members' negative attributions and expectancies are not all inaccurate, and the goal of a cognitive–behavioral approach is to foster *realistic* rather than Pollyanna thinking. It is important to help family members identify and modify inaccurate cognitions, but it is equally important to identify accurate perceptions and plan other methods for modifying real problems. When a parent's attribution that his new spouse feels strong hostility toward his children is accurate, it is the spouse's feelings that need attention, not the attribution.

Modifying Behavioral Deficits

A number of behavioral interventions are particularly relevant to the needs of remarried families. Given that these techniques have been reviewed elsewhere (see Chapter 1), our description focuses on how they are tailored to this particular type of family.

Parenting skill training. It is fairly common in remarried families to find that one of the two adults lacks experience parenting children of a certain age or lacks parenting experience at all. The techniques of skill training are standard, including didactic instruction (e.g., "minilectures" by the therapist, assigned reading such as Patterson's [1975] book), modeling by the therapist, behavioral rehearsal, and performance feedback. However, the therapist also must be aware that progress in this training could be impeded if 1) the individual being trained perceives this as a threatening indication of his or her inadequacy, or 2) the biological parent forms a coalition with the therapist, serving as a "co-trainer" and thus placing the stepparent in a one-down position. Although similar issues can arise in parenting skill training with families other than the remarried, we find that they are more common following remarriage. Thus the therapist must help the new couple deal with discrepancies in their parenting skills and experience in a constructive manner that builds "teamwork" rather than eliciting competition.

Communication training. Given their past experiences in different families, members of remarried families often lack the shared "shorthand" expressions and the shared meanings for words and gestures that develop among members of a family who have spent many years together. Consequently, they often benefit from practicing basic expressive and listening skills such as those in Guerney's (1977) Relationship Enhancement program. The therapist can introduce a rationale for training the family in such skills when he or she is able to point out instances of the family's faulty communication during therapy sessions. The family should practice the new skills during therapy sessions before attempting them outside as "homework," in order to maximize their chances of success in the home setting.

Problem-solving and negotiation training. Training remarried families in these skills (described in Chapter 1) must take into account the possibility that family members used different problem-solving strategies in their former families and the possibility that any discussions about alternative solutions to a problem may be impeded by issues specific to remarried family life. For example, one may have difficulty getting a couple to "brainstorm" possible solutions to the problem of how to deal with a noncustodial parent who is unreliable in picking up and returning the children on time if the stepparent believes strongly that the custodial parent should have little or no direct contact with his or her former spouse. Thus the basic skill training procedures often must be accompanied by interventions designed to alter dysfunctional cognitions about "appropriate" roles in a remarried family.

Time management. As noted earlier, remarried families must cope with complex schedules that often involve activities of people in at least two households. They often have not had prior experience with budgeting and scheduling time to the degree necessary in their new family. Consequently, they find themselves stressed and frustrated by their inability to meet all of their obligations and set aside leisure time as well. The therapist can be of assistance by making the family aware that time management is a common problem in remarried families and by providing some training in basic time management skills, including prioritizing tasks and making realistic, systematic daily schedules.

Intimacy-building exercises. An additional type of behavioral intervention that often is especially relevent for remarried families involves *intimacy-building exercises.* Such exercises may be appropriate for new spouses, for stepparents and children, and for stepsiblings. In contrast to "forced blending" (Isaacs, 1982) in which family members attempt to impose intimacy (e.g., the mother who tells her child that her new spouse "will be your new father, and you must call him 'dad' "), these exercises are designed to provide family members with some shared pleasant activities. The goal is to allow individuals to get to know one another and perhaps discover mutual interests in a context without pressure. For example, stepsiblings might be given an opportunity to spend time together at an amusement park, or a stepparent and stepchild may plan a "special outing" together. Such intimacy-building exercises may be most effective when conducted after the therapist has explored any unrealistic beliefs that family members have held regarding the development of love and cohesion in remarried families.

JOINING WITH THE FAMILY

On the whole, a cognitive–behavioral approach to treatment of remarried families raises few unique issues regarding the establishment of rapport and an effective therapeutic relationship with the family. Whatever unique issues do arise have been described in our earlier descriptions of assessment and clinical intervention, but we summarize here what we believe are the special issues to which a therapist must be sensitive in order to establish a therapeutic relationship with remarried families. First, it is important for the therapist to clarify family boundaries by including particular people in sessions and perhaps excluding others, and this practice may produce some tension if the family members have other preferences. Certainly a therapist may not want to jeopardize the therapy by insisting on the inclusion or exclusion of a particular person. It is always possible to renegotiate this issue with the family later, once a more solid therapeutic relationship has been established. Meeting a family's request regarding session membership need not stop a therapist from discussing with the family the importance of attending to family boundaries. For example, a family may insist that there is no reason to include a child who "only visits on weekends" because they see the problem as the tension between the stepfather and a child who lives in the house. The therapist can remind them of the role that individual plays in family interactions by posing questions such as "If John was here right now, how do you think that would affect the argument that you are having about responsibility for doing chores?"

Second, given the hypersensitivity that members of some remarried families have to loyalty issues, the therapist should be judicious in his or her use of the technique of aligning with particular members. However, this does not preclude the therapist's support of efforts to establish a constructive boundary around a particular family subsystem (e.g., supporting the couple's attempts to spend some "intimacy-building" time alone together in the face of protests from the children).

Concerns regarding alignment are particularly relevant when one uses individual sessions with family members. Although we generally interview families conjointly, occasionally we notice that one or more members of a family seem inhibited in discussing their thoughts and feelings about the presenting problems. At such times we use individual interviews judiciously, emphasizing to the entire family that we will not hold secrets shared in these sessions and that it is our intention to provide individual members a forum for experimenting with expressing themselves before they do so in front of the family.

Finally, because many remarried families do not enter therapy conceptualizing their problems as linked to their special family structure, it is often the therapist's task to draw their attention to the possible association between remarriage issues and a specific presenting problem such as an acting-out child. In doing so, the therapist should be sensitive to possible defensiveness, or even denial, on the part of some family members who hold unrealistic beliefs that remarriage should present no obstacles to the instant development of family cohesion and happiness. A therapist who challenges this belief too forcefully at the beginning of treatment risks damaging rapport. We find it best to approach *any* firmly held unrealistic belief first by briefly noting to the family that a large proportion of remarried families experience some "rough spots" with certain issues as they form their new families. Later in therapy they often are more open to seeing their beliefs as part of the problem, once we have helped them plan some specific beneficial behavioral changes and have brought to their attention some data that are inconsistent with their beliefs about family life.

SPECIAL CLINICAL ISSUES IN THE TREATMENT OF REMARRIED FAMILIES

The treatment techniques used with remarried families do not differ significantly from those used in cognitive–behavioral therapy with any type of family. However, a few special clinical issues often arise.

First, although cotherapy offers a number of advantages in family therapy, we do not recommend it in work with remarried families unless the cotherapist pair has a well-established history together. Given that the therapy deals with the merging of two families, if two therapists also are struggling with the formation of their own relationship, we believe that this can be a disruptive force. Also, if each of the cotherapists forms a consistent alliance with one of the two merging families, this could interfere with the blending process.

A second unique clinical situation involves the utility of the beliefs and interaction patterns that members of remarried families bring to their new family. Although all people who enter family therapy are faced with changing their ways of thinking and behaving, those in remarried families face the prospect of changing patterns that may have "fit" quite well in a previous family experience. For example, a parent may have previously believed that nuclear family members always "come first" in each other's lives. However, a stepparent who has joined this nuclear family may have children who do not live in the household and who will be as important to him or her as the members of the nuclear household.

When a parenting problem is presented by a remarried family, and often when a child behavior problem is presented, the first major issue that arises typically is "What is the role of the new spouse in disciplining and parenting the stepchildren?" The couple generally must agree on an answer to this question (and deal with any cognitions that interfere with their reaching such agreement) before they are able to collaborate on solving the presenting problem, even though the problem is distressing to them. Although several arrangements involving the parent and stepparent are possible, the critical issue is that the marital partners agree on what the stepparent's role will be and make this decision clear to the children. Although it often is suggested that the adults need to be equal "co-parents," we have found that the sharing of the parenting role is not always the best solution. The important considerations are that the parenting arrangement is clear to all family members and that all parties feel comfortable with it.

Finally, because remarried families still live in a vacuum of sorts when it comes to clear societal definitions of appropriate family roles, support groups (such as the Stepfamily Association of America) can be valuable for providing them validation and "normalizing" of their experiences. As noted earlier, we recommend these groups highly, and we suggest that when none are available locally therapists consider forming one as an adjunct to therapy for their clients.

REFERENCES

Anderson, J.Z., & White, G.D. (1986). An empirical investigation of interaction and relationship patterns in functional and dysfunctional nuclear families and stepfamilies. *Family Process, 25,* 407–422.

Beck, A.T., Rush, A.J., Shaw, B.F., & Emery, G. (1979). *Cognitive therapy of depression.* New York: Guilford Press.

Berman, C. (1981). *Making it as a stepparent: New roles/ new rules.* New York: Bantam.

Bray, J.H., & Berger, S.H. (1986, August). *Children's social and behavioral development in new stepfamilies.* Paper presented at the annual convention of the American Psychological Association, Washington, DC.

Bryan, L.R., Coleman, M., Ganong, L.H., & Bryan, S.H. (1986). Person perception: Family structure as cue for stereotyping. *Journal of Marriage and the Family, 48,* 169–174.

Burgoyne, J. (1983) *Stepfamilies in a changing society.* Paper presented at the Stepfamily in Britain Conference, London.

Cherlin, A. (1978). Remarriage as an incomplete institution. *American Journal of Sociology, 84,* 634–649.

Cherlin, A. (1981). *Marriage, divorce, remarriage.* Cambridge, MA: Harvard University Press.

Clingempeel, W.G., (1981). Quasi-kin relationships and marital quality in stepfather families. *Journal of Personality and Social Psychology, 41,* 890–901.

Ellis, A. (1962). *Reason and emotion in psychotherapy.* New York: Lyle Stuart.

Ellis, A. (1977). The basic clinical theory of Rational-Emotive Therapy. In A. Ellis & R. Grieger (Eds.), *Handbook of Rational-Emotive Therapy* (pp. 3–34). New York: Springer.

Fincham, F. (1985). Attribution processes in distressed and nondistressed couples: II. Responsibility for marital problems. *Journal of Abnormal Psychology, 94,* 183–190.

Glick, P.C. (1984). Prospective changes in marriage, divorce, and living arrangements. *Journal of Family Issues, 5,* 7–26.

Guerney, B.G., Jr. (1977). *Relationship enhancement.* San Francisco: Jossey-Bass.

Hacker, A. (1983). *U/S: A statistical portrait of the American people.* New York: Viking Press.

Hetherington, E.M., Cox, M., & Cox, R. (1982). Effects of divorce on parents and children. In M.E., Lamb (Ed.), *Nontraditional families: Parenting and child development.* Hillsdale, NJ: Lawrence Erlbaum Associates.

Isaacs, M.B. (1982). Facilitating family restructuring and relinkage. In L. Messinger (Ed.), *Therapy with remarriage families* (pp. 121–143). Rockville, MD: Aspen Systems Corp.

Johnson, H.C. (1980). Working with stepfamilies: Principles of practice. *Social Work, 25,* 304–308.

Kent, M.O. (1980). Remarriage: A family systems perspective. *Social Casework, 61,* 146–153.

Pasley, K., & Ihinger-Tallman, M. (1982). Remarried family life: Supports and constraints. In N. Stinnett, J. DeFrain, K. King, H. Lingren, G. Rowe, S. Van Zandt, & R. Williams (Eds.), *Family strengths: Vol. 4, Positive support systems* (pp. 367–383). Lincoln: University of Nebraska Press.

Patterson, G.R. (1975). *Families: Applications of social learning to family life.* (rev. ed.). Champaign, IL: Research Press.

Pretzer, J.L., Fleming, B., & Epstein, N. (1983). *Cognitive factors in marital interaction: The role of specific attributions.* Paper presented at the World Congress on Behavior Therapy, Washington, DC.

Sager, C.J., Brown, H.S., Crohn, H., Engel, T., Rodstein, E., & Walker, L. (1983). *Treating the remarried family.* New York: Brunner/Mazel.

Visher, E.B., & Visher, J.S. (1978). Common problems of stepparents and their spouses. *American Journal of Orthopsychiatry, 48,* 252–262.

Visher, E.B., & Visher, J.S. (1979). *Stepfamilies: A guide to working with stepparents and stepchildren.* New York: Brunner/Mazel.

Visher, E.B., & Visher, J.S. (1985). Stepfamilies are different. *Journal of Family Therapy, 7*(1), 9–18.

6

A Cognitive–Behavioral Approach to the Treatment of Conduct Disorder Children and Adolescents

Ray DiGiuseppe

Most clinicians I know or supervise do not enjoy working with conduct disorder (CD) children. These children have been described as aggressive (Patterson, 1974), disobedient, defiant, noncompliant (Forehand & King, 1977), oppositional (Wahler, 1969), and sometimes antisocial (Quay, 1979). Conduct disorder children usually have poor self-esteem (Patterson, 1986), and they sometimes are impulsive. More often than not, they do not desire or cooperate with treatment. Conduct disorder children make up the bulk of outpatient child referrals to mental health practitioners, and they are the diagnostic group most likely to develop psychopathology in adulthood if they remain untreated (Quay & Werry, 1979). Longitudinal studies have found that such children do *not* outgrow their problems and that measures of childhood aggression are as stable as measures of intelligence (Olweus, 1979, 1980). Thus a child therapist will be almost sure to encounter this population, which is both difficult and in great need of treatment.

This chapter represents my attempts to formulate a treatment program for conduct disorder children, adolescents, and their families. The picture of conduct disorder presented here has emerged from my clinical work with this population since the mid-1970s. It is a synthesis of cognitive, behavioral, and family systems approaches. Although the theories underlying all of these approaches have been used to address the problems and treatment of conduct disorder, no one theory appears adequate to explain the phenomenon fully or to guide its treatment.

Any discussion of conduct disorder that fails to consider the family context would be inadequate, because the entire family is affected by the presence of a conduct disorder child and because parents are the primary socializing agents. A family approach to this problem is suggested because many studies have demonstrated that parents of conduct disorder children treat these children differently from the way that parents of normals treat theirs (Patterson, 1986). Also, evidence has emerged suggesting that parents of conduct disorder children treat these children differently from the way that they treat their children who do not have conduct disorders (Anderson, Lytton, & Romney, 1986). Moreover, there has been a lack of empirical evidence to support the effectiveness of individual psychotherapy with conduct disorders (Levitt, 1971). Most successful treatments have included the family members (Haley, 1980; Kazdin, 1985; Patterson, 1982). A family systems conceptualization suggests which parameters of family functioning are likely to promote pathology (e.g., absence of a hierarchy of authority between parents and children) and how they should be changed. Chapter 2 provides a detailed discussion of this model.

Although family factors appear to be important in conduct disorders, the common systems view that presenting problems such as a child's aversive behavior serve functions in maintaining family equilibrium appears to have a notable limitation. Therapeutic interventions designed to remove the utility of problematic symptoms (e.g., symptom prescription in the strategic approach) do not take into account the fact that family members actively interpret and alter information provided by others in their daily interactions. Support for the assumption that merely shifting the family interaction pattern (e.g., by means of therapist directives) will produce new subjective experiences for the family members and eliminate chronic responses that family members have had to one another has been limited. In fact, there is a growing body of evidence that family members misperceive or discount behavioral changes made by other members (see Chapter 1). Thus the use of cognitive interventions by systems-oriented therapists can help family members alter their information processing in a manner that facilitates constructive changes in the structure and organization of their interactions.

Cognitive factors involved in conduct disorders tend to fall into two major categories: those cognitions of the child that contribute to negative behaviors and those of the parents that interfere with their use of effective child management skills. Children who exhibit conduct disorders have been hypothesized to have deficits in self-instructional cognitions and in social problem solving. The self-instructional model posits that impulsive behavior develops because of a child's inability to develop verbal mediation of his or her behavior (Camp & Ray, 1984; Kendall & Braswell, 1985; Meichenbaum, 1977). The social problem-solving model suggests that conduct disorder children do not display adequate social problem-solving skills (e.g., the ability to conceptualize alternative solutions to problems or adequately assess the consequences of alternatives) or they only conceptualize aggressive alternatives to social problems (Camp & Ray, 1984; Spivack & Shure, 1974). In addition, the rational–emotive therapy approach proposes that people with impulse disorders maintain an absolute demand that they must attain their desires and further believe that they cannot tolerate the discomfort of frustration (Bernard & Joyce, 1984; DiGiuseppe, 1983; Ellis, 1985).

Although cognitive theories have demonstrated great utility in helping us understand what occurs (or does not occur) in the mind of an impulsive child, use of cognitive interventions alone has not produced *behavioral* change in clinical populations (Abicoff, 1979, 1985). It appears that the clinician who treats severely disturbed conduct disorder children cannot rely on cognitive procedures alone.

Parental cognitions that may influence the development and maintenance of conduct disorders in their children include beliefs about child rearing that lead parents to choose not to use particular child management techniques, as well as cognitions that produce levels of aversive emotions that disrupt parenting behavior. Although no research data exist yet to determine whether cognitive interventions with parents can change parenting behavior and the conduct disorder child's symptoms, my clinical experience suggests that such an approach greatly enhances the effectiveness of behaviorally oriented parenting skill training.

The fine-tuned interventions developed by behavior therapists offer family therapists specific techniques for altering problematic interactions between a conduct disorder child and the other members of the family. For example, these interventions can address a variety of specific factors that could impede successful interaction between the conduct disorder child and his or her siblings. Such factors might include the following. First, the conduct disorder child may lack behavioral self-control (e.g., he or she is unable to inhibit impulsive behavior that angers the siblings). Second, the conduct disorder child and siblings as a group may lack negotiation skills, which leads to repeated conflict (e.g., they escalate fights about what movie to see or what game to play). Third, the conduct disorder child's tantrum behavior may be firmly established in his or her behavioral repertoire because it has been reinforced for years by producing other family members' compliance with his or her wishes, and the reinforcement has occurred on an intermittent schedule, which is a pattern that typically results in responses that are highly resistant to extinction (Bandura, 1969). Thus the addition of behavioral techniques greatly increases the family therapist's armamentarium of interventions for bringing about change.

Patterson's (1976) coercive family process model, which is based on operant learning principles, posits that negative reinforcement shapes the conduct disorder child's symptoms. It suggests that both the parent and the child engage in coercive behaviors which are aversive to each other. The parent or child gives in to the demands of the other in order to avoid the aversive stimuli, thus experiencing negative reinforcement. For example, when a child whines to receive a reward such as a toy from the parents, the parents can end the child's whining by supplying the reward. This is negatively reinforcing for the parent, because it stops the unpleasant whining. However, it is simultaneously positively reinforcing for the child because he or she receives a treat for whining.

Research based on the coercive family process theory has found that when compared to parents of normal children, parents of conduct disorder children are less effective in stopping their children's deviant behavior (Patterson, 1982, 1986), more vague in giving commands (Forehand, King, Peed, & Yoder, 1975), more likely to be involved in long sequences of coercive behavior with their children (Patterson, 1982, 1986), less likely to perceive deviant behavior (Bogaard, 1977; Reid & Patterson, 1976), more likely to provide attention and positive consequences for deviant behavior (Snyder, 1977), more punitive (Patterson, 1982; Snyder, 1977), and more likely to issue commands (Lobitz & Johnson, 1975). The treatment devised from this model is parent training which focuses on increasing parental monitoring of the child's behavior, avoiding positive reinforcement of deviant behavior, extinguishing coercive behaviors, and reinforcing prosocial behavior (Patterson, 1974; Patterson, Chamberlain, & Reid, 1982; Patterson & Reid, 1973).

Behavior therapy has provided me with the most data and the most specific techniques for changing conduct disorder children and adolescents. However, behavior therapy also has proven inadequate alone, because it fails to address the issue of parents' frequent failure to *use* the techniques described and practiced in therapy sessions which would produce change in their child. It also commonly does not take into account the degree to which each person's behavior influences the behavior of each other family member. Parents are conceptualized as lacking the parenting skills necessary to control their children (Patterson, 1986), but the effects that an individual's spouse and children can have on his or her ability to exercise parenting skills often receive minimal attention. The addition of cognitive procedures to a treatment package for conduct disorder provides a technology to help parents use the powerful behavioral strategies, and the addition of a family perspective helps one conceptualize the complex interactions that shape each member's behavior. It appears that only by integrating cognitive and behavioral approaches, within the context of a family interaction perspective, can we develop a comprehensive (and I hypothesize more effective) treatment for conduct disorders.

A COGNITIVE–BEHAVIORAL FAMILY MODEL OF CONDUCT DISORDER

Conduct disorder children, their parents, and sometimes their siblings and extended family members arrive in therapists' offices at times of extreme crisis. The family's response to the problem at hand provides the justification of approaching conduct disorders with the most comprehensive treatment package available. Because conduct disorder children almost never self-refer, assessment and treatment can almost never be directed at the identified patient alone. On the other hand, failure to focus on the identified patient's idiosyncratic way of being the family's problem probably will result in unsuccessful treatment as well.

As a parent knows, all infants are born with no frustration tolerance and no ability to delay gratification. As neonates mature, some develop the ability to tolerate frustration and delay gratification for longer periods better than others.

Hypothetically, conduct disorders could develop for the following reasons. First, a child could fail to develop delay of gratification and frustration tolerance skills because the parents fail to expect them, fail to teach them, or fail to reinforce them in the child from an early age. Second, the parents' process of teaching these skills may be interrupted at a certain point. Third, the child may have a difficult temperament or particular handicaps that make him or her more resistant to learning these skills. The model presented here accounts for the reciprocal nature of family members' cognitions, affect, and behavior, as well as for each individual's *unique* contribution to the system by way of temperament and external factors. Each proposed process in the development of conduct disorders is discussed below.

Failure to Teach Frustration Tolerance

Parents may fail to teach frustration tolerance skills for a number of reasons: 1) their inappropriate, erroneous child-rearing philosophies, 2) their values regarding desirable behavior, 3) their ignorance regarding appropriate child management skills, 4) their own psychopathology, and 5) interference from psychosocial stressors which disrupt their abilities.

All of these factors can result in the child failing to learn delay of gratification and frustration tolerance. By not experiencing frustration and by controlling one's parents so well with the coercive process (Patterson, 1976, 1982), the child fails to learn problem-solving strategies and coping self-statements. Also, the parents' willingness always to please the child reinforces rather than disputes the child's irrational demand for pleasure and comfort. As the child matures and fails to learn delay of gratification or frustration tolerance skills, his or her behavior becomes successively more disturbed and age-inappropriate with each passing year.

Parental values and standards. Frequently it is entrance into school that brings about the referral for treatment. Before the child attended school, the parents may not have perceived his or her behavior as problematic or deviant. However, school requires a new set of behavioral demands which previously were absent at home.

Under certain circumstances, a child who is in the process of developing a conduct disorder may not be identified as such when he or she enters school. First, the child may have developed minimal delayed gratification and frustration tolerance skills, which barely meet the behavioral requirements at school. Second, a child may be intelligent enough to earn good grades with minimal effort. Finally, the parents may discount the school personnel's complaints, because the parents accept the child's minimal or failing grades. In these cases, the parenting strategies which develop inadequate delayed gratification and frustration tolerance skills will continue. Each year the child will again fall a little behind his or her peers in these skills, but still the family may not perceive the problem.

However, eventually the child will lack the skills necessary to inhibit behaviors that conflict with the values and standards of the parents. The parents may then see the problem as having a sudden, recent onset, even though in these cases of "latent conduct disorders" the failure to achieve delayed gratification and frustration tolerance skills has been developing for years. For example, Sheri, age 12 years, was taken to therapy by her parents for unexcused school absences in the first semester of junior high school. The parents believed that the child should attend school and "do the right thing." They were shocked at their daughter's defiance over attendance. However, the school records indicated marginal or failing grades for years and poor classroom behavior as rated by her teachers. Upon questioning, the parents revealed that their daughter failed to do chores, answered back to them, and was generally noncompliant. However, none of these behaviors was of concern to the parents, because of their belief that their daughter was special and should not be required to do things that displeased her. It was only when she cut class and violated a strongly held value of theirs that they noted a problem.

Adolescents usually develop a desire for more independence and increased contact with peers. Latent conduct disorders frequently emerge into full-blown serious problems at this age. After years of controlling parents coercively about minor issues, the new adolescent desires a new range of behaviors, which may include freedom, sex, and use of alcohol and drugs. The conduct disorder child is not accustomed to inhibiting desires or submitting to authority. At this point, the conflict between the child and parents escalates.

Parents' skills at child rearing are likely to be influenced both by their knowledge of alternative child-rearing techniques and by their beliefs about what are proper and effective strategies. Parents commonly have implicit (and sometimes quite explicit) theories of child development on which they base their child-rearing strategies. Some parents unwittingly reenact the child-rearing strategies that their own parents used with them, whereas others tend to use a polar opposite approach in their attempt to reject a model they found aversive during their own upbringing. Parents' child-rearing philosophies also can be influenced by prevailing behavioral and social science theories popularized through the mass media.

Therapists need to take into account the range of parents' personal child-rearing theories. Some parents who believe "Spare the rod and spoil the child" may seem hard, angry, and aggressive to some therapists but may in fact be very loving (and not abusive) and may only be behaving as they think best for their child. In contrast, some parents say, "If only I could get my child to understand . . .," based on the belief that understanding always precedes and leads to behavior change. As a result, these parents may reject all punishment and instead may lecture to their children. Other parents believe that their children will automatically do the right thing when they are ready, and they tolerate the child's inappropriate behavior, believing that maturation will correct the problem.

Many parents today believe that children should not be frustrated, that all punishment is wrong, and that children should always be free to express themselves. Regardless of the influences that have shaped these permissive attitudes, it appears that they represent the source of many parental difficulties.

It is difficult to raise children without denying them some rewards, without limiting their behavior in some way, or without punishing some behavior. Consequently, it is not enough for therapists to teach parents behavioral child management skills. It is also important to foster in the parents a philosophy of child-rearing that emphasizes the desirability of teaching frustration tolerance, the importance of setting limits, and the advantages of inculcating appropriate social skills in compliance with demands of others.

Parental neglect and rejection. Clinicians who work in residential treatment settings, foster care agencies, or who treat cases of child abuse or neglect often see cases of conduct disorder children who have experienced substantial rejection and emotional neglect. Such severely neglected children commonly display extreme depression, hopelessness, and/or diffuse anger. It is easy to hypothesize that the conduct disturbances of these children are an "acting out" of their intense emotions over being rejected. However, I believe that it is more accurate to view these children as having two separate yet interacting problems. Because they have been neglected and rejected by parents and guardians, it is likely that they were not taught frustration tolerance and delayed gratification skills. As a result, they will exhibit the poor impulse control typical of conduct disorders. In addition, they will be likely to display depression as a result of being rejected and neglected by adults. It is easy for such children to conclude that they must be worthless, because a series of adults rejected them.

Dysfunctional parental emotions and cognitions. Some parents have disturbed emotions that interfere with their parenting. The emotions of guilt, anger, and discomfort anxiety commonly surface when parents have difficulties with their children. The following is a description of these emotions and the irrational ideas that elicit them.

When parents feel *guilty* about their child's behavior, they are most likely to engage in two cognitive processes. First, they attribute the child's misbehavior or problem to themselves, and second, they condemn themselves for being responsible for the problems. *Attributions of self-blame* may derive not only from the parents' inability to handle the child's behavior, but also from their inability to prevent frustrating or unpleasant events that may have befallen the child. For example, some single parents may believe that their inability to remain married has inflicted a divorce and the loss of one parent unfairly on their children. Such loss, the parent believes, is catastrophic for the child. Parents of sick children (even if the illness occurred years ago), learning-disabled children, retarded children, and handicapped children may believe that they are partly responsible for their child's misfortune. They may dwell on thoughts that perhaps there was something that they could have done to prevent the child's problem. Even if the parent does not view himself or herself as responsible for causing the child's problem, she or he may feel guilty for having been unable to prevent the problem, or for being unable to ameliorate or remove the problem immediately.

Many parents who experience guilt not only make negative attributions regarding responsibility for the problems but also hold *beliefs* that their child has been frustrated or wronged, and that the child does not deserve and/or cannot bear other misfortunes and frustrations. They often believe that their child needs special consideration to make up for past inequities. The child is seen as unable to tolerate normal parental discipline. For example, a parent may believe that it would be cruel and unjust punishment to have their physically handicapped daughter miss television because she has not completed her homework. Even such small, inconsequential, frustrating events inflicted in normal child rearing are seen as too catastrophic for the child to stand.

High levels of *anger,* not just annoyance, are frequently experienced by parents of children with conduct disorders. It can be especially difficult to deal with anger in these families. The parents usually view their anger as functional. They yell, scream, or lecture their children. They often perceive this behavior as punishing the child, and they assume that the punishment will suppress the behavior that angered them. Not only is the anger commonly initiated by the parents' irrational belief that the child *should* behave better and deserves the aversive punishment, but their *expectation* that the anger will be an effective child management tool reinforces the emotional state.

Many parents do not take action until they are angry. These parents use their emotional arousal level as a cue to discipline their children. Here, the child's behavior is ignored initially, but not long enough to be extinguished. As the behavior increases in force or persists over time, so does the parents' irrational thinking. Ultimately, the parents' emotion reaches a threshold of anger, and they react aggressively to stop the child's behavior. The parents believe that their emotional state is the appropriate signal to discipline their child and that angry outbursts are an effective child-rearing strategy. The parents leave the interaction confident that they have had an impact on the child. However, the situation looks different from the child's perspective. The parents have tolerated the child's misbehavior for a length of time before becoming angry. For example, a child may learn that she can tease her siblings several times before eliciting parental retribution. Similarly, a child may learn that he can ignore his parents' requests to do chores for 20 minutes, but that a 30-minute delay will produce an unpleasant response from the parents. Parents commonly are aware of the ineffectiveness of their use of anger in child rearing, and that little change is likely to occur until they modify their own responses to their children. What is necessary to alter the parents' unrealistic view of using anger expression as a disciplinary technique is to provide them with specific behavioral criteria for identifying undesirable child behaviors, which they can use as cues for initiating discipline procedures. The goal is for the parents to respond to the problem behaviors and not to their own momentary emotional upset about the behaviors.

Much of parents' upset at their children will, on closer examination, turn out to be *discomfort anxiety* or low frustration tolerance (Ellis, 1980). Many parents seem to have a rather romantic notion about offspring and child rearing. Although the rewards of procreation are many, the frustration, hardships, and hassles can be significant. Possibly the most trying hassle of child rearing is its omnipresence. Although there are regular vacations from work and even a few from one's spouse, children usually take 20 years to grow up. Parents may believe that they are overwhelmed by the constant stressors provided by their children. At such times it is easy for the parents to give their children just what they desire so that they will stop their aversive behavior. The parents believe that they cannot tolerate the discomfort involved in confronting their children's stressful behavior.

Parents with such discomfort anxiety often start following behavioral contracts devised by therapists but quickly give up if change in the children's aversive behavior is not immediately forthcoming. Their children usually know this about them. Response cost or extinction procedures are likely to cause an "extinction burst" of increased aversive behavior before the child changes in a positive direction: "If I behave bad now, Mom will give up." It is important to prepare the parents for these extinction bursts and to help them realize that their children may be purposely testing them and trying to get them to succumb to parental low frustration tolerance by behaving more obnoxiously.

Parents caught in coercive family processes appear to judge the effectiveness of their parenting interventions by the short-term outcome. When asked to consider the long-term outcome and imagine that they forgo immediate relief, they often reveal a case of "I can't-stand-it-itis." They focus on all of the difficulties in raising their children and conclude that they are just too weak or tired to stand up to the children's whining and other aversive behavior. They also may believe that they do not deserve such a difficult task and may persist in the irrational belief that child rearing *"should"* be easy.

Interrupted Development of Frustration Tolerance

Another cause of conduct disorders is the interruption of the parents' efforts to teach delayed gratification and frustration tolerance skills. In such families the parents may have been doing a fine job of child rearing, but a crisis (e.g., marital difficulties or separation, illness, financial or job problems, development of parental psychopathology) stops the process. The child will have developed age-appropriate delayed gratification and frustration tolerance skills, as well as age-appropriate behaviors, until the age when the disruption took place. At that point the parents may be too preoccupied with their own problems or emotional disturbances to attend to child rearing. As a result, they stop raising their expectations for the child's level of maturity and/or increased delayed gratification and frustration tolerance skills during the period of interruption. The crisis causing the interruption might even be severe enough that the parents stop enforcing rules altogether, and the child's behavior might regress.

Difficult Temperament

Chess and Thomas (1984) demonstrated that children are born with fairly stable and consistent patterns of behavior, which they label temperament. The correlation between difficult temperament and later onset of antisocial behavior has been documented in several longitudinal studies (Kellam, Brown, Rubin, & Ensminger, 1983; Kellam, Ensminger, & Turner, 1977; Sameroff & Seifer, 1983; Werner & Smith, 1977). Chess and Thomas (1984) proposed that psychopathology does not develop solely as a result of temperament or solely as a result of the way a child is raised, but rather because of a mismatch of the two. Proper development occurs because of the "good fit" between the parents' child-rearing strategies and the child's temperament. One type of temperamental pattern that Chess and Thomas (1984) described is the "difficult child temperament." Such children are characterized by low rhythmicity (e.g., they do not show rhythms in biological functions such as eating and sleeping), high-intensity reactions to any stimuli, and withdrawal from new stimuli. Children of this temperament present more of a challenge than others, especially to a parent of a different character. For example, a child who displays irregular rhythmicity, high distractibility, a low responsiveness threshold, negative moods, and a short attention span could prove problematic for a relaxed, reflective parent. This child's response pattern repeatedly will violate parental values. The parent will have to enforce rules about conduct, be more vigilant in monitoring the child's behavior, and expend more energy in child rearing than would be required with an easy temperament child.

Parents may be less likely to expend the energy needed to raise such a child if they have low frustration tolerance themselves or if they maintain irrational expectations of the child. They may believe that they should not have to use forceful, high-impact discipline, or that they should not have to repeat themselves to the child. In short, they believe that their child should be similar to them and that parents should not have to work so hard. Thus a cognitive model would postulate that it is not only the mismatch between the child's and the parents' temperaments that causes the problem, but also the parents' cognitions about the temperamental difference.

Summary of the Model

The model just presented assumes that parents and children are influenced by and influence each other's behavior. However, it recognizes that each also brings to the family behavioral predispositions in the form of temperament, as well as cognitions such as beliefs and expectations. It also acknowledges that stressors from outside the family system affect family members' behaviors. The basic task of the parents is to socialize the child: to teach him or her to comply with social rules and develop the frustration tolerance and delay of gratification skills that will enable the child to cope with the world. Children will differ in their willingness and ability to accept this training, and parents will vary in their skill and persistence in training their children in the face of this resistance or limited responsiveness from the children. Parents will require a certain set of skills to raise their children effectively. Parents may fail at effective parenting through a lack of skills, emotional upset concerning the hassles of child rearing (associated with their dysfunctional cognitions about children and child rearing), the imposition of stressors from inside or outside the family, and so on. The child may desire total and immediate gratification, may resist imposition of rules, and actively may try to discourage the parents from applying consistent child management strategies.

ASSESSMENT

Assessment of Problematic Child Behaviors and Characteristics

The first task in designing a treatment plan for a conduct disorder child is to assess adequately the child and family. A most important early step in the assessment is the completion by the parents and teachers of an objective, well-normed scale for rating the child's behavior. Not only does this reveal how the parents see the child, but it also provides a baseline for determining whether the identified patient's behavior is truly deviant compared to age and sex norms. If such an assessment reveals normal behavior, the problem may not be a conduct disorder but rather a problem of unrealistic expectations by the parents. Assuming that the identified patient's behavior is deviant, the assessment provides a baseline with which to compare future measurements to determine whether treatment has been effective.

By far the most inclusive and perhaps the best standardized and validated scale is the Personality Inventory for Children (Lachar & Gdowski, 1979). This scale includes validity scales which assess whether the parents are exaggerating the child's behavior or are defensive. This information alone is most helpful for treatment planning. This measure also includes subscales for 12 types of problems. The major drawback is its length—600 items. The parents' completion of this measure as part of the therapy intake process clearly can help the clinician gauge their motivation for treatment.

Another good scale is the Louisville Behavior Checklist (Miller, 1984). This scale has several subscales which help distinguish between conduct disorder children who are socialized and those who are unsocialized. This can be an important distinction, because the unsocialized children are more difficult to treat due to their inability to form close interpersonal relationships.

Another useful scale is the Walker Behavior Checklist (Walker, 1983). This scale is not as well standardized, but its strength lies in its ease of administration, and for that reason it is good to use with teachers, who usually do not object to filling it out several times during treatment.

Another behavioral scale is the Child Behavior Checklist (Achenbach & Edelbrock, 1983). The instrument is well standardized, has been used in hundreds of research studies, and has the added advantage of having separate forms and norms for parent, teacher, and child self-report versions.

It is also important to assess the duration and degree of the child's symptoms. Specifically, the therapist should ask questions about problem behaviors which the parents have not identified as the reason for the treatment referral. For example, the parents might not have identified noncompliant behaviors as deviant before the child violated their values, and there may have been a long history of such problematic child behavior, with the parents indulging the child or avoiding dealing with the problems. *Specific* questions can help in such an assessment. Has the child done well in school? What were his or her grades for the last several years? Did the child attend school?

How often did he or she cut school? Did he or she complete homework? Have the teachers complained? Does the child come in the house when he or she is told to do so? Does the child complete chores? What does the child do when denied things?

In addition to behavioral assessment, personality assessment of the child by means of objective inventories also can be helpful. The Millon Adolescent Personality Inventory (Millon, Green, & Meagher, 1982) may be the most helpful. It provides scales to assess basic personality traits, areas of concern (issues about which the adolescent is worried), and behavioral prediction scales. The personality scales help one determine if the adolescent is psychopathic, immature, or exhibiting a burnt child (neglect) reaction. Conduct disorder children and adolescents usually score high on scales measuring forcefulness, poor self-concept, intolerance of others, poor family rapport, poor impulse control, social disconformity, and scholastic underachievement. The more psychopathic client will have the same elevated scores, as well as a high score on confidence (actually measuring narcissism). The "burnt child" will have the same elevated scores as the conduct disorder child, with additional high scores on subtests measuring introversion, inhibition, and passive-aggressiveness.

The downward versions of the 16 PF (Cattell & Eber, 1965), the Children's Personality Questionnaire (Porter & Cattell, 1979), and the High School Personality Questionnaire (Cattell & Cattell, 1975) are also helpful for gaining information concerning the child's basic personality characteristics. Typically conduct disorder children and adolescents score low on factors measuring superego strength—or conformity to social rules—and self-discipline, and possibly high on dominance and demandingness. The burnt child is likely to have the same pattern of characteristics and also score low on ego strength.

Assessing the Family Structure

After the therapist has defined the child's problematic symptoms clearly, the next assessment issue concerns the family structure. Who makes the rules in the family? Who sets the limits on whose behavior? Are there rewards for compliance? Are there any response costs for noncompliance? Who monitors the child? Does each parent apply his or her own rules? Do the parents agree about the consequences of noncompliance? Are there any alliances between either parent and the identified patient? Do the siblings exhibit any problematic behaviors? How do the siblings get along with the conduct disorder child? Do the parents apply different child-rearing strategies with the conduct disorder child than with the siblings? Are there any grandparents involved in the child rearing? If so, how much power do they have? Are the parents afraid to disagree with the grandparents?

The best way to assess the emotions and behavior of the family members is to have them attempt to solve a problem during a session. The therapist can ask the parents how they could correct one of the child's disruptive behaviors. Here one can assess the parents' problem-solving abilities. If they do not devise an appropriate solution, the therapist could suggest one, especially one that has the parents assert their role in relation to their power in the family. When the therapist asks the parents if they will follow through with the intervention, often the child erupts in an emotional display of force. Here the therapist could stop the action and ask both the parents and the child what they were feeling and thinking during the interchange.

Also important to know is what strategies the parents have tried in order to correct the child's behavior. If they have been in therapy, what type? What did the therapist do with them, and with the child? Most parents report that they have "tried everything," but careful questioning regarding their *persistence* usually reveals that they tried each strategy for a very brief time.

The next task is to assess the parents' feelings and cognitions. It is most important for the therapist to assess the parents' philosophies of child rearing, as well as their persistence at following them. Here one can ask what they think and feel when they are confronted with the child's transgressions and what they think and feel when they attempt an intervention. This is often the most important part of the assessment and therefore should be given the most time. However, because the parents have brought their child as the indexed patient and commonly do not see themselves as part of the problem, it is crucial to conduct this assessment in a manner that does not convey to the parents that the therapist thinks they are the sole cause of the problem. One way to accomplish this part of the assessment is to do it at a later point in the treatment. The best time may be after the therapist has given the parents some behavioral strategies to try, and they have failed to follow them or did not enact the procedures well. In their frustration at failing to control their child, they are likely to talk about exactly what they felt and thought during the attempt or when they decided not to follow the therapist's suggestions.

The final part of the assessment concerns the child. Does this child express any remorse about the broken rules? What does he or she feel and think just prior to a transgression? Can the child conceptualize the consequences of the behavior before acting? And finally, how does the child feel and think about the parents' discipline and attempts to limit his or her behavior?

JOINING WITH THE FAMILY

Children with conduct problems almost never desire to change. They would rather be watching televison or playing with friends than going to therapy. The children usually will complain to their parents to stop attending therapy. Because the parents have sought help, will bring the child for treatment during their free time, and will pay for the treatment, it is important to address their concerns.

Building Rapport with the Parents

Supervisory experience has suggested to me that many therapists (especially young professionals who do not yet have children) tend to blame the parents for their child's behavior problems. Their focus on the parents may be due to their own clinical impressions or their awareness of research evidence (Robinson, 1985; Robinson & Eyberg, 1981) that the parents of conduct disorder children often are overly demanding and critical or lack warmth toward their children. Many therapists with a family systems orientation also seem to focus on the parents' own marital relationship, based on the hypothesis that the child's behavior is symptomatic of a disturbed marriage. For example, Harbin (1977) believes that the child's symptoms are an outlet to focus attention away from marital tension. Vogel and Bell (1968) and Bell (1975) have argued that a disturbed child often serves as a scapegoat onto which parents can project their negative feelings and anger. Byng-Hall (1980) suggested that the child's symptoms serve the function of regulating the distance between the parents. However, although clinicians continue to assume that the parents' marital problems are a causative factor in conduct disorders, major reviews of the research literature on this topic (Loeber & Dishion, 1983; Patterson, 1986; Robinson, 1985; Rutter & Giller, 1983; Wilson & Hernstein, 1985) have failed to confirm this assumption. Clinical experience suggests that tension in the couple's relationship can be a result of coping with child problems, as well as a cause of such problems.

Parents who have sought professional help for their child may be insulted, angered, defensive, or alienated if the therapist immediately places issues concerning their marital relationship on the agenda. Blaming the parents may only lead to quick termination. Convincing parents to work on their own relationship problems or individual psychological problems (e.g., discomfort anxiety) when the therapist has evidence that these factors do play a role in a child's conduct disorder is a particularly delicate matter. A collaborative relationship with the parents designed to explore the causes of their child's problems and collectively to investigate solutions is a good first step in developing rapport.

With conduct disorder families, the parents are distressed and concerned about their child's behavior. It appears most helpful for the therapist to assume that the parents are ignorant of how to control their child's behavior more effectively, or that they would like to change any of their own emotional disturbances that disrupt their parenting skills. It is important that the therapist communicate understanding of the parents' concern for their child. The therapist notes that sessions are not intended to fix the parents, but rather to help them cope with the child and learn how to change the child's behavior.

I prefer to explain to the parents that individual therapy has not been demonstrated to be effective for the problem of conduct disorders. The present and most successful approach is to help the parents learn how to structure rewards and penalties which are therapeutic. This is more likely to meet with acceptance than informing the parents that it is a family problem and that they are part of the problem which must change as well. During the course of therapy, the parents' failed attempts to follow assigned behavioral strategies are discussed during sessions. The parents become aware of their own inability to follow through on the therapist's recommendations. When this occurs, the immediate focus is on what they felt when they attempted the behavioral strategy and what they were thinking when it was time for them to act. In this context their thoughts and emotions that interfere with their using more successful parenting strategies become grist for the mill of therapy.

The most obvious limitation to the effective use of the treatment described here is families with parents who are *unwilling* to participate. Such cases are frequently referred for treatment by courts and social service agencies or are treated by school psychologists and social workers in the school. The alternative treatment usually tried in such cases is supportive therapy or individual cognitive–behavioral therapy with the child. I do not advocate not treating conduct disorder children whose parents are uncooperative, but my clinical and supervisory experience leads me to be a pessimist about such treatment unless some social agencies apply pressure on the parents to change the child.

When parental lack of cooperation with therapy results from severe marital problems, one parent may wish to undermine the authority of the other by undoing the treatment contingencies with the child or by instituting opposite ones. Conjoint therapy for the parents can be tried, with the goal of stopping the parents from using the child as a weapon against each other. Marital harmony need not be restored in order to bring about effective parenting. The therapy would help the parents become aware of how their behavior exacerbates the child's behavior and would help them to reach an agreement to treat the child consistently and similarly, for the best interest of the child they both love, even though they have their own differences. If this strategy does not work one of the parents still can work with the therapist to enforce whatever rules he or she can. Although this strategy obviously is flawed, at least the child may learn to discriminate and behave differently for each parent.

Building Rapport with a Resistant Child

At this point, the reader may question whether therapy can proceed if rapport has not been established with the child. Most psychotherapies with children stress the importance of trust and rapport in building a therapeutic relationship. However, how realistic is it to expect children to be nondefensive and self-disclose when the therapist monitors their misbehavior and makes sure that the parents follow their contract to penalize the child or deny rewards for such misbehavior?

The groundwork for developing rapport with the child has been set throughout the therapy. In setting the goals of therapy, the parents and the therapist have discussed what the parents' long-term fears are: "How will she ever finish high school?" "How will he ever cope with a job if he can't cope with school now?" "How will she ever keep friends or earn a living when she can't even get out of bed on time in the morning and can't get along with us?" The therapist makes it clear from the outset that he or she and the parents have the child's long-term interest in mind even as the child objects to their rules because of the short-term losses. While setting up a behavior management system for a family, the therapist constructs a system not only of response costs but also of *rewards*. In addition, the response costs system is organized and specific. The child knows exactly what to expect from the parents. The child may perceive this consistency as less aversive than the inconsistent, arbitrary, and capricious punishment that the parents have used. The behavior management system also results in a reduction of the verbal assault and nagging incidents between parents and child. The therapist thus has led the way to a more positive parent–child interaction. The therapist also has corrected many of the parents' misconceptions about parenting and has challenged their irrational beliefs that have elicited dysfunctional emotional and behavioral responses toward their child. These procedures communicate to all of the family members that the child is not the only one who contributes to the problem. This process helps the therapist establish rapport with the child.

Occasionally, rapport appears to wither and children remain silent during the therapy sessions. Perhaps the child directs only unpleasant words toward the therapist. At this point, several decisions are required. Is therapy more likely to succeed if meetings with the parents are stopped and the behavioral management component is abandoned? Perhaps meeting with the children alone and waiting for a trusting relationship to grow between them and the therapist will result in their willingness to discuss their problems and to seek help. I think not! If I had to choose, I would rather that the child remain silent, or even express dissatisfaction about coming to therapy sessions, than that the parents abandon the behavioral treatment components. The therapist can provide the child with rationales for such a procedure (e.g., the behavior management procedures communicate from the parents and therapist that they believe the child is able to change and to tolerate the frustration provided—it is an affirmation of faith in the child).

CLINICAL STRATEGIES AND TECHNIQUES

Starting Treatment

The first task of treatment is choosing the first target behavior. This takes considerable clinical judgment for the following reason. The child wishes to sabotage the process. The first target behavior to be changed will elicit a contest of wills. The issue is not only symptom change but also power. A failure to change the first target symptom will reinforce again the child's coercive process and sense of power, and it will reinforce the parents' sense of hopelessness. Thus the first target should be one for which the parents can monitor and control the reinforcers readily. The target also should be one that the parents clearly want to change and for which they are willing to expend the energy to succeed.

The older the child, the more aversive his or her coercive attempts can be. An adolescent can harm the parents physically, run away, damage property, or embarrass the parents. The therapist and the family should try to predict what coercive strategies will be used by the child, and then they can plan how the parents will react. Therefore, before the parents actually carry out a strategy, they and the therapist (with the identified patient present) problem-solve. What reactions can they expect from the child? What have they done before when the child acted that way? Was their response effective in changing the child's behavior? How could they react differently so as to produce better results? Which alternative reaction would be best? What emotions of theirs would interfere with following that plan of action? What are some of the thoughts they would have that would elicit those emotions? Are those thoughts illogical, irrational, or lacking empirical evidence? What thoughts could replace the dysfunctional thoughts?

This phase of therapy is the most crucial, and it is advisable to continue the sessions focusing on the preceding issues until the parents believe that they are capable of handling the child's or adolescent's coercion in a successful manner. When this is accomplished, the therapist and parents inform the child or adolescent that the new behavior management rules will begin on a specific day.

The therapist also represents a rationale for the new rules and consequences, such as the following. The therapist and parents will acknowledge that the child will not like the rules and that the new procedures are a change from the parents' past behavior. However, the reason for setting the new rules is that the child's present mode of behavior is likely to lead to more serious transgressions in the future and poor adjustment in adult life. The changes are not cruel or capricious. It is because of the parents' concern for the child's future that they have thought through these rule changes. Although the child may not believe this reasoning and may make numerous arguments why it is false, the therapist persists in telling the child the reason for the intervention. The child may come to believe that the parents and therapist have his or her long-term best interests at heart, even though he or she desires immediate gratification. Such an attitudinal shift is helpful, but not necessary for treatment to proceed.

Behavioral Interventions

Behavioral interventions are at the heart of any change project with conduct disorder children. One difficulty that clinicians frequently encounter with this patient population is that the application of positive reinforcers is ineffectual. The family already may have given the child many reinforcers for coercive behaviors unwittingly, or so many reinforcers have been noncontingent or free that new reinforcers lack power to alter a child's behavior. The solution to this problem is to make the noncontingent reinforcers contingent on compliance with the new rules. Most parents do not realize the number of noncontingent rewards their children (and all children) receive. These include maid service, laundry service, chauffeur service, meals, favorite treats and snacks, new clothing, television, and telephone, just to name a few.

The behavioral strategy I find most successful is to withdraw all or some of the foregoing reinforcers and then to provide them as the child "earns" them back by complying with the rules. Alternatively, one can use a response cost procedure and withdraw these privileges for violations of rules, with the privileges being reinstated when the child complies with the rules.

Whatever behavioral terminology the therapist uses to describe such strategies, the conduct disorder children view them as negative and coercive. However, the use of such negative or coercive procedures may be unavoidable. Patterson and Fleischman (1979) reported that the use of noncoercive methods (i.e., positive reinforcement, extinction of antisocial behavior, and negotiating prosocial behavior) are insufficient for the task. They reluctantly concluded that it is the parents' effective use of punishment (time out, withdrawal of rewards and privileges, work details, and overcorrection) which is most likely to be maintained by the parent from parent training. Therefore, the primary mechanism of change identified in these studies is still coercive punishment. The shift in parental behavior involves a change in what is punished. Prior to treatment, these parents ignored or punished a large proportion of their children's prosocial behaviors and tolerated aggressive behavior. As a result of treatment, the parent extinguishes or punishes aggressive behavior and reinforces more prosocial behavior. Patterson and Fleischman (1979) conclude that it appears necessary for the parents to use punishment more successfully. They suggest that this can be done by 1) lowering the absolute level of punishment, 2) making the punishment more contingent on specific behaviors, and 3) using punishments that are likely to be effective and not merely an annoyance.

The last suggestion by Patterson and Fleischman may be crucial. Parents often need help in learning to conceptualize what will be coercive to their child. Frequently parents punish their children by sending them to their rooms. An inspection of the child's room may reveal a television, stereo, computer, telephone, games, and so on. Although the child is annoyed and inconvenienced by this limitation, it is by no means costly. To ensure that the experience resembles "time out," it is best to advise parents to remove all of the enjoyable things from the room first, starting with those that the child enjoys most. Parents provide a host of such noncontingent reinforcers to their children; these can be contingent on desirable behavior.

Cognitive Interventions with Parents

As noted, many parents will be ill prepared to follow the behavior contingencies that they have agreed to enact. Thus considerable time will be spent disputing the beliefs which cause the emotions that dethrone the parents from the top of the power hierarchy in their family.

The disputing of the parents' dysfunctional cognitions usually is done *before* they actually attempt to implement *any* behavioral contract which has been planned in therapy. This ensures that the parents adhere to the procedure and thereby increase the probability that they will be reinforced for using good child management skills. For this reason, this stage of therapy lasts as long as needed. The more irrational the parents, the more time spent at this stage of treatment. Moving ahead too fast (i.e., before the parents see the errors in their thinking) will result in an escalation of the family conflict.

Some disputing of irrational beliefs will take place both while the therapist is convincing the parents to take action and reinstitute their role at the head of the family hierarchy and when the behavioral targets and reinforcement contingencies are being set. Both of these processes in the behavioral contingency component of treatment are impeded by the parents' beliefs about what is socially acceptable or developmentally appropriate behavior.

For example, a girl of age 13 may wish to stay out until 1:00 AM, and her parents are unsure about their decision that this is too late. They take no action and do not mention a curfew to the child. The parents express their concern about the child's hours by their facial grimaces when the therapist brings up the topic. When asked if they approve of the 1:00 AM time, they report that they are unsure that it is their place to say—but no, they do not like it. The therapist has to help them dispute the erroneous belief (reinforced by their daughter) that they have no right to set limits on the child. Once they are convinced that her coming home at this hour is an appropriate target behavior for change, the daughter complains. The child says that all of her friends stay out this late and that the parents will ruin her social life if they institute an earlier curfew. At this point the therapist is a resource of developmental information about appropriate behavior. Also, the therapist helps the parents with the guilt they feel when they set such a change in a target behavior, particularly by challenging beliefs such as "We are bad parents if we cause our child any emotional pain." For these reasons, the therapist will always be alternating between behavioral and cognitive interventions.

The following is a more detailed description of how the therapist works to dispel the irrational beliefs which lead to the emotions that interfere with child management.

Guilt. In disputing guilt-eliciting cognitions, several important points can be emphasized to the parents. First, the parent often erroneously assumes that he or she is the sole cause of the child's past problems, or the sole possible protecting force. Such parents can be reminded that they can never be so omnipotent as to prevent a learning disability or diabetes. It is helpful to list specifically the many other factors that may have caused the child's problems. A second key irrationality embedded in these parents' guilty thinking is the notion that some past or present adversity is so unpleasant and awful that their child cannot be expected to live normally, and that restitution must be made to the child for this event. However, examples abound of children with similar problems who have adjusted well and who live normal lives. A therapist can recount such stories to help parents challenge their own irrationality. It is also helpful to dispute their idea that the adversity suffered by their child inevitably weakens all children (perhaps noting how adversity commonly strengthens people's abilities to cope with inevitable future life stresses).

The most destructive aspect of guilt-producing parental thinking, however, is the idea that children are too labile to tolerate frustration. Such is the stuff of self-fulfilling prophecies. Some parents believe that their children cannot handle frustration and therefore give them reduced practice in developing frustration tolerance and reinforce the child's catastrophizing about hypothetical disastrous effects of enduring frustrations. Frequently the parent uses present behavior problems as evidence that the past activating event devastated the child (i.e., "I can tell Jack's illness had a terrible effect on him; he still gets upset when I ask him to do something"). It is most important for the therapist to stress the resilience of children and to show repeatedly the function that the parents' guilt serves in maintaining the present problem. It also is helpful to ask the parents how long they expect to live and care for their child. Because the parents believe that their offspring cannot cope, do they believe that their child will require constant care? If the parents do expect the child to develop frustration tolerance someday, how do they expect this to occur? Coping skills do not develop magically when a child reaches maturity.

The type of guilt that is most resistant to change usually occurs when the parents blame their parenting skills for producing the aberrant behavior of their child. Here again, the guilt leads to short-term restitution in the form of relaxed discipline. The parental logic usually is "I'm a lousy parent, ergo I'm a lousy person." All the disputes suggested by Ellis (1985) against such self-worth and self-rating beliefs apply here. If philosophical disputation does not produce a satisfactory solution, empirical disputes may be more helpful. Minimizing the parents' exaggerated sense of responsibility can be achieved by a detailed discussion of the many factors (e.g., genetic, physiological, cultural, educational, peer) that shape the child into an adult.

Anger. The first lesson to teach parents about anger is that they should not punish out of anger but because the child has transgressed a rule.

The first step in reducing the anger is to convince parents that this emotion will not help them or their children. Many parents punish their children solely by means of angry outbursts of yelling. However, the verbal expression of anger by the parents usually is not considered aversive enough by the children to suppress their inappropriate behavior. They can do as they please and have to suffer only the moderate irritation of 10 minutes of yelling. Parents often feel better after yelling and also delude themselves into thinking that they have done something about the problem. Response cost and extinction procedures seem to be more effective ways of controlling children's behavior than yelling.

Another problem with anger, besides its ineffectiveness, is that it usually begets more anger. Children are more likely to become more angered by their parents' verbal aggression than they are by standard, basic behavior management techniques. Among other reasons for the child's reciprocal anger, yelling is more personally insulting and degrading than behavior managment procedures.

Once the parents understand that anger at their children will not change their children, they may be more willing to look at their own irrational beliefs which get them angry. According to Ellis (1977), anger usually follows from "demanding" rather than "desiring" philosophies. Parents' anger at children is no exception. They can demand all they want that their child behave nicely, but obviously there is no objective rationale (law of the universe) for insisting that what they wish to happen *must* occur. Children, after all, tend to be mischievous, ignorant, and partly unsocialized—because they are children. It is helpful to point out to angry parents that at some point *they* were unruly children. Only through learning, supervision, and parental controls did they learn to behave less obstreperously. Their children will require the same effort. If the parent remembers being a well-behaved child, the therapist might comment that some children are better behaved than others, but that a large percentage of children are more unruly than their parents might wish that they would be. The therapist then could add that it may seem unfair that the child's unpleasant behavior necessitates extra child-rearing work by the parents, but this is such a common situation that therapists are swamped with inquiries from parents who are interested in suggestions about new strategies they could use to improve their children's behavior.

Discomfort anxiety. Discomfort anxiety and low frustration tolerance can be dealt with by stressing that the short-term pain of listening to the child's whining will produce long-term gains by helping the parent to extinguish the child's negative behavior. The result is that both parents and children experience better rapport, because the parents spend less time dealing with the child's whining and more time engaging in positive interactions. Will they give up first, or will the child? It is helpful to have the parents stand next to the child and ask the child who is going to be in control and who is going to have psychological strength.

Philosophical disputes that focus on the parents' low frustration tolerance can deal with the obvious strengths that parents have shown in many previous child-rearing situations. Especially relevant is convincing them that they can tolerate frustration and that it is not imperative for them to be cool, calm, and collected at all times. Regardless of what disputational strategies the therapist chooses, the reduction of low frustration tolerance is likely to be a crucial step in getting the parents to adhere to behavioral contracts.

Cognitive Interventions with the Children

Once the parents adhere to the behavioral strategies, the child has some motivation to talk privately with the therapist. The cognitive strategies that the therapist teaches now have some meaning and purpose for the child. The child may wish to avoid response costs or to seek additional rewards.

At this stage of therapy, I usually meet with the parents and the child at the beginning of each session. We discuss the child's progress on the target behaviors, the parents' adherence to the behavioral regime, and any changes that are required in the behavioral contract to shape the child's behavior progressively to the ultimate goal (e.g., requiring a higher percentage of homework completed). This review of progress, then, becomes the "meat" of the session with the child. By knowing that Johnny did not finish his homework three nights and had fights with other boys after school, the therapist focuses on the emotions and cognitions that caused the disruptive behavior.

Disputing and challenging the irrational aspects of the thinking of children with conduct disorders can be somewhat more difficult than dealing with middle-aged neurotic clients. As with all children (DiGiuseppe, 1981), it is important to make sure that they have a schema and a vocabulary for the emotions that the therapist would like them to develop; that is, a conceptual awareness that a certain emotion can occur in certain situations. Children often have limited schemata concerning emotional reactions to events. They may have either a limited repertoire or a fixed notion of the appropriateness of an emotion for a specific event.

An example of this principle is Jeff, a 16-year-old referred after being expelled from school for classroom pranks and fire setting. Jeff was at the top of his class in a prep school, and he had aspirations to be a physician. However, Jeff came from a working-class family, and he had many conflicts and fights with his father, whom he displeased. Jeff was angry at his father because he believed that his father's lack of social polish and his working-class roots would somehow prevent Jeff from achieving his aspiration. In disputing Jeff's condemning attitude toward his father, it became apparent that Jeff was unable to give up his anger at his father because he could not conceptualize how to feel toward his father if he acknowledged his father's faults. In his mind, one felt either respect and love *or* disdain. He could not conceptualize a positive feeling toward a father that did not include aspects of respect or viewing the person as a role model. We discussed the separation of feelings he might attain. He could feel grateful toward his father for what he provided for Jeff; he could feel fondness for his father for all of the good times they had together. However, those feelings did not necessitate that he consider his father a role model for all things. Once Jeff concluded that accepting or even liking his father did not mean that he had to hold him as a role model, it was easier for him to develop more accepting and less condemning attitudes toward his father.

Conduct disorder children are characterized by their cognitive deficits. They frequently do not think before they act. Because of this the therapist may dispute the child's underlying demand for comfort and satisfaction by providing him or her with rational self-statements to be rehearsed in situations which previously elicited impulsive dysfunctional behavior. Although anger is the most frequent problematic emotion with conduct disorder children, the cognitive therapy literature regarding anger control is sparse. The most helpful approach for our young clients is Novaco's (1975) stress inoculation procedures. Some preliminary research suggests that this approach can be adapted successfully to conduct disorder children of preadolescence and early adolescence (Sackles, 1980; Schlichter & Horan, 1981). The children are first taught the appropriate use of anger, as well as the role of irrational beliefs and thinking styles in generating and maintaining anger. However, because these children are impulsive, they usually do not recognize their irrational beliefs and dispute them *in vivo*. Self-instructional training is used to get them to stop and think more rationally before they act.

The importance of self-instructional training in stopping dysfunctional thoughts and promoting constructive thoughts cannot be overemphasized for this population. Anger and impulsivity do not lend themselves to reflective disputing. When angry clients confront a difficult situation, they start experiencing demanding thoughts (e.g., "He *must* do it my way or I can't stand it!"). This process leads to anger. Anger is likely to motivate quick action and to lead to physically or verbally aggressive behavior. In a short period of time, the entire incident is over. The angry client has not tried any cognitive disputing and has not experienced any success in coping.

Disputing one's own upsetting cognitions takes time and practice. Because of the impulsive nature of behavioral expressions of anger, the conduct disorder child does not take the time to think. Some latency-extending or response-delaying strategy is needed to slow the client's reactions, so that disputing can start before the coping trial is complete.

In summary, then, the individual sessions with the child focus on the following:

1. The occurrence of the problematic target behaviors since the last session, as reported by the parents.
2. Discussion of actual situations in which the child experienced the emotional or behavioral problems.
3. Expansion of the child's emotional vocabulary to include ways to describe positive and negative emotional reactions, with a goal of motivating the child to see the desirability of reducing his or her negative emotional responses to life events.
4. Identification and disputation of the irrational beliefs causing the disturbed emotions and behaviors.
5. Teaching specific self-instructional statements to inhibit immediate responding, to focus on cognitive disputing, and to guide appropriate behavior and emotions.
6. Teaching social problem-solving skills (i.e., generating alternative

solutions and consequential thinking) in order to provide the child with more adaptive ways of responding to previously problematic situations.

SPECIAL CLINICAL ISSUES

Motivation for Change

Conduct disorder children and adolescents are notorious for being unmotivated for treatment. Most therapists report trying to build rapport with them to facilitate the children's revealing the nature of their problems. However, why should these children want to relinquish power in the family? It is hypothesized here that the conduct disorder child will be unwilling to participate in a therapy that he or she views as effective. Some adolescents will even report misleading their parents that they are happy with a therapy that in fact is ineffectual, in order to make the parents continue the treatment so that no other change strategies will be implemented.

When a therapist suggests limiting the child's power, or curtailing his or her benefits, the child will attempt to get the parents to leave therapy. Some frequently used strategies are attacking and slandering the therapist, purposely escalating misbehavior in order to convince the parents that treatment will not work, leaving the therapy session and refusing to return, and expressing an interest in individual therapy so that he or she can talk about problems.

Many therapists are stymied when the identified patient refuses to come for therapy. However, therapy need not stop. The parents are part of the problematic family interaction pattern, because of their beliefs which keep that system operating. It is important to show them that their reactions to the child's resistance have contributed to the maintenance of the pattern by reinforcing the child's negative behavior. Therapy can focus on changing their cognitions and behaviors toward the child in a manner that will help the parents reassert their place in the family hierarchy. The parents then will set rules and contingencies to shape the conduct disorder child's behavior.

For example, Kate, a 16-year-old, was referred for truancy, stealing, and frequent running away from home. She loudly protested that she did not need therapy. She claimed that her behavior was normal, and that there would be no problems if not for her parents' "stupid rules" that she attend school and keep a curfew. She added that her parents did not give her enough money. When contingencies for rule violations were discussed, Kate would protest loudly, swear at the therapist and her parents, and storm out of the office, slamming the door behind her. The parents expressed concern that Kate needed therapy to help control her angry outbursts and failure to recognize her behavior problems. Kate's outbursts had the effect of focusing the parents on her upset and away from her transgressions and any consequences for them. The therapist persisted in explaining how Kate had gotten what she wanted—a focus away from her behavior. As the therapist helped the parents locate and challenge their beliefs that caused them to feel guilty about Kate's outbursts, they were able to follow through on the behavioral contingencies that had been generated during the therapy sessions. In a matter of weeks, Kate's behavior started to improve, and she returned to therapy.

The therapist need not despair when high levels of resistance occur. Rather, the more extreme the resistance, the more the therapist can be assured that the intervention chosen is one that will work if it is applied consistently.

REFERENCES

Abicoff, H. (1979). Cognitive training interventions in children: Review of a new approach. *Journal of Learning Disabilities, 12,* 123–135.

Abicoff, H. (1985). Efficacy of cognitive training interventions in children: A critical review. *Clinical Psychology Review, 5,* 479–512.

Achenbach, T.M., & Edelbrock, C.S. (1983). *Manual for the Child Behavior Checklist and Revised Child Behavior Profile.* Burlington, VT: University Associates in Psychiatry.

Anderson, K.E., Lytton, H., & Romney, D.M. (1986). Mothers' interactions with normal and conduct-disordered boys: Who affects whom? *Developmental Psychology, 22,* 604–609.

Bandura, A. (1969). *Principles of behavior modification.* New York: Holt, Rinehart and Winston.

Bell, J.E. (1975). *Family therapy.* New York: Jason Aronson.

Bernard, M.E., & Joyce, M.R. (1984). *Rational-emotive therapy with children and adolescents: Theory, treatment, strategies, preventive methods.* New York: Wiley-Interscience.

Bogaard, L. (1977). Relationship between aggressive behavior in children and parent perception of child behavior. *Dissertation Abstracts International, 37* (12-A, Pt. 1), 7625.

Byng-Hall, J. (1980). Symptom bearer as marital distance regulator: Clinical implications. *Family Process, 19,* 355–365.

Camp, B.W., & Ray, R.S. (1984). Aggression. In A.W. Meyers & W.E. Craighead (Eds.), *Cognitive behavior therapy with children* (pp. 315–350). New York: Plenum.

Cattell, R.B., & Cattell, M.D. (1975). *Handbook for the High School Personality Questionnaire.* Champaign, IL: Institute for Personality and Ability Testing.

Cattell, R.B., & Eber, H.J. (1965). *The Sixteen Personality Factor Questionnaire* (3rd ed.). Champaign, IL: Institute for Personality and Ability Testing.

Chess, S., & Thomas, A. (1984). *Origins and evolution of behavior disorders: From infancy to early adult life.* New York: Brunner/Mazel.

DiGiuseppe, R. (1981). Cognitive therapy with children. In G. Emery, S. Hollon, & R. Bedrosian (Eds.), *New directions in cognitive therapy* (pp. 50–67). New York: Guilford Press.

DiGiuseppe, R. (1983). Rational-emotive therapy with conduct disorders. In A. Ellis & Bernard (Eds.), *Rational-emotive approaches to problems of childhood* (pp. 111–132). New York: Plenum.

Ellis, A. (1977). *Anger: How to live with and without it.* Secaucus, NJ: Citadel Press.

Ellis, A. (1980). Discomfort anxiety: A new cognitive behavioral construct. *Rational Living, 15,* 25–30.

Ellis, A. (1985). *Overcoming resistance: Rational-emotive therapy with difficult clients.* New York: Springer.

Forehand, R., & King, H.E. (1977). Noncompliant children: Effects of parent training on behavior and attitude change. *Behavior Modification, 1,* 93–108.

Forehand, R., King, H., Peed, S., & Yoder, P. (1975). Mother–child interaction: Comparison of a non-compliant clinic group and a non-clinic group. *Behavior Research and Therapy, 13,* 79–84.

Haley, J. (1980). *Leaving home.* New York: McGraw-Hill.

Harbin, H.T. (1977). Episodic dyscontrol and family dynamics. *American Journal of Psychiatry, 134,* 1113–1116.

Kazdin, A. (1985). *Treatment of antisocial behavior in children and adolescents.* Homewood, IL: Dorsey.

Kellam, S.G., Brown, C.H., Rubin, B.R., & Ensminger, M.E. (1983). Paths leading to teenage psychiatric symptoms and substance use. In S.R. Guze, F.S. Ferns, & J.E. Barrett (Eds.), *Childhood psychopathology and development* (pp. 17–51). New York: Raven Press.

Kellam, S.G., Ensminger, M.E., & Turner, R.J. (1977). Family structure and the mental health of children. *Archives of General Psychiatry, 34,* 1012–1022.

Kendall, P.C., & Braswell, L. (1985). *Cognitive-behavioral therapy for impulsive children.* New York: Guilford Press.

Lachar, D., & Gdowski, C. (1979). *Actuarial assessment of child and adolescent personality: An interpretive guide for the Personality Inventory for Children.* Los Angeles: Western Psychological Services.

Levitt, E.E. (1971). Research on psychotherapy with children. In A.E. Bergin & S.L. Garfield (Eds.), *Handbook of psychotherapy and behavior change: An empirical analysis* (pp. 474–494). New York: Wiley.

Lobitz, G.K., & Johnson, S.M. (1975). Parental manipulation of the behavior of normal and deviant children. *Child Development, 46,* 719–726.

Loeber, R., & Dishion, T.S. (1983). Early predictors of male adolescent delinquency: A review. *Psychological Bulletin, 94,* 68–99.

Meichenbaum, D. (1977). *Cognitive behavior modification: An integrative approach.* New York: Plenum.

Miller, L.C. (1984). *Louisville Behavior Checklist manual* (rev. ed.). Los Angeles: Western Psychological Services.

Millon, T., Green, C., & Meagher, R. (1982). *Millon Adolescent Personality Inventory manual.* Minneapolis: National Computer Systems.

Novaco, R. (1975). *Anger control: The development and evaluation of an experimental treatment.* Lexington, MA: D.C. Heath.

Olweus, D. (1979). Stability of aggressive reaction patterns in males: A review. *Psychological Bulletin, 86,* 852–875.

Olweus, D. (1980). The consistency issue in personality psychology revisited—with special reference to aggression. *British Journal of Social and Clinical Psychology, 19,* 377–390.

Patterson, G.R. (1974). Interventions for boys with conduct problems: Multiple settings, treatment and criteria. *Journal of Consulting and Clinical Psychology, 42,* 471–481.

Patterson, G.R. (1976). The aggressive child: Victim and architect of a coercive system. In E.J. Mash, L.A. Hamerlynck, & L.C. Handy (Eds.), *Behavior modification and families* (pp. 267–316). New York: Brunner/Mazel.

Patterson, G.R. (1982). *Coercive family process.* Eugene, OR: Castalia.

Patterson, G.R. (1986). Performance models for antisocial boys. *American Psychologist, 41,* 432–444.

Patterson, G.R., Chamberlain, P., & Reid, J.B. (1982). A comparative evaluation of a parent-training program. *Behavior Therapy, 13,* 638–650.

Patterson, G.R., & Fleischman, M.J. (1979). Maintenance of treatment effects: Some considerations concerning family systems and follow-up data. *Behavior Therapy, 10,* 160–185.

Patterson, G.R., & Reid, J.B. (1973). Interventions for families of aggressive boys: A replication study. *Behavior Research and Therapy, 11,* 383–394.

Porter, R.B., & Cattell, R.B. (1979). *Handbook for the Children's Personality Questionnaire* (rev. ed.). Champaign, IL: Institute for Personality and Ability Testing.

Quay, H.C. (1979). Classification. In H.C. Quay & J.S. Werry (Eds.), *Psychological disorders of childhood* (pp. 1–42). New York: Wiley.

Quay, H.C., & Werry, J.S. (1979). *Psychopathological disorders of childhood* (2nd ed.). New York: Wiley.

Reid, J.B., & Patterson, G.R. (1976). The modification of aggression and stealing of boys in the home setting. In E. Ribes-Inesta & A. Bandura (Eds.), *Analysis of delinquency and aggression* (pp. 123–145). Hillsdale, NJ: Lawrence Erlbaum Associates.

Robinson, E.A. (1985). Coercive theory revisited: Toward a new theoretical perspective on the etiology of conduct disorders. *Clinical Psychology Review, 5,* 597–626.

Robinson, E.A., & Eyberg, S. (1981). The dyadic parent–child interaction coding system: Standardization and validation. *Journal of Consulting and Clinical Psychology, 49,* 245–250.

Rutter, M., & Giller, H. (1983). *Juvenile delinquency: Trends and perspectives.* New York: Guilford Press.

Sackles, J. (1980). *Three treatment programs for anger control in young adolescents.* Unpublished doctoral dissertation, Hofstra University, Hempstead, NY.

Sameroff, A.J., & Seifer, R. (1983, April). *Sources of continuity and parent–child relations.* Paper presented at the meeting of the Society for Research in Child Development, Detroit.

Schlichter, K., & Horan, J. (1981). Effects of stress inoculation on the anger and aggression management skills of institutionalized juvenile delinquents. *Cognitive Therapy and Research, 5,* 359–366.

Snyder, J.J. (1977). A reinforcement analysis of interaction in problem and non-problem families. *Journal of Abnormal Psychology, 86,* 528–535.

Spivack, G., & Shure, M. (1974). *Social adjustment of young children: A cognitive approach to solving real-life problems.* San Francisco: Jossey-Bass.

Vogel, E.F., & Bell, N.W. (1968). The emotionally disturbed child as the family scapegoat. In N.W. Bell & E.F. Vogel (Eds.), *A modern introduction to the family* (pp. 412–427). New York: Free Press.

Wahler, R.G. (1969). Oppositional children: A quest for parental reinforcement control. *Journal of Applied Behavior Analysis, 2,* 159–170.

Walker, H.M. (1983). *Walker Problem Behavior Identification Checklist: Revised edition manual.* Los Angeles: Western Psychological Services.

Werner, E., & Smith, R. (Eds.) (1977). *Kauai's children come of age.* Honolulu: University Press of Hawaii.

Wilson, J.Q., & Hernstein, R.J. (1985). *Crime and human nature.* New York: Simon and Schuster.

7

Problems in Families of
Older Adults

Sara H. Qualls

The theoretical focus of cognitive–behaviorism on an analysis of cognitive and behavioral functioning has been well received within the gerontological community because of its similarity to gerontologists' analyses of the behavior of older adults in a contextual, functional framework. The cognitive–behavioral model emphasizes the reciprocal causality of person–environment interaction and the role of both "objective" environmental characteristics and cognitive processes of perception in determining human behavior. Similarly, gerontologists emphasize the importance of assessing the person, environment, and person–environment match in order to perform a functional analysis of the person's behavior (Lawton, 1983).

The goal of this chapter is to consider how therapists working with the elderly and their families can use the basic tenets of the cognitive–behavioral framework to guide their case conceptualization, assessment, and intervention in a wide variety of specific situations.

A COGNITIVE–BEHAVIORAL VIEW OF THE ELDERLY IN A FAMILY CONTEXT

A basic tenet of the cognitive–behavioral perspective is that human behavior is determined by environmental contingencies as processed cognitively. In other words, thought processes are the guidance mechanism by which humans adapt to the environment. Emotions as well as behaviors are considered to be functionally related to the environmental contingencies as perceived by the individual (Mahoney & Arnkoff, 1978).

Cognitive processes perform the tasks of taking in environmental information (e.g., sensory and perceptual mechanisms), storing that information (e.g., memory), and anticipating, evaluating, and comparing new information with previous knowledge. Behavioral attempts to maximize reinforcing experiences and minimize aversive experiences are guided by cognitive processes operating both within and outside of awareness.

A cognitive–behaviorist often must look at an older person's family not only to understand the real environmental contingencies within which an older client is operating, but also to discover important components of the client's cognitive framework. "Cognitive framework" refers to the structure of knowledge and beliefs within which an individual's cognitive processes must function. Conscious thoughts are the "surface" manifestations of a deeper structure of assumptions and beliefs which organize our understanding of our world. Given that behavior is mediated by cognitive processes operating both within and outside of conscious awareness, the behaviors of family members can be thought of as demonstrations of the beliefs and expectations each member carries into interactions. Furthermore, the behavioral cues and contingencies provided for the older person by family members are mediated through the older adult's cognitive framework. Family members' actions serve to reaffirm or stimulate change in the framework, depending on the degree of consistency between the belief structure and the observed behavior.

Beliefs shared by members of a family function as family "rules," often unspoken but behaviorally constraining (Jackson, 1965). It is common for beliefs about the range of "respectful" behaviors to constrain children's actions toward parents, sometimes in maladaptive ways. Adult children may constrain their actions toward a demented parent for fear that they will not be acting respectfully. Consider as another example the couples who behave in accordance with the shared belief that husbands and wives should maintain their social world as a couple. These couples often cease all social contact if illness impairs the ability of one partner to continue participating. If the unimpaired wife of an Alzheimer's patient is encouraged to initiate a social event, she is likely to express considerable discomfort with the thought of leaving her demented husband. This discomfort reflects a discrepancy between the client's cognitive framework and the adaptive behavior. Several belief structures could create the distress in this context. Distress could be rooted in a fear that her husband might engage in inappropriate behavior while an alternate care provider was present. In this case the fear reflects an underlying belief that the wife is somehow responsible for her demented husband's behavior. Another belief that could block a spouse's independent socializing would be simply that it is inappropriate for one partner to have fun if the other cannot. The therapist may be unaware of the beliefs creating this distress and will need to assess which specific cognitive framework evokes the distress before choosing an appropriate intervention.

As families have grown increasingly complex (due, for example, to the simultaneous existence of four or five generations and the high rate of divorce and remarriage), simple generalizations about the context or cognitive frameworks of families with older members are impossible. It is critical to examine closely the familial context of each client in order to understand the functions served by each relationship and to identify particular components of the cognitive framework of the family members which are relevant to the identified problems.

In addition to information about contexts and cognitive frameworks, cognitive–behaviorists are interested in cognitive processing. Although older adults demonstrate considerable variability in cognitive processing, it is normative for persons in their seventies and eighties to experience deficits in cognitive processing (e.g., attentional process, abstract reasoning skills, and memory processes; Poon, 1985). The degree of deficit varies greatly across individuals. Cognitive–behavioral therapists must acknowledge the impact of a particular client's deficits on his or her adaptation to the environment. Some deficits impair the older adult's ability to perceive environmental cues and contingencies accurately, whereas other deficits impair the problem-solving abilities once information is perceived. Thus the cognitive–behavioral model requires a therapist to assess *how* information is processed as well as *what* information is processed.

Conceptual Model of Etiology

Within the cognitive–behavioral framework there are two ways for a behavior problem to arise: 1) a person can learn maladaptive behaviors (awkward, unskilled thought, behavior, and affect patterns that meet his or her needs in a very narrow array of contexts), or 2) the environment can change in such a way that previously learned behavior no longer is effective. A further distinction can be made between behaviors that were learned *recently* to facilitate adaptation to a new situation but are not fully adequate, and *long-term* thought, behavior, or affect patterns which have never allowed the person to function well (comfortably and/or effectively at meeting a broad range of his or her needs). It seems useful when working with individuals with a long personal history to attempt to differentiate between long-term and recently acquired behaviors and to determine the recent changes that brought the person into therapy.

Factors Producing Behavioral Dysfunction

In the tradition of the reciprocal determinism paradigm, it is useful to categorize the factors that produce distress sufficient for intervention in terms of *changes in the environment* and *changes in the person*. Changes in the person can be in the person's physiology, cognitive framework, and/or behavior. Environmental changes can occur in the "objective" or real characteristics of the physical environment and social environment, the subjective perception of the environment, and the function of the environment. Retirement is a common example of a contextual change that requires adaptation. Retirement produces changes in the structure of one's day, in the array of stimuli and contingencies on which one bases judgments of self-worth, and in the frequency and types of interaction with one's spouse. The social losses which permeate the later part of life (changes in the environment) can require that a person adapt either by learning to live in a more restricted social environment or by building a different social world. Both adaptation strategies require skills: in the first case, the skill of satisfying needs with limited resources, in the second case, skills of social network building. Even a person who has excellent social network *maintenance* skills may now be in the position of needing to learn social network *acquisition* skills. These changes evoke a need for revised cognitive, behavioral, and affective patterns even in the most well-adapted individuals.

There are three specific types of change which frequently (almost normatively) occur and require adaptation in the person or the environment.

Changes in physical health. Most pervasive in our culture of increased life expectancy are changes in physical health during the later part of life. Increasingly, geriatric physicians are emphasizing that it is chronic rather than acute illness which plagues older adults (typically *multiple* chronic illnesses). Living with chronic illness can be thought of as a series of adaptations to altered physical functioning, changing self-image, and a functionally different environment. Both patient and family are required to change as the patient's physical functioning changes.

Patients and/or families who do not understand the implications of a disease process often experience significant practical or emotional problems for which they seek help. Patients may attempt levels of independent living and activity which are inappropriate. In contrast, ignorance concerning the disease can leave the patient assuming that she is to reduce her activity level, forcing the environment (often the family) to provide more services than may be necessary (i.e., premature dependence). Patients often become depressed as the sources of positive stimulation and events are reduced.

Family members respond to their beliefs about the patient's illness in a variety of ways. Some create and foster inappropriate dependence. Others reinforce the patient's fears that unless she does everything for herself, all functioning will be lost. Either extreme can result in harm to the patient.

When an older adult with a diagnosed illness seeks help from a therapist, a full assessment of behavior (self-care, recreational, social) and beliefs (patient's and family's) must be carried out to clarify the actual nature of the reported problem. For example, families of Parkinson's disease patients often struggle with how much help to provide the trembling, unsteady patient. When balance is precarious it is tempting to reduce the possibility of falling by arranging the patient's life so that he does not have to leave a chair. Exercise, however, is important to slowing the deteriorating effects of the disease. In a specific case where family conflict is arising over the patient's behavior, a therapist will need to gather information about the patient's physical functioning, the patient's beliefs about his physical functioning, and the family's beliefs about the patient's functioning. Beliefs about the need to provide support and the dangers of not providing support are usually central to the conflict. In many instances, once information about the disease is available to them, family members can modify their cognitive frameworks independently in ways that alter the patient's and family's behavior to reduce conflict and promote health. When an adequate framework is in place therapists may need to teach specific skills (e.g., structuring specific contingency contracts for promoting physical activity). Behaviors which "make sense" within the client's current cognitive framework may be introduced without cognitive intervention. There are other cases, however, in which information alone does not produce behavior change. Cognitive restructuring of beliefs may be required before the family can behave in ways that promote the older adult's maximal functioning. Less obvious beliefs and assumptions (e.g., very basic beliefs concerning dependence or nurturance) may deter the family members' motivation to change or their ability to decide on specific new behavior goals (see Intervention section below).

Changes in children's lives. Increasingly, we are becoming aware of the intergenerational effects of changes in the lives of one generation (Hill &

Mattesich, 1979). Changes in children's lives may adversely alter the behavior, thoughts, and feelings of older adults. Midlife divorce, for example, has been demonstrated to affect the life of the divorcees' parents in numerous ways (Hagestad, Smyer, & Stierman, 1984). Even very elderly parents often provide emotional and sometimes financial care for the divorcee, a responsibility that may occur at the time when the parents are concerned about the adequacy of their resources to care for themselves. Pruchno, Blow, and Smyer (1984) use the term "life-event web" to characterize the network of relationships which is affected by an event in a single life. Events vary in the breadth of their impact and in the visibility of their effects on other lives in the web. A midlife woman returning to work when her children are in high school may dramatically alter the behaviors of her own household. Her parents may be less obvious members of the web whose lives are nonetheless affected by their anxiety concerning who will now be available to care for them if they become physically dependent. A social worker whose only contact is with the elderly parents may be confused by their attempt to enter a nursing home before it is appropriate. In this instance, the parents' behavior demonstrates their belief that working daughters cannot provide the care that parents require as their health declines. The attempted admission to the nursing home is a way of taking responsibility for their own care, a responsibility they now assume their daughter cannot share. This assumption may or may not be accurate, and it may or may not be shared by the daughter. The social worker needs to assess (or ask the older couple to assess) the daughter's beliefs about her role in her parents' care, in order to help the couple make appropriate decisions.

Beliefs about the actions of "good children," the roles of the oldest generation, the frequency and timing of family interactions, and the transfer of family assets from older to younger family members are among the common cognitive structures that affect older adults' reactions to changes in their children's lives. Once again, we see how important it is to assess major changes in the lives of other members of the web as we conceptualize the older adult's problems.

Although less obvious to an observer than changes in behavior, changes in children's *perceptions* can alter intergenerational communication. As children watch their "strong" parents age physically, their observations often conflict with unspoken beliefs about parents' invincibility. If the basic belief about parents' "strength" is altered, children may begin interacting with their parents so differently that familiar patterns of communication are interrupted. Children who fear their parents' health decline may withdraw to avoid dealing with daily concrete evidence of dysfunction. On the other hand, middle-aged children may expect so much from themselves as "caregivers" that they prematurely take over their parents' lives. In these two examples, cognitive–behavioral interventions would focus on the beliefs and assumptions about the parent–child role, helping the client family sort through its thoughts and feelings about changing intergenerational roles. Typical questions to address include: Are adult children supposed to "parent" their parents? When is it respectful to overrule one's parents' preference (e.g., for housing or for driving) to ensure their safety? How can one intercede in one's parents' decision-making process without being disrespectful?

Even when changes in the children are not the explicit reason for seeking intervention, a therapist may need to assess intergenerational relations before assuming intervention should be targeted only on the elder. A common scenario is a family seeking help with decision making concerning an elderly member who is showing signs of physical decline. The children may enlist a therapist's aid to convince Mother that she should come and live with them so she does not have to go to a nursing home. Assessment in such cases may include not only Mother's functioning, but the children's perceptions, beliefs, and expectations concerning aging (especially cognitive decline) and concerning ways of taking care of one's parents. Children commonly believe that "good children" are supposed to take such good care of their parents that the parents do not experience cognitive decline, and that only "unloving" children would "abandon" their parents to a nursing home. Quotation marks are used in the previous sentence to highlight words that mask important beliefs (those representing an absolute value judgment which is likely to produce strong negative thoughts and emotions and restrict the range of appropriate behaviors). For many very frail older persons, a nursing home is the only appropriate placement. Housing options with fewer services would endanger the life of the older person. In these situations it could hardly be "unloving" or "abandonment" to place one's parents in a nursing home.

Treatment often involves helping the children question their assumptions concerning "appropriate" aging and develop specific problem-focused models for their concerns. Labels such as "dependent" are applied to behavior as a result of assumptions held concerning responsibility and control. A mother who makes a daily phone call to her adult daughter may be perceived as "dependent" if the daughter believes that her mother calls her because she is lonely. A different set of assumptions (more likely to occur in early adulthood) could lead the daughter to be angry at her mother for "checking up on her." Thus whereas changes in children's behavior can force older adults to reexamine their assumptions about the late-life "parent" role, children also frequently need to alter the assumptions on which their behavior toward their parents is based.

Changes in sociocultural context. The current elderly cohort has lived through "future shock" (Toffler, 1970)—during their lifetime the rate of sociocultural change has been dramatic. Many of these changes require adaptation. Higher rates of divorce and remarriage have altered the cross-generational family structure. Increased life expectancy as a result of advances in treatment of acute illnesses has created a situation in which most of us can anticipate experiencing multiple chronic illnesses which will erode our range of functioning in our advanced years. Each aged individual must adapt to these and other recent sociocultural changes without the benefit of modeling from the previous generation.

Many problems for which older adults and their families seek treatment reflect the challenge of changing from the cognitive model their parents used and creating a model with more accuracy for today's world. Therapists must be prepared to help a family expand its view of housing options, for example, from "own home, children's home, or nursing home," to incorporate inter-mediate levels of supportive housing services (e.g., congregate living facilities). Some families may need assistance in expanding their view of the role of a "good child" to include a role for "good long-distance child." Many older adults are challenged to develop a meaningful concept of leisure time after retirement. Leisure typically is defined as activity you do in your "free time." However, after retirement, time is not as neatly divided into work time and free time as is typical prior to retirement. In addition, one's parents may have provided no model for retirement if their version of good aging was to "work until you die." Problem behaviors often are simply behaviors that follow "old rules," regardless of current realities.

Interplay of Individual and Family System Factors

As outlined, many of the changes that accompany aging have an impact on *individuals* across generations. Family *systems* also experience the impact of the changes outlined. A system is characterized by the specific rules of interaction among its elements (Jackson, 1965). Systems theory states that changes in one element in the system will result in reverberating changes throughout the system because of the intense interconnectedness of system members. For example, when a husband retires, his altered behavior patterns will communicate to his wife different messages concerning the husband–wife relationship than those communicated by his behavior as a working man. This change in his behavior can be expected to alter his wife's thoughts, feelings, and/or actions. If her concept of "husband" was defined by behaviors in which he engaged as a working man (e.g., financial provider), she will be required to alter her framework (and likely some of her behaviors) to maintain her perception of him as "husband" when he retires.

Changes in one person or in one person's environment in later life often result in alterations in the rules of interaction in that person's major relationships (Gallagher & Frankel, 1980). Individuals experience thoughts and feelings as a function of physiological, cognitive, or environmental change, and the behaviors of individuals may change the "rules" by which an entire system operates. Consider, for example, a family that has maintained a set of rules such as: "Be polite to your parents. Never interrupt them or correct them. Be respectful." The onset of combative, angry behaviors in a demented mother requires an alteration in these rules, particularly for the daughter who lives with and cares for the mother. It is likely that her beliefs about "good daughters" have incorporated those interactional rules, so that she is in the apparently hopeless dilemma of being a "bad daughter" for restraining her mother's combative behavior, or a "bad daughter" for letting her mother behave inappropriately in front of guests. The daughter will experience great stress until she finds a way to alter the rules to resolve the dilemma.

Rules of interaction typically are embedded in each individual's assumptions of "how it is supposed to be" if you are good. The daughter just described, caught in the unresolvable dilemma of her own belief structure, is likely to be sufficiently stressed by living with a lack of hope that she can ever be a "good daughter" that she develops an ulcer, becomes depressed, or tears into a rage when a sister criticizes her decision to place Mother in a nursing home. This example illustrates the link between what family systems theorists refer to as "rules" and what cognitive–behaviorists refer to as assumptions or beliefs. Rules of interaction exist in the minds of the system members in the form: "This is how it should be done, or else bad things will happen." The internal form of this rule language is exactly what the cognitive–behaviorist elicits from clients (using the term "belief") and teaches clients to question.

ASSESSMENT

When working with older adults, a therapist continually must be aware of the heterogeneity of the older population, especially the diversity of changes that occur in varied combinations in the domains mentioned previously. Assessments must be focused on the behavior of particular persons in particular contexts in order to elicit the information needed to determine contingencies that maintain the problem behaviors.

The tradition of a broad-based functional assessment is well ingrained in geropsychologists (Lawton, 1986). Lawton (1986) identified four areas to address when doing a full functional assessment: 1) *behavioral competence*—information about physical health, functional health (activities of daily living, ability to maintain financial independence), cognition, time use (including recreation and creative innovation), and social behavior; 2) *perceived quality of life;* 3) *psychological well-being*—life satisfaction, morale, positive and negative affect, happiness, depression, and self-esteem; and 4) *objective environment*—physical environment, personal environment, community environment, social environment, and life events. In addition, he notes the importance of assessing three areas that have relevance to planning long-term care: caregiver's needs for support, formal and informal caregiving resources, and client preferences concerning services.

An important step in assessing an older family is to determine whether the family's problem has been labeled as a problem of one particular older family member, the "identified patient" (IP). If the psychological or physical well-being of an elderly person is in question, the therapist must obtain accurate information concerning that individual's health and functional capability (e.g., ability to perform activities of daily living) before attempting family therapy. A variety of initially presented concerns (e.g., Mom's forgetfulness, Dad's depression) should raise red flags for the therapist concerning possible organic causes of the dysfunction, which must be ruled out before a therapist can focus on environmental contingencies. The therapist can shift the focus from the IP somewhat by observing the ways in which the family interacts as they obtain appropriate physical health and functional assessments. Although it makes some family therapists uncomfortable to follow the family's lead in labeling one member as the IP, it is nonetheless critical in the case of older families to work with accurate information concerning the capabilities of older family members. This information places the therapist in the position of questioning how family members' beliefs and thoughts about the older person influence their behavior.

Instruments which are useful in assessing the range of functioning of the older adult and the salient personal and environmental factors which affect functioning are presented next.

Standard Instruments

Broad functional assessments. Several major assessment packages are available to measure the broad spectrum of human functioning (Lawton, 1986). Most popular is the Duke Older American Resources and Services (OARS) Multi-dimensional Functional Assessment Questionnaire (Duke University Center for the Study of Aging, 1978), which has well-sampled normative data for comparison (Fillenbaum & Smyer, 1981). A time-consuming but fully comprehensive assessment package is the Comprehensive Assessment and Referral Evaluation (CARE; Gurland, Kuriansky, Sharpe, Simon, Stiller, & Birkett, 1977). The Philadelphia Geriatric Center Multilevel Assessment Instrument (MAI; Lawton, Moss, Fulcomer, & Kleban, 1982) offers a range of functional information on its full, mid-length, and short forms. A brief but comprehensive self-report scale that is psychometrically strong is the Self-Evaluation of Life Function Scale (SELF; Linn & Linn, 1984). Although these four packages did not arise from the cognitive–behavioral tradition, they provide the range of information critical to therapists working with the multifaceted problems of elderly.

Cognitive–behavioral assessments. In addition to these broad packages, several assessment tools used with other populations are useful with the elderly. For example, the Beck Depression Inventory (BDI; Beck, Ward, Mendelson, Mock, & Erbaugh, 1961) and Beck's Hopelessness scale (Beck, Weissman, Lester, & Trexler, 1974) are quick self-report measures of relevance to therapists in a variety of settings who need to assess a patient's mood quickly. The BDI has been demonstrated to have acceptable reliability and validity with samples of older adults (Gallagher, Breckenridge, Steinmetz & Thompson, 1983; Gallagher, Nies, & Thompson, 1982) but must be interpreted cautiously when used with physically ill older adults because of the number of items that refer to physical symptoms that may be more related to the illness than the depression (see review of depression assessment instruments in Kazniak & Allender, 1985).

Cognitive processes can be assessed with the Dysfunctional Thought Record (DTR), which is used to record specific thoughts in specific situations (Beck, Rush, Shaw, & Emery, 1979). Although use of the DTR requires training, my experiences suggest that the DTR provides a useful structure for teaching older clients to identify thoughts, note the resulting feelings and actions, and learn to alter their own cognitive structure. Older clients may require more trials to learn to use the DTR effectively, so the pace of cognitive therapy may proceed more slowly than with younger clients.

Hussian (1981) describes strategies for assessing several specific problem behaviors of older adults. He emphasizes traditional behavioral assessments focusing on observation and measurement of antecedents and consequences of specific behaviors. Although his clinical examples are primarily institutional examples, their applicability to other systems (e.g., families) is clear. Specific behavioral assessment strategies are presented for problem behaviors such as chronic screaming, urinary incontinence, wandering, and combativeness (problems which families of organically disordered older adults find particularly stressful).

Family Assessments

There are no measures of family interactions of older couples or families available for therapist use. The assessments described thus far focus on the functioning of the individual older adult. Assessment of *functional contexts* is where the family becomes involved. Herr and Weakland (1979) provide outstanding examples of assessment of the family's role in maintaining (and sometimes creating) the behavior dysfunction. Their model follows closely the problem-focused family therapy approach of the Palo Alto MRI tradition, which is consistent with the traditional behavioral model of documenting exactly what thoughts and behaviors of which people proceed, follow, and are believed to respond to the targeted problem behavior.

The assessment of the functional context of the IP's problem behavior requires inquiry into behavior patterns of other family members. Specifically, it is important to consider how the family chose to handle what was perceived to be the elderly person's behavior problem. The MRI model emphasizes that families' unsuccessful efforts to "solve" the problem, although well intentioned, often serve to maintain it.

A typical example presented by Herr and Weakland (1970, pp. 100–112) is the case of a "grandfather" who was recovering from an illness in his daughter's family's home. Grandpa became increasingly reclusive in his room despite the family's best efforts to encourage him to come out. The family assessment focused on the behaviors of family members which might be maintaining the excessive withdrawal. Questions focused on exactly how frequently and under what conditions family members had observed Grandpa leaving his room. This careful questioning of family members' interactions with Grandpa elicited the information that all of Grandpa's needs were being met within his room, including the need for social interaction.

The therapist's efforts to understand what maintained the family members' behavior patterns (of inappropriately serving Grandpa) led to questions concerning behaviors and feelings (e.g., "When Grandpa got angry how did you feel?" "What did you do that seemed helpful in solving this problem?"). In the process of piecing together the results of various strategies to get Grandpa out of his room, it became apparent that the daughter had experienced considerable shame, embarrassment, and frustration regardless of her father's behavior (his behavior on various occasions included tears, anger, and compliance). The therapist then probed for the thoughts that evoked the daughter's strong negative feelings (and which were likely to be maintaining her behavior). He noticed that the daughter had been telling herself that she had tried everything, that nothing she did would please her father, that only her determination was keeping her going (a belief that encouraged her to try harder the same "failed" solutions). To complicate matters further, other family members' behaviors also were determined to be "maintaining" the social withdrawal. Even though everyone in this family verbally encouraged Grandpa to come out of the room, each person also responded to his or her own skeptical thoughts concerning Grandpa's ability to take care of himself within the family. Each member of the family was visiting Grandpa in his room, inadvertently reinforcing his withdrawal behavior.

This case illustrates nicely the importance of assessing family members' thoughts and assumptions as well as their actual behaviors. The daughter's beliefs about "good daughters" and about the small potential for change were producing excessive caretaking behaviors, which were maintaining her father's dependent behaviors. Other family members' beliefs about the "duty" of relatives to comply with older family members' requests were maintaining Grandpa's social withdrawal. This family needed to work through some of its unrealistic and inaccurate beliefs about Grandpa (e.g., that it is awful for daughters to cause father's distress, that Grandpa was unable to leave the room, that Grandpa was greatly disappointed in the family) in order to comply with a treatment plan that involved changing behavior.

Systematic Assessment

It bears repeating that when doing cognitive–behavioral therapy with older adults, professionals must perform a broader assessment than is necessary with younger adults. The comprehensive assessment instruments mentioned previously provide the therapist with adequate psychosocial background information. In addition, a complete physical exam (or information available from an exam done in the last two to six months) is warranted in cases involving a decline in daily functioning. Using this broad array of data, a therapist often will become aware of more than one arena (e.g., physical health, memory deficits, or economic resources) in which the individual's functioning is limited. Ideally, an interdisciplinary team is then available to follow through with more thorough assessments and interventions in appropriate areas. More than with any other population, it is critical for therapists to consult with other health care professionals concerning their elderly clients because behavioral symptoms and syndromes so often are interrelated with other domains of health (e.g., use of medication, chronic illnesses).

Once the therapist is certain that all data are available and the physical health condition is clearly understood, he or she can begin the traditional cognitive–behavioral assessment. Often all that is required is integrating information already available into a cognitive–behavioral formulation of the problem. In other cases additional specific information is needed. In addition to observation of behavior frequencies and behavior contingencies, tools developed for use with other populations can be adapted for older adults. For example, Lewinsohn's Pleasant Events Schedule and Unpleasant Events Schedule have been adapted to include events appropriate to the later part of life and can be used to monitor the presence and frequency of daily activities when treating depression (Gallagher, Thompson, Baffa, Piatt, Ringering, & Stone, 1981).

The systematic assessment strategy which begins with a broad-based assessment and focuses in on specific problems is illustrated in the case of Mrs. J. Mrs. J, an attractive, healthy-looking 68-year-old, was taken to a geriatric clinic by her husband for treatment of her "nerve trouble." Mrs. J reported tingling and burning in her arms and legs, and difficulty breathing. A complete physical exam, including a neurological exam, ruled out a physical cause for the symptoms. Neuropsychological testing revealed no significant cognitive deficits. Mrs. J was diagnosed as having an anxiety disorder with panic attacks. A full psychosocial history revealed that the symptoms had begun three years previously, a few months after her husband retired. Within the past five years one daughter had divorced, another daughter's son was regularly using illegal drugs, and Mrs. J's oldest sister (with whom she had never been at peace) moved into the same neighborhood. Mr. and Mrs. J reluctantly described their marriage as having been seriously conflicted for decades. Mr. J was a traveling salesman who was on the road for one- to two-week intervals. Apparently these breaks away from each other kept the conflict over daily activities at a minimum. Upon retirement Mr. J wanted to "relax," and spent most of his time in their home or at the club pool.

Using the data available from this broad assessment, the therapist formulated several hypotheses. First, it appeared that Mrs. J had always been an anxious person. The current symptoms were an exacerbation of her generalized anxiety due to cumulative stress. Second, the conflict in Mr. and Mrs. J's relationship was a major cause of the current symptoms. Specifically, the increased amount of time spent together within what had previously been defined as Mrs. J's domain (her home) was creating the opportunity for several small conflicts each day. In addition, Mr. J had not replaced his major sources of positive social interaction (sales contacts) and appeared to be mildly depressed. Third, Mrs. J's concern for the well-being of her extended family had expanded to include a vague sense of responsibility for improving their troubled lives. Note that these hypotheses focus on environmental events and dysfunctional beliefs as causes of behavior problems, a focus that could be used only after organic causes of the anxiety symptoms had been ruled out.

These hypotheses guided the next level of assessment. Mr. and Mrs. J both began to keep daily logs of pleasant and unpleasant events. Mrs. J monitored her anxiety, and Mr. J monitored his mood. In the process of recording these data, the couple became aware of various specific beliefs and assumptions each held concerning their relationship and their preferences for a retired lifestyle, including preferences for relationships with the family. Mrs. J believed Mr. J should be active in retirement, helping out in their children's households (and leaving her house to her!). Mr. J believed retirement was a time of freedom from responsibility, a time for passive leisure activities. He wanted Mrs. J to join him in relaxing and preferred to help her with housework so she could join him for leisure activities.

In the process of discussing beliefs and assumptions, communication skill deficits became apparent. The J's would argue about the plans for the day or about their children's problems until she "got a spell," which terminated the argument. Neither person had the communication skill to facilitate productive problem solving of these basic belief differences about retirement or about the conflicting beliefs that had troubled their marriage for years. This case illustrates the progression from broad assessment of several domains of functioning (physical, cognitive, relational) to specific assessments of particular domains.

Assessment of cases involving more than one generation proceed similarly. Adult children who bring their depressed, forgetful, or simply cantankerous parent for treatment will almost always identify the parent as the IP. It is critical for the therapist to assess the extent to which the medical sick role is appropriately applied to the older adult before looking at the particular problematic behaviors which motivated the children to seek treatment at this time. Once physical health has been assessed, the therapist can proceed to assess how this particular family is choosing to respond to the older person whose behavior has been labeled as problematic (i.e., assess the functional context of the behavior).

In summary, a broad-based assessment is particularly important when working with older adults because of their vulnerability to physiological, social, and cultural changes. Data from a broad assessment (using one of the comprehensive packages described above or integrating data from a physical exam, neuropsychological assessment, and social work assessment) can then be framed within a cognitive–behavioral model. Specific problems may require additional assessment of cognitive or behavioral contingencies. Family interactions are likely to be involved in the etiology and/or maintenance of problem behaviors.

CLINICAL STRATEGIES AND TECHNIQUES

Believing the Change Is Possible

It is appropriate to begin this section with a few comments about the importance of therapists believing that change is possible. Historically, therapists have seen far fewer older clients than the mental health needs within the elderly population warrant (VandenBos, Stapp, & Kilburg, 1981). Several reasons for the low usage rate have been postulated (Schaie & Willis, 1986). Among them, therapists' beliefs about the ability of older persons to change must rank high. Specifically, two aspects of aging that are susceptible to negative attitudes are the beliefs that older adults are cognitively rigid and that they experience so many losses that mental health and happiness are impossible.

Freud took the position that the increasing rigidity which accompanies aging precludes the effectiveness of as pervasive a change process as psychotherapy (Zarit, 1980). He lent professional sanction to the popular assumption that older people, like old dogs in the familiar adage, cannot learn new tricks. Subsequent data have demonstrated that the elderly are perfectly capable of learning (Schaie & Willis, 1986). The learning context may need to be arranged to accommodate sensory deficits and/or changes in rate of cognitive processing, but we lack conclusive evidence that the range of material they are able to learn is different from that of younger adults.

Psychoanalysis also set the tone for viewing only broad personality change as valid psychotherapy. Clearly many of the clients of any age seen in psychotherapy have not come seeking pervasive change, so that brief, limited interventions have been developed within several therapeutic frameworks that are effective for a range of behavior problems. Older clients, similarly, may or may not seek pervasive change. It is inappropriate to assume that persons not wanting broad personality changes are not good candidates for therapeutic intervention.

Clinicians may perceive that older clients' lives are so full of losses that depression and degeneration are inevitable. Despite the inevitable occurrence of losses in late life, the grief that accompanies loss need not result in depression or degeneration. Research on grief emphasizes the roles that change and adaptation play as part of the grief process (Bowlby, 1980; Parkes, 1972). Grief appears not only to be an emotional reaction to a perceived loss, but also involves the development of a cognitive framework which accounts for the loss and prepares the individual to live without the lost person or lost function. Therapists with an appropriate model can see interventions with the grieving as having the potential for growth (e.g., the development of more adaptive belief structures, a wider range of behavior patterns, or a richer array of experiences).

Having worked with the assumption that older persons can learn new behavior and thought patterns, even in the social context of multiple losses, we should extend this hopeful perspective to include the belief that change can occur in older persons' relationships. Families experience culturally age-graded social changes (e.g., empty nest), and typically adapt quite well. Obviously, family relationships can—and do—change. A family is likely to seek help from a therapist when it finds itself unable to generate a systemic change (a change in the way family members behave and communicate as they accomplish family tasks) to accommodate changes in individual members' behaviors. It is critical for the therapist to believe that systemic change is possible and to be able to conceptualize conditions under which that change is likely to occur.

In clinical work with the elderly, it is important to choose carefully the standards used to measure change. Measurable changes are useful feedback to the therapist (and the client) that changes are, in fact, occurring. Older clients may progress more slowly toward the goals than younger clients, so therapists must be prepared to measure small increments of change and not to abandon a treatment plan too soon. Careful control over the therapist's thoughts about the progress of therapy (e.g., "This may be slow, but we are making progress") is critical to maintaining hope when therapeutic progress is slow.

Older adults often live with severe restrictions (e.g., physical disabilities, fixed incomes). It is very important for therapists to set goals that are small enough for success to be achieved, even within very restrictive circumstances. Treatment goals that are stated in specific, quantifiable terms are easily monitored and offer the therapist a way of charting progress. For example, a 74-year-old woman with a history of multiple hospitalizations for schizophrenic episodes is referred along with her "schizophrenic" lover to a cognitive–behavioral therapist as she is being discharged from an inpatient unit. The therapist is informed that the discharge is therapeutically premature but administratively necessary (i.e., the hospital has no beds available). Is this a hopeless cause? Not if the therapist can create a treatment plan that is problem-specific (e.g., keep the patient and her lover out of the hospital for six months), with measurable units of progress toward specific treatment goals (e.g., number of social contacts per week; number of negative self-statements per day; number of couple conflicts per week). Both therapist and clients can experience success if the treatment goals are defined by small increments of thought and behavior change.

There are clients (e.g., depressed clients) for whom hopelessness is pervasive, and even specific, measurable treatment goals do not incite an optimistic response. Three principles seem to be effective in such cases. First, the therapist must stay focused on the treatment rationale and plan so as to maintain his or her own hope. Collegial supervision can be particularly helpful in maintaining an unwavering belief that change is possible through problem-focused treatment methods, even when progress is slow. Second, clients do not have to believe in the efficacy of a particular intervention for the intervention to work. Therapists may only need to contract with clients for change, not belief in change. Clients may not be optimistically involved in treatment goal-setting until a small change has occurred which can serve as the basis of hope. Third, therapists can solicit a commitment for treatment with family members whose involvement with the problem behavior may be indirect (e.g., a niece, sister, or son who lives nearby), but whose belief in the possibility and importance of change is strong enough to keep the family in treatment long enough for changes to occur.

In sum, I would like to suggest that a therapist's belief in the possibility of change is a necessary, although not sufficient, condition for productive therapy. Strong beliefs that change is possible are more likely when measurement of small increments of progress toward the overall goals can be incorporated into the intervention. Clients as well as therapists benefit from concrete evidence that learning is occurring and behavior is changing.

Maximizing Functioning

A common treatment goal for families with an older adult identified patient is to help the family learn to encourage (by their words and actions) the highest possible level of functioning in the older family member. For example, therapists often are approached by adult children who are distraught over their parents' diminished sensory, cognitive, or physical capacities. If these adult children perceive that the parents' health has declined sufficiently to place the parents in danger (e.g., vision deficits endanger driving), the children will respond to their assumptions concerning appropriate ways to protect their parents. The parents, however, may be afraid to receive help because of their belief that receiving help indicates dependence. Thus family conflict may be created when the children step in to "help out." As a general rule, in cases where competence is an important issue in the family conflict, it is helpful to assess thoroughly the IP's physical and cognitive limitations as soon as possible. This provides the information the therapist needs to address inaccurate beliefs (held by the IP or family members) about the IP's appropriate range of independence.

Physical incapacity due to a chronic illness or stroke is a difficult challenge to family members wanting to be supportive of independent functioning or helpful in areas where the patient is in need of aid. The following case illustrates the complex assessment tasks and case formulations required of a family therapist working with an ill older adult.

Mrs. S, a 54-year-old Hispanic woman, was referred by a physician who was frustrated and confused by her frequent reports of neurological symptoms (headache, vision blurring, limb numbness) and anxiety symptoms (inability to focus attention, panic attacks). A physical exam (including neurological examinations) had revealed a complex medical history which included childhood brain trauma from a car accident, a history of alcoholism (which had ended five years previously), and a moderately severe left-sided stroke four years earlier. Her current symptom reports were accompanied by requests for medication to resolve the symptoms, specifically requests for tranquilizers.

A psychologist was asked to assess Mrs. S for psychological dysfunctions that might influence her ability to report accurately her symptoms and to manage her distress without using medication. In addition, she was asked to assess the extent to which the family might be exacerbating the distress and reinforcing the sick role. Specifically, the physician suspected that Mr. S might be content in his role of caregiver, so that improvement in Mrs. S's health would upset the balance of their relationship. Mrs. S's children, on the other hand, were pressuring the physician to eliminate from her treatment all tranquilizers because of their anger at her history of substance abuse. The physician requested guidance in determining when to respond with medication to her undiagnosable reports of pain and anxiety.

The data from a cognitive assessment suggested that Mrs. S had multiple sources of brain damage which produced a significant expressive aphasia, mild receptive aphasia, and considerable difficulty maintaining attention in verbal tasks, which diminished her abilities to do verbal problem solving. In addition, she showed very poor cognitive self-control during problem-solving tasks as well as during normal conversation. Apparently she had used physical symptoms as her primary mechanism of experiencing and expressing her distress (i.e., she somatisized her anxiety and depression) throughout her life.

An assessment of family interaction was conducted in a family interview. During the interview Mr. S responded to the children's inquiries as to the legitimacy of Mrs. S's symptoms by angrily pointing out how many major illnesses and injuries she had endured. The daughter quickly and angrily retorted that her mother had always played the "poor me" game and used it to justify her alcoholism and child abuse. The daughter demanded that her mother begin to take responsibility for herself instead of using pills. As she listened to this interchange, Mrs. S began to tremble, and, placing her hands over her eyes, she claimed to have a terrible headache that disrupted her vision and ability to think. The therapist proceeded in the interview to focus on each family member's beliefs about Mrs. S's ability to function given her current physical condition. It became apparent that Mr. S believed that his wife's symptoms indicated she was about to have another stroke any minute, and that the children were hostile and unloving when they questioned their mother's symptom reports. The children believed their mother was using physical symptoms to escape responsibility, and that she could function quite well if only she were not being reinforced for her sick role behaviors.

The therapist began the family intervention by sharing information concerning Mrs. S's impairments. Specifically, she suggested that Mrs. S was cognitively impaired in ways that limited her ability to control her symptom expression as well as her ability to cope with anxiety-provoking thoughts (e.g., "People will think I'm stupid if I can't produce a common word in normal conversation"). The family was then invited to share in the process of making decisions about how to help her cope in ways that produced the greatest independence on her part. The therapist complimented Mr. S for his dedicated service to Mrs. S and encouraged him to push himself to give even more by engaging in this family problem-solving session. He responded that he was willing to go another mile if it would help her. The children expressed surprise at the extent of the cognitive impairment and began to reevaluate their reactions to her "crazy talk." Intervention with this family proceeded to focus on 1) demonstrating to family members the impact of their behavior on Mrs. S's mood, behavior, and ability to solve problems independently, and 2) helping family members identify various ways each could respond to her frequent symptom reports which would not exacerbate anxiety-induced symptoms but also would not ignore organically based symptoms.

This family's dilemma is common to families dealing with chronic illnesses: how to help appropriately. In this case, conflicting beliefs among family members about appropriate patient functioning and appropriate help were producing behavioral interaction patterns that accelerated tension and complicated the medical treatment of an ill woman. It is not unusual for healthy family members to believe themselves to be responsible for sick members and therefore either deny sickness in others so they do not have to carry such a burden (as the daughter did in this case) or assume the ill person's responsibilities beyond what is necessary (as Mr. S did). Errors in either direction lead family members to present an incomplete or distorted portrayal of the ill person's functioning. A functional assessment clarifies the exact range of behavioral functioning so the therapist can move with confidence to clarify levels of support needed to maintain the highest possible level of functioning in the older adult. Once the range of functioning is known, therapists and families can work together to determine the types of supports needed and to clarify the meanings of "dependence/independence" for everyone involved.

Empowering Family Members to Choose

Therapists frequently work with families toward the goal of making decisions. The need to make decisions concerning health care, housing, and intergenerational relationships is among the reasons families with older adult members seek help from psychosocial professionals. Three ways therapists can facilitate family decision making are by providing information, teaching decision-making skills, and clarifying family rules (common beliefs) about the process of making good decisions.

Providing information. The simplest level of therapeutic intervention is to provide information. Because it is simple to accomplish, it is probably one of the most frequently used and most powerful interventions. Many of the problems with which families in late life struggle are new to this cohort. The increasing life expectancy has created problems for members of the current elderly cohort with which no other member of their family may have dealt. For example, for the first time a large number of mentally retarded individuals are living into old age. Typically, mildly to moderately mentally retarded individuals have been cared for by their parents until their deaths in middle adulthood. With a considerable portion of the current cohort living into old age, a new problem arises for the siblings of older mentally retarded persons once the parents die. It is common for family members to choose to institutionalize a family member because that is the only choice about which they are knowledgeable. When a therapist can provide information about other levels of housing (e.g., board and care) or in-home services, a family can often proceed to make appropriate decisions. In many cases it is not the decision-making skills that are lacking, but knowledge of the range of options.

A powerful example of the impact of information has occurred over the past several years in the care of Alzheimer's patients and their caregivers. It has become increasingly clear that families provide a tremendous amount of care to Alzheimer's patients. Support groups for the caregivers and family members have evolved into one of the most popular modes of support for maintaining the demented person in the home as long as possible. One reason for the importance of the support groups is that members share information about managing the demented patient and, equally important, about managing their own stress. Both pieces of information place the family in the position of deciding how they will cope with the disease. Families without this information spend a lot of effort trying to solve behavior problems that cannot be changed, an effort which adds further stress to the caregiver when the burden of providing care is not understood.

The later part of life is full of events and changes (e.g., retirement, illness, and death) that can be frightening and mysterious. Information has the power of "normalizing" these in ways that reduce stress, anxiety, and depression.

Teaching decision-making skills. The decision-making skills needed by older families may be lacking for a number of reasons. Some families never learned good skills but were not faced with difficult decisions demonstrating their absence. Other families never learned them, and thus have a history of poorly made decisions that lead everyone in the family to dread facing future decisions.

One difficulty that often arises when multiple generations are involved in decision making is that families needing to make decisions concerning elderly family members often must work together in small groups in which they have never before tried to make decisions. For example, a mother and her adult son may need to make a decision concerning family finances while a father is recuperating from a stroke. This late life event may be the first time the two generations have worked together as colleagues with equal power. When working with peers in making decisions, communication strategies are quite different from those used in authoritative context. Although Mother may know how to communicate well with peers, she may need some cognitive intervention to encourage her to function with her son as a peer.

The simplest decision-making models seem to be the best for teaching families who are under time pressure and considerable stress how to work through a difficult decision. For example, D'Zurilla and Nezu (1982) present a simple, useful model for social problem solving. The steps include defining the problem in behavioral terms, checking previously attempted solutions, generating a range of possible solutions, evaluating the effects of each option, choosing the "best" option, creating a plan for implementation, implementing the plan, evaluating its effectiveness, and making appropriate modifications. There are many points in this process that may be stumbling blocks for a particular family. As with individuals and families of any cohort, a therapist's structured guidance can be most useful in clarifying the point at which they are blocked and teaching them skills to accomplish a particular step in the process.

Revising family rules. Families have rules governing both the process of decision making (which may need to be modified as noted above) and the range of acceptable ("good") outcomes of decision making. Most families develop acceptable ways (or rituals) for making decisions. There may be only a limited number of people in the family "allowed" to have the final say. There may be certain members whose roles are to criticize any and all options.

Some circumstances require that decisions be made in unfamiliar ways (i.e., in ways that break the rules for how "best" decisions are made). Many unexpected life events alter at least the familiar time frame for decision making, if not also the people available to make the decision. A decision made under less than optimal circumstances may be perceived to have been a "bad" decision (i.e., have produced a bad outcome) simply because the decision-making process was believed to be inadequate. Family members may feel guilty about placing Mother in a nursing home, even if that was the only realistic option, if the decision was made quickly or without input from all members of the family.

As mentioned previously, family rules about how tasks should be accomplished are usually embedded in the minds of individuals in terms of "right" and "wrong." Guilt, anxiety, and depression may result from individuals being pushed into making decisions in a way that feels "wrong." Cognitive interventions are needed to challenge the assumptions behind the blanket negative judgment and to begin the revision of individual beliefs and family rules. A therapist may ask the client to record her automatic thoughts that precede the guilt or depression. Examples of such thoughts include: "I shouldn't have stepped out all on my own. Maybe someone else in the family could have figured out something better. I was just being lazy to take the simple solution of putting Mom in the nursing home. I was putting my own pleasures above her well-being." These thoughts can then be analyzed for the accuracy of their content. For example, the source of the "should" could be questioned by considering the emergency nature of the decision, which did not allow others' input. In this case, the client can begin to sort out her realistic sadness about the nature of the required decision (nursing home placement for her mother), as distinct from unnecessary negative feelings about how the decision was made.

Therapists often need to question the family rules concerning who is and who is not allowed to make decisions. As the oldest generation's health, financial, and social resources decline, there are often changes in the pool of decision makers that is available. There may also be changes in the status of certain members of the pool. A previously passive wife may, upon her husband's death, allow her children to make decisions for her simply because she does not think of herself as a decision maker. A therapist observing the family's process may suggest that because the woman has no impairment in her ability to think and choose, it would be most appropriate for her to assert herself with her children and regain the responsibility for making choices relating to the estate. It is not unusual for a therapist to play the role of advocate for the oldest family members in cases where younger members carry inappropriate beliefs concerning the older person's capabilities, roles, and preferences. As an advocate, a therapist may focus on developing the older person's ability to think and act independently, by providing either skills training or cognitive interventions to challenge the individual's beliefs that he or she can or should enact behaviors that are within his or her repertoire. Therapists also may choose to be advocates for older clients by intervening directly with family members' beliefs and assumptions. In an advocacy role, a therapist can use a cognitive therapy strategy of gathering data to evaluate the validity of a particular belief or of questioning the logic of an overgeneralized belief. In the case of the passive widow just described, the family may be challenged to provide empirical evidence of the mother's inability to make a certain set of decisions (e.g., to demonstrate that she does not make *any* independent decisions in a given week, or to have a psychologist evaluate her competence to make decisions). An alternative strategy for questioning the family's assumption is to use logic to challenge their belief that because Mother did not make major decisions when Father was alive, she cannot do so now.

Siblings often have difficulties orchestrating decisions concerning their parents' care. A therapist may be asked by one sibling (the full-time caregiver) to call other siblings and request their help if the caregiver has tried to enlist help without success. Some of the most bitter family quarrels occur when a distant relative questions or criticizes the judgment of the caregiver. A large family meeting in which specific issues relating to the parents' care are enumerated, and a structured problem-solving approach is used, may be required to teach previously uncooperative peers a strategy (or rules) for working together.

Clinical Decisions

Is the patient really the patient? One of the questions that arises frequently when working with families of older adults is whether the older adult is the patient, or whether the family system is the patient. Usually the appropriate answer is that both ways of defining the patient are appropriate. As has been emphasized throughout this chapter, most situations involving older adults as patients relate to a real or perceived discrepancy between the older person's functional capabilities and the support available in the environment. It is critical for the professional to make an independent assessment of any functional deficits that make it appropriate to think of the older person as a patient in need of care.

On the other hand, it may be that the older person's deficits are a problem only because of the family's inadequate strategies for solving the problems generated by the older person's limitations. Once the older person's functional

capacities have been determined, the family may appropriately become the
targeted identified patient. In the latter case, the therapist's task is to raise
the question of how the family has created difficulties for itself by not engaging
in effective problem solving.

Who should be included in therapy? The simplest rule is that all those
involved in the problem should likely be involved at least in the assessment
phase. Involvement can be measured by determining 1) who has the right
to make family decisions, 2) who is involved in the daily functioning of the
targeted IP (e.g., the cleaning lady, transportation volunteer), 3) who controls
family resources (e.g., the lawyer from Uncle Jim's estate, the neighbor who
provides dinner every night for Grandma), and 4) who is *perceived* to hold
family power (e.g., a social worker or physician, or a long-distance daughter).
As a general rule, the more people involved in assessment, the better; constraints
usually come from the therapist's schedule rather than from a lack of
cooperation of those involved. All persons involved may not need to be
present in one meeting. Multiple smaller meetings are more useful for some
purposes (e.g., a therapist may meet with the client and his physician concerning
health care issues and with the client and his children concerning housing
issues). During intervention, decisions as to who to include are more varied,
and relate directly to the treatment goals. If the older person (IP) lives with
a spouse, it is wise to include the spouse. Older couples who are likely to
share many hours together each day have tremendous influence on each other's
thoughts, feelings, and behaviors. Otherwise, my bias is to include in regular
meetings only those most relevant to creating the changes. Usually all members
of a household are included, but since many elderly live alone, the therapist
must decide who are the relevant change agents and involve them in the
therapy. Family therapy with older families may appear to an outsider as
individual or couples therapy—it is the breadth of the assessment and the
conceptualization which encourage me to think of most of my therapy as
family therapy. Several meetings with individuals with various family members
may work more smoothly than a large family meeting. Periodic larger system
meetings can be useful in generating feedback on changes perceived from
different vantage points within the system, and to check on the need for
modifications in the original plan.

The therapist's role. As with any population, the therapist's role is determined by a combination of factors including the therapist's theoretical orientation to intervention, the client's beliefs about the therapist, and any
constraining factors the therapist's agency imposes. Therapists operating within

a cognitive–behavioral model typically think of themselves as teachers, program developers, and program evaluators. With older adults, supporter and advocate may also be appropriate roles.

The current cohort of older adults tends not to be very sophisticated concerning mental health professionals, and brings into therapy a wide variety of beliefs concerning the therapist's role (Zarit, 1980). Although I have not always found it critical to socialize clients into the traditional ways of thinking about being a client, I have found it important to clarify the contract for change. One client referred to me as "that nice young student who needs me to help her with some research." After working for a while on the issue of who was helping whom, I discovered the client was willing to contract with me for change (in the informal sense of contract) even though she was not willing to think of herself as anything other than a "helper" with my research. Later in the therapy we were able to look back on her condition when we first met and agree that she, in fact, had wanted help to work on a variety of problems. It is not always necessary, or even desirable, to label your contact with families as "counseling" (Herr & Weakland, 1979). Families who need help may not be able to tolerate the concept of "counseling." Unless it is interfering with obtaining a working commitment to change, it is almost always best to use the client's language (e.g., "I need some information," "to see what someone else thinks about this," or "we're going to try to make things work more smoothly for everyone").

The therapist's job context may constrain the roles available to him or her. In community mental health centers the number of sessions therapists can spend with one client may be limited. Therapists in an outpatient medical clinic may be limited to consultative and referral roles. On the other hand, an administrator at a senior center may have considerable latitude in deciding on the depth of intervention he or she is willing to engage in with a particular client. When working with the elderly, therapists often see more needs than can possibly be met with the staff provided by a particular agency. Furthermore, private practitioners often see needs of individuals who have no financial resources to pay for treatment. Herr and Weakland (1979) emphasize that professionals making contact with the elderly frequently encounter individuals and families that appear to be appropriate for intervention, and that simply making the encounter is not sufficient cause for choosing to initiate that intervention. One must decide how available he or she is able to be; to step beyond one's availability is a set-up for burnout.

The structure of therapy. Special rules concerning the structure of therapy with older families are needed primarily under three conditions: 1) when one or more of the clients exhibit cognitive deficits (even mild deficits can require changes in the learning environment); 2) when clients are extremely naive concerning psychotherapy; and 3) when clients are physically impaired in ways that preclude the use of the traditional 50-minute hour in the therapist's office.

As mentioned previously, normal aging typically takes some toll on cognitive processing. To compensate for cognitive losses, it is helpful to slow the pace of therapy and to increase the number of repetitions of any new learning experience. Structured homework often is useful because it provides additional repetitions of newly learned skills or strategies. Structured homework assignments that involve more than one family member provide family members with additional opportunities for observing existing family rules (shared beliefs and behavior strategies that govern interaction), experimenting with new rules, and practicing new rules. It is particularly important to have older clients practice new behavioral and thought strategies actively within the session before sending them out to practice their homework assignments due to the need for an increased number of learning trials.

Because fewer older adults have received mental health care than members of other cohorts, older families seeking help may need special accommodation to therapy. When working with a 94-year-old man and his 88-year-old wife concerning the panic attacks the man was experiencing, it became a therapeutic ritual to restate at the beginning of each session the purpose and contract for therapy as distinct from the more passive medical interventions with which they were familiar. Over a period of weeks the couple began to think of our work as active experimentation with their thoughts and behaviors, but it took a cognitive intervention to change their expectations concerning our respective roles. There are therapy-naive clients in all age groups; older families simply are in the cohort that is least likely to have received mental health services previously.

Some of the behavior problems encountered by older adults are secondary to physical illness. Chronic illness patients and their families may require unique structure for their therapy sessions. For example, the length of a session may be determined by a patient's capacity to focus attention or to maintain bladder control. Transportation limitations resulting from physical incapacity may provide such a major barrier to seeking mental health services that gerontologists may practice in a medical clinic, a patient's home, or a senior center in order to minimize that barrier. In fact, facilitating the clients' use of public transportation to get to the therapist's office may be an early goal of therapy. The most basic rule for structuring sessions appears to be flexibility.

Chronic illness patients (and their families) seem to be particularly hungry for information concerning the behavioral components of their diseases. Bibliotherapy often is extremely useful. Local chronic disease associations and support groups can provide therapists with a suggested reading list of books which their participants have found helpful. Even for the generally healthy, books such as *You and Your Aging Parent* (Silverstone & Hyman, 1982) provide information that adult children may find useful in anticipating planning with their parents, and in thinking through their own beliefs about aging.

TECHNIQUES FOR JOINING WITH THE FAMILY

Joining with an older family is in most ways similar to joining with a younger family. It is critical to the process of joining with any family that a therapist be able to reframe the problem in ways that help the family see themselves as normal people struggling with common problems of living, that empathize with the pain of living with the problem(s), and that complement the efforts already invested in solving the problem(s).

Using the Clients' Languages

One of the first challenges in initiating a collaborative relationship with older families is finding languages that fit the clients' models for defining their problems. Although this process occurs in therapy with any family, there are cohort-specific languages that are more familiar to this cohort of older adults and therefore more likely to facilitate joining. Consider the difference between "low" and "bummed" as descriptors of depression. The former is much more likely to open doors of communication with the elderly. Of course, language is indicative of a larger framework for "explaining" emotional or behavior problems. The therapist's use of a "wrong" word can let clients know that they are not understood. For the current cohort of older adults some terms which depict increasing reliance on others (e.g., "lacks responsibility for self," or "is dependent") may be interpreted as implying failure to care for self as a moral weakness, much as would have been the case at age 30. The client's response (e.g., "I take care of myself—nobody is responsible for me but me") corrects the therapist's errors in use of language. Considerable distress can be avoided by using the client's language to whatever extent possible in wording questions and devising interventions (e.g., "need a little help," "given all you've been through, it sure seems like time for others to lend you a helping hand").

Offering Realistic Hope

A common complication of the process of joining with older families is the therapist's confusion concerning the relationship between hope and reality. The social and physical circumstances of the elderly can appear, especially to young therapists, to offer little hope for an acceptable quality of life. Consider an 85-year-old woman who lived alone since her husband's death five years ago, and who is depressed. She lives with chronic pain, relies solely on a social security pension for income, and has sensory and physical impairments that make it difficult for her to leave her home. Her only daughter and son-in-law live 500 miles away. Her major social contact is with the woman who brings her meals once a day. It is the children who contact you to help their mother. Where is the hope?

A cognitive–behavioral therapist has been trained to think of problems in behavior-specific ways. As noted, specificity enables the therapist to measure small gains. It also teaches a therapist to think in terms of the smallest possible changes in a client's behavioral repertoire, cognitive framework, or environment that can produce positive changes in a person's mood. In this case, the therapist began working within Lewinsohn's model for conceptualizing and treating depression (Lewinsohn, Youngren, Munoz, & Zeiss, 1978). The client learned relaxation skills and imagery techniques for pain management. With encouragement she identified a variety of potentially pleasant events which required minimal activity. She easily identified a set of frequent negative self-statements. The goals of increasing the frequency of pleasant events *and* her ability to enjoy them (by controlling the degree to which her pain was the center of her attention) were primary. The therapist decided that the client needed some experiences (even small ones) which demonstrated her ability to control some aspect of her life. In this case the frequency of pleasant activities was an easily measured variable which would provide rapid, concrete feedback. Once the client began attempting pleasant activities, her negative thoughts began to intrude. DTRs were used to monitor negative thoughts, and Beck's model for cognitive intervention was used to identify the relationship among the thoughts, mood, and tendency not to initiate pleasant activities (Beck et al., 1979). This woman was able to regain some control of her activities, thoughts, and mood under extremely adverse circumstances. The family was involved in this treatment as sources of information about activities she had found pleasant earlier in life. In this case it was also important to teach the family appropriate ways of responding to her complaints of pain (e.g., to remind her of her pain control strategies). Even at a long distance this family was a strong mediator of the client's mood.

In other cases similar to this one, more drastic interventions could be appropriate (e.g., helping the family decide to move the client to a housing facility with supportive services and built-in social networks). Clients who cannot manage to feed, bathe, and clothe themselves or who are too depressed to care for themselves need to be placed in a more supportive, structured environment which ensures their physical safety before treatment of the depression would be appropriate.

Therapists working with the elderly for the first time inevitably encounter their own helplessness when attempting to help those with multiple problems. Although wide-eyed optimism is inappropriate, the therapist's hope is critical. When joining with a family, a therapist needs to find small, concrete goals which are clearly within immediate reach to elicit positive client expectations.

Acknowledging Age Differences

Most therapists working with older families are significantly younger than their clients. In the "joining" phase of therapy this age discrepancy may be referred to explicitly ("You are just a child—you couldn't possibly understand what it is like to lose a spouse") or implicitly ("Your generation can't imagine what it was like during the Depression"). Therapists who have wondered about their ability to empathize with older adults because they have not "walked in their clients' shoes" must first work out a rationale for themselves (e.g., "I've never been schizophrenic, alcoholic, or phobic either, but I have skills, knowledge, and caring that enable me to work effectively"). The therapist may then decide it is useful to broach the subject with the clients. Herr and Weakland (1979) note that arguing about one's ability to understand completely is silly. As an alternative, they suggest acknowledging the age difference and inviting the client to help the therapist understand. In some circumstances I have found it useful to acknowledge the unfortunate circumstance in mental health care whereby we lack elderly therapists. The general task is to acknowledge clients' concerns, to invite their involvement in working to overcome the barrier, and simply to clarify your willingness to work with the clients to whatever degree they wish to involve you.

SPECIAL CLINICAL ISSUES

Multidisciplinary Perspectives

The importance of integrating information from a variety of disciplinary perspectives cannot be overemphasized. Older adults' lives are complex, usually incorporating multiple problems. Multiple physical illnesses, low social status, diminishing social networks, special housing needs, and fixed incomes that often are inadequate for basic self-care all contribute to the complex mental health needs of this population. As stressed previously, a broad, careful assessment of physiological and social bases of psychological dysfunction is critical. Meetings and phone calls involving practitioners from several disciplines (in addition to written reports) are advantageous in cases of even moderate complexity.

Low Rate of Positive Social Reinforcement

A major problem in late life is the diminution of sources of positive feedback and self-esteem. I sometimes find it useful to switch between individual sessions, where we can work intensely on learning new behaviors and thought patterns *and* where I can load the socially impoverished patient with positive feedback, and family sessions in which we can examine inter-actional patterns which maintain ineffective behavior and thought patterns. Although I know of no data to warrant this decision, switching back and forth seems to portray to the clients the critical symbiosis between the individual's adaptation and the structure of relevant environmental contin-gencies. Most families seem to hear both parts of the message: 1) that the older person must adapt to the familial environment, *and* 2) that family members can facilitate or impede the success of that adaptation by changing their behaviors.

Unveiling Family Secrets

Individual family members introduce family secrets into therapy with older adults for much the same reason that they do so in any family: to inform the therapist that family members' ways of thinking about the problems at hand are more complex than the therapist realizes. Two common types of family secrets involve sibling conflict and long-term marital conflict.

Most cases in which children must make decisions regarding a dependent parent are presented to the therapist because of family conflict. It is not unusual for one sibling to call to "explain" the system to the therapist. As with most "secrets," it is ideal to convince the sibling to contribute his or her ideas to a family session where everyone relevant to the IP is present. Of course, this ideal often is not met either because such individuals refuse to join such meetings or because they participate in meetings and remain silent, withholding their "secret."

In either case it is important for the therapist to stay focused on the problem at hand. If a practical decision concerning, for example, housing must be made, other issues may be irrelevant. The critical issue is to explore options for making the decision and working with the family on issues related to mobilizing the family. The secret information may have been interesting or even useful, but if it is not relevant to the problem at hand, it is unnecessary for *this* particular session.

There are times when a family member will share a secret over the phone regardless of the therapist's desire for a family conference. It is not unusual to hear something like, "I simply couldn't be in the room with my sister. It eats all over me to watch her playing 'dutiful daughter.' I want you to know that she has never given my mother anything but grief since she was born. Now she pops on the scene wanting to make all these decisions. Even though my husband and I have visited my mother every Sunday, taken her food, cleaned her house and done her laundry, we will *not* get involved with my sister, so we won't be at your 'family meeting'!"

Now that the "secret" of serious sibling conflict is known to the therapist, a decision must be made about how best to address the original problem (concerning the parent). Certainly the secret information clues the therapist into some parameters in the process of problem solving, but in most cases it should not be allowed to divert family members' attention from the task at hand. Clearly, the sister who shares this information carries some strong beliefs about how daughters ought to treat their parents (e.g., "Dutiful daughters should take care of mother's daily needs") and about the right to make decisions ("Only dutiful daughters should be allowed to make major decisions"). Identifying these beliefs may help the "dutiful" sister decide how she wants to deal with the "pampered" sister in making decisions about their mother.

Marital "secrets" involving conflict, infidelity, and incest may also be offered in the course of therapy. A 60-year-old couple sought sex therapy for the problem of impotence. A physical exam revealed several potential physiological reasons for the impotence (history of cardiovascular disease including several bypass surgeries). As the therapist proceeded in several sessions to work with the couple's beliefs about the relationship between intimacy and sexuality, the man began to cry. He left the session and called the therapist the next day to explain that his wife had engaged in a series of affairs over the past 20 years, only to return and proclaim him "her best lover." He was convinced that sexual activity was his only chance of holding her in the marriage. This "secret" placed his previous resistance to reframing sexuality as only one expression of sensuality (and not necessarily the most important one) in a different light. The therapist was forced to deal with his sexual functioning as conceptually related not only to intimacy, but also to commitment.

This man was able to introduce into the therapy sessions his fear that without sexual intercourse in their relationship his wife would not believe she had a complete marriage and might turn to others for sexual contact. Even though no explicit statement of her previous affairs was made, the issue of commitment to the relationship was brought into a prominent position in their sex therapy. The man's fear of acknowledging the affairs kept him from discussing them overtly, but he was able to identify and articulate several of his fear-evoking thoughts which had induced him to seek therapy. Specifically, he discovered that when he anticipated sensual or sexual activity he automatically started thinking that he was inadequate to satisfy his wife and that without sexual intercourse their relationship would not last. The therapist helped him gather information from her concerning the accuracy of his automatic thoughts. The conversation that ensued focused on the issue of commitment to the relationship. Once it was clear that she was committed to the relationship regardless of his impotence, he was able to change the focus of his thoughts during sensual moments. He focused his thoughts on a series of statements she made to him which reassured him that she was committed to the marriage. When he had mastered using these alternative thoughts, he was able to begin teaching her to enhance his sensual pleasure, a process which resulted in increased intimacy in the relationship and successful completion of her sexual response.

A therapist's first response to secrets must be to question their role in altering the goals of therapy. Even in cases where the goals are not altered, the secret information is likely to alter the process of treatment by introducing more complex cognitive frameworks for the therapist to use in conceptualizing the problem. There are occasions when the "secret" information reveals dysfunctional beliefs which must be modified before treatment can proceed.

Conflicted Families

Although the preferred arrangement for working with conflicted families (e.g., the "dutiful" and "pampered" sisters described previously) is to have everyone present, it just may not be possible regardless of the therapist's outstanding persuasive skills. Once again, flexibility is the hallmark of working with the complex family constellations so often confronting a gerontologist.

A first step in arranging meetings with conflicted families may be deciding how to decide who to exclude from which portions of the decision making. In the case of the angry sisters it may be most appropriate for the current caregivers (the "dutiful" daughter) to have a major role in determining which level of supportive housing Mother needs, and for the "pampered" daughter to be involved in other decisions. The therapist may enlist help from the family in making that choice or may offer it as the therapist's terms for working with the family. Therapists must recognize the constraints offered by the family structures within which they must work. A divided and conflicted family is not likely to allow Mother's therapist to resolve decades of division. Family members may, however, accept that the therapist is only able to work toward solving Mother's problems under certain conditions, and that if they fail to meet those conditions the therapist will have no services to offer them. Once again, clarifying the specific problem with which you are enlisting their involvement and the specific conditions under which you are able to work offers them the option of using your services on your terms or resolving the problem on their own.

Self-Help Groups

Concurrent use of self-help groups is especially useful when the clients' major concerns center around issues relating to chronic illnesses. The Alzheimer's Disease and Related Disorders Association offers local self-help groups for family members of patients with Alzheimer's disease. Local hospitals often offer groups for family members of patients with specific disorders as well as for the patients themselves (e.g., heart disease, osteoporosis, Parkinson's disease, cancer). Self-help groups offer the opportunity for clients to accept their own family experiences and to develop a way of thinking about the adequacy of their responses to the current stress. These are particularly wonderful adjuncts to cognitive–behavioral therapy for caregivers for whom considerable stress results from unfamiliarity with an IP's disease (etiology, course, prognosis) and with the normal range of emotional responses in caregivers. Concrete problem solving may occur in these groups, drawing on the array of experiences represented in the group. The family therapist is then available to deal with other issues relevant to family functioning.

Financial Concerns

Private practitioners and agency administrators deal daily with the difficulty of working out payments for elderly clients who typically are on fixed incomes, with Medicare or Medicaid as their primary health care funding. Hospitalized patients needing nursing home placement are very often caught in untenable situations in which the only source of funding is Medicaid, and Medicaid requires the liquidation of all but the most basic assets the family may have worked so hard to save. I know of no magic cures for this problem which arises so often in work with older families. My rule of thumb is to work hard with members of other generations to generate as broad a list of alternative funding sources as possible. There have been occasions when older parents living in a child's home could be covered under the child's health insurance. More often, the children coordinate payments among themselves. Sometimes a local organization (church or civic club) will sponsor the health care of a particular family.

Most gerontological mental health practitioners I know choose to offer a portion of their services to indigent clients, but the portion never matches the need. Some practitioners choose to work in multidisciplinary settings where their services can be billed under a physician's name so that Medicare and Medicaid will reimburse them. (Note, however, that the restrictions are difficult to work within. Medicaid and Medicare require physicians to be on the premises when services are offered and require allied health practitioners to be "supervised" by the physician. Furthermore, treatment of only a very restricted set of disorders will be reimbursed. Medicare has a very low ceiling on the reimbursements for mental health services within a year.) Perhaps this is an area that will best be dealt with on a political level rather than a case-by-case basis. Under the current government policies, mental health care of the elderly is severely impeded by the poor provisions of Medicare and Medicaid.

CONCLUSION

The cognitive–behavioral model provides a useful structure for identifying, evaluating, and intervening with problems that frequently arise in older families. Physical, social, and cultural changes that occur in late life affect the behavioral functioning of the older individual and his or her family members because of their impact on the functional capabilities, perceived capabilities, or environmental supports of the older person. Assessments which cover an array of factors relevant to the functioning of older adults are the first critical step in treatment. Data generated from a functional assessment can be organized within a cognitive–behavioral framework to identify specific thought and behavior patterns which warrant more detailed assessment. Interventions with the elderly require the therapist to clarify his or her beliefs and values regarding change in late life and to focus the interventions toward specific, measurable changes that maximize older adults' independent functioning and empower families to make decisions. Most therapy process issues that arise when working with older families are dealt with as they are with younger families. Intergenerational family involvement, the cognitive deficits that can result from physical illnesses, and the stress of losses in late life are specific concerns that often alter the therapy process with older families. Therapists must exercise some caution in determining when cognitive–behavioral interventions might interfere with a normal developmental process or serve as a politically coercive force that would not maximize older adults' functioning.

REFERENCES

Beck, A.T. (1967). *Depression: Clinical, experimental and theoretical aspects.* New York: Harper and Row.

Beck, A.T., Rush, A.J., Shaw, B.F., & Emery, G. (1979). *Cognitive therapy of depression.* New York: Guilford Press.

Beck, A.T., Ward, C.H., Mendelson, M., Mock, J., & Erbaugh, J. (1961). An inventory for measuring depression. *Archives of General Psychiatry, 4,* 561–571.

Beck A.T., Weissman, A., Lester, D., & Trexler, L. (1974). The measure of pessimism: The hopelessness scale. *Journal of Consulting and Clinical Psychology, 42,* 861–865.

Bowlby, J. (1980). *Attachment and loss: Vol. 3. Loss: Sadness and depression.* New York: Basic Books.

Duke University Center for the Study of Aging (1978). *Multi-dimensional functional assessment: The OARS methodology* (2nd ed.). Durham, NC: Duke University.

D'Zurilla, T.J., & Nezu, A. (1982). Social problem-solving in adults. In P.C. Kendall (Ed.), *Advances in cognitive–behavioral research and therapy* (Vol. 1, pp. 201–274). New York: Academic Press.

Fillenbaum, G.G., & Smyer, M.A. (1981). Reliability of the OARS multidimensional functional assessment questionnaire. *Journal of Gerontology, 36,* 428–434.

Gallagher, D., Breckenridge, J., Steinmetz, J., & Thompson, L. (1983). The Beck Depression Inventory and Research Diagnostic Criteria: Congruence in an older population. *Journal of Consulting and Clinical Psychology, 51,* 945.

Gallagher, D., & Frankel, A.S. (1980). Depression in older adult(s): A moderate structuralist viewpoint. *Psychotherapy: Theory, Research and Practice, 17*(1), 101–104.

Gallagher, D., Nies, G., & Thompson, L.W. (1982). Reliability of the Beck Depression Inventory with older adults. *Journal of Consulting and Clinical Psychology, 50,* 152.

Gallagher, D., Thompson, L., Baffa, G., Piatt, C., Ringering, L., & Stone, V. (1981). *Depression in the elderly: A behavioral treatment manual.* Los Angeles: USC Press.

Gurland, B.J., Kuriansky, J., Sharpe, L., Simon, R., Stiller, P., & Birkett, P. (1977). The comprehensive assessment and referral evaluation (CARE)—Rationale, development, and reliability. *International Journal of Aging and Human Development, 8,* 9–41.

Hagestad, G.O., Smyer, M.A., & Stierman, K. (1984). The impact of divorce in middle age. In R.S. Cohen, B.J. Cohler, & S.H. Weissman (Eds.), *Parenthood: A psychodynamic perspective* (pp. 247–262). New York: Guilford Press.

Herr, J.H., & Weakland, J.J. (1979). *Counseling older adults and their families.* New York: Springer.

Hill, R., & Mattesich, P. (1979). Family development theory and life span development. In P.B. Baltes & O.G. Brim (Eds.), *Life-span development and behavior* (Vol. 2, pp. 162–200). New York: Academic Press.

Hussian, R.A. (1981). *Geriatric psychology.* New York: Van Nostrand Reinhold.

Jackson, D.D. (1965). The study of the family. *Family Process, 4,* 1–20.

Kazniak, A.W. & Allender, J. (1985). Psychological assessment of depression in older adults. In C.M. Chaisson-Stewart (Ed.), *Depression in the elderly: An interdisciplinary approach* (pp. 107–160). New York: Wiley.

Lawton, M.P. (1983). Environment and other determinants of well-being in older people. *Gerontologist, 23,* 349–357.

Lawton, M.P. (1986). Functional assessment. In L. Teri & P.M. Lewinsohn (Eds.), *Geropsychological assessment and treatment* (pp. 39–84). New York: Springer.

Lawton, M.P., Moss, M., Fulcomer, M., & Kleban, M.H. (1982). A research and service-oriented Multilevel Assessment Instrument. *Journal of Gerontology, 37,* 91–99.

Lewinsohn, P.M., Youngren, M.A., Munoz, R.F., & Zeiss, A.M. (1978). *Control your depression.* Englewood Cliffs, NJ: Prentice-Hall.

Linn, M.W., & Linn, B.S. (1984). Self-Evaluation of Life (SELF) Scale: A short comprehensive self-report of health for the elderly. *Journal of Gerontology, 39,* 603–612.

Mahoney, M.J., & Arnkoff, D. (1978). Cognitive and self-control therapies. In S.L. Garfield & A.E. Bergin (Eds.), *Handbook of psychotherapy and behavior change* (pp. 689–722). New York: Wiley.

Parkes, C.M. (1972). *Bereavement: Studies of grief in adult life.* New York: International Universities Press.

Poon, L. (1985). Differences in human memory with aging: Nature, causes, and clinical implications. In J.E. Birren & K.W. Schaie (Eds.), *Handbook of the psychology of aging* (2nd ed., pp. 427–462). New York: Van Nostrand Reinhold.

Pruchno, R.A., Blow, F.C., & Smyer, M.A. (1984). Life events and interdependent lives: Implications for research and intervention. *Human Development, 27,* 31–41.

Schaie, K.W., & Willis, S.L. (1986). *Adult development and aging* (2nd ed.). Boston: Little, Brown.

Silverstone, B., & Hyman, H.K. (1982) *You and your aging parent: The modern family's guide to emotional, physical, and financial problems.* New York: Pantheon.

Toffler, A. (1970). *Future shock.* New York: Random House.

VandenBos, G.R., Stapp, J., & Kilburg, R.R. (1981). Health service providers in psychology: Results of the 1978 APA Human Resources Survey. *American Psychologist, 36,* 1395–1418.

Wechsler, D. (1945). A standardized memory scale for clinical use. *Journal of Psychology, 19,* 87–95.

Wechsler, D. (1981). *WAIS-R manual.* New York: Psychological Corporation.

Zarit, S.H. (1980). *Aging and mental disorders.* New York: The Free Press.

8

Cognitive–Behavioral Approaches to Family Treatment of Addictions

Stephen E. Schlesinger

The direct and indirect costs of addictions impose a formidable burden on the economy and social fabric of the United States. Alcohol abuse has been recognized officially for nearly two decades as one of this country's major health problems (National Institute on Alcohol Abuse and Alcoholism, 1971). The abuse of other drugs remains significant, alarmingly so among younger Americans. Smoking, long linked to a variety of debilitating and lethal health complications, continues in the public eye as a major source of preventable primary and secondary illness. Other addictive behaviors—most notably eating disorders and compulsive gambling—have come into the public spotlight somewhat more recently.

Self-help movements and ideologies were the first to offer addicts rehabilitative options, and they remain the most prevalent influence on treatment. While individual and group therapy approaches to addictive problems have been in use for some time, the addition of family therapy techniques to the treatment arsenal is only relatively recent. This is now considered an option for treating addiction to alcohol and other drugs (Coleman & Davis, 1978), although one which may be used infrequently (Regan, Connors, O'Farrell, & Jones, 1983). It does not appear that family treatment is as widespread in treatment of other addictive disorders, such as gambling, smoking, and eating disorders. For this reason, the focus of this chapter is on family treatment of addictive disorders involving alcohol and drugs. Therefore, in this chapter "addict" refers to those physically or psychologically dependent on and those who abuse drugs and alcohol. "Addictive families" refers to the families of addicts.

Family approaches to treatment of addictions have been based on systems theory (e.g., Ablon, 1976; Baither, 1978; Berenson, 1976; Bowen, 1974; Davis, 1977–78; Davis, Berenson, Steinglass, & Davis, 1974; Distasio & Harbin, 1977; Fram & Hoffman, 1973; Harbin & Mazier, 1975; Hinkle, 1983; Kaufman & Pattison, 1981; Klagsburn & Davis, 1977; Lawson, Peterson, & Lawson, 1983; Stanton, 1979; Stanton, Todd, and Associates, 1982; Steinglass, 1977, 1980), psychodynamic principles (e.g., Paolino & McCrady, 1977), principles of transactional analysis (e.g., Steiner, 1971), holistic approaches (e.g., Rosenberg, 1981/82), and behavioral principles (e.g., James & Goldman, 1971; Miller, 1976; Noel & McCrady, 1984; O'Farrell, 1982). Structural family therapy techniques seem to predominate among current approaches to the treatment of addictive families, though there is some debate about their efficacy (e.g., Olson, Russell, & Sprenkle, 1980; Sowder, Dickey, & Glynn, 1980). From this systems perspective, addictive behaviors function as part of a network of interactions, and they both result from and perpetuate certain dysfunctional aspects of family life. Some view the addictive behavior as the ingredient which maintains the family's homeostasis by providing a focus for family interactions which diverts attention from other, less palatable family problems (e.g., Stanton et al., 1982). Others suggest that addictive family systems are rigid and that addicts exploit the rigidity in some manner in order to maintain their addictive behaviors (e.g., Wegscheider, 1981, 1983), although the incentive for addicts to do so is sometimes obscure.

Cognitive–behavioral treatment of families is infrequently mentioned in general in the literature and almost never in family treatment of addictions. This chapter considers such treatment.

Treatment of addictive families presents several special issues which are discussed later in the chapter. I want to comment on one here, however. It concerns the matter of who is involved in treatment. My *preference* is to work with the whole family, including the addict. However, *necessity* sometimes dictates working only with nonaddicted family members if an addict is unwilling to participate, is organically impaired, or is simply too disruptive for treatment. It is common in families whose addicts refuse to participate in or are excluded from treatment to see family change bring about a change of attitude in the addict resulting in his or her inclusion in treatment later in the therapy.

Addictive family life typically is chaotic. Chaos stems in part from the addict's behavior and in part from the family's interpretations of and responses to that behavior. Addicts frequently use a lot of money to support their habits and diminish or deplete family resources. One cocaine addict, for example, used all of her family's $42,000 savings in the six months before she entered treatment. Family members frequently cannot rely on addicts. The mother of a 6-year-old could not plan anything for her mid and late weekday afternoons because her husband was often too intoxicated to pick the child up at school. Addicts often deplete family members' emotional resources. "I can't go through this again with you. I don't know how to explain your junkie friends to the kids any more. I've reached the end of the line," was the way one exasperated father described his predicament to his barbiturate-addicted wife. Some families are embarrassed by the public behavior of their addicted relatives and withdraw into the isolation of their homes. One family's social life "dried up because we couldn't take the humiliation when John would get drunk at friends' houses or out in public."

Family members frequently feel insecure about their future as a family, devote increasing amounts of time and energy to thinking about the addict, and are uncertain about when the next crisis with him or her will occur. One 14-year-old's school and extracurricular lives "took a nosedive because I always think about Dad. Will he show up at school and make a scene? Is this the day the police will come and take him away again? Boy, is that embarrassing! I can't stop thinking about it." Often family members perceive the addict as malicious (e.g., "Why is he *doing* this to us?" or "He's drinking to hurt us") or lacking in care (e.g., "If he really loved us, he wouldn't be doing this"). Some see the addict's behavior as evidence of a major family flaw (e.g., "You don't see this sort of thing in healthy families").

A COGNITIVE–BEHAVIORAL VIEW OF ADDICTIONS IN A FAMILY CONTEXT

An addictive family's dysfunction can be approached from the perspective of the nonaddicted family members or from the perspective of the addict. Usually the former is the one that brings the family to treatment.

The family's problems can be viewed initially with respect to three areas: members' beliefs about family life, their expectations concerning the likelihood that certain unpleasant events will recur, and the manner in which members explain the nature of their predicaments.

Beliefs about family life involve a set of hopes and aspirations about "ideal" family life which members develop in part from families of origin (parents) and in part from observations of other families and representations of family life in various media. Family members typically report frustration and diminished hope in the face of a clash between their images of the ideal and their current family experiences.

As a result, family member's *expectancies* are frequently formalized about the likelihood that certain unpleasant events and patterns will recur. The past becomes prologue in their eyes, and members begin to predict that they have only chaos to anticipate. Expectations of change—or of the capacity to change—by family members or the addict frequently diminish. Family members form assumptions about the addicted relative's actions, and they often place those actions in order of seriousness. One family, for example, measured the severity of their predicament by the method by which the addict became intoxicated. When he drank, family life "seemed to be eroding," but his eventual intravenous injection of other drugs signaled "complete debauchery" on the part of the addict and a profound deterioration of family values. Preoccupation with the addict and his or her drug-taking behaviors distorts the family's vision and cements members' negative expectancies about family life.

To explain the apparent disintegration of family life, members develop *attributions about the causes of their turmoil.* In addictive families, these frequently focus on the addict, often to the exclusion of other factors not related to his or her addiction-related behaviors. Family members often begin to think alike, and the collective family ability to see alternatives to its dilemmas suffers.

Each family member observes relationships with and among other family members, and he or she frequently sees chaos. Relationships, patterns of contact, and communication opportunities tend to be inconsistent. The ability to predict and influence important aspects of the family declines, and with this goes part of each individual's sense of efficacy as a member of that family. Communication skills and opportunities often are impeded as the addiction draws more and more of the family's attention, further precluding resolution of these deficits. Those problem-solving skills on which the family otherwise might draw frequently are submerged. Taken together, these forces leave many addictive families exhausted and demoralized. It is in this state of cognitive depletion that families often come for help.

ASSESSMENT

Assessment of addictive families varies somewhat according to the manner in which they present themselves for treatment. Initial assessment issues are standard. First is the matter of whether a family presents itself for treatment of problems related to addictive behaviors of one or more members or for treatment of other problems. Assessment always includes inquiry into drug and alcohol use of all members, and it is frequently important to focus first on any active drug or alcohol abuse. It is generally accepted by those treating addictive problems that whatever other family problems may exist cannot be resolved while the abuse continues actively, including those related to the addict's behavior. In some cases addictive families request treatment for other problems, and it is important for therapists to help them focus on the identified addiction-related problems as well. For this reason, it is important to inquire about addictive problems as part of the comprehensive initial assessment.

Further assessment hinges on whether the family appears with or without its addictive member and on whether the addict is actively involved in his or her addictive behavior.

Families that include their addictive relatives in treatment frequently identify that member as the cause of much of their trouble. Although it is important for the therapist not to underestimate the impact of an addictive process on the family, so too it is important not to subscribe at the outset wholly to the family's inclination to cite the addict as both its demon and its savior. A comprehensive picture of the addictive behavior is desirable, including the role of family matters in the mediation of the behavior.

Assessment of addictive behaviors can be done handily in the presence of other family members, but if it has not been accomplished prior to the family's involvement in treatment, it is not necessarily appropriate to undertake in the first family session. To do so may elevate the addict's behavior implicitly to a position of prominence in the family's turmoil before the therapist has had a chance to evaluate the family's overall level of functioning.

The assessment of addictive behaviors is most useful when it is specific and helpful in describing the addict's behavior as both the response to certain contingent circumstances (including cognitive appraisals) and the stimulus for future appraisals both by the addict and by family members. The Comprehensive Drinker Profile (CDP; Miller & Marlatt, 1984) is an example of such an interview guide. The CDP asks a detail about a drinker's pattern of alcohol consumption and yields a view of his drinking in standardized units for comparison across beverages whose absolute alcohol content varies. It also identifies typical circumstances which precede (and may seem to trigger) drinking episodes and those which are associated with the termination of such episodes. This is helpful for putting the addict's behavior—in this case drinking—into its context, identifying factors that precipitate and maintain it, and for describing its relationship to family functioning.

Several other matters are of interest when the family presents itself for treatment. First is the status of interactions in the family. Some families appear for therapy at a point at which interactions are still intact but are in danger of deteriorating; others appear only after interactions between members have been distorted. Characteristics of families in the latter category include cognitive factors such as confused attributional styles and belief systems, impaired communication skills, dysfunctional negotiation strategies, and faulty problem-solving abilities.

Assessment of Cognitive Factors in Addictive Families

No comprehensive instruments exist which measure cognitive factors specific to addictive families. Nevertheless, several types of cognitions are the foci of initial assessment: *attributions* family members make about the causes of their problems, *beliefs* members have about family life in general, and *expectations* about their own family's life, about the course, tempo, and outcome of treatment, and about family life once the addictive behavior ceases. Before treatment begins, the therapist must have formulated the family's perspectives in each of these areas.

Attributions about family problems. Family members both define and explain family problems for themselves. It is important to probe the family's matrix of attributions for what has caused and is maintaining the family's difficulties. In this regard, the first attribution to be voiced frequently is blame directed at the addict's disruptive behavior. Initially, however, it may not be possible for the therapist to develop a sufficiently comprehensive picture of the family's behavior to evaluate whether the addictive behavior results from or has caused family turmoil, whether there has been some combination of the two causal processes, or whether the addiction is independent of family matters.

One family was referred for treatment by their 41-year-old, amphetamine-abusing father/husband's individual therapist, and they came without J (the addict). For several reasons, the family and J agreed that he would not join them in treatment. His wife and three children described a family life that was "just about as perfect as you can get" until J started using drugs. With his therapist's concurrence, J agreed to talk individually with the family therapists and described a traumatic adolescence and early therapeutic experience. He viewed his marriage and early family life as peaceful and fulfilling and described his drug use in the same way as his family had. He used drugs at work for two years to get through long days in his high-pressured job, but eventually he began using them at home as well. As drug use increased, J used more money to maintain his habit, and the family became more and more isolated in order to avoid being embarrassed by his behavior in public. In this case, the therapists treating the family concluded that family problems seemed to be more the result of than contributors to J's drug use.

For M's family, however, the conclusion was different. She was a 16-year-old marijuana user whose drug connections were made in her high school. Her behavior began to deteriorate two years before the family came for treatment. She was doing poorly academically, despite being extremely capable. Her social life evaporated, despite her past popularity. The precipitant that brought the family to treatment was M's arrest for marijuana possession, an arrest which occurred in a manner that was extremely humiliating for the family.

The family initially described a chaotic set of family circumstances which her mother, father, younger sister, and younger brother attributed to M's drug use. Her older brother, however, gradually described a chaos merely made worse by the marijuana use, but originating earlier in marital discord and its resultant "hard feelings and hard times" over many years prior to M's drug use. In this family's case, treatment began as the therapist helped members clarify the family's problems and understand M's drug behavior as an outgrowth—and an important one at that—of prior family difficulties. Prominent among these was the difficulty her parents had resolving their own problems. Their communication styles prohibited an accurate initial airing of each other's positions. As they both became aware of the deterioration of a particular effort to discuss a problem, they switched their attention to M so as not to face the collapse of the effort ("If we had, what would that have said of us?"). M perceived this unwanted attention as unbearable ("What was I supposed to do, just stand there? Solve their problems?") and turned to her friends and their drugs for relief.

Beliefs about family life and family roles. Beliefs each member has about family life and the roles each member "should" play constitute an important reference point against which members compare their current functioning, progress in treatment, and the outcome of their efforts to change. In many cases, however, these basic beliefs are not expressed openly by family members. Several are of particular interest in a cognitive assessment. First is an assessment of beliefs each member has about who should be doing what in the family (who cooks, cleans, earns money, provides technical support, is available for emotional support, etc.; "In a functional family, fathers do . . ., mothers do . . ., and children do . . ."). Addictive families frequently describe radical violations of these beliefs as drug and alcohol use increasingly impaired the addicts' functioning in the family. One woman agreed before her marriage that her husband would "work and I would do the housework and raise our kids." They had two boys and two girls, and the children's initial functions in the family followed analogous gender lines (e.g., the girls helped Mom cook and clean, and the boys took out garbage and helped with home repairs). As the husband drank more and more, the family's income declined as he was demoted and then fired from his job. At that point, his wife went to work to support the family and attributed her involuntary role switch to what she called her husband's "defects."

A second important category of belief involves how the family should be handling problems ("When problems arise, families should . . ."). It has been my experience that addictive families frequently at once believe that families *should* be handling problems in some effective manner, but that theirs *cannot* deal with their problems successfully because of the drug use. In this regard, it is important to know, for example, whether families believe that they and subsequent generations are doomed to disruption, regardless of their efforts, because, in the words of one father, "This is like a disease that is passed on from parents to their children. We can't stop it!"

It also is important to assess beliefs about how in general the family should be functioning. One family came for treatment with its opiate-addicted member (the father) and a long history of general dissatisfaction by family members with family life preceding his use of drugs. Primary among the factors influencing the chronic dissatisfaction was what the wife came to call the "Brady Bunch Factor"—families were "supposed" to be virtually problem-free and able to overcome even potentially catastrophic problems with dispatch. Those families that could not were irretrievably damaged, as she, her addicted husband, and their three daughters believed of themselves.

Beliefs about family life and family roles frequently are learned in members' families of origin and applied to their subsequent families of procreation. In some cases, they are the products of other influences such as the media (e.g., movie or book themes) or observed relationships among members of other families. However acquired, they prescribe for an individual certain aspects of family life against which to measure his, his relatives', and the family's overall performance.

Expectations. Expectations addictive families bring with them into treatment tend to be of four general types. First are expectations each has about the

motivation and capacity for change of other family members, particularly the
addicted relative. Frequently these are negative with respect to the addict and
take the form of "We've been through this so many times and it hasn't
worked"; or "He says he'll try, but we've heard that before"; or "He's said
it so often, I don't think he could do it if he tried."

Past experience aside, the extent to which family members assess negatively
the addict's determination and ability to change influences their predictions
about the potential futility of their investment in treatment. Probing their
assessments in this area begins the process of explicating their expectations
for future family life and determining the potential that negative predictions
may confirm themselves.

The second set of expectations to be assessed are those concerning *treatment
itself.* These fall broadly into three categories: the course of treatment, its
tempo, and its outcome. Discussion of family members' views of the course
of treatment focuses on their and the addict's hopes for treatment, for
members' involvement in the treatment process, and, often, the implicit wish
that therapy—and specifically the therapists—will "fix" the addict, who may
be seen as the "broken" cog in the family wheel.

Family members often have global expectations for the *course of treatment*
which may not include their participation, for example, in an examination
of their own cognitive appraisal mechanisms. One family came for treatment
and stated explicitly, in response to one therapist's invitation to describe their
views of family functioning, that "It's him [the addict], not us. He's doing
what he's always done, and it's tearing us apart. When he stops, we'll be
OK. There's not much we can do in the meantime, is there?"

Family members often harbor ideas of how long it will take to complete
treatment. The family of one cocaine-addicted executive came to the first
session, minus the addict, and announced their "full faith that we'll be able
to wrap this up in a couple of visits." Ideas about the *tempo of treatment*—
rate of change and total time to resolution—form a timetable which guides
members in their ongoing assessment of progress in and their satisfaction with
treatment. Their expectations are best elicited early in treatment and evaluated
with family members in realistic terms.

The third of this triad of expectations concerns the *outcome of treatment*—
where will it lead? Will the family be together or not? Will the addict still
be a member of the family if it is? Will he or she still be an addict? Will
the family still have problems? Sometimes members enter treatment with
expectations of its outcome based loosely on hopes, assumptions, and prior
beliefs about family life and the obstacles to its enjoyment. Where these

exist, expectations of gloom and Nirvana can be equal impediments to adequate involvement in treatment.

The final expectation to probe during assessment concerns family members' visions of *family life after the addictive process stops.* To the extent that family members perceive their problems to be related fundamentally to the addiction, their expectation for change may turn on the sole criterion of interruption of the addictive cycle. Discussion of postaddiction life gives the therapist an idea both of how narrowly focused the family is on the addictive process and of how realistically it views the process of recovery of adequate functioning after the addiction stops.

The assessment process gathers information not only on the cognitive styles of addictive families but also on their behavioral styles and deficits. The following is a summary of behavioral factors typically covered in such an assessment.

Assessment of Behavioral Factors in Addictive Families

Behavioral assessment focuses on family members' communication styles, the abilities to express their needs and dislikes effectively, and their ability to identify, tackle, and solve problems effectively.

Communication styles. The assessment of communication styles and the identification of potential deficits in communication start with an exploration of which topics tend to form the core of family interactions (the content of communication). In families with a disruptive addictive process, much of the interaction among members stems in some way from that addiction. Frequently little else rivals the amount and type of interaction stimulated by the addict(ion). The therapist may conclude that the proportion of the family's interactions devoted to the addiction, the cognitive content of those interactions, or both, will be matters to address early in treatment.

The second focus of assessment concerns the communication pitfalls which afflict family members' attempts to talk to one another (their style of communication). The following 10 pitfalls occur with striking regularity: interrupting, jumping to conclusions, diversions to unresolvable matters (including fixing blame, establishing the "truth," trying to make others feel guilty, and calling other people names), mind reading, predicting futility, use of extreme terms, use of vague language, turning statements into questions, responding in ways which inhibit further discussion (including summing up too soon, reverting prematurely to proverbs, and attributing one's own or another person's behavior to unalterable personal characteristics), and tackling too much at once.

The presence of one or more of these pitfalls may impede not only the family's ongoing interactions but also its ability to negotiate solutions to its most pressing problems. As the pitfalls appear, the therapist offers explanations of them to families and returns to them later in treatment as the issues recur. Although these can apply to *any* family, my experience has been that they arise commonly in addictive families. Schlesinger and Horberg (1988) discuss these pitfalls in greater detail.

Expression of needs and dislikes. This next focus of assessment involves the degree to which each member can tell the others what he is thinking and feeling. One aspect is how assertive each can be with other family members. This may be an area of future treatment focus. At this point the succinctness of members' expressions, the degree to which they state or ask for something clearly, and the extent to which verbal and nonverbal messages are compatible are the foci of observation. Addictive behaviors introduce distractions into a family's life and frequently impair members' abilities to state clearly what they want from other members. In part this results from a preoccupation with the addict's disruption. In part it results from the strong emotions (e.g., anger, frustration) which that disruption engenders in family members and which obscures members' previous abilities to express themselves effectively. Schlesinger and Epstein (1986) proposed several aspects of assertive behavior (e.g., clear statements of feelings and requests) which the current assessment seeks to illuminate.

Problem-solving and negotiation skills. Some families are unable to identify family problems successfully and to generate and negotiate effective solutions. These difficulties are perhaps exacerbated in addictive families because of the chaos which the addictive process frequently injects.

Unfortunately, a comprehensive system for observing in detail and coding an addictive family's systematic problem-solving and negotiation abilities would be quite cumbersome for clinical applications. Nevertheless, attention to this area is vital, in part because these family skills will influence members' abilities to implement planned changes in the family as therapy progresses.

There are several aspects of problem solving that the clinician should observe. First, how systematic are family members in identifying the crux of a problem? Can they make it concrete enough to operationalize it? Second, how well do family members brainstorm alternative solutions? Do they restrain others' contributions or seem to censor their own expression of potential solutions? Third, can they evaluate systematically each of the generated alternatives and negotiate among themselves to choose the most acceptable to all? Fourth, can they implement, evaluate, and if necessary change solutions which they choose? Observation of assigned behavioral tasks is most helpful in this endeavor. Choosing a small problem described by the family and asking members to work on possible solutions affords the therapist an opportunity to view the family's problem-solving and negotiation abilities in action and hints at family members' capacity to perform adequately in solving problems outside of the therapy.

The clinician should observe two aspects of the family's problem-solving efforts. If the addict is present in treatment, it is important to note whether a diminution of his cognitive faculties (likely largely related to his drug or alcohol use) impedes his ability to contribute adequately to the family's efforts. The second aspect can apply whether or not the addict is present. It concerns the degree to which the family focuses its attention solely on the addict and his or her behavior. Although attention to this major aspect of family life is understandable, the success the family ultimately will have in resolving its problems may rely on its ability to see beyond the addiction.

In sum, assessment of addictive families focuses on addictive behaviors of family members; the generic and addiction-related cognitions pertinent to family problems, life, and roles; and expectations of treatment and of life beyond treatment. Behavioral factors of importance are communication styles, expressive capacities, and skills of problem solving and negotiation.

The concept of family "enabling" behaviors which support the addictive process is missing from the preceding discussion. Enabling is a primary concept in some family views of addictions (see, for example, Wegscheider, 1981, 1983). It refers to acts by family members which protect the addict from the consequences of his or her behaviors and thereby permit (or encourage) perpetuation of the addictive process. Some such acts may seem more active (e.g., buying beer for the drinker, bailing the addict out of jail) than others (e.g., providing room and board for an addicted child), but their effects are seen as the same.

From a cognitive–behavioral perspective, "enabling" is not *one* aspect of the family's functioning. Rather, it is incorporated into the behavioral and cognitive life of the family and discussed in the part of treatment which deals with the addictive process itself. The negative reinforcement paradigm represented by a wife's call to her husband's boss to explain a "blue Monday" as "the flu" is placed in the context of its ability to reinforce the addict's weekend drinking by relieving him of the anxiety of calling his boss. But attached to her actions are the wife's cognitions. These cognitions represent themselves in the addiction-related behavior (the phone call), but they typically influence other aspects of family life as well (e.g., "A good wife is supposed to do what her husband asks, even if she doesn't like it"). In this sense, instances of "enabling" *behaviors* may yield an incomplete picture of an addictive family's dysfunction if separated from the *cognitions* with which they interact and by which the behaviors are influenced.

Let us turn our attention now to the strategies and techniques of treating addictive families.

CLINICAL STRATEGIES AND TECHNIQUES

Initial Decisions

The first decisions about treatment usually concern who will be treated. Typically, these decisions focus on the roles addicts, children, and members of families of origin will play in treatment.

Will the addict be included in treatment? The decision about whether addicts join their family members in treatment involves all of the principals. The addict may remove himself or herself from candidacy by refusing to participate. In this event, the addict's behavior becomes an issue in treatment as the family extracts itself from involvement in the addictive process and normalizes its functioning apart from the addiction.

Alternatively, families sometimes elect to enter treatment without their addicted relatives, in many cases after several previous unsuccessful attempts to approach solutions to their problems jointly with the addicts. They exclude the addicts in part because of their frustration and in part because of their increasing conviction that joint treatment will be unproductive.

Some families come for treatment without a *nonaddicted* member whose participation in treatment and whose role in the addictive cycle is crucial in the therapist's opinion. In such an event, the therapist must decide initially whether family treatment is feasible without that member. If not, the therapist can try to invite the member for an individual session to hear his or her perspectives on the addictive process, on other family problems, and on his or her reluctance to join the rest of the family for treatment. If the member is, in the therapist's opinion, inextricably involved in the family's problems and therefore indispensable for treatment, the therapist can try to persuade the member to join the therapy. If the member still declines to join the family for treatment, the therapist should consider terminating treatment for the family. In this event, the therapist should refer members for individual or group treatment to deal with identified problems.

Whether exclusion of addicts is by their own or their families' hands, treatment in their absence frequently allows family members the opportunity to detach themselves from the addictive cycle and may eventually serve as an impetus for the addict to become involved in treatment later, sometimes at the family's invitation. Although it might be argued that because of the effect his or her addiction has on the addict, treatment of a family in the absence of its addicted member is unlikely to progress very far, it is important for many families to strengthen themselves before tackling the task of reintegrating the addict. Addictive families tend to be disorganized, emotionally depleted, and distracted from using skills they have or could learn and bring to bear on their difficulties. Frequently families can profit from the opportunity to develop their strengths without their addictive relatives.

Will children be included in treatment? The issue of whether children should be involved in treatment is relatively easy to answer. Yes, they should be, with two exceptions. First, children are best not included if they are too young to participate in or understand the treatment sessions. Usually, however, children in an addictive family are able to describe and react to family disruption at a surprisingly early age, and the danger may be that young children are too readily *excluded*. Second, children who are included in treatment generally may be excluded for specific portions of the treatment which focus on intimate aspects of their parents' relationship.

Some families are concerned that bringing young children to treatment will expose them to the addictive behavior and in some way predispose them to the unacceptable aspects of the addict's lifestyle. This amounts to a fear of contagion or corruption of youngsters. Whether the addict is an adolescent whose parents fear an undue influence on younger siblings or a parent whose spouse is concerned about the "example" he or she may set for the children, the concern is usually based on an assumption that the children know little about the addict's behavior. In my experience, children have proven to be savvy observers of their relatives' behaviors, and they deny themselves the opportunity to talk about their views openly with other family members. They know what is going on. However, children often misattribute the addict's inconsistent and unreliable behavior to some personal fault in the child. Including them in treatment allows children an outlet for their observations, for clarifying their attributions, and for garnering support from other family members.

Will families of origin be included in treatment? Deciding to include members of families of origin in treatment is sometimes appropriate but usually cumbersome. Frequently family problems arising from an addictive disorder are related to attitudes and behaviors learned by members during their formative years. To the extent that a family's difficulties are related to issues in a family of origin, it may make sense to include members of the extended family in treatment.

Generally there are two considerations that influence such a decision. One concerns the extent to which members of the extended family have direct influence on the problems presented by the addictive family. The greater the influence, the stronger is the rationale for including them. In this regard, the family to be treated is the "family of relevance," a unit which includes those whose involvement with the addictive family's current problems is compelling and influential.

The in-laws of one alcohol-addicted family head were included in treatment because they lived with the drinker and his three children and were intimately involved in the family's life. For example, they frequently passed messages between their drunken son and his wife or children which minimized or distorted the seriousness of his drinking, and they stepped in at times when their daughter-in-law sought to confront her husband about the extent of his drinking and its impact on the family. Their intent was to minimize "friction in the family, which is not good." The set of behaviors stemming from this belief was unacceptable to the family and, in treatment, the in-laws concluded that their actions were unproductive, however well intentioned.

The second consideration undertaken in the process of deciding whether to include members of the extended family is a practical one. Increasing the number of family members in attendance frequently renders the treatment unmanageable, however appropriate it may be to include additional members. A larger number of participants crowds the treatment area, but it also increases geometrically the interrelationships to which the therapist's attention is drawn, and it magnifies the cognitive complexity of the treatment. Although it might be argued that seeing the complexity is vital for therapists and that cotherapy is an alternative to handle this potential problem, at some point it may render treatment immobile.

Clinical Strategies

Broadly conceptualized, treatment strategies resolve themselves into three areas. The first is *to clarify family members' initial conceptions of the flow and product of treatment* by eliciting their expectations of treatment itself. It is at this point that the therapist elicits expectations noted at the assessment stage for consideration by family members.

Frequently family members enter treatment without much knowledge of the addictive process impinging on them. Their attention has been focused on disruptive aspects of the addict's behavior and on the attendant confusion the family experiences. Typically the family has no clear standards for realistic expectations regarding the course, tempo, and outcome of treatment. A steady course at a fast pace toward an ill-defined but "better" family lifestyle are objectives commonly voiced.

However, such family goals are insufficient for treatment purposes. Several items need clarification for the family. First, the therapist needs to explain the *course of treatment,* including the components discussed later. This socialization into treatment also includes appropriate education about the effects of alcohol or drugs as used by the addict, the nature of addictions, and family roles in addictive processes. Frequently families of addicts anticipate treatment vaguely as a set of instructions to help them, in the words of one child, "climb out of our pit." The common expectation that the family's role in treatment will be passive ought to be dispelled early in therapy.

Second, families often expect that the *tempo of treatment* will be rapid, that treatment will proceed at an even pace, and that their involvement in treatment will be brief. Although this is sometimes a reasonable expectation, often it represents an impatience borne in part of frustration; that is, "The problem is [the addict's]; why should we spend a lot of time talking about it? Let him solve it." This expectation also may stem partially from the family's tendency to minimize dysfunctional aspects of their interactions other than those associated with the addictive process. That turned out to be the case in the family of the adolescent (M) mentioned earlier whose previous family discord played a role in her marijuana use.

The *outcome of treatment* is the focus of the last set of the family's initial expectations the therapist should probe in treatment. Often these concern family members' conceptions of the nature of family functioning following treatment and the role the addict will play in the posttreatment family. Implicit in many families' assignations to treatment is the belief that treatment will "improve" life by making things "better." Although these are laudable goals, their vagueness invites disappointment both with treatment and with its outcome. Clarification of these hopes, often frustrated in the past, involves the therapist providing a description of specific treatment objectives, including intermediate steps on the way to the family's end goals and criteria which operationalize "improvement" and "better functioning" in behavioral terms. One family, for example, was aided in describing some objectives which pertained to their addicted teenager (e.g., "He will be attending school regularly with no suspensions for six months"; "He will participate in family activities like dinner and vacations") and some which addressed other areas of family problems (e.g., "Mom and Dad will talk together for 10 minutes a day"; "In the next three months, we will restart our social life by inviting the R's and the G's [whose invitations they had wanted to reciprocate for six months] for dinner").

The role of the therapist at this stage of treatment is less directive than it becomes at later stages. As described in Chapter 1, it involves probing the three areas described above, encouraging as much family input as possible. A Socratic method of step-by-step logical inquiry is helpful at times as a way to clarify concepts that challenge the family. At other times the therapist can introduce interpretations (e.g., "You seem to want something immediately") to clarify issues. The goal is to help the family members draw a clear picture of their expectations and place these into a realistic framework for evaluating their and the treatment's progress and outcome.

The second strategy in treatment is *to increase effective communication and negotiation skills* among nonaddicted family members (and among them and addicts, when addicts are included in treatment) and to shift the focus of attention from the addiction to family functioning. This is not to say that the addictive process is not a legitimate focus of part of the treatment effort; clearly it is, to the extent that the family must wrestle with an active addict's daily behavior and their responses to it. An initial step in "getting better," however, is a shift by the family from a preoccupation with the addictive process, which most frequently remains beyond the family's direct control, to changes in its own functioning, which decidedly *are* in its control. This involves learning a set of skills, and it involves an active, sometimes educative role for the therapist. As the family increases the effectiveness of its skills, members often find that the impact they have on the addict increases. At this point family members can focus on their interactions with the addict.

At this stage of treatment three areas are appropriate foci of treatment. One concerns the attributions family members have formulated, the second focuses on communication and negotiation skills, and the third concerns setting and adhering to limits.

Attributions. Members of any family draw conclusions about their relatives which help them explain why the others act the way they do. Often this is a means of producing more manageable, simplified summaries of the causes of the large number of pleasant and unpleasant events which occur among members.

Addictive families frequently focus on negative attributions to explain interactions among members, particularly with addicts. The chaos common in addictive families obscures both clear analytical efforts by members and accurate perception of relevant data. Negative actions by other family members are frequently attributed to global traits (e.g., "He's a self-centered bum") and pernicious motives (e.g., "All he ever wants to do is argue and pick fights with me"), whereas potentially positive actions are rendered suspect (e.g., "He does that when he wants something from me"), much as Baucom, Bell, and Duhe (1982), Fincham and O'Leary (1983), and Holtzworth-Munroe and Jacobson (1985) described in relationships of distressed couples. Missing from this attributional process is the ability to identify and capitalize on the sometimes subtle fluctuations in their relatives' actions which, if exploited, could provide a foundation for change in the family. Addictive families often have developed rigid patterns of thought and interaction, so the ability to observe deviations in their patterns and to incorporate these observations into their interactions is a significant initial achievement.

Awareness of fluctuations in relatives' behaviors helps break established patterns of inflexibility, fear, and hopelessness by providing cues for family members to implement skills learned in treatment. Partly as a result of members' reactions to the long-term stress of living with an addict, including experiences with their relatives' past relapses, attributional styles in addictive families frequently lead members to attend selectively to the negative (or potentially negative) behaviors of their relatives, to ignore or discount positive behaviors, and to generate irrationally pessimistic conclusions about the worth of treatment ("What's the use?") and the durability of positive changes during therapy (e.g., "She's set in her ways. She'll change back to the way she was.").

The first steps in reversing this insidious process are for the family members to define the network of attributions they have made about each other and about relationships among other members, and then to learn to gather data to evaluate the accuracy of those shorthand explanations of their relatives' behaviors and motives. The latter objective involves *discrimination training,* the process of helping family members become better observers of their own and their relatives' behaviors (see, e.g., Liberman, Wheeler, & Sanders, 1976). This focuses on the application of improved observational skills to the assessment and, where applicable, reformulation of conclusions drawn about relatives. The object is to help family members become more accurate observers of each other and to draw rational conclusions about each other's behavior.

Discrimination training begins after the nature of each member's attributions about the others has been defined. It is accomplished typically by homework assignments followed by analyses in sessions. The therapist offers an explanation about the genesis and role of attributions in family life and about the selective negative attentional processes that sometimes distort the observational abilities of members of addictive families. Of particular interest are attributions members make of each others' actions in the therapy sessions, which the therapist can elicit with members as a model for families to use between sessions. The therapist then can help each family member select one of his or her negative attributions concerning another family member as the focus of the homework to follow. Frequently members choose conclusions they have made about the addict. These are best avoided initially, especially if the addict is still actively drinking or using drugs.

Family members are instructed to keep journals of observations of the "target" relatives' behaviors, both positive and negative, as they bear on the selected attributions. Journals are brought to the subsequent session for analysis. For example, in an initial family therapy session, the 20-year-old sister of a cocaine addict attributed her mother's concern about her college grades to "her view of me. She doesn't think I can make it on my own. She always harps on me; she never shows me she believes in me." A subsequent weekly journal revealed several observations this young woman made that she believed supported her conclusion (e.g., "She asked me if I had enough gas in my car"; "She told me I shouldn't hang around with Betty") and several more that suggested otherwise (e.g., "She asked my advice on buying a dress she wanted"; "She complimented me on getting a summer job").

Initial analysis of each journal's entries is for applicability to the target attribution. Subsequent analysis consists of weighing each relevant entry as evidence which supports the identified attribution or challenges its accuracy.

Communication training techniques. Communication training techniques typically begin with exposure to listening and expressive skill development and then proceed to assertiveness and negotiation skill techniques. Because family members often see communication as taking place mainly in dyads, the initial focus here is on structured techniques of interacting with family members singly. The rationale given to the family for this approach at this stage is that the contributions each member makes to family life depend on his or her skill as an effective communicator, as both expresser and listener; the more skillful each becomes, the higher the probability that he or she will contribute constructively to the family's life. Sometimes a member asks, "What does this have to do with X's drinking?" In this case, the point is reviewed that family members are affected by the drinking and can benefit from becoming more skillful in these areas, and that only by becoming more skillful can they realistically hope to have an impact on the addict.

The focus on listening and expressive skills starts with Guerney's (1977) Relationship Enhancement techniques. These are highly structured, interactive procedures through which family members learn to listen actively to others, to communicate their understanding of others' expressed thoughts and feelings, and to acknowledge their respect for their relative's good will, in spite of any disagreements of differences of opinion. Homework involving listening skills and techniques for offering nonthreatening feedback is a frequent adjunct to therapy sessions. During sessions, the therapist is active and directive in teaching principles and in formulating exercises to implement those principles. Cotherapist pairs may model these skills for family members. The interested reader will find Guerney's (1977) book an excellent source on the theory and techniques associated with Relationship Enhancement skills.

Gottman, Notarius, Gonso, and Markman's (1976) book on communication is another excellent source both for therapists and for family members for a related set of techniques. Gottman and his colleagues have developed strategies for couples which help them reduce communication pitfalls that derail partners' communication and perpetuate distortions and misunderstandings. These strategies combine attentive listening skills with effective feedback techniques, and they focus on helping each member engender and communicate a sense of good will to the other. Although the skills Gottman et al. (1976) describe were developed for couples, they readily can be applied by all family members to alter their dysfunctional communication patterns and distorted perceptions of one another.

Assertiveness training techniques with addictive families follow from the clinical observation that, in part because of the disruption of the addictive cycle, members cannot be assertive effectively. Addicts frequently are seen as avoidant, unassertive, or, alternately, as manipulative. Family members often have difficulty setting limits on addicts or on their own involvement with them. Sometimes family members become angry or frustrated and try to induce changes in addicts by means of aggressive actions. As their relatives become aggressive, addicts perceive these interactions as aversive and do not respond in the manner that the relatives had hoped. Family members need help to develop more effective communication styles, both with addicts and among themselves, when their communication has become aversive and ineffective.

It is important for therapists to ascertain from nonaddicted family members how assertive they are with each other and to understand both how assertive they are with the addict and how assertive he or she is with them. Frequently communication with addicts is hostile.

As described in Chapter 1, the therapist describes a two-component model of communication to the family. Because the *nonverbal component* is often the less obvious to family members than the *verbal* components, therapists model assertive communication to illustrate consistent (verbal and nonverbal agree) and inconsistent (verbal and nonverbal disagree) communication.

Among the components that emerge as members begin to identify the nonverbal aspects of their own communication are *eye contact, facial expressions, body posture, gestures, quality of voice* (often referred to as a paralinguistic channel of communication), and *timing*.

Families are asked to focus on three aspects of the verbal portion of assertive communication when organizing their thoughts before speaking. Because an important goal of assertive communication is to be brief and to the point, they are encouraged initially to generate a series of three-sentence messages: 1) a statement of the topic one wants the listener to consider, 2) a statement of one's emotional reaction to the topic (with emotions clearly distinguished from thoughts), and 3) a statement of what one wants of the listener. If a family adopts this three-step model, hostile verbal interchanges can be reduced as family members learn to state their reactions to specific situations explicitly.

The wife, two daughters, and son of an amphetamine addict were distressed because he frequently arrived home under the influence of the drugs he obtained at work. His tenure at work was protected by his influential position, and little pressure was exerted by his employer to stop his use of "uppers." Family members had tried to tell him of their displeasure with his evening (and frequent weekend) drug use, but to no avail. With assertiveness training, they collaborated to fashion a three-sentence request: "When you use drugs, you act crazy at home and you ignore us. We feel angry and hurt that you seem to prefer the pills to us. We want you to stop using drugs, and we will not be involved with you any time you're high." It took several attempts to get their message across to him, including the use of the "fogging" technique described later when he reacted belligerently.

Family members sometimes have difficulty reducing a thought to three sentences and may feel awkward when they hear themselves speak succinctly and directly to others. The experience, however, is more important than feeling awkward at first. It is the substance; the form can be adjusted later for personal comfort.

These new skills initially are practiced during therapy sessions by means of role plays. Role-play situations are best chosen from among a family's past experiences rather than generated by the therapist. Family members frequently offer the negative when asked to think of examples of communication problems. That is, they suggest a matter in which one member has reacted negatively and wants another to *stop* something. Although this is an appropriate application of assertiveness training, another point is sometimes overlooked; improved communication among family members typically requires both asking others to do *less* of what is abrasive or disruptive and giving them positive feedback by asking them to do *more* of what a family member *does* like. Learning to ask for what they want can have an important impact on members' expectations of what they can reasonably expect from their relatives.

Part of assertiveness training with addictive families involves an introduction to several ancillary techniques. Two concern ways to deal with responses to assertive messages. A third involves negotiating with relatives. The therapist cautions the family that just because one formulates and delivers a well-crafted, assertive message does not guarantee success. Others may not appreciate or respond to these efforts in the manner one desires. Sometimes relatives ignore the assertive efforts.

The first ancillary technique, the "broken record" technique (Smith, 1975), may be appropriate for this situation. When the receiver of a message changes the topic, the sender is encouraged to use the concept of timing (e.g., to wait until the other completes the response) to provide a summary of his or her understanding of the receiver's reply using the techniques of Relationship Enhancement described by Guerney (1977). When the receiver acknowledges that the sender has understood his or her reply accurately, the sender is encouraged to restate the original three-step message ("I understand that; however . . . "). This refocuses attention on the original topic and allows both family members to feel satisfied that they have been understood.

Sometimes in addictive families responses to assertive messages may be a good deal more hostile, perhaps in the form of personal insults or verbal attacks. Such insults and attacks frequently are offered as bait to derail and deflect communication on a particular issue. The assertive response to this, the "fogging" technique, is a modification of the "broken record" (Smith, 1975). Senders are encouraged to acknowledge (though not necessarily *accept*) such insults or replies as the receiver's opinion, then to return to the original message. A typical response might start with "It may *seem* that I'm incompetent, but . . . [original message]."

The third ancillary technique is called the "workable compromise" (Smith, 1975). It helps family members view step three of the verbal response (the stated request) as an opportunity to open negotiations with each other by offering (or responding with) suggestions of compromise. Such compromises often resolve what might otherwise develop into an impasse. An important application of the workable compromise technique is to develop flexibility in communication and to avoid becoming rigid in an assertive manner. Negotiation is the goal, and compromise is its key.

Practice of assertiveness skills in sessions and in homework assignments seems most fruitful when it involves recent family problems. Behavioral rehearsal is designed to provide experiential learning of the techniques, with feedback from therapists. Family members can hear themselves speaking directly to one another in new ways which allow each to be heard accurately.

Having taught families the skills of assertive communication and, through homework, having helped them apply the skills practically to their everyday lives, one has completed their exposure to communication skills. Before moving on to the next component of treatment, as a preventive measure the therapist presents them with a description of a series of potential obstacles to change. The therapist does not predict that these will occur but notes that they are important to recognize if the family experiences a lack of progress. Eight types of problems typically faced by families during the course of treatment are fear of the unknown, fear of change, getting over the hump, losing sight of the goal, getting hung up on details, embarrassment, dysfunctional communication, and inertia (see Schlesinger & Horberg, 1988).

The eight problems are presented to families in treatment as they begin to implement new skills. They are not intended as a listing of problems either which *will* occur in every family or which will occur in the order in which they are presented. Frequently they are identified in the course of treatment as families report being discouraged that, in the words of one father, "It's not as easy as I thought. By now, I thought we'd be on Easy Street." When these problems occur in the course of treatment, it has been my experience that discussing their implications with families is usually enough to restore the members' determination. The intervention is of the nature of a "fine tune" rather than a major overhaul of the family's efforts.

For example, one family discussed the increase in unacceptable behavior of their addicted member and concluded that it was "like you told us he would probably do when we started talking to him directly." They reported a decrease in both the anxiety and building sense of futility that had accompanied the initial observation of his behavior. Another family was discouraged when members' social lives did not improve "enough for us to notice." A brief discussion of their continued embarrassment and the cognitions which elicited it was sufficient, in the words of the 20-year-old son, "to get us back on track."

Setting Limits

The chaos reported by addictive families typically stems in part from an inability to formulate, set, and maintain effective limits on proscribed behavior. For those with relatives still actively drinking or using drugs, limits typically apply to the terms of the addict's relationship to the family. For those whose addicts are no longer drinking or using drugs, limits pertain both to acceptable non–drug-related behavior and to possible relapse. Setting limits is usually a more cogent issue for acceptable non–drug-related behavior. Helping family members set limits aids them in reducing their preoccupation with an addict's behavior and refocusing their attention on other matters.

Setting limits is presented as a series of steps, with appropriate exercises at each step to help families operationalize the process of instituting a set of limits (Schlesinger & Horberg, 1988). In step one, *families experience pain but often are unable to see specific problems that perpetuate the pain.* At this stage families typically feel overwhelmed and experience themselves in crisis. Despair, fear, anxiety, and demoralization quickly follow, as does a diminution of the family's skills of rational observation. This creates confusion, and the family members feel paralyzed in their attempts to deal with the addict. Identifying the relationship between their overwhelming feelings and their reactions to the confusion and sense of paralysis leads to step two.

In step two, *family members identify what hurts.* This is done by helping the family evaluate the addict's addiction-related behaviors systematically (e.g., intoxication at home, arguments about drugs and alcohol, physical abuse, sexual abuse, job problems) and rating the pain each type of behavior causes for the family (ranging from none to unbearable pain and worry).

In step three, *family members formulate limits to prevent the repetition of pain*. This follows from step two. Members are encouraged to look over their pain ratings, to define which level on their rating scale constitutes unacceptable pain, and to identify items rated at or above that level as behaviors which exceed their limits. At this point families have established inviolable limits.

In step four, *families learn to see themselves and their futures as separate from the addict*. This is an important step because, if family members cannot conceive of their future happiness without a close relationship with the addict, they will not risk alienating the addict. If the implicit "bottom line" is that the family will not separate from the addict as a final option, the range of options the family allows itself is truncated.

The process of helping family members work through this stage begins with an examination of their assumptions about the addict's current and future role in the family. The family is encouraged to examine assumptions concerning the addict's indispensability and, with techniques of imagery, to explore a future without him or her. Frequently the untested assumption of indispensability creates a great deal of anxiety, which, in turn, dissipates as imagery creates new possibilities for future family functioning without the addict.

For some family members the task at this stage triggers a sense of guilt at seemingly abandoning their addicted relative. Guilt typically follows from cognitions concerning what "good" and "bad" people do about addicted parents, spouses, and children. If this occurs, the therapist can help the family reexamine the rationale for setting limits in general (to help the family and likely have an impact on the addict) and for this step in particular (setting limits likely cannot be accomplished if the limit setter ultimately relies on the addict's acquiescence in areas that might offend the addict). Further, the therapist can examine directly with family members both the cognitions on which the "guilt" is based (e.g., "Good parents are available for their kids no matter what") and the conclusion that seeing themselves as separate actually constitutes "abandoning" their relative.

Step five involves helping *family members develop support for their (possible) separation from the addict and for the limits they set*. Support from outside sources helps family members cope with the stress which frequently accompanies their decisions to fashion future family life without the addict. In times of doubt, supporters help the family recall past pain and provide the family validation and encouragement concerning their plans for change. At this step therapists actively explore the establishment and maintenance of social support which is independent of the addict.

In step six, *family members communicate the limits to the addict.* This can be frightening, but as part of the family's effort to restructure itself without the chaos of the addiction, it is necessary. Limits are best communicated to addicts in simple, straightforward terms. Limits are rules (e.g., no drinking when driving; no drug use in the home; no more extramarital affairs) with clearly stated consequences for violation (e.g., loss of use of the family car; find someplace else to live; divorce). They are best communicated in a manner that is *brief and to the point* and tells the addict *one thing at a time.* Issues of safety (e.g., Will he react violently?) are important to explore with the family.

Having communicated the limits to the addict in step six, *family members recognize they must adhere to their limits* in step seven. Implementing new limits means acting differently toward the addict, and acting differently can be stressful. Family members are encouraged to call upon their supporters for help if their determination wavers during the period in which they feel uncomfortable. Therapists frequently are excellent sources of temporary support for the family as they "get over the hump."

The process of helping the family formulate, set, and maintain limits rounds out the second strategy in treatment. The third strategy is *to increase effective problem solving* among nonaddicted family members and, if possible, with the addict. This addresses the difficulty addictive families often have in making sense of their problems and constructing adequate strategies to solve them. Problem-solving training techniques are applicable in this regard.

Problem-Solving Training

Addictive families often lack the skills to analyze and understand their problems. Components of their difficulty contaminate one another, and members may be left with the impression that they are helpless in the face of hopeless problems. Problem-solving training addresses itself to these feelings and their sequelae.

Problem-solving training is applied to the treatment of addictive families in three phases. In phase one members operationalize—or define clearly—their problems. In phase two they learn to brainstorm for possible solutions. In phase three they choose an agreed-upon solution. The material covered along the way is consistent with the work of Falloon, Boyd, and McGill (1984), Jacobson and Margolin (1979), Platt and Spivack (1975), and Stuart (1980), and it is described in greater detail in Chapter 1.

Structure of Therapy

The next sections of the chapter concern the structure and function of treatment and related issues. The first issue to be considered concerns who will treat the family.

Use of cotherapists. The use of cotherapists in treating addictive families is beneficial to therapy. When cotherapists work together with the family, several things become practical which otherwise would not be possible. For example, therapist modeling of the techniques described earlier (problem-solving, communication, and negotiation skills, for example) is feasible. Such modeling can be instrumental in bringing otherwise foreign skills to life for the family, in part by providing family members a style to emulate in their interactions.

The use of cotherapists may be contraindicated in some cases in which the addict is not included in treatment. In cases in which the addict may join treatment later, the addition of a cotherapist at that time often aids the addict's assimilation into treatment. In effect, the cotherapist, like the addict, is "new" to the treatment and is often perceived by the addict as a potential ally in dealing with alliances among the family members that have been established or strengthened by the treatment.

A helpful option is to employ "consultants" rather than (and in some cases in addition to) cotherapists in the treatment of certain families. Consultants can introduce additional perspectives into treatment and, as discussed later, can be a tool for overcoming a family's resistance to treatment.

Consultants typically are other clinicians who have expertise in the area in which they are invited to participate. In the case of one family, for example, I joined the treatment for two sessions to help the family overcome difficulties they had implementing some problem-solving strategies. The consultant's specific involvement was successful in helping the family past its block, and it reassured the family that their therapist was willing to draw upon other resources for assistance. It has been my experience that consultants can be helpful and not disruptive to the treatment effort if used judiciously.

Structure of therapy sessions. Typically, families are seen weekly for one and one-half or two hours at the start of treatment. Such regularity helps establish a cadence to treatment. Intervals greater than a week seem too long to develop momentum.

As is typical of cognitive–behavioral approaches to family problems in general, therapy sessions with addictive families tend to involve considerable activity by both the therapist and the family. During periods of work on acquisition of one or another skill, the therapist provides a lot of didactic explanation. Role-plays, involving family members and often therapists, are used, and family members are encouraged to make notes during and between sessions, particularly concerning concepts and skills learned and questions they may want to ask. Liberal use is made of homework assignments in which the family practices specific observational or other skills. Homework is assigned at the end of practically every session, and it becomes the focus for the start of subsequent sessions, providing not only practice of new skills but also continuity in the treatment. When appropriate to supplement work in treatment sessions, reading material is suggested for family members (among others, Burns, 1980, for cognitive principles; Schlesinger & Gillick, 1985, for alcoholism information; Schlesinger & Horberg, 1988, for a discussion of family recovery; and Burns, 1985, for a cognitive perspective on relationship difficulties).

TECHNIQUES USED IN JOINING WITH THE FAMILY

Families tend to have a spokesperson when they come for treatment. It is the spokesperson to whom therapists can turn at the start of treatment for an explanation of the family's presence in therapy. Following the spokesperson's introductory description of the family's difficulties and hopes, therapists ask for perspectives of other family members (e.g., "How do things look from your angle?" "How do you see what's been going on?" "Why does it continue?"). At this point, the aim is to listen to each member and assure each that his or her viewpoint has been heard accurately. Striving to use each member's linguistic style (e.g., mode of expression and slang) is very important in this endeavor.

In the case of a family that comes without its addictive member, a major task is to assess family strengths and to encourage members to capitalize on those strengths. For example, family members have attended selectively both to their own negative actions and failures and to their impact on family life, and they may describe a chaotic and dysfunctional family life. They can recount only the chaos and not the occasional inroads they may have made to reduce the chaos. These frequently escape the family's attention. Helping members focus on such accomplishments is a first step in the direction of joining with the family on its journey to recovery.

The use of case histories (altered to preserve confidentiality and introduced in pertinent outline) has been helpful in creating a sense of safety—that family members can trust that therapists have experience treating these types of difficulties. Family members usually describe their predicament by telling stories describing a painful but decidedly downward trajectory into an abyss of unknown depth. Their involvement in the addictive process, in their view, has no happy ending. Case histories allow me to talk about families whose distress began similarly but whose members ultimately were able to influence some trends which previously had seemed irreversible. Although therapists must be careful not to appear to be painting a picture in which families live happily ever after, case histories allow family members to evaluate therapists' understanding of and experience with problems the family brings to treatment. Families may also use case histories to assess their therapists' investment in helping them and to decide how willing they are to allow therapists to join them in that effort.

In some cases, however, the therapist's treatment efforts may be met with particular problems of resistance. These are best addressed early in treatment. Resistance may appear in two basic ways. First, many families come to treatment with a skepticism that treatment will lead to constructive change or that changes will last. Many times this skepticism arises from their perceived past failures. In the words of one adolescent son of a cocaine-addicted father, "Why should I think this will work any better this time than the last two times we went to see a shrink?" Therapists can use a second concept of resistance to treatment, which I have labeled the "Three R's" (Schlesinger, 1984), to explore such family skepticism.

The Three R's constitute a cognitive trilogy through which nonaddicted family members commonly pass, and its resolution is a prelude to treatment. Engagement in treatment often is blocked by the residuals of prior trauma experienced by a family, whose members attribute their suffering to actions by (and possible "bad faith" of) their addicted relative. Schlesinger (1984) suggested a useful model for helping the "victimized" family members come to terms with the obstacles to their engagement in treatment.

The first R is *retribution*, the fantasy family members often bring to treatment of inflicting pain on their addicted relatives commensurate with their own suffering during the active addictive periods. The fantasy of *restitution* is the second R. It refers to an expectation of "repayment" from addicts for family members' suffering. The third R is *refuge*, the desire family members have to guard against future disruptions occasioned by an addict's relapse. It comes to the fore when families move past the frustration of the two previous fantasies. A more detailed description of the Three R's and their clinical utility can be found in Schlesinger (1984) and Schlesinger and Epstein (1986).

The Three R's can be an invaluable aid in joining with the family, particularly its nonaddicted members. Because they are such common themes, they allow the therapist to "predict" the family's concerns and emotions when these may be poorly formulated and typically helps family members believe, in the words of one mother, "You know *us* and *our* type of problem." Working through the Three R's with families does not guarantee that the issues will not recur later in treatment, but it does lay the foundation for interpreting their impact should they reemerge.

SPECIAL CLINICAL ISSUES IN THE TREATMENT OF ADDICTIVE FAMILIES

The following are special issues that arise in the treatment of addictive families.

1. *Treating individual families versus groups of families.* In theory, treatment of any sort in groups offers certain advantages. This applies as well to group treatment of families. Group treatment of families allows individual families to observe and imitate the adaptive behavior modeled by other family units, exposes family members to the influence of their peers in other families, and offers families support for the problems they experience in the course of treatment (e.g., Bartlett, 1975; Berger, 1973; Hindman, 1976). Some authors suggest that participation in multifamily therapy improves addicts' adjustment to outpatient treatment and reduces recidivism (e.g., Hendricks, 1971; Kaufman & Kaufmann, 1979).

In practice, however, groups of families can be unwieldy. Assembling even the minimum recommended three families (Kaufman, Roschmann, & Woods, 1984) may mean accommodating 15 to 20 people in a room. Kaufman (1985) describes one family group session in which 40 people filled the room. As the number of people expands, the complexity of treatment increases and its value may suffer proportionately.

2. *Which is the appropriate family for treatment?* At the outset of treatment, it is necessary to agree with family members about the relevant participants in treatment. In most cases members of the addict's immediate family circle are appropriate participants. In some cases others appropriately may be included as well. Although it is a matter of some debate (e.g., VanDeusen, Scott, & Stanton, 1980), the issue of whether to involve the adult addict's family of procreation, family of origin, or both, seems to resolve itself into a decision

to include the family of "relevance." For example, treatment of one family included the 40-year-old addict, his wife and two children, and the addict's mother, who had considerable influence on her son's family life. The addict's father, however, did not join the treatment endeavor because he and other family members deemed his involvement in the "problem" to be unimportant. In general, the rule of thumb is to involve as many members beyond the immediate family as may be involved in the addictive process or, with the family's agreement, who may petition for inclusion in treatment.

The issue of whether the addict will be involved in treatment arises in this regard as well. The preferable alternative is that the addict accompany his or her family to treatment. In cases in which the addicts exclude themselves, the therapist explains to the family that his or her participation will be desirable when the addict agrees to come for treatment. In the event the family excludes the addict, the therapist must make an assessment of the family's reasoning. If family members wish to come for treatment without the addict because they are seeking a way to reconstitute the family without him or her and have given up hope of a cooperative effort by all members to resolve family problems arising from the addict's behavior, the therapist explores this with the family in the absence of the addict. The goal of this exploration is to assess the degree to which the family has resolved to separate itself from the addict. Factors that play a role in this assessment include the emotional reactions accompanying the family's decision (e.g., family rage) and members' expectations of treatment in the addict's absence (e.g., "If we come for help and get ourselves together, maybe it will have an impact on him and he'll straighten out his act"). Although it is desirable for addicts to be involved in treatment of their families, therapists may agree either to delay or to abandon their inclusion if the resistance of other family members is strong, as in the case of persistent rage directed at the addict.

Therapists should always seek to include the addict's perspective in their assessment of family problems. It is consistent with the current approach to treating addictive families for the therapist to see the addict separately. In cases in which the eventual inclusion of the addict in the family therapy is possible, these individual sessions can be preliminary to that inclusion. In other cases the therapist considers in such sessions the desirability of referring the addict for further treatment with another clinician. Under either condition, however, therapists see addicts individually only for a few sessions, in part so as not to divert the course of family treatment by becoming the intermediary between the family and the addict.

3. *Should abstinence be required of the addict before treatment commences?*

This is an important question, and it has several answers. For families who come for treatment without their addicted relatives, the question does not apply, at least until the addict joins the treatment process. In this case, the family's reaction to continued drug or alcohol use is a central part of therapy, but actual use is not.

For families whose addicts accompany them for treatment, abstinence is encouraged during treatment, among other reasons because the addict can neither attend to nor contribute to treatment fully if he or she continues to use drugs. Abstinence obviates an unfruitful and unproductive debate about the limits of use and excess. For those cases in which an addict may have trouble remaining abstinent on his or her own, alternatives for assistance can be explored, including blood alcohol or breathalyzer tests for alcohol consumption, disulfiram therapy to prevent drinking, and periodic urine screens for other drug abuse. To minimize interference with treatment objectives, monitoring services can be arranged through outside sources.

4. *Are the prognoses for treatment different depending on whether the addict's participation is coerced or voluntary?* The answer is "Yes and no." Coerced treatment (e.g., by courts, employers, or the family itself) generally is more difficult to begin and maintain than "voluntary" treatment, and experience suggests that it may be less effective. First, families and addicts are rarely hurt by exposure to treatment, even if that treatment is not effective. In cases in which addicted relatives are forced into treatment, addicts and other family members are frequently defensive, well protected against what they predict will be treatment's assaults. This initially may render treatment efforts impotent. On the other hand, the coercion that may bring an addict to treatment may also keep him there long enough for the family to let down its guard and participate in therapy. "Voluntary" treatment, by contrast, may be the result of implied, but less rigidly enforced coercion (e.g., from other family members) and may terminate prematurely.

5. *Does treatment differ if families have several and/or periodic addicts?* The precipitant for treatment of some addictive families is the constant and, in some cases, long-term disruption of family life caused by an addict's drug use or drinking. For other families, drug use may not be as chronic, or several addicts may contribute to family stress. Treatment in theory does not differ if there is more than one addict or if the addictive behavior is periodic rather than constant. However, certain practical matters may vary.

Having several addicts in a family sometimes complicates decisions made in therapy. These include decisions about whether all, some, or none of its addicted members will be invited to join treatment, whether addicts will be ejected if they begin to use drugs again, and whether family life can continue if several of its members persist in their use of drugs. These matters differ from issues considered by one-addict families. They tend to be more intricate because several addicts can influence many more aspects of family life.

For families with several addicts and with addicts who use drugs or drink only periodically, the issue of abstinence remains unchanged. Abstinence throughout treatment and beyond for drug addicts is routinely requested, and, depending on their patterns and severity of drinking, at least through the bulk of treatment for periodic drinkers. It has been my experience that some drinkers who came for treatment early in their drinking career (e.g., before physical and psychological damage develops) have returned spontaneously to moderate levels of drinking after treatment, except in cases in which abstinence became a negotiated condition for desired family membership.

6. *When might it be appropriate for treatment to focus on single family members' thought processes and behaviors?* When family changes cause adjustment difficulties for an individual member because of that member's individual psychological makeup, it may be appropriate to focus for a time on that person's distress. In most cases this eventuality is best handled in the context of family treatment rather than outside family sessions. Exceptions include problems concerning intimate aspects of marital relationships, which are best discussed by spouses in the absence of other family members.

My guidelines for handling such individual problems are that they be addressed specifically and in the shortest time possible. For example, the wife of an alcohol-dependent father of five children became increasingly anxious as treatment progressed and her husband was reintegrated more and more fully into the family. She found it difficult to talk without stuttering, she started to pace around the treatment room, and on one occasion she started to hyperventilate in a therapy session. Her anxiety became an obstacle to further progress as the family increasingly focused on and deferred to her anxiety; that, in turn, made her even more anxious about the direction family life was taking. After 10 sessions in which family issues were discussed, two sessions were devoted to her anxiety. The cognitive roots of her emotional responses to family change were traced to a series of self-derogatory cognitions and subsequent negative predictions of her ability to cope in her "new" family. Her participation in previous family sessions gave her the "language" to discuss, clarify, and dispute her individual thought processes and to influence her behavior. Thereafter, family work continued.

7. *When is it appropriate to see family members individually?* I try to avoid this in work with addictive families, in part because requests for

individual sessions may represent attempts to manipulate the family treatment. But at times I will agree to see a family member individually if he or she persists in stating that an issue requires an individual hearing. I insist, however, on an agreement with the individual member that no "secrets" will be discussed with me but kept from the rest of the family. In one case, this rule was as unacceptable to the individual family member as continued family treatment with my knowledge of his "secrets" was to me. He entered individual treatment with another clinician, but the family elected to continue treatment with its addicted mother.

In some cases individual treatment may be indicated for a family member particularly to resolve past individual traumas. In those cases I make referrals to other clinicians for separate individual treatment, while those members continue with family treatment. This has established family treatment as treatment of the whole, with ancillary treatment for truly individual problems handled separately.

8. *How are self-help groups used in treatment?* Addicts and their families have a number of self-help groups from which to choose. These groups are available to families should they decide to seek the support of a group of people who have shared their problems with an addiction or an addict. Alcoholics Anonymous (AA) and its ancillary programs (Al-Anon, Alateen, and Alatot) focus on alcoholism, Narcotics Anonymous and its ancillary program Naranon focus on narcotics abuse, Cocaine Anonymous and its recently developed family companions focus on cocaine abuse, and Families Anonymous focuses on a variety of addictive and abusive problems. Generally, these self-help programs follow the model of AA and are organized into a series of "steps" through which addicts and family members pass as they "work the program" (Alcoholics Anonymous, 1953, 1955).

Self-help group participation is not only compatible with family therapy but also highly desirable in most cases. I encourage addicts and families to attend self-help group meetings. They are a good source of support and provide an opportunity to focus regularly and directly on the addictive behaviors themselves. In many cases this obviates the need to focus on these in therapy, a welcome benefit for treatment which otherwise may be diverted to a discussion of the addiction itself. Although the addictive process contributed directly to the family's problems, it may not be the exclusive source of difficulty. To the extent that addicts and families find other chances to focus on the details of addiction, therapy can concentrate more directly on the family's interpersonal functioning.

9. *Does a family's "disease" orientation preclude cognitive–behavioral treat-*

ment? If a family is wedded to the "disease model" of addictions and perceives
a cognitive–behavioral approach to be antithetical to their beliefs and, in the
view of the therapist, if its use would remove the supports from an otherwise
brittle family, this approach is certainly not appropriate. It may be appropriate,
however, to explain to family members that how they conceive of their
predicament adds to the stress of coping with what they have defined as a
disease.

SUMMARY

Although perhaps not yet widely used, cognitive–behavioral techniques
offer alternatives to help addictive families approach and resolve the problems
which result from or are exacerbated by the addictive processes in their midsts.
The multifaceted approach to treatment described in this chapter is readily
tailored to the needs of individual families and easily modified as conditions
warrant. The future of these techniques in the treatment of addictive families
seems promising.

REFERENCES

Ablon, J. (1976). Family structure and behavior in alcoholism: A review of the
literature. In B. Kissin & H. Begleiter (Eds.), *Social aspects of alcoholism* (pp.
205–242). New York: Plenum.

Alcoholics Anonymous (1953). *Twelve steps and twelve traditions.* New York:
Alcoholics Anonymous World Services.

Alcoholics Anonymous (1955). *Alcoholics Anonymous.* New York: Alcoholics Anonymous World Services.

Baither, R.C. (1978). Family therapy with adolescent drug abusers: A review.
Journal of Drug Education, 8(4), 337–343.

Bartlett, D. (1975). The use of multiple family therapy groups with adolescent
drug addicts. In M. Sugar (Ed.), *The adolescent in group and family therapy*
(pp. 262–282). New York: Brunner/Mazel.

Baucom, D.H., Bell, W.G., & Duhe, A.D. (1982, November). The measurement
of couples' attributions for positive and negative dyadic interactions. Paper
presented at the annual meeting of the Association for the Advancement of
Behavior Therapy, Los Angeles.

Berenson, D. (1976). Alcohol and the family system. In P.J. Guerin (Ed.), *Family
therapy: Theory and practice* (pp. 284–297). New York: Gardner Press.

Berger, M.M. (1973). Multifamily psychosocial group treatment with addicts and
their families. *Group Process, 5*(1), 31–45.

Bowen, M. (1974). Alcoholism as viewed through family systems theory and family
psychotherapy. *Annals of the New York Academy of Science, 233,* 115–122.

Burns, D. (1980). *Feeling good.* New York: New American Library.

Burns, D. (1985). *Intimate connections.* New York: William Morrow.

Coleman, S.B., & Davis, D.I. (1978). Family therapy and drug abuse: A national survey. *Family Process, 17*(1), 21–29.

Davis, D.I. (1977–78). Family therapy for the drug user: Conceptual and practical considerations. *Drug Forum, 6*(3), 197–199.

Davis, P., Berenson, D., Steinglass, P., & Davis, S. (1974). The adaptive consequences of drinking. *Psychiatry, 37*, 209–215.

Distasio, C.A., & Harbin, H.T. (1977). Family systems theory and therapy: A logical approach to counseling in the addictions. In G.F. Waldorf (Ed.), *Counseling therapies and the addictive client* (pp. 95–112). College Park: School of Social Work, University of Maryland.

Falloon, I.R.H., Boyd, J.L., & McGill, C.W. (1984). *Family care of schizophrenia: A problem-solving approach to the treatment of mental illness.* New York: Guilford Press.

Fincham, F., & O'Leary, K.D. (1983). Causal inferences for spouse behavior in maritally distressed and nondistressed couples. *Journal of Social and Clinical Psychology, 1*, 42–57.

Fram, D.H., & Hoffman, H.A. (1973). Family therapy in the treatment of the heroin addict. *Fifth National Conference on Methadone Treatment, 1973 Proceedings, 1*, 610–615.

Gottman, J., Notarius, C., Gonso, J., & Markman, H. (1976). *A couple's guide to communication.* Champaign, IL: Research Press.

Guerney, B.G., Jr. (1977). *Relationship enhancement.* San Francisco: Jossey-Bass.

Harbin, H.T., & Mazier, H.M. (1975). The families of drug abusers: A literature review. *Family Process, 14*, 411–431.

Hendricks, W.J. (1971). Use of multifamily counseling groups in treatment of male narcotic addicts. *International Journal of Group Psychotherapy, 21*(1), 84–90.

Hindman, M. (1976). Family therapy in alcoholism. *Alcohol Health and Research World, 1*(1), 2–9.

Hinkle, L.M. (1983). Treatment of the family system damaged by alcoholism. Paper presented at the annual meeting of the Alcohol and Drug Problems Association of North America, Washington, DC.

Holtzworth-Munroe, A.S., & Jacobson, N.S. (1985). Causal attributions of married couples: When do they search for causes? What do they conclude when they do? *Journal of Personality and Social Psychology, 48*(6), 1398–1412.

Jacobson, N.S., & Margolin, G. (1979). *Marital therapy: Strategies based on social learning and behavior exchange principles.* New York: Guilford Press.

James, E., & Goldman, M. (1971). Behavior trends of wives of alcoholics. *Quarterly Journal of Studies on Alcohol, 32*, 373–381.

Kaufman, E. (1985). *Substance abuse and family therapy.* New York: Grune & Stratton.

Kaufman, E., & Kaufmann, P. (1979). Multiple family therapy with drug abusers. In E. Kaufman & P. Kaufmann (Eds.), *Family therapy of drug and alcohol abuse* (pp. 81–93). New York: Gardner Press.

Kaufman, E., & Pattison, E.M. (1981). Differential methods of family therapy in the treatment of alcoholism. *Journal of Studies on Alcohol, 42*(11), 951–971.

Kaufman, E., Roschmann, J., & Woods, B. (1984). A likable couple: The use of interwoven family groups in the treatment of a blended alcoholic family. In E. Kaufman (Ed.), *Power to change: Family case studies in the treatment of alcoholism* (pp. 267–291). New York: Gardner Press.

Klagsburn, M., & Davis, D.I. (1977). Substance abuse and family interaction. *Family Process, 16*(2), 149–164.

Lawson, G., Peterson, J.S., & Lawson, A. (1983). *Alcoholism and the family.* Rockville, MD: Aspen Systems Corporation.

Liberman, R.P., Wheeler, E.G., & Sanders, N. (1976). Behavioral therapy for marital disharmony: An educational approach. *Journal of Marriage and Family Counseling, 2,* 383–395.

Miller, P. (1976). *Behavioral treatment of alcoholism.* London: Pergamon Press.

Miller, W.R., & Marlatt, G.A. (1984). *Comprehensive Drinker Profile.* Odessa, FL: Psychological Assessment Resources.

National Institute on Alcohol Abuse and Alcoholism (1971). *First Special Report to the U.S. Congress on Alcohol and Health.* Washington, DC: U.S. Department of Health, Education and Welfare.

Noel, N.E., & McCrady, B.S. (1984). Behavioral treatment of an alcohol abuser with the spouse present. In E. Kaufman (Ed.), *Power to change: Family case studies in the treatment of alcoholism* (pp. 23–77). New York: Gardner Press.

O'Farrell, T.J. (1982, August). Marital and family therapy for alcohol problems. Paper presented at the annual meeting of the American Psychological Association, Washington, DC.

Olson, D.H., Russell, C.S., & Sprenkle, D.H. (1980). Marital and family therapy. *Journal of Marriage and the Family, 42,* 973–994.

Paolino, T.J., & McCrady, B.S. (1977). *The alcoholic marriage: Alternative perspectives.* New York: Grune & Stratton.

Platt, J.J., & Spivack, G. (1975). *Manual for the means-end problem-solving procedure (MEPS): A measure of interpersonal cognitive problem-solving skill.* Philadelphia: Hahnemann Community Mental Health/Mental Retardation Center.

Regan, J.M., Connors, G.J., O'Farrell, T.J., & Jones, W.C. (1983). Services for the families of alcoholics: A survey of treatment agencies in Massachusetts. *Journal of Studies on Alcohol, 44,* 1072–1082.

Rosenberg, D.N. (1981/82). Holistic therapy with "alcoholism families." *Alcohol Health and Research World, 6*(2), 30–32.

Schlesinger, S.E. (1984, August). 3 R's in the marital treatment of alcohol abuse. Paper presented at the 92nd Annual Meeting of the American Psychological Association, Toronto, Ontario.

Schlesinger, S.E., & Epstein, N. (1986). Cognitive–behavioral techniques in marital therapy. In P. Keller & L. Ritt (Eds.), *Innovations in clinical practice: A source book,* Vol. 5 (pp. 137–156). Sarasota, FL: Professional Resource Exchange.

Schlesinger, S.E., & Gillick, J.J. (1985). *Stop drinking and start living.* Blue Ridge Summit, PA: TAB Books.

Schlesinger, S.E., & Horberg, L.K. (1988). *Taking charge: How families climb out of the chaos of addiction . . . and flourish.* New York: Fireside Books/Simon & Schuster.

Smith, M. (1975). *When I say no, I feel guilty.* New York: Bantam.

Sowder, B., Dickey, S., & Glynn, T.J. (1980). *Family therapy: A summary of selected literature* [DHEW Publication No. (ADM) 80-944]. Rockville, MD: National Institute on Drug Abuse.

Stanton, M.D. (1979). Family treatment of drug problems: A review. In R.L. Dupont, A. Goldstein, & J. O'Donnell (Eds.), *Handbook on drug abuse* (pp. 133-150). Washington, DC: National Institute on Drug Abuse.

Stanton, M.D., Todd, T.C., & Associates (1982). *The family therapy of drug abuse and addiction.* New York: Guilford Press.

Steiner, C.M. (1971). *Games alcoholics play.* New York: Grove Press.

Steinglass, P. (1977). Family therapy in alcoholism. In B. Kissin & H. Begleiter (Eds.), *Treatment and rehabilitation of the chronic alcoholic* (pp. 259-299). New York: Plenum.

Steinglass, P. (1980). A life history model of the alcoholic family. *Family Process, 19*(3), 211-226.

Stuart, R.B. (1980). *Helping couples change: A social-learning approach to marital therapy.* New York: Guilford Press.

VanDeusen, J.M., Scott, S.M., & Stanton, M.D. (1980). Engaging "resistant" families in treatment. I. Getting the drug addict to recruit his family members. *International Journal of the Addictions, 15*(7), 1069-1089.

Wegscheider, S. (1981). *Another chance: Hope and health for the alcoholic family.* Palo Alto, CA: Science and Behavior Books.

Wegscheider, S. (1983). Chemical dependency: A system illness. *Focus on Alcohol and Drug Issues, 6*(2), 2-3, 30.

9

Treating Depression and Suicidal Wishes Within the Family Context

Richard C. Bedrosian

A COGNITIVE-BEHAVIORAL VIEW OF DEPRESSION AND SUICIDAL WISHES IN A FAMILY CONTEXT

Causal Factors

Depression is probably best understood as a "final common pathway" (Akiskal & McKinney, 1975), reflecting the joint influence of various combinations of etiological factors. In any given case, a unique configuration of biochemical, psychological, and interpersonal factors may unite to produce and maintain the depressive symptomatology. Since the depressed person participates in an ongoing, continuous process of reciprocal influence with the environment (including his or her significant others), it is necessary to view the causal process as circular, as opposed to unidirectional. Although it may be useful at times to focus on either organismic or contextual influences separately for descriptive or therapeutic purposes, in reality these two factors never operate completely independently of one another.

Organismic variables that influence depressive symptoms include the following. *Biochemical factors* such as a genetic predisposition to depressive spectrum disorders, neurotransmitter imbalance, substance abuse, and secondary effects of other physical malfunctions (e.g., underactive thyroid) tend to place limits on the expected efficacy of any psychological treatment, especially if the appropriate medical interventions do not occur. *Cognitive factors,* including basic assumptions for living or schemata, expectations, interpretations, fantasies, imagery, and so on, may or may not be within the patient's immediate awareness. Although many patients distort the meaning of or fail to respond to a substantial portion of external stimuli, even the most rigidly organized cognitive system is constantly bombarded by contextual influences. Because cognitive processes organize and stimulate behavior, they directly influence (and in turn are influenced by) interpersonal relationships. *Behavioral excesses and deficits* include lack of assertiveness or other communication difficulties, extreme social withdrawal, habitual procrastination, inappropriate angry behavior, and so on. Although a depressive episode caused by other factors certainly might give rise to such responses, individuals who tend to behave habitually in certain ways (e.g., unassertively) may be more prone to create life circumstances for themselves in which depression becomes an inevitable result. Within the individual, cognitions and behaviors constantly influence one another.

Contextual variables that promote depressive symptoms include the following. *Extreme life stresses* can have direct effects on depression. Although cognitive factors certainly play a role in mediating the individual's responses to such stressors (Abrahms, 1981), traumatic events such as combat, rape, the death of a child, or chronic illness assault the physical and psychological integrity of the organism, particularly if they occur repeatedly. *Relationship problems with significant others,* such as chronic family or marital conflict, pathological psychological adjustment of a family member, chronic illness or physical disability on the part of a family member, or dysfunctional family structure commonly elicit depression. The affective states, behaviors, and cognitions of each member of a family system tend to resonate together in a continuous process of reciprocal influence.

Cognitions, Relationships, and Depression

It is clear from a large number of research studies that there is a substantial disturbance in thinking present in depressive disorders, as exemplified by Beck's (1976) concept of the "cognitive triad," the negative view of the self, the world, and the future. According to the cognitive model, distorted thinking may not "cause" a depressive episode, but it certainly may play a crucial role in the maintenance of dysphoric affect and other symptoms. The depressed person becomes trapped in a vicious cycle, in which dysfunctional ideas are constantly reconfirmed, thereby maintaining and reinforcing the depressed mood. If an individual perceives the self as worthless, the world (especially one's family) as devoid of warmth and/or opportunity, and the future as offering no hope for change, then suicide may begin to look like a desirable solution. A number of studies have demonstrated the strong association between hopelessness and suicidal intent (Bedrosian & Beck, 1979). As the depression grows more severe, the patient's ability to perceive nonsuicidal options diminishes, which in turn generates more depressive affect and continued suicidal thinking.

Cognitions play a key role in family and marital relationships on a number of levels. Cognitions about the self (and the self in relationship to others) 1) guide the selection of individuals and relationships to which one is attracted, 2) influence the individual's style of relating (e.g., unassertive, demanding), 3) heighten sensitivity to particular behaviors of others (e.g., guilt induction or criticism), and 4) set the internal standards which regulate the enactment of one's role in the family (e.g., "I must make those around me happy at all times"). Cognitions about others 1) determine whether their behavior will be attributed to situational factors ("He's been too depressed to work this week") as opposed to stable personality traits ("He's lazy, just like his father"), 2) generate predictions (sometimes self-fulfilling prophecies) and expectancies regarding their actions and attitudes ("My wife can't be counted on to keep any of her promises to me"), and 3) set the affective tone (e.g., anger, distrust, warmth) for interactions with the individual(s) in question. Cognitions about relationships 1) prescribe roles and behaviors in a family or marriage ("A man is king of his castle"; "Men are weak and need women to look after them"; etc.), 2) set standards against which current interactions are evaluated (e.g., "In a good marriage, the spouses never fight"), and 3) generate expectations of oneself and one's significant others ("If someone really loves you, they'll know what you want without having to be asked").

Clinical experience indicates that patients differ greatly from one another in the degree to which pervasive, longstanding basic assumptions about the self and others play a role in generating and maintaining the current depressive episode. At one end of the continuum is the individual with good premorbid adjustment, realistic expectations of himself or herself and others, and a history of constructive responses to frustration, who may experience a brief depressive reaction to a highly stressful life event, such as the sudden death of a child. This type of individual may experience a temporary disruption in both self-esteem and interpersonal relationships during a depressive episode but will quickly revert to more constructive patterns of thinking and behavior with the assistance of a therapist.

At the other end of the continuum is the individual with a history of recurrent depressions, a chronically poor self-image, and a string of abusive relationships, whose current difficulties seem to stem directly from his or her basic assumptions for living and the associated habitual patterns of behavior.

As in the two case histories described later, such an individual often develops a distorted belief system about the self and others as a result of experiences in a disturbed family of origin and subsequently forms relationships with unsuitable partners throughout his or her lifetime. The new dysfunctional families thereby created by such an individual then proceed to generate their own symptoms, which in turn serve to compound the chronic depression and/or other symptoms within the individual. The dysfunctional cognitions of the members in such families often interlock and resonate with one another so powerfully as to prevent more adaptive beliefs and/or behaviors from emerging on anyone's part, as the following case vignettes illustrate.

Teresa grew up as the only child in a very close-knit family of Italian descent. Both of her parents were high achievers, active and prominent in community affairs. They were consistently supportive of their daughter, to the point of having indulged her at times. She idealized her parents and was generally motivated by a sense of fair play to conform to their wishes and expectations. Teresa never remembered any indications of overt conflict in the home while she was growing up. Signs of hostility or conflict in the family were suppressed to the point where her parents never even criticized Teresa explicitly. Instead they would express their dissatisfaction with her indirectly, often through subtle nonverbal gestures, such as a raised eyebrow. Such gestures were never followed by discussion or elaboration of any kind. The rather strict parochial education she received from kindergarten through high school also failed to provide Teresa with any realistic norms for the expression of anger and the resolution of interpersonal conflict.

As an adult, Teresa had a very low tolerance for conflict of any kind. Not surprisingly, she tended to be unassertive in a variety of situations. After graduation from college, she married Louis, a quiet man who seldom expressed dissatisfaction of any kind. For seven years the couple had the sort of peaceful, conflict-free existence Teresa had assumed marked the ideal marriage. Then without prior warning of any kind, Louis one day announced that he no longer loved her, packed his things, and moved into an apartment with a female co-worker. In retrospect, it appeared that the inability of both spouses to tolerate and work through conflict of any kind had contributed to the ultimate dissolution of the relationship.

Louis had left Teresa with two young children, Michael and Donna, who were 6 and 4 respectively at the time of his departure. Over the next 10 years, Louis would miss child support payments for long periods of time, despite the fact that he was financially solvent. Teresa responded stoically to her financial hardships, declining to take legal action against her former husband, because she was afraid that he would retaliate by moving out of state or otherwise alienating himself from his children.

As time passed, Teresa's extreme aversion to conflict resulted in more than just money problems for her and her children. Louis eventually married his former co-worker and adopted her young son. Although he lived in a nearby town, he saw very little of his own children, at one point even failing to make contact with them for nearly two years. Visitations on holidays and birthdays were sporadic and unpredictable. Finally, when the children were teenagers, Louis explicitly terminated their Christmas visits to his home, blaming his actions on what he described as their negative attitudes, and on the fact that he now had a family of his own. Michael, now 16, had always blamed himself for the failed relationship with his father and had shown signs of chronic depression (school underachievement, social withdrawal, and poor self-esteem) since early adolescence. Louis' latest rejection only deepened his despair and sense of worthlessness. His level of social and academic functioning, already problematic, dropped precipitously, and he reported to a school counselor that he was beginning to think about suicide. He firmly believed that if he had been a better son, his father would not have rejected him. He became obsessed with trying to understand what he had done to alienate his father.

Teresa had always wanted her children to admire and respect their father, so she had never alluded to his infidelity or to his financial irresponsibility in their presence. She had tried her best to prevent them from resenting Louis, to the point of making excuses for his lengthy absences and his many failures to acknowledge milestones in their lives. At times she even had pretended that gifts she had purchased for them were from their father. In her efforts to preserve whatever positive elements existed in the relationship between Louis and the children, she had inadvertently nurtured unrealistic ideas about him and sowed the seeds for Michael's self-punitive response to his father's neglectful behavior. Because Michael had been told all his life that Louis was a good, kind, loving man, it seemed logical to him that he must be to blame for his father's actions. From his point of view, only a rotten son would cause such a wonderful father to behave in such a rejecting manner.

A similar interlocking relationship pattern is exemplified by the case of Peter and Sherry, a couple in their middle thirties. Although they sought treatment for marital distress, it was clear that both of them experienced recurring periods of significant depressive symptoms. Peter's mother had been a chronic abuser of both alcohol and prescription drugs throughout his childhood and adolescence. He remembered having played a caretaking role for her as far back as grade school. In early adolescence, he often experienced anxiety while at school during the day, worrying about what kind of situation he would find when he returned home in the afternoon. Instead of participating in extracurricular activities or socializing after school, he felt compelled to rush right home, to make sure that his mother was safe. While his other siblings had separated themselves, both physically and psychologically, from the family situation at a young age, Peter remained in close contact with his mother. As a husband, a father, and a businessman, he was compulsive, anxiety-ridden, overly serious, and responsible to a fault. Sherry, on the other hand, had been diagnosed a juvenile diabetic at a young age, and as a consequence had been pampered and overprotected by her parents. She grew up viewing herself as fragile, ineffectual, and unable to take substantial risks of any sort. On the other hand, she expected, and often received, constant support and nurturance from others, without experiencing a strong need to reciprocate. As an adult, she tended to be unassertive and overly dependent.

While Peter believed that he was directly responsible for the thoughts, feelings, and behaviors of those he loved, Sherry was often willing to abdicate her responsibility for herself. By being so willing to do things for Sherry which she should have been doing for herself, Peter constantly reinforced her sense of helplessness and incompetence. Since Peter thought it was his duty to make Sherry happy, her tendency to blame him for her own shortcomings and dissatisfactions strengthened his view of himself as a failure and stimulated depressive affect. When Peter became overtly depressed and anxious, his wife would alternate between panic because her protector was failing her and anger at him because he no longer seemed to be the strong man she had married. Such reactions on Sherry's part either exacerbated Peter's negative feelings about himself or spurred him on to greater heights of caretaking behavior toward her. Not surprisingly, it was nearly impossible for Sherry to escape a sense of despair, chronic anger, and a poor image of herself as long as Peter insisted on supervising her every move.

Summary of the Model

The present cognitive–behavioral model proposes that depression and suicidal wishes in individual family members commonly result from both organismic and contextual factors. On the one hand, the individual may be predisposed to depression due to biochemical factors as well as dysfunctional cognitions and behavioral excesses and deficits that had roots in his or her upbringing in the family of origin. Such organismic factors can produce depression directly (e.g., when organic factors produce depression in the absence of notable precipitating life events) or by impeding the individual's ability to cope with contextual factors such as life stresses outside the family (e.g., job, school) and within it (e.g., marital conflict, parent–child conflict).

On the other hand, severe stresses within the family can elicit depression and suicidal wishes in individuals who do not have notable biochemical, cognitive, and behavioral vulnerabilities to affective disorders. Chronic aversive interactions among family members that appear to the members to be insoluble can produce a strong sense of hopelessness and helplessness in the individual, leading to depression and the consideration of suicide as an option to escape from the distressing situation.

Commonly the organismic and contextual factors exert mutual influences on each other in eliciting and maintaining depression and suicidal wishes. Individuals with predispositions to depression often form dysfunctional families in which members have shared or complementary depressogenic cognitions, and in which the behavioral interactions of the members are stressful (e.g., aversive interactions, poor problem solving). Thus the individual with vulnerabilities to depression helps to shape a family that fosters depression, and poorly functioning families create an environment of stress and hopelessness that breeds depression. Consequently, the efficacy of treatment of depression and suicidal wishes often calls for attention to both intrapersonal and interpersonal family factors.

ASSESSMENT

Depression and Suicide Ideation

Several valid and reliable paper-and-pencil measures of depression are available. I have utilized the Beck Depression Inventory (Beck & Beamesderfer, 1974) with good results for nearly a decade. In addition to obtaining a global indication of the severity of the depressive episode, it is vital for the clinician to determine whether "vegetative signs" (e.g., early morning awakening, significant appetite and/or weight loss, excessive fatigue, disrupted concentration, deficits in short-term memory, and loss of libido) are present in sufficient number and intensity to suggest that antidepressant medication might be helpful. The Hamilton Rating Scale for Depression (Hamilton, 1967), an interview-based instrument which is strongly weighted toward physical symptoms, provides a useful outline for the kinds of questions the clinician needs to ask in order to determine whether the patient might benefit from medication.

A thorough investigation of the patient's suicidal cognitions is essential in order for the clinician to estimate the degree of suicidal risk present. The Scale for Suicide Ideation (Beck, Kovacs, & Weissman, 1979) provides an excellent outline for the initial assessment of suicidal thinking. As described in greater detail elsewhere (Bedrosian, 1986; Bedrosian & Beck, 1979), several aspects of suicide ideation require investigation: 1) the relative strengths of both the wish to live and the wish to die; 2) the content of any passive suicidal wishes (e.g., skipping insulin injections), if present; 3) the patient's conception of suicide and what it offers him or her; 4) the patient's emotional response to the suicidal thinking (e.g., fear, anger, comfort); 5) the patient's sense of control over the suicidal impulses, the nature of the control mechanisms employed, and the presence of any factors which might disrupt self-control in the future (e.g., substance abuse, agitation, psychotic symptoms); 6) the presence and nature of any deterrents to suicide; 7) the nature and extent of any suicide plans, the lethality and availability of the method(s) involved, and details of any actions undertaken by the patient in anticipation of death (e.g., making a will, giving away possessions); and 8) the degree to which the patient has communicated suicidal wishes to significant others, and the manner in which those individuals responded to the patient's communications (e.g., supportively, angrily, with denial).

The clinician needs to bear in mind that the nature and extent of an individual's suicidal thinking may fluctuate considerably over time and/or across situations. Contextual factors, especially marital and family relationships, can exert a profound influence on the strength of the suicidal impulses. Risk assessment can be complicated when the comparative security of a therapist's office or the separation from family problems provided on an inpatient unit diminish the intensity of the suicidal ideation. Consequently, it is necessary to conduct a careful situational analysis of the suicidal cognitions. Such an analysis frequently provides the first clues of ongoing pathology in the family system.

For example, Helen, a severely depressed factory worker in her forties, experienced prolonged episodes of suicidal thinking, which sometimes lasted as long as two or three days. Initially she was unable to account for the source of her suicidal ruminations, beyond a global sense of despair and hopelessness. Continued questioning by the therapist over two or three sessions revealed that each episode of suicidal ideation was preceded by conflict between Helen's husband and her 20-year-old son by a previous marriage. Since the son had entered adolescence, she found herself in the middle of such conflicts, which on occasion escalated to violent proportions. Helen's description revealed the young man to be a chronic substance abuser who was clearly suicidal at times, and possibly psychotic as well. Subsequently, the therapist worked to provide entry into treatment for the son and the family as a whole.

Research studies conducted with a variety of clinical populations have supported the hypothesis that hopelessness plays a crucial role in stimulating suicidal intent and ideation (Beck, Kovacs, & Weissman, 1975; Bedrosian & Beck, 1979). To eliminate the suicidal risk in a given case, it is necessary to identify and change the unique chain of reasoning which leads the individual to conclude that life is no longer worth living. The therapist needs to determine whether the hopelessness relates more to an immediate stressor ("I'm better off dead because I'll never find a job in this economy") or to a more pervasive basic assumption ("I've been a worthless loser all my life"). If the suicidal wishes are based on chronic, persistent beliefs, the risk will persist, even after the immediate crisis has passed. Further, strongly held beliefs are more resistant to change, produce more intense affective reactions, and may stimulate more pressure to act in a self-destructive manner.

History

Cognitive–behavioral treatment is not typically associated with any particular developmental model, nor does it explicitly require that the therapist aid the patient(s) in making connections between childhood events and current symptoms of psychological distress in every case. Nonetheless, even in cases where subsequent treatment interventions never refer explicitly to historical material, it is difficult to imagine the therapist working in a sensitive, thorough manner without some awareness of how earlier events have helped to shape the current difficulties and the associated belief systems. A good historical overview often enables the therapist to identify dysfunctional basic assumptions and behavior patterns quickly (Guidano & Liotti, 1983) and to understand more clearly why family members are unable or unwilling to fulfill their expectations of one another. The case of Peter and Sherry, described earlier, is a good example of the way in which historical material facilitates an understanding of the belief systems which stimulate the current distress. I prefer to make such historical connections salient for patients during treatment, especially when reaction patterns learned in one's family of origin are persisting inappropriately in current relationships.

In the course of the initial interview(s) with individuals, couples, or families, the clinician should strive to investigate the following areas:

1. *Structure and characteristics of family of origin.* Occupational, economic, ethnic, and religious status of the parents. Birth order and sibling relationships. Nature and extent of alcohol abuse or other psychopathology among members of family of origin. Child-rearing practices and basic values of parents. Occurrences of physical, sexual, or psychological abuse during childhood or adolescence. Nature of current relationships with members of family of origin. Current stressors experienced by family of origin (e.g., physical illness, divorce).

2. *Level of academic and social functioning in childhood and adolescence.* Nature and extent of extracurricular interests, particularly those which might have offered a sense of mastery and/or social competence. Parental reactions to level of achievements. Quality of self-image in childhood and adolescence. Dating and sexual history.

3. *History of medical and/or psychological complaints.* Presence of untreated or unrecognized psychological symptoms. Nature of previous psychiatric treatment and patient's perception of its effectiveness. History of miscarriages or abortions in female patients. Prior occurrences of alcohol or drug abuse, impulsive behaviors, or antisocial actions.

4. *Vocational/achievement history in adulthood.* Nature and extent of career progression, including job stability. Degree of satisfaction with career and possible regret over past vocational decisions. Nature and extent of any achievement-oriented activities not directly connected with employment (e.g., amateur theater, show dog breeding).

5. *History of current family configuration.* Circumstances of meeting and bonding with spouse or partner. Reactions of families of origin to marriage. Health history and level of psychological functioning of current family members, with particular emphasis upon ongoing substance abuse or other psychopathology.

Cognitive Distortions

Although several psychometrically sound measures of cognitive distortions have been developed (e.g., Eidelson & Epstein, 1982), I am most experienced in the use of direct interaction with the patient(s) to elicit the ideation which stimulates dysphoric affect, self-defeating behaviors, and/or problematic interactions with others. Through a series of gently probing questions the therapist will elucidate the idiosyncratic chain of thinking that led to a particular affective state or interpersonal interaction. The therapist frequently interrupts the questioning process to offer the patient capsule summaries of his or her cognitive processes and, as therapy progresses, looks for opportunities to link current distortions with themes elicited in previous discussions. The more chronic and severe the difficulties, the more necessary it will be to recognize each individual's basic assumptions for living which lead him or her to make the same cognitive errors over and over again.

With couples or entire families present in the session, the therapist has the opportunity to elicit each individual's cognitions in response to transactions occurring with others. In addition to aiding the therapist in assessing cognitive distortions, such a process may also serve as a valuable therapeutic intervention for the family, as discussed in greater detail later. A fairly typical investigation of cognitions occurred during a session with Peter and Sherry, a couple described earlier:

Sherry: I know I shouldn't, but I keep comparing myself to other couples who seem to have so much more than we do.

Peter: See! She blames me for that.

Therapist: How do you know that? Has she ever told you she was disappointed in you for not making more money?

Peter: No, she's never said anything, but I know she feels that way. Who else would be at fault for us not having the things that some of our friends have?

Therapist: Do you blame yourself for not having more material success?

Peter: Of course I do. If I had more drive, I'd be more successful. A lot of the time I consider myself a failure.

Therapist: What does it mean to you, to be a failure?

Peter: It means I haven't lived up to my responsibilities as a man, to take care of my family, to make my wife happy.

Therapist: What if you do fail at those things? What will happen then?

Peter: I wouldn't do anything to myself, but I'd pretty much feel like I didn't deserve to live.

In the course of this dialogue, Peter's perfectionistic and overly responsible attitudes came to light. It became clear that the unrealistically high expectations he set for himself led to considerable self-blame and a tendency to project the same sort of critical attitudes toward him onto others, particularly his wife. Later in this discussion the therapist elicited more information about Sherry's responses to the success of their friends. It became clear that the issue behind comparing herself to others was one of her own perceived inadequacy, not Peter's. She assured her husband that she viewed him as a success, although he characteristically had difficulty believing her. Subsequently the therapist began to explore some of the cognitions associated with Sherry's poor self-image by directly questioning her and encouraging dialogue on the subject between the spouses. Clearly, both Peter and Sherry's reactions to their financial status (which was comfortably middle class) stemmed from the dysfunctional basic assumptions they had about themselves. Both of them had experiences in their families of origin which could well have given rise to such negative beliefs.

Cognitive therapists use role-playing, imagery, self-monitoring, and a variety of other tactics to enhance access to belief systems. Since the ability to recognize one's thought processes is a skill that develops over time, patients may receive a variety of homework assignments designed to increase their awareness of their cognitions. Such assignments may be especially useful with individuals who initially find it hard to identify what they are thinking. For example, Tyrone and Satira sought treatment after he had slapped and pushed her during an argument. Normally a quiet and withdrawn man with no history of even remotely similar behavior, Tyrone was unable to describe the thought processes which had led to the angry outburst. In fact, he was unable to identify many substantive areas of dissatisfaction with his wife, although the therapist was strongly convinced that there were a number of points of tension between the spouses. Consequently, the therapist asked Tyrone to watch carefully for even the slightest dissatisfaction with Satira's behavior and to note how he responded to each situation. As time went on, he was able to identify a number of recurring areas of annoyance with his wife. Moreover, he became increasingly aware of his tendency to withdraw immediately if provoked.

Family Interaction Patterns

A number of family therapists emphasize the utility of having the couple or family enact their dysfunctional relationship patterns during the treatment session (Haley, 1976; Minuchin & Fishman, 1981). Without the benefit of a live performance, the therapist is limited to the accounts of family members, which are likely to be biased, self-serving, limited by lack of insight, or simply hampered by unintentional inaccuracy. Moreover, therapeutic interventions seem to have a refreshing immediacy and intensity if they are in response to experiences shared by all participants in the present moment.

Consequently, it is desirable for the therapist to become less central a focus of interaction in the session, in favor of allowing family members to speak directly to one another. Such an arrangement may be awkward at first for the family members, who may prefer to direct their remarks to the clinician. Also, therapists with training and experience primarily in individual treatment at first may find it difficult to take a less central role. Given sufficiently compelling content and minimal interference by the therapist, many of the family's characteristic interaction patterns will emerge. In observing such interactions, the therapist seeks to determine the behavioral repertoire of the family, the expectations (both implicit and explicit) family members have of one another, the belief systems (both shared and individual) which govern the family functioning, the habitual interpretations family members make regarding one another's actions, and the interactional sequences which most typically trigger symptoms of distress. Consequently, the clinician should attempt to answer the following questions:

1. How do the family members respond to the depressive symptoms? Do significant others attempt to reassure the patient or argue against the negative cognitions? Do family members show signs of responding to the depressive symptoms with an angry or rejecting attitude toward the identified patient? Does the depressed individual become even more hopeless or helpless in response to certain behaviors by the family members? What beliefs and interpretations on the part of family members play a role in such repetitive cycles? How does the identified patient perceive the actions and attitudes of the rest of the family?

2. What is the structure of the family? Is there an identifiable hierarchy? Who makes the decisions in particular areas? Which coalitions seem to occur repeatedly in the family? Do any coalitions interfere with family functions such as parenting? Is the identified patient caught in a chronic triangle, involving perpetual conflict between two of the family members? What dysfunctional beliefs help to keep the patient in such a position? Are the boundaries between the generations appropriate, with clear and consistent role expectations for both parents and children? Are the spouses' expectations of one another and of the family in general relatively compatible? Is the identified patient's depression part of being caught in a chronically helpless or incompetent position in the family? How do ineffective structures and dysfunctional beliefs maintain one another in the family?

3. What is the communicational style of the family? Is there an atmosphere of openness, or one in which frank discussions are discouraged? Are conflicts typically resolved in some constructive fashion or do they lead to denial or excessive escalation? Are there any particular issues which no one seems able to discuss? Who seems to divert discussion away from sensitive areas, and how is the diversion accomplished? Which family members seem most assertive? What sort of responses do they receive from the others? Which family members tend to withdraw in the face of conflict, and how are they responded to by the others? What are the belief systems underlying the communicational styles of the individual family members, as well as the family as a whole?

The reader will note that some of the family issues described in the preceding paragraphs, especially those involving belief systems, cannot be investigated thoroughly unless the therapist interrupts ongoing interactions during the session. I prefer to intersperse "enactments" or family interactions in the treatment sessions with dialogue between the participants about the interactions just concluded. Such an arrangement is preferable to holding repeated extensive discussions of interactions which have taken place outside of the session, since the therapist will have a more complete data base for transactions which have occurred in his or her presence.

CLINICAL STRATEGIES AND TECHNIQUES

Treatment Options

As noted earlier, a significant proportion of depressed individuals come from dysfunctional families of origin and go on to form problematic families of their own. For many of these individuals, stressful interpersonal relationships coexist with the depressive symptoms. Thus it is not uncommon to encounter a depressed adult entering treatment who describes problems with an abusive or alcoholic spouse, a drug-dependent child, a chronically demanding aging parent, and so forth. Upon further questioning, it becomes clear that the identified patient belongs to a highly distressed family system in which perhaps several individuals are experiencing significant psychological symptoms.

In contrast, in the course of treating a family or marital problem (e.g., parental friction with an acting-out adolescent, stepparenting difficulties, severe conflict between spouses), the therapist may observe that one or more members of the dysfunctional system are suffering from various configurations of depressive symptoms, up to and including vegetative signs and suicidal ideation. Where should the therapist intervene?

On the one hand, my treatment model for depression assumes that changing the identified patient's cognitions is a necessary but often not sufficient condition to achieve both symptom relief and long-term prevention of similar psychological distress. Clinical experience indicates that a depressive episode which occurs within the framework of a highly constructive family system is relatively infrequent, except in cases of catastrophic stress or a definite biochemical etiology. Even an otherwise "normal" person who happens to have a biological predisposition to recurrent severe depressive episodes will have a profound effect on the outlook and behavior of the other family members, regardless of how well adjusted they are. In most instances when an individual seeks treatment for depression, it is desirable for the therapist to assist the family members, as well as the identified patient, to change their cognitions, their behaviors, and ultimately their habitual patterns of interaction. Consequently, an ideal treatment plan involves contact with significant others. As the succeeding sections demonstrate, my treatment approach to couples and families places a major emphasis on the belief systems underlying the dysfunctional transaction patterns.

On the other hand, there are disadvantages to making the family system the exclusive focus of treatment. Even when treatment has enabled the family system to support a higher level of functioning on the part of all concerned, there may still exist inner cognitive barriers which prevent the depressed patient, and others in the family as well, from making optimal use of the improved interpersonal atmosphere. In the most severe cases of depression, the identified patient may have such a distorted outlook that he or she is unable to perceive changes in family interactions and communication patterns accurately, despite repeated therapeutic interventions designed to highlight them. Moreover, unless the identified patient is able to communicate with complete openness in the presence of other family members, the therapist who utilizes only family sessions may be unable to monitor the level of suicidal risk accurately over the course of treatment.

The clinician also needs to be sensitive to any indications that the depressed individual is suffering from a disorder that requires medication (e.g., bipolar disorder, schizoaffective disorders) or substance abuse which interferes with the intellectual processes necessary for successful therapeutic outcome. In such cases, real therapeutic work on the cognitive components underlying the depression does not begin until the individual's other symptoms have been brought under some degree of control.

Consequently, it is often desirable to treat depression with a combination of individual and family interventions. The extent of individual treatment required depends on the degree of current and longstanding cognitive distortions experienced by the identified patient as well as his or her motivation for therapy. Similarly, the degree of family treatment is determined by the level and chronicity of the dysfunction in the system and by the willingness of the members to participate.

Clarifying the Meaning of Depressive Symptoms

Clinical experience indicates that nearly all patients and significant others benefit from some degree of education regarding depression and suicide. Depressed individuals and their families need to understand that one cannot simply "snap out" of a depressive episode through an act of sheer will. Patients often make statements such as "I must not want to feel better" or "I must be getting something out of being depressed." Family members, who may be frustrated by a lack of positive response to their attempts to energize and reassure the identified patient, may express similar sentiments as well.

The therapist should attempt to block any scapegoating of the depressed individual which may be occurring. Similarly, family members need to know that they cannot realistically expect the depressed individual to respond positively to reassurance and/or advice. Without such information, significant others may repeatedly engage in futile efforts to change the identified patient's dysfunctional thinking, only to withdraw eventually from that person in frustration, thereby reconfirming the depressed individual's negative self-image.

One way to address the issues described in the preceding paragraphs is for the therapist to orchestrate interactions between family members and the depressed individual revolving around the latter's symptoms, particularly his or her cognitive distortions. By examining the cognitions of everyone involved in the transaction, the therapist enables new interpretations and behaviors to emerge. A typical example involves Peter and Sherry, a couple described earlier in this chapter. Peter frequently described himself as a failure, despite his substantial career accomplishments. The therapist allowed Sherry to attempt to reassure him by enumerating his achievements. As her efforts continued to fail, Sherry grew more and more frustrated with her husband. When asked what she was thinking, she replied, "He's wallowing in it. He doesn't want to feel better." Meanwhile, her husband's response was to think, "She really doesn't think very much of me, and now her true feelings are coming out." The therapist then began an extensive exploration of Peter's feelings of inadequacy, which had begun long before he had even met his wife. It became clear to both spouses that since he had such chronically negative views about himself, there was no way he could accept that his wife viewed him any differently. Peter was able to recognize that while there were areas in which his wife was dissatisfied with him, he typically projected many of his own self-esteem issues onto her. Subsequently, the therapist worked repeatedly to assist Peter in discriminating between Sherry's complaints about him and his own dissatisfactions with himself. Although it did distress Sherry to recognize how negative her husband's self-concept was, she was able to dissipate much of her anger toward him by realizing that he had no desire to be depressed. Sherry also came to recognize that her own sense of inadequacy and incompetence caused her to panic at the sign of any weakness on her husband's part, since it suggested that he might not be able to take care of her. The therapist encouraged her to listen to him empathically, without setting herself up for failure by attempting to talk him out of his negative cognitions. Consequently, she was able to respond to him in a sensitive, understanding manner, without ultimately becoming angry and inadvertently reinforcing his poor self-image.

While assisting the identified patient and the family members to understand more about depression, the therapist assumes the role of an expert, and may work from a more didactic stance than usual. The reader should note, however, that in the ideal cognitive therapy interaction, the therapist teaches not through lecturing but by leading the family member step-by-step through a socratic dialogue (as described in greater detail in the following section on changing cognitions). Learning through an experience in therapy always seems more durable than learning through the weight of the therapist's authority. Similarly, information in print generally seems more credible to patients than information offered verbally by the therapist. Consequently, it is extremely useful to encourage the identified patient, and any family member interested enough, to read a good popular text on depression and/or cognitive therapy (e.g., Burns, 1981, or Emery, 1983).

The therapist needs to orchestrate experiences that will enable the identified patient and the family members to understand the factors which caused the current depressive episode. In some instances the precipitating factors are obvious to everyone. In other cases the depressed person and/or the significant others may make a variety of incorrect attributions about the causal factors behind the depressive symptoms. A common situation involves the spouse who blames himself or herself or the marriage for the psychological distress, when the depression is actually either endogenous or a reaction to circumstances outside the home.

The clinician frequently encounters instances in which a focus on depressive symptoms diverts attention from the major issues (e.g., marital conflicts) which need to be resolved in order for lasting therapeutic gains to be achieved. The therapist needs to stimulate interactions in the session which underscore the connections between family relationships and depressive complaints. In the case of Peter and Sherry described earlier, the therapist was able to demonstrate repeatedly that whenever the husband increased his protective, controlling behavior toward his wife, even when his motives were benign, she responded with more helplessness and depressive affect. The more depressed and inadequate Sherry appeared in the session, the more her husband continued to "help" her, with consistently negative effects.

Changing Cognitions

The process of enabling patients to identify and evaluate the validity of their beliefs constitutes the core of cognitive therapy. The reader is referred to the detailed clinical literature describing the use of cognitive therapy with depression and related disorders (Beck, 1976; Beck, Rush, Shaw, & Emery, 1979; Bedrosian, 1986; Bedrosian & Beck, 1980; Bedrosian & Epstein, 1984; Guidano & Liotti, 1983). As each family member's beliefs and interpretations unfold, the therapist aims to orchestrate experiences which enable the individual to assess the validity of his or her cognitions, and/or to sample alternative points of view. In addition to enabling family members to identify distortions in their cognitive responses to particular situations, it is vital for the therapist to foster an awareness of how basic schemata or assumptions for living stimulate repeated difficulties for the individuals involved. Many different treatment interventions can be correctly identified as "cognitive," so long as the therapist's explicit goal is to modify the thinking which accompanies psychological symptoms, self-defeating behaviors, and dysfunctional interaction patterns with significant others.

One typical cognitive strategy involves the use of questioning (or a "Socratic dialogue") to enable the individual to discover information discrepant with the dysfunctional cognitions. It is often useful to assist the family member to achieve psychological distance from the current situation, so that he or she can view the ideas involved with greater objectivity. To encourage distancing, the therapist may ask questions such as "If I were a friend of yours and the same thing happened to me, would you think that I had deserved it?" Similarly, the therapist may ask the patient to reverse roles and play the therapist. Another alternative might involve orienting the person to a similar situation he or she had coped with more successfully in the past, in order to rekindle the style of thinking which predominated at that time.

When the therapist meets with a couple or an entire family, he or she has the opportunity to encourage the participants to test their beliefs and interpretations about one another directly. Often such beliefs are embedded in the statements family members make, so that the therapist needs first to make the underlying cognition explicit. For example, a husband may say to his wife, "I did things just the way you wanted over the weekend, and you still got mad at me." The therapist could begin by asking him what he did for his wife, and how he knew what it was she had wanted from him. Did he try to guess what she wanted, without asking her directly? The therapist may then invite the man to question his wife directly regarding exactly what her expectations were. Was the wife indeed angry? Did she communicate directly to her husband about what had upset her? What does the episode say about the style of communication in the marriage, and/or the specific vulnerabilities of either spouse? Given individuals who are motivated to improve their relationships, such dialogues help to improve communication skills and allow family members to perceive one another in less threatening or malevolent terms. The therapist will repeatedly ask the family members to check out any implicit assumptions (e.g., "She's probably mad at me for what happened last Monday," "He thinks I'm not doing enough to help myself," or "I know she won't believe me when I say this") with one another before proceeding with a particular conversation.

As described earlier in this chapter, problematic marital or family relationships usually involve interlocking patterns of negative thinking and behavior on the part of all the participants. During conjoint sessions, family members can become aware of how their own cognitive distortions are triggered by particular types of interactions and how their behaviors stimulate dysfunctional thinking in others. In working with couples or families cognitively, the clinician needs to go beyond doing "serial individual therapy" by stimulating ongoing dialogue among the participants and using it as a springboard for examining the cognitions of all concerned.

Teresa, a woman described in an earlier section, sought family treatment after she was notified by a high school guidance counselor that her son, Michael, had reported suicidal ideation. The therapist met with Teresa, Ben (her second husband), and Michael, age 16. Michael was well aware that his depression had been triggered by a series of rejections by his father, but he persisted in shouldering all the blame for the failure of the relationship. When the mother seemed to hedge about the circumstances surrounding her divorce from Michael's father, the therapist decided to meet with the couple separately, without the son present. During the interview with Teresa and Ben, the therapist learned of the father's infidelity and his failures to meet his financial commitments, as well as the mother's repeated attempts to cover for him in the eyes of the children. As she described her many attempts to enhance the father's image, Teresa was able to recognize that her behavior had served to nurture and perpetuate false hopes, thereby ultimately triggering greater disappointment and self-blame on the part of her children. When asked whether he had made similar observations on his own in the past, Ben replied that he had, but he had not shared them with his wife. The therapist directed Ben to explain to Teresa why he had not given her more candid feedback regarding the situation with her former husband. He cited fears of hurting her feelings, intruding into areas that were none of his business, and being perceived by his wife as "too hard line." Contrary to Ben's expectations, Teresa accepted his feedback positively and asked him to let her know if he noticed her behaving in a similar manner in the future. The therapist and the couple agreed that it might be helpful if Michael learned more of the facts regarding the divorce and his father's behavior.

During a subsequent session, the therapist asked Michael to open a dialogue with his mother about his father and their marriage. Ben played a supportive role, by encouraging his wife to continue in her narrative when she seemed to be faltering, and by suggesting additional questions for Michael to ask his mother. Although she had spent years hiding information from him, Teresa herself was quite surprised to discover how little Michael really knew about his father. The revelations, which were offered in an extremely even-handed manner by the mother, enabled Michael to begin to perceive the relationship with his father in a new light. Although he experienced justifiable anger toward his father, and an understandable sense of loss over a father–son relationship that never was, Michael had begun to free himself from the burden of responsibility for the breakdown in communication which had taken place. He stated to his mother in no uncertain terms that he did not want her to shield him from the truth ever again. The dialogue with Michael, and the conversation with Ben which had preceded it, caused Teresa to begin to question her attitudes toward confrontation and conflict.

Once an individual recognizes an idea as invalid or irrational, the therapist may strive to place the significance of that particular cognition into some broader perspective. Does the individual tend to make the same type of cognitive error in other situations? Does the distortion relate to a pervasive set of beliefs (e.g., perfectionism, dependency, or overresponsibility) which lie at the core of his or her difficulties? Is there historical information (e.g., alcoholic family background) which ties in with the individual's beliefs? How do spouses or family members habitually trigger misinterpretations and/or reinforce dysfunctional beliefs on one another's parts? Can the individual anticipate situations in which he or she will be more likely to think in a similarly negative manner, and begin to practice more adaptive responses to such situations? Can family members learn to avoid triggering distorted thinking in one another?

The therapist may assign a wide variety of *homework assignments,* to perpetuate awareness of distorted thinking, to enable the patient(s) to test certain cognitions, to stimulate behaviors which support new beliefs, and to provide opportunities to practice new thinking patterns. For example, Andre, a man who was seen by the author in marital therapy, stated in a session, "I'm not a good father. I never do anything enjoyable with the kids. I'm always withdrawing from them, so I can be alone to watch TV and do other selfish things." The therapist immediately asked him to solicit an opinion on the topic from his wife, Diane. The wife, who certainly had other complaints about her husband, was quite positive about Andre's behavior as a father. Ironically, the fact that Diane was often so negative in her attitude toward him made her favorable remarks about his fathering more credible to Andre.

To enable Andre to test further the validity of his beliefs, the therapist asked Andre to chart both his activities with the children and his "selfish" behaviors for several weeks. Andre found that although he spent more time watching television than he (or his wife) thought was necessary, it usually took place after the children had gone to bed. The data he collected indicated that nearly all the time he spent at home was devoted to activities with the children. Subsequently, the therapist asked him to log other areas in which he criticized himself. Over time, Andre was able to recognize his relentless perfectionism and resist the tendency to berate himself more frequently, thereby decreasing his vulnerability to depression.

By monitoring his thoughts when he found himself withdrawing from others in the family, Andre discovered that he tended to pull away from others most during periods of intense dissatisfaction with himself. This information enabled Diane to begin resisting the idea that her husband's distant behavior represented a rejection of her.

As they begin to recognize their cognitive distortions, family members can learn to dispute their negative ideas actively. Because the rational responses which the individual uses to counter the distortions need to be believable and realistic, they must flow from the insights gained in treatment. Never does the therapist spoon feed responses that are not based on the family member's previous discussions of his or her thought processes during earlier treatment sessions.

Translating Depressive Symptoms into Systems Issues

Several particular themes seem to appear with regularity in the interactions between depressed patients and their families. The therapist may choose to address the issues involved with a combination of interventions focusing on cognitions and the behavioral interaction patterns among family members.

Overresponsibility. It is not unusual for the family member who serves a caretaking role for others who suffer from substance abuse and/or other psychological problems eventually to request treatment for depression. A major factor in such a depressive episode is the patient's misplaced sense of responsibility and exaggerated loyalty to the family member(s) in question. Often the identified patient is the adult child of an alcoholic parent, with a lifetime of experience in the caretaking position. The therapist works to make the identified patient's beliefs about being able to change others as explicit as possible, in hopes of shedding some doubt on the validity of such ideas. The therapist also attempts to generate family interactions, during sessions as well as at home, which illustrate for the patient again and again the futility of his or her caretaking position. For example, these family interactions may demonstrate that family members do not wish to change, refuse treatment for their problems, resent the identified patient's intrusions, are capable of making their own decisions, can tolerate the stresses in their own lives without assistance, and so on. It also is useful to elicit and begin to modify the beliefs that keep the other family members entrenched in overly dependent roles or lead them to project blame inappropriately onto the depressed individual's shoulders. Furthermore, the therapist looks for opportunities both within and between sessions to increase psychological (if not physical) distance between the caretaker and the relevant family members.

Lack of assertiveness. Many depressed patients complain bitterly about family conditions in individual sessions, but they remain almost mute when face to face with the significant others involved. The identified patient may remain in a chronically helpless role, unwilling to articulate his or her expectations or dissatisfactions, while experiencing a paralyzing level of anger and despair. Moreover, for any number of reasons, the family may be structured in a manner that keeps the depressed individual in the helpless role. In some cases the entire family or marital system suffers from a paucity of communication of any sort. Consequently, lack of assertiveness should be viewed by the clinician as just one manifestation of more generic problems in the family system, such as pervasive denial of problems, excessively rigid roles, or lack of equity in the marital relationship.

To ensure lasting prevention of depressive symptoms, it is vital for family members to learn gradually to communicate their complaints and expectations directly, without excessive guilt or fear. Increasing assertive communication requires the ability to learn new behaviors and to resist the pull of dysfunctional beliefs (e.g., "I shouldn't have to ask for what I want," "Terrible things will happen to me if I displease another person," "A good family never quarrels"). Such changes, especially on the part of the depressed individual, have the potential to produce immediate turbulence in the family system in a number of ways. The identified patient may find that other family members refuse to honor direct requests, thereby precipitating overt conflict. Similarly, the identified patient may begin to threaten others by assuming a more adequate role or by raising issues that were previously taboo. The therapist needs to be careful not to elevate the depressed patient to an assertive position which he or she really cannot sustain independently. Unless the depressed person develops assertive skills gradually, he or she will be unable to remain focused on the issues long enough to resolve them, and a loss of credibility with other family members for both the therapist and the identified patient will ensue. Similarly, it is vital for the therapist to show empathy with the concerns of all family members, not only those who happen to be less assertive.

Dysfunctional expectations of the marital relationship. Because many depressed patients suffer from chronically low self-esteem, it is no wonder that their expectations of their spouses appear self-defeating and/or unrealistic. In turn, spouses of depressed individuals may have their own problems with self-image, resulting in similarly distorted expectations. Some individuals tolerate physical or psychological abuse from their partners because they simply cannot conceive of any other type of relationship, believe they do not deserve better treatment, or continually hold themselves responsible for their spouses' hostility. Other patients, particularly those who also appear to have personality disorders, may approach the marital relationship with a strong sense of entitlement, leading to constant anger and/or disappointment with a spouse whose efforts to please are never quite enough. The therapist's task is to make such expectations explicit at every turn, not only to facilitate an examination of their accuracy but also to explore the underlying beliefs, about oneself and about the nature of relationships, which maintain the cognitions. The therapist may attempt to block conflict and guilt induction between the spouses, so that they have an opportunity to ask themselves the crucial questions: Are my expectations of relationships realistic? Are my expectations of my particular partner realistic, given his or her track record, psychological makeup, and motivation to change? Can I live with the departures from my "ideal" in my present relationship without chronic anger or depression? How do I reinforce and/or strive to live up to the unrealistic expectations my spouse has of me?

The reader should bear in mind that from a systems point of view, the therapist's job is far from over once a spouse recognizes an unrealistic set of expectations of his or her partner. It is necessary to provide both spouses with an awareness of how their cognitions and behaviors interlock, as well as to enable them to generate alternative viewpoints and behaviors. For example, in the case of Peter and Sherry discussed previously, Sherry was able to recognize how her expectation that a man would take care of her led to a stifling, unsatisfying relationship with her husband. The therapist repeatedly asked her to monitor between sessions any instances in which she allowed Peter to make decisions for her and/or involved him in tasks which she could have handled acceptably on her own. Gradually she began to show more assertive and independent behavior. On the other hand, Peter's lifelong belief that the woman in his life would be unable to function independently made it necessary for him to learn to restrain himself from imposing unwanted advice and unsolicited help on his wife. The therapist consistently pointed out instances in which his wife was more self-reliant than he would have expected, and set up dialogues in the session in which he practiced listening empathically to Sherry's complaints about her life, without offering solutions or advice to her. To enable the spouses to change their expectations of one another further, the therapist looked for opportunities to have them reverse their habitual roles, with Sherry acting as a helper to Peter.

Suicidal wishes. Different types of families dictate the use of sharply contrasting strategies by the therapist in response to suicidal wishes. Minuchin's (1974) distinction between enmeshed and disengaged families provides a helpful framework for generating treatment interventions. In his view, enmeshed families are characterized by intense involvement, rapid communication of affective states, and often blurred boundaries among the members. Such families frequently offer nurturance, support, and a sense of belonging, at the expense of promoting independence and growth, particularly on the part of offspring. From a cognitive point of view, members in enmeshed families are "overvigilant" in that they are constantly alert for signs of trouble (e.g., anger, depression, disloyalty) in the other members. On the other hand, disengaged families are characterized by sparse communication, minimal nurturance, low overt emotional arousal, and increased psychological distance among members. Such families offer sample opportunities for separation and growth but may sacrifice warmth and support in doing so. From a cognitive perspective, members of disengaged families often learn how to practice selective attention to a fault, by avoiding thinking about or discussing painful topics, by refusing to attend to signs of friction with one another, by using withdrawal as a means of resolving conflict, and so on.

In enmeshed families, the suicidal ideation may occur in a climate of overinvolvement, high emotional arousal, and open conflict. The identified patient may feel overwhelmed and guilty about the family conflicts and may view suicide both as a punishment for his or her bad behavior and as the only available solution to the interpersonal difficulties. To maintain the safety of the identified patient in such cases, the therapist needs either to block the family transactions which seem to exacerbate the suicidal wishes or to take other steps, such as hospitalization, which will create more secure boundaries among the individuals involved in the conflict. The therapist may attempt to mute the responses of family members to the suicidal wishes and other depressive symptoms, so as to increase distance between individuals and reduce the dysfunctional level of affect in the family.

In a disengaged family the initial attempts by the depressed patient to reveal the extent of his or her distress may provoke little or no overt reaction. Although at first blush the members of a disengaged family system may not seem to be very involved with the suicidal individual, it is important for the therapist not to give up too quickly on such a system. Family members may care deeply about the suicidal patient but may lack the ability to respond to the identified patient's distress with what most of us would consider an appropriate degree of warmth and support. The therapist must challenge the disengaged system by creating a crisis over the suicidal wishes, in order to determine whether the family members are simply distant and impervious to social cues or whether they actually are rejecting the identified patient. The therapist needs to provide data so that the family members can accurately recognize the suicidal risk posed by the identified patient. Tentativeness or understatement by the therapist with regard to the suicidal wishes may only encourage the maladaptive pattern of psychological distance in the disengaged family. Family members may persist in denying the risk, or in dismissing the suicidal threats as manipulative, but unless the therapist literally bombards them with information and emotional stimulation he or she will never know if they are capable of responding more adequately to the situation. The therapist will need to elicit the family members' cognitions about the identified patient and to push constantly to make unstated attributions and expectations on everyone's part more explicit, especially those which involve suicidal wishes and other depressive symptoms. Members of disengaged families may be too quick to think that the crisis is over and reestablish a distant relationship with the identified patient. Again, only sustained pressure from the therapist will provide the identified patient with sufficient contact with family members to determine whether a greater degree of involvement is possible.

Triangles. It may be clear to the therapist that the depressed patient is participating in triangulation, either by serving as a buffer between two conflicting family members (e.g., parents or spouse and child), or by detouring his or her conflict with another family member (most likely a spouse or a parent) through a third party (e.g., a child or a lover). It is not uncommon to find depressed adults well into middle age who are still struggling with being triangulated by their parents. Early and persistent induction into parental conflicts seems to produce individuals who are guilt-ridden, overresponsible, and unable to separate themselves from destructive relationships. Suicide offers such individuals an escape from the helplessness and conflicting loyalties associated with the go-between position. In such cases the therapist's goal is to disengage the depressed patient from the triangle and to get the conflicting parties to fight directly with one another. Achieving this goal will require behavioral or structural changes within the family (bringing the conflicting family members into more direct contact with one another, isolating the depressed individual from their transactions, etc.), as well as cognitive changes on the part of at least the identified patient, who must learn to resist the impulse to get involved again in the conflicts.

Treatment Format Issues

The manner in which an individual, couple, or family presents a request for treatment may dictate varying strategies on the part of the therapist. This section addresses some of the issues that arise in matching treatment modalities to presenting complaints when depression is part of the clinical picture.

An individual seeks treatment for depression. In the course of working with a depressed patient, I am most likely to use some combination of individual and family work. Severely depressed persons are rarely seen solely on an individual basis, particularly if they are suicidal. Similarly, it is unlikely that a severely depressed patient will not be involved in some individual therapy during the course of treatment, even when the family system is the major focus of the therapist.

At a minimal level of involvement in treatment, family members will provide data on the identified patient, receive information on the nature of depression, and be encouraged to interact with the depressed person in a supportive manner. As described earlier in this chapter, the therapist will need to assess the quality of functioning in the family system and to intervene whenever possible to correct dysfunctional processes which either stimulate or maintain the depressive symptoms. Initial contact with significant others should occur as early as possible in the treatment process. From there, the therapist may utilize the presenting complaint of depression as a means of entry into the family system, for the purpose of changing the cognitions and dysfunctional interactional styles of its members. Although what begins as an individual therapy case may well end up as a marital or family treatment case, the author recommends making such transitions carefully, and with the informed consent of the participants (see the subsequent section on therapeutic contracts).

The therapist's decision to include each family member in treatment should be based on a clear rationale. For example, young children may not be included routinely in therapeutic work with a depressed parent unless the agenda involves their growth and development. On the other hand, members of the family of origin with whom the patient no longer lives may well become a part of the treatment process, because of their involvement in the formation and maintenance of the depressed individual's basic belief system. Family members who are invited to treatment sessions but are obviously not part of the central focus of the therapeutic work may justifiably become resistant and thereby weaken the therapist's future leverage and credibility.

A couple or family seeks treatment for problems other than depression. In the course of working with such cases, the therapist may identify significant depressive symptoms on the part of one or more family members. The therapist will need to decide whether improvements in the family would be sufficient to produce changes in the depressive symptoms or if it would be useful to provide individual treatment for the depressed member(s). I tend to assume that the more severe and unremitting the depression, the greater the potential need for some individual therapy as an adjunct to family or marital treatment.

TECHNIQUES USED IN JOINING WITH THE FAMILY

Creating a Clear Therapeutic Contract

Any family member who participates in treatment needs to know why he or she in particular is involved in therapy, and what the goals of the therapy are. Writers such as Haley (1976) emphasize the need for the therapist to work within the framework of the family's presenting complaint, particularly in the early stages of treatment. Therapists who plunge too quickly into unsolicited family or marital interventions run the risk of being perceived by the identified patient and his or her family members as nonsupportive, disrespectful, and/or incompetent. When an individual has sought treatment for depression, most family members enter a consultation with a therapist expecting to address legitimate concerns about the identified patient. The more the therapist honors such expectations at the outset, the more leverage and credibility he or she will have later in treatment, because of the atmosphere of trust and forthrightness which has been established. Paradoxically, then, anchoring early treatment interventions in the presenting complaints ensures a broader focus (which may include previously taboo subjects) as therapy progresses. As the therapist's credibility grows, he or she should be alert for opportunities to underscore data which indicate the need to explore and resolve additional issues in the family system. As in other cognitive interventions, the therapist should strive to create experiences for the family members in which the data that argue for additional therapeutic interventions essentially speak for themselves. The therapist should also exercise similar caution when offering individual therapy to a depressed person who had originally sought treatment for a family or marital problem.

Serial Alliances

The therapist needs to ensure that each participant in the treatment sessions plays a useful role and has an opportunity to air his or her concerns. If the therapist has spent several individual sessions with the identified patient, it may be necessary to make some special gesture to join with the spouse or significant other(s) who are now becoming involved in treatment. "Special gestures" may range from an effusive greeting and expressions of gratitude for the person's involvement in treatment to a period spent meeting alone with the therapist. The therapist needs to communicate to the other family members that they are not being held responsible for the identified patient's depression, and that treatment will not necessarily jeopardize valued relationships in the family. It may be helpful to point out how the other family members' very presence in the session indicates a high level of concern for the identified patient, and to stress that the therapist's role is not to attack but to offer assistance that will enable them to be even more helpful to the depressed individual. Without demeaning either the identified patient or the family, the therapist can point out that depression is often baffling for the lay person to deal with, particularly without guidance from a professional.

The therapist must become adept at constantly shifting alliances from moment to moment in the treatment sessions. For example, when identifying a cognitive distortion on the part of one family member, I always try to point out complementary distortions on the part of the other family members as well. The goal should be for all participants to perceive that they have received an equitable amount of all the things that therapy and the therapist have to offer: empathy, support, confrontation, pressure, and so on. It may be desirable for the therapist to tell the couple or the family that he or she is striving for a sense of balance among the participants in treatment and that their feedback would be welcomed any time they perceived that the therapeutic "goods" seemed to be distributed unequally.

SPECIAL CLINICAL ISSUES IN THE FAMILY TREATMENT OF DEPRESSION AND SUICIDAL WISHES

Clarifying the Therapist's Responsibility

Although they require continuous scrutiny and caution on the part of all professionals involved with them, suicidal patients often create needless anxiety for the therapists who treat them. The very life-threatening nature of a suicidal depression gives the therapist a clear mandate to protect the patient above all else. How much of a subjective sense of risk does the therapist tolerate before he or she takes some action (e.g., hospitalization, notification of significant others) to ensure the patient's safety? The following rule of thumb should help when in doubt. If you feel uncomfortable about having the patient leave your office without some intervention, then exercise the options available to you (e.g., notifying family, arranging for hospitalization) to protect the individual. Whatever damage that occurs in the therapeutic relationship as a result of taking such actions can generally be undone subsequently by emphasizing a sincere and abiding interest in the patient's welfare, but the damage generated by a suicide attempt may be irreversible, even if the attempt is unsuccessful.

Therapists who regularly treat individuals who pose a high risk of suicide may need to keep the following points in mind. First, do not allow yourself to underestimate the level of risk involved in a particular case. Prepare yourself for the potential worst-case scenarios. Although you want to impart a sense of hope to the patient, you need to protect yourself with a realistic expectation of what you can accomplish. Your awareness of the limitations of your influence will help inoculate you against the possibility of losing a patient. Second, ask for consultation and/or moral support from supervisors or peers whenever you need it. Make sure you have someone you trust and respect readily available to assist you in the event of a crisis. Because averting suicide is our highest priority as mental health professionals, never hesitate to interrupt someone if you need immediate input. Third, do not bear the responsibility for preventing self-destructive behavior alone. Involve significant others, whether they are family members, friends, clergy, neighbors, or supervisors, in the effort to maintain the patient's safety. If necessary, the therapist can remain in close telephone contact with family members who live far away from the identified patient.

Suicidal Threats and the Family

Family members (or mental health workers for that matter) who dismiss suicidal threats as halfhearted or manipulative are in dire need of education. Many readers are well aware that even the most manipulative or attention-seeking individual is capable of successfully completing a suicide attempt inadvertently. Unless the family and any other caretakers can be moved to take the suicidal ideation seriously, the identified patient may be in severe jeopardy. Family members should be told by the therapist in no uncertain terms that all suicidal ideas on the part of the identified patient should be taken seriously.

The family members need to be fully informed as to the options available to respond to a suicidal crisis. The therapist must emphasize that in responding to such a crisis, the first priority is maintaining the depressed patient's safety. Family members should never be put in the position of having to estimate suicidal risk without professional consultation. I routinely give my home telephone number to all suicidal patients and their families, so as to increase the chances of being available to respond immediately to the crisis. Family members are often instructed to proceed directly to a nearby hospital emergency room if the therapist is not accessible, so that they can at least receive a professional evaluation of the situation. Family members frequently express guilt or confusion over the advisability of taking actions which might antagonize the suicidal patient. The therapist may respond by asking, "How will you feel later on if something does happen and you didn't take the actions you had planned?" Hospitalization may be the safest course when the therapist questions the ability of the family to ensure the identified patient's safety.

It is vital for the therapist to help the family members create and sustain a climate in which the identified patient can speak openly about the suicidal wishes. The clinician can begin this process by modeling such an open dialogue with the depressed individual in the session. The therapist must focus immediately on any transactions within the family which tend to undermine openness or encourage a spirit of secrecy. Because some families with a suicidal member tend to be secretive and closed to outsiders, only sustained therapeutic pressure will succeed in maintaining open communication. No matter how open the family seems to be, however, the therapist should still use individual interviews with the suicidal person as the customary means of assessing risk.

Depressed individuals at times are hesitant to disclose their suicidal wishes to significant others, for fear of the hurt and anxiety such information might cause. On the other hand, many suicidal patients also believe that their families would be happier if they did kill themselves. With the therapist's guidance, the depressed individual can receive the message repeatedly from family members that although they are distressed about the suicidal thinking, they would be far more traumatized by a successful suicide. Not all families will be able to provide such reassurances to the suicidal member, of course. In the least benign instances, the family interaction may not support more adaptive behavior on the part of the depressed person, to the point where he or she receives the implicit message that perhaps suicide would be a desirable option for all concerned. Such a nonsupportive family environment often indicates that only hospitalization will assure the suicidal patient's safety, at least on a short-term basis. In such unfortunate situations, effective aftercare following hospitalization may well require prolonged separation between the identified patient and his or her family.

CONCLUSION

This chapter has attempted to illustrate how a cognitive orientation can aid in the treatment of depression, particularly in work with couples and families. As described in the previous sections, many of the family processes that often accompany depressive symptoms are associated with dysfunctional belief systems. The cognitive approach seems to provide patients with both insight into dysfunctional thinking patterns and a means of generating more adaptive responses to future stressors. If treatment succeeds in changing both beliefs and behaviors in a distressed family, then it will have greatly reduced the probability of similar difficulties occurring in the future.

REFERENCES

Abrahms, J. (1981). Depression versus normal grief following the death of a significant other. In G. Emery, S. Hollon, & R. Bedrosian (Eds.), *New directions in cognitive therapy* (pp. 255–270). New York: Guilford Press.

Akiskal, H.S., & McKinney, W.T. (1975). Overview of recent research in depression: Integration of ten conceptual models into a comprehensive clinical frame. *Archives of General Psychiatry, 32,* 285–305.

Beck, A.T. (1976). *Cognitive therapy and the emotional disorders.* New York: International Universities Press.

Beck, A.T., & Beamesderfer, A. (1974). Assessment of depression: The Depression Inventory. In P. Pichot (Ed.), *Psychological measurements in psychopharmacology: Modern problems of pharmacopsychiatry* (Vol. 7). Basel, Switzerland: Karger.

Beck, A.T., Kovacs, M., & Weissman, A. (1975). Hopelessness and suicidal behavior: An overview. *Journal of the American Medical Association, 234,* 1146–1149.

Beck, A.T., Kovacs, M., & Weissman, A. (1979). Assessment of suicidal intention: The Scale for Suicide Ideation. *Journal of Consulting and Clinical Psychology, 47,* 343–352.

Beck, A.T., Rush, A.J., Shaw, B., & Emery, G. (1979). *Cognitive therapy of depression.* New York: Guilford Press.

Bedrosian, R.C. (1986). Cognitive and family interventions for suicidal patients. *Journal of Psychotherapy and the Family, 2*(3/4), 129–152.

Bedrosian, R.C., & Beck, A.T. (1979). Cognitive aspects of suicidal behavior. *Suicide and Life-Threatening Behavior, 9,* 87–96.

Bedrosian, R.C., & Beck, A.T. (1980). Principles of cognitive therapy. In M.J. Mahoney (Ed.), *Psychotherapy process: Current issues and future directions* (pp. 127–152). New York: Plenum.

Bedrosian, R.C., & Epstein, N. (1984). Cognitive therapy of depressed and suicidal adolescents. In H. Sudak, A. Ford, & N. Rushforth (Eds.), *Suicide in the young* (pp. 345–366). Littleton, MA: John Wright.

Burns, D.D. (1981). *Feeling good: The new mood therapy.* New York: New American Library.

Eidelson, R.J., & Epstein, N. (1982). Cognition and relationship maladjustment: Development of a measure of dysfunctional relationship beliefs. *Journal of Consulting and Clinical Psychology, 50,* 715–720.

Emery, G. (1983). *Own your own life.* New York: New American Library.

Guidano, V. & Liotti, G. (1983). *Cognitive processes and emotional disorders.* New York: Guilford Press.

Haley, J. (1973). *Uncommon therapy.* New York: Norton.

Haley, J. (1976). *Problem solving therapy.* San Francisco: Jossey-Bass.

Hamilton, M. (1967). Development of a rating scale for primary depressive illness. *British Journal of Social and Clinical Psychology, 6,* 278–296.

Minuchin, S. (1974). *Families and family therapy.* Cambridge, MA: Harvard University Press.

Minuchin, S., & Fishman, H. (1981). *Family therapy techniques.* Cambridge, MA: Harvard University Press.

Rogers, C.R. (1951). *Client-centered therapy.* Boston: Houghton Mifflin.

10

Cognitive–Behavioral Treatment of Adult Sexual Dysfunctions from a Family Perspective

Susan R. Walen and Richard Perlmutter

SEX THERAPY AND COGNITIVE THERAPY: A MARRIAGE

Although psychotherapists have long been interested in the topic of sexuality, the field of sex therapy is relatively new. Through the beginning of this century, the concept of sexual problems was unidimensional. All problems (from fetishes to phobias and performance difficulties) were grouped together as "sex problems" and all were treated in an undifferentiated way with whatever was the prevailing mode of therapy. In earlier times the treatment was likely to be a nonspecific dietary or rest cure, and success rates for treatment were not impressive (Kaplan, 1979). In this century, until the 1960s, the predominant approach to the treatment of sexual problems was psychoanalytic. Sexual problems were viewed as symptomatic of emotional conflicts originating in early childhood and, according to the theory, would persist until the conflict could be resolved and the personality of the individual restructured. In addition to being time-consuming and expensive, analytic treatment often left the individual with insight but with the sexual problem unresolved (Allgeier & Allgeier, 1984).

The next major step in the development of the field of sex therapy occurred as the definitions of sexual dysfunctions began to be refined. Kaplan (1979), tracing the history of the diagnosis and treatment of sexual dysfunctions, points out that a biphasic notion of sexuality was described in the 1950s and a triphasic notion in the 1970s. The biphasic notion acknowledged that problems of arousal (e.g., erectile dysfunction) were separable from problems of orgasm (e.g., premature ejaculation), and that different and specific treatment procedures could be applied to each. The triphasic notion added the dimension of desire-phase problems; in such cases the individual may have an intact arousal and orgasm system but have little or no desire for sex.

While diagnostic discriminations were improving, treatment options were being developed, primarily in behavioral modalities (e.g., Annon, 1974; Masters & Johnson, 1970; Wolpe, 1982). Specific behavioral prescriptions were becoming available, particularly for arousal and orgasm problems as well as phobic problems such as vaginismus. Somewhat less success was being reported for desire-phase problems and relationship-based problems, however (Kaplan, 1979). Clearly, a more "psychotherapeutic" approach with a broader viewpoint was often needed in addition to the behavioral prescriptions.

A cognitive approach, such as Ellis' Rational–Emotive Therapy, seemed to fill this gap neatly because it offered an avenue to the "internal dynamics" as well as the behavioral problems of the client. In his many writings on sexuality, Ellis has drawn an important distinction between *sexual dysfunctions* and *sexual disturbances* (e.g., Ellis, 1976). Sexual dysfunctions, which Ellis asserts are an occasional and inevitable part of every individual's sex life, need not cause undue emotional distress. For example, data collected by Kinsey and his associates indicate that 75% of all men ejaculate within two minutes of vaginal penetration (Kinsey, Pomeroy, & Martin, 1948). Similarly, researchers speculate that premature ejaculation may well be a recurrent problem for as many as 20% of all American males (Masters, Johnson, & Kolodny, 1982). Behaviors (such as rapid ejaculation) need not produce emotional distress or precipitate further sexual problems, but when they do, the resulting sexual disturbance may well be the more important clinical problem. The sexual disturbance is the consequence of "disturbing thinking" and thus falls within the working arena of the cognitive therapist.

Using the descriptive language of Ellis' Rational–Emotive Therapy, it is not the Activating Event (A) which causes the Consequence (C) of emotional and behavioral distress. Rather, it is how that event is perceived and evaluated by the individual, what "meaning" it has to the individual, and how the event compares to the individual's expectancies that determine the C. In short, it is the client's Belief System (B) that forms the network of cognitions that is the immediate precursor to the resultant emotional turmoil.

As sex therapists have long pointed out, our sexuality is perfectly natural— but rarely naturally perfect. Certainly aspects of sexuality can be negatively affected by biological events as well as environmental events, but perhaps the most pernicious effect on healthy sexual functioning is exerted by strong negative emotions such as anxiety, guilt, anger, and depression.

The theoretical model underlying cognitive–behavior therapy asserts that these strong negative emotions are largely caused by the erroneous or dysfunctional cognitions which precede and accompany them. Perhaps the most significant contribution a cognitive therapist can bring to the topic of sexuality, therefore, is to remind us that our most important sex organ is between our ears, not between our legs! Our sexual functioning can largely be conceived of as a set of attitudes and beliefs, often acquired very early in life, which can profoundly affect our sexual feelings and our sexual behavior.

The family context is important for two reasons. First, it is that context in which faulty beliefs are often learned originally; and, as adults, it is in that context that they are frequently played out, perpetuated, and passed on to a new generation (e.g., Darling & Hicks, 1983). Our families of origin are the sites in which much of our important early sexual learning takes place, by conditioning, by modeling, and by direct or indirect instruction (Calderone, 1979). Second, the family context reminds us that sexual attitudes and behaviors have an interpersonal and interactive component. The behavior of each individual in a couple (or larger family context) can serve as a stimulus (or Activating Event), which will be processed through the receiver's Belief System of expectancies and attitudes (Epstein, 1986). Thus both "cross-generational" cognitions and "systemic" (within the current family system) cognitions may have impact on the adults' sexual functioning.

This chapter describes a cognitive–behavioral framework for understanding the origin and maintenance of adult sexual dysfunctions and outlines cognitive–behavioral procedures for assessing and treating such problems. The application of this approach to sex therapy is later illustrated with a case description.

SEXUALITY: A COGNITIVE–BEHAVIORAL VIEW IN A FAMILY CONTEXT

Sex Education in the Family

When sexually troubled adults come for sex therapy, we typically ask them about the messages they received from their parents about sex. Frequently such clients disclaim this factor, saying, "I never got any negative messages about sex at home . . . why we never talked about it at all!" No communication is not the absence of a message. In fact, it can be one of the strongest messages of all. Many topics that are never mentioned are the "taboo" ones, and the strident message is, "That's so distasteful a subject that we won't even talk about it!"

In point of fact, education about sexuality begins from the earliest days of a child's life. Much of the teaching is nonverbal at first, as was discovered by a young working mother after she picked up her infant from the babysitter's house. When she unpinned the baby's diaper at home, the child reached for her own genitals but looked up at her mother with a playful, "testing" look. After a few such incidents, this attentive mother decided to ask the babysitter how she handled diaper rituals and, specifically, if she punished the child for touching herself. The kind and matronly sitter was shocked. "Why, I'd never punish her," she exclaimed. "I just whisk away her hand and pull up the clean diaper very quickly." This, of course, is teaching, and the message is: "That's something we don't do; we don't touch the electric outlets, the pretty knickknacks, or our genitals." This mother chose to do some reeducating. She asked the babysitter to follow her mothering model, and when the baby's diaper was next changed and the baby reached for her genitals, Mom smiled and soothingly said, "That feels good, doesn't it, dear? You can take a few minutes for pleasure."

In another family, the mother trained her children to wash their bodies with a washcloth but carefuly instructed them to use a separate cloth for their genitals. The attitude that these children acquired was that their genitals were "so dirty that they should not be touched at all." As the reader may easily imagine, negative attitudes such as these are not good preparation for the development of a comfortable adult sex life. In fact, two sisters from this family were seen in therapy, as adult women, and each presented a problem of sexual avoidance.

In these ways we acquire many messages about various aspects of sexuality from our families of origin, including concepts about sex roles, body awareness, sensuality, pleasure seeking, and love and caring. We learn, for example, how males act, how females act, how people show affection, and what kinds of sexual pleasuring activities are acceptable. Typically, some of our family's sexuality messages are negative (e.g., "Don't touch yourself, that's bad!"), some are positive (e.g., the excitement at daughter's first "training" bra), some are contradictory ("Sex is dirty" and "Save it for your beloved on your wedding night"), and some are conditional ("That's all right, but only after you're married").

Most informal sex education is of a negative slant: what *not* to do or touch or experience. Even those parents whose stated objective is to provide their children with a better sex education and more positive sex messages than they themselves received have a hard time. If their own training was negative and if they are still working through their own negative values, these parents can be confusing teachers at best. One such mother gave her daughter a very upbeat and informative lecture about sexual intercourse but was overheard to say, as she summarized, "And so, darling, when sex rears its ugly head. . . ." These messages are heard by children loudly and clearly.

One major study on parents as sex educators (Roberts, Kline, & Gagnon, 1979) pointed out in detail how poorly the job often is done. A sample of 1400 parents was interviewed about how they discussed sexual topics with their 3- to 11-year-old children. Most simply reported that they were silent. For example, less than half of the parents of 11-year-old children had even mentioned intercourse to their children. Among girls approaching the age of menarche, almost 40% had never heard of the topic from a parent. Less than 2% of the fathers had discussed wet dreams with their sons. In fact, many of these parents stated that they did not even display physical affection toward one another in front of the children. Presumably the parents' notion was that what their children do not see, they will not ask about. Apparently the children received that message; by the age of 9 or 10, questions on sexually related topics had virtually ceased.

It is the contention of the cognitive therapist that negative, contradictory, and conflictual attitudes about sexuality are at the heart of sexual disturbances. It is the work of cognitive therapy to help individuals identify and then modulate or correct dysfunctional attitudes and beliefs. Although a variety of cognitive and behavioral strategies may be used in treatment, the final common pathway leads to cognitive change which will result in lowered emotional tension and improved sexual functioning.

Secrets of Sex in Families

Because sexuality is such a difficult topic for many individuals to discuss, many aspects of sexuality remain as "secrets." Secrets are not necessarily bad, because some can encourage healthy interpersonal bonds and boundaries. For example, siblings often strengthen their relationships by sharing secrets to which the parents are not privy, and the parents do likewise. *Sexual* secrets and sexual privacies are not necessarily troublesome either. Many aspects of sex are private in most societies, and parents certainly need to socialize their children that certain behaviors and topics—sexual or not—are not appropriate in public places.

Troublesome secrets. When some other aspects of sexuality are kept a secret, the secretiveness can cause later problems even though the behavior is normative. For example, one such "secret" is about the *pleasure of sex.* Many parents readily express negative attitudes about sexuality while their positive attitudes are hidden securely away. Sex as a procreative act may be taught, in the home or in the schools, but sex as recreation, as a joyful expression of health or happiness or affection, is usually not mentioned.

Masturbation is one of the big "secrets" that exist within many couples, and both members may be reluctant to reveal this activity for fear that the act is so shameful that it will turn off the partner or cause the partner to feel rejected. Masturbation in children is not typically seen as a sign of normal, healthy sexual pleasuring in most families. The inhibition of masturbation ranges from subtle discouragement (e.g., abruptly removing a baby's hand from his or her genitals during diapering) through direct disapproval (e.g., scowls and statements) to severe and often cruel punishment. Sometimes these inhibitory messages effectively stop the behavior, and at other times the masturbation continues, now accompanied by shame, guilt, and anxiety. In either case, negative parental responses to a child's masturbation can produce sexual problems in the ensuing adult years.

Families commonly treat *childhood sexuality* as a "secret." Mary Calderone (1976), the noted sex expert, suggests that by the time children are 5 years old they have acquired at least one sexual problem: the feeling that there is something seriously wrong with them for asking questions about where babies come from or for finding pleasure in touching their own sex organs—or both! Although research (e.g., Money, 1976) suggests that sexual rehearsal play in childhood is essential to the development of adequate adult reproductive functioning, parental suppression of childhood sexuality continues. Children, however, are born sexual and remain sexual. What they do learn is to hide their sexuality; they appreciate the parents' messages that sex is simply too difficult a topic for the adults to handle. The kids muddle along in secret.

That *adolescents are sexual* is often treated as a "secret." If parents have remained secretive about sex and have not prepared their children to be able to discuss sexual impulses, then the time of adolescence can represent a continuation of the child's sexual secrets.

That *parents are sexual* is often a "secret." In some families, aspects of adult sexuality such as nudity, sexual play, or even signs of affection have become enveloped in a cloud of mystery and privacy. In families with children, such activites may go on only behind the parents' closed door.

Serious secrets. There are other types of sexual secrets that are predictably associated with problems, disturbance, and unhappiness. Included in this list are secrets about unusual object choices or sexual acts (paraphilias), gender dysphoria (e.g., transsexualism), rape, and incest. Each of these sexual issues may pose special problems for families, but the added burden of cognitive distortions and misattributions may exacerbate emotional turmoil for any family member.

For example, in incest the secret can become a central part of the family relationship. The child is placed in an impossible position in which she fears being the instrument of destruction of her family unit if she divulges the secret. This guilty thought, coupled with fear of punishment if she tells, imbues the child and her secret with a sense of much power and pain. The secret is also kept because of a complex attachment to the victimizer and a growing belief in the child that she has been doing something wrong (Swanson & Biaggio, 1985).

Over the last few years, the widespread prevalence of this particular secret has been entering public awareness and a great deal of public education has ensued. Much of this education has been directed at the children, through the schools and the public media, and has been largely aimed at correcting misattributions of responsibility and helplessness. For example, the authors of *A Better Safe Than Sorry Book* teach the following:

> The really bad thing is that sometimes even when you say "NO!" a grown person might force you to do things you don't want to do. If this happens, it is NEVER your fault, even if you can't say "NO." It is ALWAYS the grownup's fault. Tell someone you trust what has happened because most grownups are nice to kids. Tell, even if you are afraid they won't believe you. The person who gave you this book will believe you. Talking about what has happened is the first thing you need to do to feel better. (Gordon & Gordon, 1984, pp. 29–30)

Similar corrective messages are also being made available for adult survivors of childhood sexual abuse, whose cognitive and emotive scars from the experience may be directly related to their current sexual problems (Kirkpatrick, 1982).

To summarize thus far, problems of sexuality can be viewed as the end products of attitudinal problems, negative attitudes often being learned in our early families and reinforced in our current families. When the burden of sexual secrecy is added, the probability of attitudinal change may be reduced. Much of the work in cognitive–behavioral sex therapy therefore entails helping sexually troubled individuals to articulate and examine their sexually troubling cognitions.

Types of Cognitions That Affect Adult Sexual Functioning

Cognitions can be divided, albeit imperfectly, into two broad categories: perceptions and evaluations. A *perception,* in turn, can be viewed as a combination of three subprocesses: 1) detection: noting the presence of a stimulus or discriminating it from other stimuli; 2) labeling: applying descriptors to classify or categorize a stimulus; and 3) attribution: finding an explanation for a stimulus event (Walen, 1980).

For example, as I glance at an attractive person at a cocktail party, I become aware of a peculiar sensation in my chest (detection). I think to myself, "My heart just skipped a beat" (labeling), followed by, "Could this be what true love feels like?" (attribution). Why choose "true love" rather than "indigestion" as the attribution? Probably a number of factors contribute to this selection, including present situational cues, current motivational factors, and past learning experiences. Perception is a process of gathering data and drawing conclusions from those data. In the sexual arena, an inability to detect sexual stimuli, incorrect labeling of them, or misattribution about their causes may significantly impair sexual performance.

Evaluation, the other major class of cognitive events, involves a rating process along a good–bad continuum (Ellis, 1962). Obviously, evaluating a sexual stimulus as positive may enhance sexual feelings, just as a negative evaluation may diminish them. When evaluations become exaggeratedly negative—what Ellis refers to as "awfulizing"—the probability of sexual problems rises. For example, if a man cannot get an erection while with his partner, he may rationally evaluate this state of affairs as unfortunate, particularly if he and his partner had hoped to have sexual intercourse. If, in addition, he irrationally exaggerates his negative evaluation and concludes that the presence of a flaccid penis is a sexual "catastrophe," he may set up such an intense cycle of anxiety and guilt that he may not only block other present sexual pleasures but future ones as well.

Walen (1980, 1985) described a model of an individual's sexual arousal which illustrates the central role of perceptions and evaluations (see Figure 10–1). The concept is one of an internal feedback loop, cognitions forming the links between sexual stimuli, sexual arousal, and sexual behavior.

A sexual cycle may begin at Link 1 with the perception of a sexual

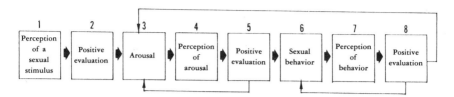

Figure 10–1. Proposed feedback loop of a positive sexual experience.
(Reprinted from Walen, 1980, p. 89, by permission of Human Sciences Press.)

stimulus, which must be noted (detection), labeled as such, and experienced as erotic (attribution), processes that seem largely to be learned in a cultural context (Ford & Beach, 1951). For example, consider how advertisements for undergarments in the Sears catalogue may be perceived quite differently by individuals from different cultures or subcultures, not only in America, but around the world.

If perceived as erotic, the next step in an arousal cycle requires that the stimulus be evaluated positively (Link 2). If a stimulus—a picture or an approach by another—is evaluated as "dirty" or "disgusting," arousal will probably not ensue.

If the results of Links 1 and 2 are positive, arousal at Link 3 will typically follow. Early stages of arousal (e.g., increases in heart rate, blood pressure, muscle tension) are quite generalized, often indistinguishable from autonomic events that accompany physical exertion or other affective states (Zuckerman, 1971). Labeling of arousal is a central concept in Schachter's (1964) formulation of emotional arousal. According to this model the two elements required for the experience of an emotion are a physiologic state of arousal and situational cues that enable the individual to label that arousal as a specific emotion. Perception and evaluation of arousal, seen as Links 4 and 5 in the current model, are related to the experience of sexual arousal and are subject to cognitive distortion.

At Link 4, perception of arousal, important differences have been noted between men and women as well as between individuals with histories of sexual problems and those without. In a nonclinical population, men seem to be quite accurate in detecting early signs of arousal (Barlow, 1977), whereas women seem far less "tuned in" to the presence of physiological arousal (Heiman, 1978). However, men with histories of nonorganic sexual dysfunction report far less sexual arousal than sexually functional men—at the same objective levels of erectile response (Sakheim et al., 1984). It seems that recognizing and responding to arousal cues is partly a function of the individual's criteria for arousal. How full must an erection be to be counted as a "sure" sign of arousal? How quickly must it occur to "count"? If the individual uses only genital signs as criteria, two errors may intrude in an arousal sequence: 1) if the signal is delayed or does not match rigid criteria, the individual may despair and abandon further attempts at a sexual pursuit, or 2) the individual may erroneously conclude that she or he is maximally aroused based on minimal cues and may experience either an anhedonic orgasm or none at all.

Increased arousal may be labeled as "anxiety" and may, in any case, often lead to heightened arousal. This phenomenon is well demonstrated in the film, *Cruising,* in which Al Pacino travels in the world of homosexual S&M "leather bars"; the film is both tense and highly erotic. Experimentally, a great many converging pieces of evidence have been accruing to indicate that physiologically elevated levels of "anxiety" can be associated with increased sexual interest and arousal (see Barlow, 1986, and Beck & Barlow, 1984, for reviews of this literature). For example, Ramsey (1943) noted that about 50% of adolescent boys responded with erections to nonerotic stimuli which involved elements of fear, excitement, or other emotional situations. Other studies have shown that experimentally induced anxiety can increase interpersonal or sexual attraction (e.g., Berscheid & Walster, 1974; Dutton & Aron, 1974). In sexually functional men, Barlow, Sakheim, and Beck (1983) demonstrated that even when told they would likely receive electric shocks if they did not get adequate erections, the direct impact of "performance anxiety" served to heighten sexual arousal.

At Link 5 in the model, arousal is evaluated. If an individual has learned to label arousal as bad, the subsequent negative emotional reactions may block further arousal. Thus the woman who thinks of her vulva as "dirty" or "smelly" and who evaluates her own lubrication as merely "sticky" or, worse, as "disgusting" may end up feeling embarrassed by her arousal and thus suppress it. If arousal is positively evaluated, however, the model suggests that arousal may be facilitated.

Once aroused, we begin or continue to behave sexually (Link 6). At this link, differences between the sexes emerge again. Women, more than men, tend to block themselves cognitively and therefore often do not "lose themselves" in the sexual encounter. Men are much more liable to time their movements and behaviors to their states of arousal than women are (Rook & Hammen, 1977). Among the reasons that have been suggested for this sex difference are 1) women have relatively less experience in producing states of sexual arousal in masturbation, 2) early heterosexual activity in women may be more gratifying for its social contact than its sexual contact, 3) female sex-role socialization stresses passivity and responsiveness to the needs of others, and 4) young women may have been preoccupied not so much with achieving sexual gratification as with monitoring access to their bodies (Gagnon & Simon, 1973). The effect of these factors may be seen in Link 7.

At Link 7 in the feedback model we observe our behavior, and it is at this juncture that a discrimination suggested by Masters and Johnson (1970) may play a key role. They discriminate "observation," which is probably inevitable and harmless, from "spectatoring," which implies a self-rating focus superimposed on a goal-oriented process. When we act as spectators, the here-and-now experience of the pleasure will be lost, and, more important, when the self-rating of the individual is critical, the results can certainly be a troublesome distraction from the arousal cycle.

Finally, and perhaps most important, at Link 8 we evaluate our sexual behaviors, and it is at this link that a sexual dysfunction can become a self-produced sexual disturbance. The resulting cognitive and emotional turmoil can inhibit current sexual functioning further and, if followed by negative expectancies, can inhibit future sexual attempts.

The important point that this representation of a sexual arousal cycle attempts to make is that cognitive events are crucial elements. Sexual arousal can be blocked at any juncture by distorted perceptions or negative evaluations. Such "unsexy" thinking can unleash a flood of anxiety, guilt, anger, or depression sufficient to derail the sexual episode.

The model also can be expanded to account for the interactive effects of partners on each other's sexual arousal. Sexual satisfaction and arousal may, in part, be a reflection of the ratio of negative to positive sexual contacts with the partner, paralleling the behavior exchange notion of marital distress (Jacobson & Margolin, 1979). Each such contact, however, has its subjective component. Consider, for example, the impact of a partner's arousal on one's own arousal. Many people report clinically what has been verified in the laboratory: if the partner is highly aroused and makes his or her sexual interest and sexual demands evident, one's own arousal can be augmented— unless a sexual dysfunction has been present. In a study by Beck, Barlow, and Sakheim (1983), clear differences were observed between sexually functional and sexually dysfunctional men when they were focusing on a partner who was highly aroused; the former showed increases in sexual arousal, whereas the dysfunctional men showed markedly lower sexual arousal. Part of the difference seemed to be "where their head was at"; the sexually functional men were focusing on erotic cues while the dysfunctional men seemed to be distracting themselves with performance worries.

One way to view the expansion of the feedback model of Figure 10–1 is to imagine two sex partners as two internal feedback systems superimposed on one another, each link in the individual system serving not only as an internal stimulus but an interactive stimulus as well. Each person not only perceives and evaluates his or her own arousal or sexual behavior but also that of the partner. As a specific example, Mr. X may have an erectile problem at Link 3, which is the stimulus not only for his perceptual and evaluative cognitions but also for those of his partner. In the best of circumstances, if he does not upset himself about the condition, he may go on to enjoy a variety of sexual behaviors at Link 6. However, if Mrs. X experiences negative perceptions or evaluations about Mr. X's genital responsiveness, she may withdraw (at her Link 6), which may set up a cycle of negative perceptions, evaluations, and emotional responses in Mr. X. The interactive nature of these cognitive, emotional, and behavioral processes is illustrated further in the case discussion to follow.

ASSESSMENT

When an individual or couple presents a sexual problem in therapy there are a number of areas in which assessments can be made. Typically, the initial aspect that is presented is the sexual dysfunction itself, and the clinician will want to evaluate the biological, psychological, and interpersonal aspects of it. Equally important, as pointed out in the previous section, is the sexual disturbance that one or both members of the couple experiences as a consequence of the dysfunction. Evaluating the disturbance entails assessing the affective and cognitive components of the distress. Sensible treatment planning also requires an assessment of the marriage in terms of commitment, expectancies, marital cognitions, and behavioral skills such as communication, assertion, negotiation, and problem solving.

Sexual Dysfunctions

Pinpointing the disorder. The *DSM-III* (American Psychiatric Association, 1980) utilizes a three-part conception of sexual dysfunctions, largely based on the work of Helen Singer Kaplan (Kaplan, 1979); this includes desire disorders, arousal disorders, and orgasm disorders. *Desire disorders* may range from merely low sexual desire (or activity) to sexual aversion. *Arousal disorders* include decreased subjective arousal and/or decreased objective arousal (e.g., difficulty achieving and/or maintaining erections). *Orgasm disorders* can include the timing of the orgasm (e.g., premature or delayed orgasm), the quality of the orgasm (e.g., anhedonic or anesthetic orgasm), or the requirements for orgasm (e.g., only in masturbation or only with a rigidly defined kind of mechanical stimulation). These disorders may also be described in terms of the longevity (e.g., throughout adult life or more recent onset) and their situational specificity (e.g., global or occurring only under certain stimulus conditions).

In addition, there are *sexual pain disorders* such as vaginismus (involuntary spasm of the muscles surrounding the vaginal entrance), dyspareunia (male or female genital pain during sexual activity), genital pain accompanying ejaculation, and pain in other parts of the body resulting from sexual activity. Finally, there are *problems with sexual frequency* (e.g., desire for more or less frequent sexual activity, or frequency disparities between partners).

Schover, Friedman, Weiler, Heiman, and LoPiccolo (1982) recommend assessing a number of other pieces of qualifying information which may affect the prognosis for sex therapy. Included in this list are unusual sexual preferences (e.g., fetishism, transvestism, sexual assaultiveness, or preference for gender other than that of the partner), history of sexual abuse (e.g., rape victim, incest victim), substance abuse, severe marital distress or spouse abuse, active extramarital affairs, and medical conditions or medications that could affect sex.

A diagnostic device that we have found particularly useful is the multiaxial problem-oriented system for sexual dysfunctions described by Schover et al. (1982). This six axis classification system enables the therapist to code problems of desire, arousal, orgasm, coital pain, frequency dissatisfactions, and the qualifying information just described. The information needed to code the patient's dysfunction(s) can be assessed in a variety of ways which are nicely reviewed by Conte (1986). Included in her review are interviews (ranging from unstructured discussions to numerically scaled problem-centered diagnostic interviews), questionnaires (ranging from short, unidimensional scales to complex multidimensional scales), and self-report behavioral records (e.g., keeping a record of one's sexual behaviors and perhaps reactions to them). Some of these devices may be more appropriate for clinical research than for the exigencies of clinical practice.

In our practice, we like to use the Sex History Form (SHF), which we try to mail to couples before their initial interview. The form contains 28 questions in multiple-choice format asking for detailed information on various aspects of sexual behavior, for each partner to fill out independently. Normative data on a sample of well-functioning couples are available for comparison purposes. (The Sex History Form and the norms are available from Dr. J. LoPiccolo at Texas A&M University, College Station, Texas 77843–4235.)

Having the SHF information in hand can help the interviewer in a number of ways: 1) the clients have an expectation that sex history information will be taken in detail; 2) a bit of desensitization to revealing sexual problems may already have taken place; and 3) the answers to the questions may help the clinician guide his or her further inquiry, particularly when there are discrepancies between the two partners. We typically obtain further assessment about the nature of the sexual dysfunction in our initial interviews with the individual, the partner, and the couple seen together. Additional details on sexual functioning may evolve as the couple begins treatment and brings back feedback from their sexual homework assignments (see below).

In the initial sex therapy interview, which typically lasts for two hours, we begin by seeing both members of the couple together (unless practical considerations, client request, or information from the referral source—e.g., very high levels of emotionality when the couple talks together—indicate otherwise). In this period we do a problem scan, guided by the SHF information, paying particular attention to how each partner views the problem(s) and to how they communicate with each other. We then ask to speak to each of them individually by saying something like: "A normal part of our procedure is to meet with each of you in private, since all of us have some areas that we wouldn't feel as comfortable discussing in front of our spouse." The intent of such a communication is to forestall any automatic negative assumptions that a partner may have about an individual session. If one partner seems uneasy with this procedure, we reiterate that it is "routine clinical practice" for us in our work with "all" couples.

During these individual meetings, under the promise of confidentiality, we ask a number of open-ended questions such as "Are there any situations, other than with your spouse, where your sexual response is different?" We inquire about sexual fantasies, sexual relationships before the current one, concurrent sexual relationships, physical attractiveness of the partner, and sexual skill of the partner. We ask about the client's conceptual understanding of the problem ("Why do you think you . . . or your partner . . . has this problem?"), and we usually end this portion of the interview by asking if the client has any questions for us.

We experience no problems with keeping these secrets and have found that the opportunity to learn these secrets is often indispensable to selecting appropriate treatment options. For example, if the individual is sexually dysfunctional with the spouse but not with another current or previous sex partner, need for further assessment will be quickly realized. In such cases, the performance contrast may significantly aid the cognitive, emotive, and behavioral assessment or may suggest other diagnostic considerations. To illustrate, in one case the outside partner was same-sexed, and the clinical issue of sexual orientation and the accompanying dysphoria was raised. In another case the male experienced inability to reach orgasm with his wife but was highly orgasmic with a lover; he was also much more verbally assertive and emotionally comfortable with the lover, and the differential assessment revealed some inhibitory attitudes he maintained toward "the wife" which had inhibited him through the course of three different marriages.

Pinpointing etiology. Years ago, sex therapists thought more dichotomously about the etiology of sexual problems. It was assumed to be either organic or psychogenic. Further, it was assumed that in the overwhelming majority of cases, sex problems such as erectile dysfunction were caused by psychological problems (Kaya, Moore, & Karacan, 1979). More recent evidence, however, suggests that as many as 50–60% of men diagnosed as having psychogenic impotence may have a relevant organic condition (Fisher, Schiavi, Edwards, Davis, Reitman, & Fine, 1979), and similar data are accruing for women (e.g., Hatch, 1981). Further, in any individual case it may be impossible to discriminate the relative importance of psychological versus somatic factors, since many individuals show both and since these factors may be highly interactive.

The importance of a complete physiological workup cannot be ignored, particularly in problems of male erectile dysfunction. A comprehensive diagnostic evaluation usually includes routine laboratory and endocrine workups, as well as morphologic, urologic, neurologic, and vascular (Doppler flow) evaluations. One procedure that has become more frequently used is the Nocturnal Penile Tumescence (NPT) study. A complete penile tumescence study may include daytime penile plethysmography while the client watches erotic films and two or three nights of NPT work at a sleep laboratory, monitoring erections that occur during rapid eye movement (REM) sleep. Detailed NPT studies such as these have been shown to be accurate in detecting organic dysfunction in about 72% of the cases, but incorrect or equivocal in 28% (Macksood & James, 1983). Less sophisticated devices (such as home-NPT monitors or the plastic-strip method) are sometimes used by urologists but are considered to have an unacceptable margin of error (Conte, 1986).

In addition to knowing of prescription drugs the client may be taking and which may impede sexual functioning, it is important to ask about alcohol and tobacco use. Longstanding use of these drugs can produce not only a short-term pharmacologic effect but also long-term vascular effects. For example, some researchers suggest that the negative effects of alcohol on sexual functioning can be demonstrated from the first drink of the evening (LoPiccolo, 1985).

Sexual Disturbances

Once the sexual dysfunction has been pinpointed, the more psychologically interesting question is: Why is the individual and/or the partner disturbed about it? In what way is it (the dysfunction) a problem for them? In fact, these are the questions we direct to the couple. These questions, themselves, may serve to begin the process of normalization and challenge the negative attitudes that surround the symptom. The questions imply concepts (which will be addressed more explicitly in therapy) such as the following: 1) it is not *necessary* to be disturbed about the symptom, 2) it is not necessary to have one's sex life made *totally* problematic by it, and 3) symptoms are not the same as dysfunctions, and dysfunctions are not equivalent to disturbances. The disturbance refers to the individuals' negative emotional and cognitive reactions to the dysfunctions and symptoms.

Most clients initially seem nonplussed by the preceding statements, because they may operate under a different belief system than the cognitive–behavior therapist. The client may believe that the sexual problem (e.g., a flaccid penis) *is* the problem, and that his penis causes his distress. Such men are asking for what Ellis (1980) calls "the inelegant solution" to their problems; they are requesting penis therapy, or a change in the Activating Event. Their thinking is based on the assumption that sex requires an erection, and thus, they believe, their distress is a "natural reaction" to their erectile dysfunction. Their problem is, they assert, that they simply do not get erections when they want them. Further, they point out, it is only in sexual situations in which they fail to get erections that they ever feel distressed. Thus, they conclude, it is the erectile dysfunction that is the source of the distress and it is only normal erectile functioning that will alleviate the distress. As one client put it, "I want a penis that gets hard on command!"

The cognitive–behavior therapist is operating under another set of assumptions and will be aiming, at least initially, for what Ellis (1980) calls "the elegant solution" or "preferential RET." This approach suggests change in the client's attitude toward the problem whether or not there is a corresponding change in the original activating event. In fact, if the therapist leaps too quickly into treatment suggestions for the penile dysfunction, the client may assume that the therapist agrees that the erection is the problem. It is primarily to counteract this belief that the elegant solution is introduced to the client before the behavioral strategies of sex therapy are even attempted. The elegant solution will thus be more than a supplement to traditional sex therapy approaches; we view it as an essential *prerequisite* component (Bass & Walen, 1986). In subsequent portions of this chapter we illustrate how we introduce this prerequisite component.

To assess the disturbance about the sexual dysfunction, therefore, we help clients to articulate their thoughts and feelings about the issues. This work may be done in session during interviews, particularly when displays of affect are present. It may be done by asking the couple to keep logs of sexual encounters and reactions to them and using these examples for discussion in session. It may also be done by using assessment instruments such as the Relationship Belief Inventory (Eidelson & Epstein, 1982).

The kinds of cognitions that are particularly relevant are those that induce strong competing affective responses (e.g., anger at the spouse, guilt, or self-doubt) or those which, as in the feedback model described previously, either distract the individual from erotic cues or suggest negative meanings to erotic events.

The Marriage

There is a complex relationship between a couple's sexual relationship and marital satisfaction. Clinically, one can find the occasional couple whose sexual relationship is minimal or highly infrequent, yet whose marriage is compassionate and content. At the other extreme are the occasional couples who get along like the proverbial "cats and dogs," yet who have a passionate and highly satisfactory sex life together. However, Sager (1976) points out that the vast majority of couples, whether complaining primarily of marital or sexual troubles, suffer both. For a time it seemed that researchers in marital therapy or sex therapy were compartmentalizing these issues so completely that they not only treated along only one dimension (marriage or sex), but assessed only one dimension. Recent research is more interactive and has demonstrated the positive impact that sex therapy can have on marital functioning (e.g., Foster, 1978) as well as the positive impact of marital therapy on sexual satisfaction (e.g., O'Leary & Arias, 1983).

The quality of the general relationship as well as the extent to which the partner is rated as sexually attractive have both been shown to be positively related to the successful outcome of sex therapy (Hawton & Catalan, 1986; Lansky & Davenport, 1975; Snyder & Berg, 1983; Whitehead & Mathews, 1977). Several useful scales to measure marital happiness are available. These include the well-validated Locke–Wallace Marital Adjustment Scale (Locke & Wallace, 1959), which provides an overall satisfaction quotient; the Relationship Belief Inventory (Eidelson & Epstein, 1982), which can help articulate some dysfunctional marital beliefs; and brief marital satisfaction questionnaires such as that used by Lazarus (1985), which asks couples to rate (0–10) their satisfaction on 12 behavioral components of the relationship (e.g., pleased with friends we share in common, in agreement with the way we are spending money). We have found the Lazarus scale useful because it can quickly pinpoint for the couple what some of their areas of dissatisfaction are, and as we work on these issues we share a common subjective reference point which can reflect immediate change. For instance, money management was a considerable issue for one couple; husband and wife both rated their satisfaction on this item as a zero or one initially. At the end of a long session in which we focused on alternative solutions to the money issue, their satisfaction ratings were much higher, and they were urged to use this simple subjective scale as they experimentally implemented their chosen solution.

Communication Skills

In addition to the consideration of the general communication skills of active listening and relevant reply (see Chapter 1), we specifically need to be concerned about sexual communication, which can include both verbal and nonverbal messages. One way to assess couple communication initially is to ask directly, "Have you and your partner been able to discuss your concerns about this problem? Do you think that your partner understands your concern?" Another is to check out this understanding: "Mary, in your own words, what do you think John's concerns are?" And, "John, how accurate is Mary's account of the issue?" Of course, the reverse dialogue is also used, having John describe Mary's issues and checking out the accuracy of his report with his partner.

Once sex therapy homework assignments get under way, the couple typically will be asked to practice giving each other verbal and nonverbal feedback on the exercises they are doing (see below, Clinical Strategies and Techniques). They can then, in turn, give the therapist feedback on their ability to do this communication work and their comfort level as they continue to practice.

The therapist, of course, will be attending to the cognitive blockades that inhibit clear and direct sexual communication and will help the individual(s) challenge those dysfunctional attitudes.

Assertiveness Skills

In addition to the general issues of assertiveness deficits described in Chapter 1, specific assertiveness issues in sexual functioning include 1) difficulties in sexual initiations and/or refusals, 2) difficulty in making or refusing sexual requests, and 3) difficulties in appropriate expression of emotion, especially loving or positive comments. Although occasionally these problems stem from skill deficits, we find that more often they are the result of cognitive blockades.

Assessment of these areas is done by clinical interview. For example, the couple, in describing a typical sexual encounter, will be asked questions such as "Who typically initiates? How does she (or he) signal interest? Are the signals clear? Is there some other signal you might prefer?" Later they will be asked questions such as "And if you are not in the mood, how do you typically let your partner know? Is the signal clear? Is there some other signal you [the receiver] might prefer?"

From our clinical work, we have learned that there are certain kinds of cognitive blockades that are very common, and to which the therapist may want to stay alert. For instance, stereotypical sex-role expectations may get in the way (e.g., "It wouldn't be ladylike to ask him for that" or "It's not manly to tell her how much I love her"). Guilt-inducing cognitions are common: "If I tell him what I want, he may feel hurt" or "She really looks interested, so I guess I should just go ahead with it even though I'm too pooped to pop!" Anger-cognitions are also very often present, especially of the mind-reading variety: "If my partner really loved me, I wouldn't have to tell her (him) what I want."

Problem-Solving Skills

Spivack, Platt, and Shure (1976) identified a number of specific problem-solving skills. For example, the therapist may assess problem-focus skills (e.g., Is the problem stated in such a way that it is potentially solvable?), solution-generating skills (e.g., brainstorming), consequential thinking (e.g., What are the consequences of each of these possible solutions?), means-ends thinking (e.g., If we want to achieve that end, what steps do we need to do?), and application skills (e.g., Exactly how shall we implement this solution?). If the attempted solution does not work, do the problem solvers "go back to the drawing board" to try out the next most likely solution or do they merely blame each other for its failure? Can they, in other words, *maintain* the problem-solving focus?

Negotiation Skills

In addition to communication skills, assertiveness skills, and problem-solving skills, couples may need negotiation skills and a positive negotiation attitude. As pointed out in Chapter 1, beliefs about the appropriateness and the value of negotiation will be as important as the behavioral aspects of negotiation. As with problem solving, negotiation frequently is not considered by couples to be a normal part of one's sex life. Sex is often put in a realm by itself because of certain other beliefs.

TECHNIQUES USED IN JOINING WITH THE COUPLE

In addition to the usual joining and engagement problems with couples, those couples presenting with sexual concerns may have special problems because of the intensity of discomfort they feel with the topic of sexuality. A useful guiding principle in the joining phases of the interview is to think in terms of modulating the level of anxiety.

Techniques for modulating anxiety vary from therapist to therapist and from school to school. A hallmark of cognitive–behavior therapy is the establishment of a *collaborative* working relationship between therapist and client(s). One straightforward approach to anxiety management, therefore, would be simply to state to clients that you recognize that many people react to certain sexual topics with some anxiety and that you will do your best to help them move at a comfortable pace. You can solicit their help in staying "tuned in" to their level of tension.

A particularly useful strategy is to spend some time on a detailed history of the life of the marriage and each individual member in the present family. Other tension-reducing strategies include the appropriate use of humor, discussions between cotherapists if both are present, refocusing on the most asymptomatic member of the couple, or simply taking breaks as needed during the interview. Throughout, the therapist strives to present himself or herself as interested, empathic, and "unshockable."

The main therapeutic stance in dealing with sexual concerns and dysfunctions is for the therapist to be "askable." The consistent nonjudgmental stance of the therapist can be an important souce of data to challenge negative automatic thoughts.

The vocabulary one uses in discussions of sexuality can be important in the "joining" phase of therapy. With very inhibited couples, we have found that playing a desensitization "word game" can sometimes help (e.g., a "brainstorming" session for "all the synonyms you have ever heard or read for X", where X is a series of specific sexual terms such as breasts, penis, vagina, intercourse, and masturbation).

Another factor that is especially pertinent in joining and engaging with couples and their sexual concerns is the concept of "normalization." An important normalization strategy may be to provide corrective information, helping clients to understand that their symptoms are common and very similar to what others have experienced (Frank, Anderson, & Rubinstein, 1978). Normalization may, in fact, be the first step toward diminishing the disturbance about a sexual dysfunction.

In summary, the process of joining with the couple and/or larger family unit on issues of sexuality primarily entails maintaining the *collaborative* approach, which is a hallmark of cognitive–behavioral therapy in general. In addition, the process may require a clinical sensitivity to the difficulty that many people feel in sharing information about their sex life and, especially, their sexual problems. By gently and nonjudgmentally helping the individuals to identify and challenge the negative attitudes that block them from doing this initial sharing—as a first phase of therapy—the stage may be set for using the same process in the clinical work to be done on the sexual problem itself.

CLINICAL STRATEGIES AND TECHNIQUES

An Initial Clinical Decision: Treating the Disturbance First

An important clinical strategy that guides the course of our therapy is based on the distinction, drawn earlier in the chapter, between a sexual dysfunction and a sexual disturbance. The former is a genital problem, whereas the latter is a cognitive–emotive problem. Our clinical strategy, which operates throughout the course of both assessment and treatment, is to focus primarily on the disturbance about the dysfunction. We do so for a number of reasons. To begin, we do not wish to collude with the client that the genital "misfunction" is a dire calamity to be addressed with all due haste.

A second reason why we treat the disturbance first is that even with a successful course of sex therapy, we expect that the client will function in a normal—that is, often imperfect—sexual manner. If the client has not learned how to remain sexually undisturbed when the body performs imperfectly, he or she is at high risk for relapse and a return to the sex clinic.

Third, our clinical experience has taught us that when the emotional distress is lowered, the genital problem often clears up by itself. Treating the secondary sexual disturbance first often obviates the need to address the primary sexual dysfunction because the individual is no longer dysfunctional.

Fourth, it has been our experience that when a couple has had a genital problem for some time and has become terribly overwrought about it, many other "couple problems" may have been created. For example, in one case involving erectile dysfunction in the husband, the distress about the decreasing penile capacity resulted in a series of frenzied attempts to find a "magic" set of stimulus conditions that would restore potency. The husband tried all manner of salves and creams, special diets and herbs, and finally turned to what his wife called "kinky sex." He insisted that she wear more revealing clothes and bought her lingerie that she found not only uncomfortable but distasteful to wear. He insisted that she pose nude for him and he sent her photo to a "swinger's" magazine. He badgered her into allowing him to try wife-swapping parties, reading pornographic material to him, and other sex practices that she found more of a "turn off" than a "turn on." She went along with these unwanted sex games for a while because, as she said, "I knew how upset he was about his problem." Eventually not only had her discomfort with these practices built up, but so had her anger. She stated, "I'm sick of having our whole sex life revolve around his damned penis. That's all he can think about, and now he wants to have an implant put in! I don't want that. Frankly, I don't care if he ever gets hard again. I hate our love life. I don't want a 'cocksman,' I want a good, tender lover!" In this case, helping the husband to become less distressed about the dysfunction was useful because he allowed himself to slow down his race to the surgeon's table and pay attention to his wife's requests for better communication and better lovemaking.

Finally, we consider treating the distress to be the initial therapy task because this strategy may facilitate empathy and communication between the sex partners. As an example, in the preceding case, the husband had no idea that his penile performance was of minimal importance to his wife in terms of her sexual satisfaction or general enjoyment. Once he was able to voice his concern that he would disappoint her sexually, she was able to reassure him quite lovingly and teach him what she did find stimulating.

Because the sexual system usually involves the couple, we view it as important that both partners agree to tackle the "elegant solution" (Ellis, 1986) first, and learn how to reduce sexual disturbances before working on sexual dysfunctions. Some clients quickly grasp this conceptual framework and readily understand the logic behind it. Other clients, particularly those whose emotional distress is very high, may take longer to agree to this therapy contract. In negotiating an agreement to this contract, the therapist has an opportunity to help the client discover some of the cognitions that make this solution seem unappealing. Often these cognitions take the form of sexual "shoulds," "oughts," and "musts."

In treating sexual disturbances, the therapist's primary tasks are to help the client 1) clarify the affective distresses, 2) elicit the relevant cognitions, 3) appreciate the connection between the two, and 4) dispute, challenge, and change the dysfunctional cognitions. In working toward the "elegant solution," the couple typically is sent home understanding that the sexual problem (e.g., his erectile dysfunction) will be with them for a while, and that their job is to see how they might enjoy one another sexually during this time. Often this therapy approach provides the first opportunity the individual or couple has had to simply be in bed with the partner without self-imposed demands to perform and perform well. For individuals who have organic causes for their genital dysfunction, the elegant solution becomes the only lasting solution to their problem. For all individuals, a lesson from the elegant solution soon becomes apparent; instead of doing a good "job" of sex, they can reach for the "joy" of sex.

The Second Step: Treating the Dysfunction

Although it would be beyond the scope of this chapter to describe the large variety of techniques used in sex therapy, we highlight a few of the more common components of sex therapy, stressing those aspects to which the cognitive therapist would pay particular attention. Caird and Wincze (1977) suggested that the majority of sex therapy programs include three general components: 1) *education,* 2) *redirection of sexual focus,* and 3) *graded sexual exposure* (via relaxation exercises or homework exercises with a partner).

A good deal of the work in treating the common sexual dysfunctions entails correcting misconceptions and providing corrective information. In essence, a significant part of sex therapy is sex education. Often this work entails teaching basic anatomy and physiology. Zilbergeld (1978) and Barbach (1975) are particularly helpful bibliotherapy sources for couples.

Among women, the most common sexual dysfunctions are orgasmic difficulties (Kaplan, 1979), and frequently these are rooted in lack of information
or incorrect information. The woman and her partner may be expecting her
to have orgasms reliably during intercourse without additional clitoral stimulation. By teaching corrective information about female pelvic anatomy and
orgasmic physiology, the woman and her partner are urged to think of her
clitoris, not the vaginal walls, as her "sex organ," the site of erotic stimulation
most likely to lead to orgasm. Of course, this teaching often has to be quite
precise. In one case, the woman assured the therapist that her clitoris was
"quite dead" and, in any case, was "very hard to reach." With the aid of
drawings and models, the therapist was able to determine that this woman
had, for years, been rubbing a hemorrhoid, not her clitoris!

In a similar way, corrective information can also be useful in questions
about intensity of orgasm. Some preorgasmic women seem to be expecting
the orgasm to be an astonishing or profoundly moving experience. Their
expectations of the orgasm make it sound more like a Hollywood version of
a seizure than the simple spinal reflex that it is. Occasionally such a woman
will discover that she had been having orgasms all along, but she did not
recognize them for what they were.

Common clinical strategies in behavioral sex therapy include suggestions
for a gradual rebuilding of the individual's or couple's sex life. Frequently
such work begins with each individual practicing the maintenance of a sensual
focus while doing self-stimulation or masturbation work. Subsequent steps
might include the gradual *in vivo* desensitization procedures generically described as Sensate Focus (e.g., nondemand touching) by Masters and Johnson
(1970). These exercises may accomplish a number of goals, both cognitive
and behavioral. By removing or lowering the demands for performance, the
individuals may be able to take the time to learn more about their own
sexual and sensual feelings. An exploratory attitude rather than a goal-directed
attitude may open avenues of communication and ultimately serve to enrich
the sexual repertoire. Sexual failures can be removed if the focus is on pleasure
rather than accomplishment. The cognitive focus we encourage is a change
from "How am I doing?" to "What am I experiencing or learning?"

As the couple brings in their "field report" on the assignments, they may
also present a rich sampling of cognitive and emotive reactions. Not uncommonly, for example, women report that it was very difficult for them to
receive sensual pleasuring passively because they distract themselves with
cognitions such as "He's probably getting bored . . . he can't be enjoying
himself just touching me without really getting sex" or "He's just sitting up

there looking at me and I feel like I'm on stage and he can see every flaw.'' Male clients often get distracted because of similar performance-based and distracting thoughts such as "I like this, but I'm not getting an erection . . . she'll probably think I'm not enjoying this . . . or that there's something wrong with me.'' A supportive partner may be an important source of data to counter these negative thoughts.

In addition to the Sensate Focus exercises, the sex therapist may want to prescribe some specific sexual recommendations for a specific dysfunction (e.g., the "Squeeze" or the "Stop–Start" procedure for premature ejaculation, teaching "orgasm triggers" for inducing a delayed orgasmic reflex, and recommending medical intervention for erectile dysfunction). Details about procedures such as these can be found in sex therapy texts and journals (e.g., LoPiccolo & LoPiccolo, 1978).

SPECIAL CLINICAL ISSUES

Sex Outside the Family

Clinically, we have occasionally found the presence of an active sexual affair to be helpful in understanding a complex sexual problem, such as a situational sexual dysfunction. These individuals may experience a sexual dysfunction in some particular situations or with some particular partners and otherwise have no sexual problem. For example, one client reported that he had no sexual dysfunction when he was with his lover but had a lifelong problem of anorgasmia or very delayed orgasm in his two marriages. Before coming to therapy, he had promised himself that he would not have sex with his lover because he feared that the "other woman" might be clouding the issue, and he remained true to his word for a number of months before— as he put it—he slipped. He was not, by nature, an introspective person and had found it difficult to identify cognitions and emotions when discussing his problems with the therapist. He continued to try to "listen to his head talk" when he was with his wife and was beginning to be able to articulate some of the distracting thoughts and attitudes that would block him sexually. After the "slip" with his lover, an encounter which was relaxed and sexually very satisfying to him (in contrast to the labored lovemaking he did with his wife), he was able to appreciate some of the cognitive differences in the two encounters. The contrasting "head talk" he discovered in himself was useful in his therapy, and he began to practice bringing some of his "lover head talk" (as he called it) home to his bedroom.

The Therapist: Sexual Attitudes and Behaviors

Clinical experiences as sex educators and sex therapy supervisors over the years has taught us an important lesson: the sexual attitudes of the therapist are often as important to assess as the attitudes of the family members. Cognitive–behavioral therapists try to maintain a collaborative empirical approach to their work, along with a sturdy nonjudgmental base. In perhaps no other area of cognitive–behavioral therapy is that stance as important as in the "delicate" area of sex therapy.

Therapists often grow up in the same kinds of families which are embedded in the same kinds of cultures as their clients. Unless they stop and assess their own attitudes about varieties of sexuality, they may not realize the impact that their own negative attitudes, restrictive values, or other sexual "shoulds" play in their therapy work. We found it useful in our own training to do some intensive study of cross-cultural aspects of sexuality and to do some training in Sexual Attitude Reassessment (SAR) courses, and we recommend the same to therapists interested in specializing in sex therapy.

Use of Cotherapy

In sex therapy, based on the early work of Masters and Johnson (1970), it was thought that cotherapy teams were important to the treatment outcome. However, empirical studies indicate that neither the number nor the gender of therapists influence the outcome of therapy delivered to couples, either in sex therapy (Arentewicz & Schmidt, 1983; LoPiccolo, Heiman, Hogan & Roberts, 1985) or marital therapy (Kaplan-Mehlman, Baucom & Anderson, 1983). In addition, it is certainly less cost-effective to use a cotherapy model. Nonetheless, therapist preference may dictate the use of two therapists either for training purposes or for professional growth and enjoyment.

Sexual Problems in a Family Context: The Wilsons

Sexual problems are generally not individual problems; rather, they interactively affect the individual and the partner and often impinge on the family unit as a whole. The interplay of individual, couple, and even multigenerational family systems can perhaps be illustrated by a case example. We present the "Wilson family," who, while they actually represent a composite of cases from our practices enable us to illustrate a sampling of clinical problems and to indicate some assessment issues and some cognitive–behavioral treatment interventions that were used.

The Wilson family consists of the following people:

Sid Wilson, a 42 year-old-engineer
Doris Wilson, 37 years old, a librarian, and Sid's second wife
Shawn, Sid's 12-year-old son from his first marriage
DiDi, the 6-year-old daughter of Sid and Doris

The initial phone call for help was made by Doris. She was in great distress and wanted to know how quickly she and her husband could be seen for sex therapy. A time was set for an initial consultation a few days hence, but Doris wanted to know if there was something she could do in the meantime to calm down. The therapist asked Doris if she would be willing to write a log of the presenting problem. She was asked to write down the event that triggered her distress and then to collect all the "thoughts and feelings which she could be aware of which were flowing through her." The therapist pointed out that it was very helpful that she was upset now, because that might make it easier for her to capture her "thoughts and feelings while they were hot." Doris was asked to bring this material to the first session so that, even if she had calmed down, they would have a clear record of what her experience had been at the time. The invitation to have Sid do the same was also extended by the therapist, but they were asked to write independently of each other and were instructed that they need not share these writings.

The purposes of this initial assessment strategy are threefold. First, it is designed to address the patient's distress about the problems that will be presented. Ellis (1986) refers to such distress as "secondary symptoms," or disturbance about disturbance," and points out that they may be more intense and prolonged than the primary problems. The exercise may thus serve a therapeutic function of instilling hope, counteracting cognitions of helplessness, and cognitively restructuring the meaning of the emotive experience of the client. Doris, for example, reported that she found it calming to do this writing because she told herself, "Well, at least there's something I can do now, and maybe it's not so terrible that I'm this upset because at least the doctor will really know how I feel inside."

Another purpose of this assignment was to begin to focus Doris on her "thoughts and feelings." This focus occupies much of the work in the cognitive–behavioral treatment and this first task may be a rough approximation in shaping the skills of discriminating thoughts from feelings and learning to accurately report both. It also enables the therapist to learn the extent of the client's skill level before therapy begins.

Finally, the preliminary task may begin to impress upon the client what has long been the philosophical watchword of the cognitive therapist, perhaps best expressed by the Stoic philosopher Epictetus: "People are not disturbed by things, but by the views which they take of them." The assignment may begin to train the client to look not only at outside events, but at internal reactions to these events.

Doris and Sid both came to the initial evaluation session. Each was seen for a private consultation period with the therapist, and then they convened as a couple to discuss the next course of action and begin to develop a therapy contract.

Doris and Sid were seen individually for their initial meeting with the therapist for a number of reasons. First, at a practical level, if one or both members of the couple were highly distressed, communication could be aided by working individually with the therapist. Second, since sexuality is such a "loaded" topic for many people, they may find it easier to speak in privacy and, if there are sexual secrets between the couple, confidentiality can be preserved while important information can be shared with the therapist. Third, and perhaps theoretically most relevant, this format can begin to teach to the couple the concept that each is disturbed in his or her own right, as individuals, and the cognitive–behavioral components of this disturbance are brought into the partnership (Ellis, 1986; Hauck, 1986). As Ellis (1986) states: "RET . . . emphasizes and teaches mating skills, but it does so within a comprehensive framework of helping each of the partners work on their individual selves too" (p. 9).

Doris came in first, and tearfully related the incident that she had written down. She stated that their sexual relationship had been very dissatisfying for a long time, and on the day that she had called the therapist she had walked into the bathroom where she found her husband masturbating. She described herself as "going crazy," which she and the therapist were eventually able to dissect into a mixture of anger, self-hatred, and fear. Some of her thoughts were: "He told me he didn't masturbate. For nine years he's been lying to me! I guess I haven't ever turned him on. I'm not sure I love him either. I feel cheated! Well, that's the end of this relationship. Oh, no . . . what will become of these children?" Doris stated that she wanted help with her anger, but that she also really was not clear about whether she wanted to remain in this marriage.

During this initial contact, the therapist attempted to assess and thereby also to teach Doris about the emotional components of her distress. The welter of emotions was so strong that Doris initially was only able to describe herself as "crazy" or "out of control," and it required some directed discussion with the therapist to break these down into more manageable components. Since the cognitive–emotive interface is the focus of much subsequent work, understanding which emotions are prominent and which cognitions connect with them is a crucial step in analysis of the problems. Doris was able to identify anger as her primary target and also determined that "underneath the anger" lay her self-doubts and fears for her future. In the A–B–C model of Rational–Emotive Therapy, the therapist was helping the client to identify a prominent C.

In Doris' case, the C turned out to be threefold. She could soon identify that she was experiencing a great deal of anger (which she rated on a 100-point SUDS, or Subjective Units of Disturbance Scale, as 95), shame (rated as 85), and anxiety (rated as 80). The behavioral component of the C was expressed as alternating withdrawal and verbal assaults on her partner. As the therapist outlined the A (partner masturbating) and the complex C on the office blackboard, Doris acknowledged that her reaction did seem overly strong and readily agreed that she needed to examine her thinking in this situation.

With a little help from the therapist, principally using the "downward arrow" strategy (Burns, 1980), Doris' list of cognitions (B's) was elaborated on the blackboard as follows:

> He told me he didn't masturbate.
> He's probably been doing it all along.
> He's been lying to me for nine years.
> That means I don't turn him on. And I never have!
> That means that there's something wrong with me.
> I'm not very sexy. No sex appeal.
> Or, he doesn't love me.
> And I don't think I love him either, then.
> This isn't the way marriage is supposed to be. I'm being cheated.
> That means I'd better end the relationship.
> But I can't support the children by myself.
> Oh, my God, what will become of them?

Doris and the therapist each made a copy of this list during the session, and put a check beside those cognitions that they agreed were the anger-inducing ones. The therapist also noted that one of Doris' cognitions indicated that she had some expectations about how marriage is "supposed to be" and that her expectations were not being met. To assess these, Doris was asked to take the Relationship Belief Inventory and the marital satisfaction scale (see Assessment) to work on in the waiting room, while the therapist met with her husband, Sid (who had filled out the same scales during his waiting period).

Sid seemed to be quite emotional when he came into the session, but with a different flavor than his wife had expressed. He was anxious, he said, since he had never been in therapy before and had never spoken to anyone about his sex problem. But he was also relieved to be there. He told the therapist that he deeply loved his wife and their family and had no interest in dissolving the marriage. He was, however, very afraid of his wife's anger, and since he did not understand it, he coped with it by simply withdrawing (literally or emotionally) from encounters that threatened to become negative. These had become more frequent, and their sexual encounters had become few and far between. The problem with that, he realized, was that since he had always had little ejaculatory control, when they did get together sexually, he had his orgasm almost immediately, sometimes even before penetration. He "knew" that was one of the reasons Doris was so angry at him. Although he had promised her years ago that he would not masturbate, he had thought that if he did masturbate, he might be better able to "perform" if he and Doris did get together sexually.

This interview with Sid validated what also was seen on the inventories he had taken: although there were many aspects of the marriage with which he was very happy, there were both sexual and interpersonal problems. Sid strongly believed that disagreement was destructive and that mind reading between partners was possible and expected. These ideas kept Sid from actively confronting and offering to problem-solve with his partner the sexual difficulty he experienced. The interview with Sid also established that many of Doris' ideas (e.g., "Sid doesn't love me") were based on her own mind reading, rather than her partner's report. During this initial meeting, Sid and the therapist agreed on some goals that Sid could work on: lowering his anxiety when his partner looked unhappy, developing assertive communication skills, lowering his distress about his sexual performance, and later working on building a richer sex life.

When the couple was reconvened for the last third of the initial appointment time, they were encouraged to share their marital satisfaction scales with each other. The therapist was aware that although there had been a great deal of emotional turmoil in the air, both Sid and Doris had indicated a number of items on which they felt reasonable degrees of satisfaction in the marriage. Later, Doris was asked to "check out" with Sid one of her beliefs—that he was not turned on to her and did not love her—ideas which he valiantly disputed, after expressing surprise that she could "even think such a thing." Doris subsequently reported that her anger was much reduced.

During this phase of the interview, the therapist was attempting to encourage some positive assertions between the partners for three major reasons: 1) for behavioral rehearsal, 2) to reinforce their belief in each other's commitment to the marriage, and 3) as a sample strategy to help the couple begin to appreciate their tendency to read each other's minds and the value of assessing the reality of their assumptions. The point of this strategy (checking out assumptions about what the partner is thinking) was shared with the couple so that they could view it as a "tool" with which it was hoped they would become facile. The therapist also asked Doris to clarify for them why she now felt less angry, and she was able to identify that Sid's responses had caused her to lessen her conviction in her negative beliefs. In the discussion that followed, the therapist was able to reinforce the A–B–C model for both partners.

The course of treatment for the Wilsons lasted for a number of months and included in-session and homework assignments designed to enhance the couple's communication skills (for both positive and negative communications) and empathy for each other's positions. Each worked on their individual overreactions by learning and practicing the A–B–C model of analysis, Sid frequently working on his anxiety and tendency to withdraw from conflict, and Doris frequently working on the "shoulds" which led her to anger or "self-downing." They had some difficult discussions about their sexual expectations and decided that they wanted to learn some more about male and female sexuality, not only for their own sex lives but so that they could be more informed and comfortable teachers for their children. When the emotional climate was lowered a bit, they began to do some Sensate Focus homework, in which they were encouraged to maintain a nondemanding approach while practicing both verbal and nonverbal communications of pleasure, learning about the partner's preferences, and identifying any distressing or distracting thoughts and feelings that interfered with the nondemanding sensual focus. Eventually Doris encouraged Sid to begin a training program to learn better ejaculatory control. He began in masturbation training, with which she was now psychologically comfortable, practicing building toward his orgasm but stopping just before the point of "orgasmic inevitability," letting the arousal fade a bit, and then resuming stimulation. This "stop–start" procedure was repeated three to five times before he allowed himself to have the orgasm; Sid practiced keeping his concentration focused on his "early warning signals" so that he could respond to them. Later Doris was invited to help in the training and they moved through a series of steps, always using the stop–start procedure: Sid with manual stimulation, Doris using manual stimulation, Doris using lubrication on her hands, Doris using oral stimulation, and, eventually, vaginal stimulation. Throughout this sex therapy procedure, Sid and Doris continued to practice their A–B–C's model and tried to maintain a problem-solving, information-sharing mental set.

During the course of these marital and sexual procedures, Sid and Doris had to wrestle with some family issues as well, since their homework required that they set aside some private, adult-only time from their busy household routine. They applied many of their new skills (both cognitive coping strategies and interpersonal communication strategies) to these issues. They learned to check out their automatic thoughts, to catch and correct the mind-reading error, to be attentive to old and often unfounded ideas and to subject them to logical analysis and/or to test them out behaviorally. In addition, they dispelled many myths and misunderstandings in the areas of sex, love, and parenting skills by doing a great deal of directed reading and discussion.

CONCLUSION

Sex therapy has come a long way, and the more contemporary, behavioral models of sex therapy have significantly enhanced treatment success rates. The addition of a cognitive therapy component to sex therapy treatment adds a sophisticated new dimension to treatment. Steger (1978) mentioned some of the uses for cognitive therapy, principally suggesting its adjunctive use to help clients do their behavioral homework, for example, when anxiety or fear stops the client from engaging in the homework procedures or when ruminative thinking or negative attitudes ("Sex is bad and immoral") block the *in vivo* treatment. In this chapter, we stressed a more integrative use of cognitive therapy, not as a supplement, but as an essential prerequisite component of therapy.

In this regard we emphasized the distinction between a sexual dysfunction (an unfortunate life event) and a sexual disturbance (the exaggeratedly negative perceptions and evaluations of this event which lead to undue emotional distress). Sexual disturbances can be highly interactive, so that even if the individual with a dysfunction is not disturbed about it, the partner may be disturbed about it, the partner's emotional distress then becoming a trigger for negative thoughts and feelings in the dysfunctional partner. Thus dealing with the sexual disturbance(s) may be considered to be the primary task in therapy, what Ellis calls the "elegant solution." When the cognitive and affective components of the problem are attended to, the remaining sexual or genital problem becomes clearer. Often the genital problem will have been resolved without direct behavioral intervention. If it is to be resolved by behavioral treatment, that treatment will likely proceed more smoothly. If the symptom is not resolvable by behavioral intervention, as is often the case with organic impairment, by reducing their distress, the couple will be able to rebuild a rich and satisfying sex life.

Thus the outcome of a successful course of therapy will lie primarily in changes in attitudes, so that sexual experiences will flow smoothly and positively for the most part. When this process occurs, the emotional climate of the individuals involved will be untroubled and sex play will be pleasant and even joyful.

REFERENCES

Allgeier, E. R., & Allgeier, A. R. (1984). *Sexual interactions.* Lexington, MA: Heath.

American Psychiatric Association (1980). *Diagnostic and statistical manual of mental disorders* (3rd ed.). Washington, DC: American Psychiatric Association.

Annon, J. S. (1974). *The behavioral treatment of sexual problems (Vol. 1).* Honolulu: Enabling Systems.

Arentewicz, G., & Schmidt, G. (1983). *The treatment of sexual disorder.* New York: Basic Books.

Barbach, L. (1975). *For yourself: The fulfillment of female sexuality.* New York: Doubleday.

Barlow, D. H. (1977). Assessment of sexual behavior. In A. Ciminero, K. Calhoun, & H. Adams (Eds.), *Handbook of behavioral assessment* (pp. 461–508). New York: Wiley.

Barlow, D. H. (1986). Causes of sexual dysfunction: The role of anxiety and cognitive interference. *Journal of Consulting and Clinical Psychology, 54,* 140–148.

Barlow, D. H., Sakheim, D. K., & Beck, J. G. (1983). Anxiety increases sexual arousal. *Journal of Abnormal Psychology, 92,* 49–54.

Bass, B. A., & Walen, S. R. (1986). Rational-emotive treatment for the sexual problems of couples. *Journal of Rational-Emotive Therapy, 4,* 82–94.

Beck, J. G. & Barlow, D. H. (1984). Current conceptualizations of sexual dysfunction: A review and an alternative perspective. *Clinical Psychology Review, 4,* 363–378.

Beck, J. G., Barlow, D. H., & Sakheim, D. K. (1983). The effects of attentional focus and partner arousal on sexual responding in functional and dysfunctional men. *Behaviour Research and Therapy, 21,* 1–8.

Berscheid, E., & Walster, E. (1974). A little bit about love. In T. Huston (Ed.), *Foundations of interpersonal attraction* (pp. 355–381). New York: Academic Press.

Burns, D. (1980). *Feeling good.* New York: Signet.

Caird, W. K., & Wincze, J. P. (1977). *Sex therapy: A behavioral approach.* New York: Harper and Row.

Calderone, M. (1976). Introduction. In G. Kelley, *Learning about sex: The contemporary guide for young people.* Woodbury, NY: Barron's Educational Series.

Calderone, M. (1979). Parents and the sexuality of their children in the "year of the child." *SIECUS Report, 8,* No. 2.

Conte, H. R. (1986). Multivariate assessment of sexual dysfunction. *Journal of Consulting and Clinical Psychology, 54,* 149–157.

Darling, C. A., & Hicks, M. W. (1983). Recycling parental sexual messages. *Journal of Sex and Marital Therapy, 9,* 233–243.

Dutton, D. G., & Aron, A. P. (1974). Some evidence for heightened sexual attraction under conditions of high anxiety. *Journal of Personality and Social Psychology, 30,* 510–517.

Eidelson, R. J., & Epstein, N. (1982). Cognition and relationship maladjustment: Development of a measure of dysfunctional relationship beliefs. *Journal of Consulting and Clinical Psychology, 50,* 715–720.

Ellis, A. (1962). *Reason and emotion in Psychotherapy.* Secaucus, NJ: Citadel Press.

Ellis, A. (1976). *Sex and the liberated man.* New York: Lyle Stuart.

Ellis, A. (1980). Rational-emotive therapy and cognitive behavioral therapy: Similarities and differences. *Cognitive Therapy and Research, 4,* 325–340.

Ellis, A. (1986). Rational-emotive therapy (RET) applied to relationship therapy. *Journal of Rational-Emotive Therapy, 4,* 4–21.

Epstein, N. (1986). Cognitive marital therapy: Multi-level assessment and intervention. *Journal of Rational-Emotive Therapy, 4,* 68–81.

Fisher, C., Schiavi, R. C., Edwards, A., Davis, D. M., Reitman, M., & Fine, J. (1979). Evaluation of nocturnal penile tumescence in the differential diagnosis of sexual impotence. *Archives of General Psychiatry, 36,* 431–437.

Ford, C. S., & Beach, F. A. (1951). *Patterns of sexual behavior.* New York: Harper and Row.

Foster, A. L. (1978). Changes in marital-sexual relationships following treatment for sexual dysfunctions. *Journal of Sex and Marital Therapy, 4,* 186–197.

Frank, E., Anderson, C., & Rubinstein, D. (1978). Frequency of sexual dysfunction in "normal" couples. *New England Journal of Medicine, 299,* 111–115.

Gagnon, J., & Simon, W. (1973). *Social conduct.* Chicago: Aldine.

Gordon, S., & Gordon, J. (1984). *A better safe than sorry book.* Fayetteville, NY: Ed-U Press.

Hatch, J. P.(1981). Psychophysiolgical aspects of sexual dysfunction. *Archives of Sexual Behavior, 10,* 49–64.

Hauck, P. A. (1986). Innovations in marriage counseling. *Journal of Rational-Emotive Therapy, 4,* 38–49.

Hawton, K., & Catalan, J. (1986). Prognostic factors in sex therapy. *Behavior Research and Therapy, 24,* 377–385.

Heiman, J. R. (1978). Uses of psychophysiology in the assessment and treatment of sexual dysfunction. In J. LoPiccolo & L. LoPiccolo (Eds.), *Handbook of sex therapy* (pp. 123–135). New York: Plenum.

Jacobson, N. S., & Margolin, G. (1979). *Marital therapy: Strategies based on social learning and behavior exchange principles.* New York: Brunner/Mazel.

Kaplan, H. S. (1979). *Disorders of sexual desire.* New York: Brunner/Mazel.

Kaplan-Mehlman, S., Baucom, D. H., & Anderson, D. (1983). Effectiveness of cotherapists versus single therapists and immediate versus delayed treatment in behavioral marital therapy. *Journal of Consulting and Clinical Psychology, 51,* 258–266.

Kaya, N., Moore, C., & Karacan, I. (1979). Nocturnal penile tumescence and its role in impotence. *Psychiatric Annals, 9,* 426–431.

Kinsey, A. C., Pomeroy, W. B., & Martin, C. E. (1948). *Sexual behavior in the human male.* Philadelphia: Saunders.

Kirkpatrick, M. (1982). *Women's sexual experience.* New York: Plenum.

Lansky, M. R., & Davenport, A. E. (1975). Difficulties in brief conjoint treatment of sexual dysfunction. *American Journal of Psychiatry, 132,* 177–179.

Lazarus, A. A. (1985). *Marital myths.* San Luis Obispo, CA: Impact Publishers.

Locke, H. J., & Wallace, K. M. (1959). Short marital adjustment and prediction tests: Their reliability and validity. *Marriage and Family Living, 21,* 251–255.

LoPiccolo, J. (1985). Lecture: Current Trends in Sex Therapy. Evaluation Research Association; Washington, D.C.

LoPiccolo, J., Heiman, J. R., Hogan, D. R., & Roberts, C. W. (1985). Effectiveness of single therapists versus co-therapy teams in sex therapy. *Journal of Consulting and Clinical Psychology, 53,* 287–294.

LoPiccolo, J., & LoPiccolo, L. (1978). *Handbook of sex therapy.* New York: Plenum.

Macksood, M. J., & James, R. E., Jr. (1983). Complete diagnostic evaluation and classification of the impotent male. *Journal of the American Osteopathic Association, 8,* 158–162.

Masters, W. H., & Johnson, V. E. (1970). *Human sexual inadequacy.* Boston: Little, Brown.

Masters, W. H., Johnson, V. E., & Kolodny, S. (1982). *Human sexuality* (2nd Ed.). Boston: Little, Brown.

Money, J. (1976). Role of fantasy in pair-bonding and erotic performance. In R. Gemme & C. Wheeler (Eds.), *Progress in sexology.* New York: Plenum.

O'Leary, K. D., & Arias, I. (1983). The influence of marital therapy on sexual satisfaction. *Journal of Sex and Marital Therapy, 9,* 171–181.

Ramsey, G. (1943). The sexual development of boys. *American Journal of Psychology, 56,* 217.

Roberts, E., Kline, D., & Gagnon, J. (1979, January). Parents' sexual silence. *Psychology Today,* 14–15.

Rook, K. S., & Hammen, C. L. (1977). A cognitive perspective on the experience of sexual arousal. *Journal of Social Issues, 33,* 7–29.

Sakheim, D. K., Barlow, D. H., Beck, J. G., & Abramson, D. J. (1984). The effect of an increased awareness of erectile cues on sexual arousal. *Behavior Research and Therapy, 22,* 151–158.

Sager, C. J. (1976). *Marital contracts and couple therapy.* New York: Brunner/ Mazel.

Schachter, S. (1964). The interaction of cognitive and physiological determinants of emotional state. In L. Berkowitz (Ed.), *Advances in experimental social psychology* (pp. 49–80). New York: Academic Press.

Schover, L. R., Friedman, J. M., Weiler, S. J., Heiman, J. R., & LoPiccolo, J. (1982). Multiaxial problem-oriented system for sexual dysfunctions. *Archives of General Psychiatry, 39,* 614–619.

Snyder, D. K., & Berg, P. (1983). Predicting couples' response to brief directive sex therapy. *Journal of Sex and Marital Therapy, 9,* 114–120.

Spivack, G., Platt, J., & Shure, M. (1976). *The problem-solving approach to adjustment.* San Francisco: Jossey-Bass.

Steger, J. (1978). Cognitive behavioral strategies in the treatment of sexual problems. In J. Foreyt & D. Rathjen (Eds.), *Cognitive behavior therapy: Research and application.* New York: Plenum.

Swanson, L., & Biaggio, M. K. (1985). Therapeutic perspectives on father–daughter incest. *American Journal of Psychiatry, 142,* 667–674.

Walen, S. R. (1980). Cognitive factors in sexual behavior. *Journal of Sex and Marital Therapy, 6,* 87–101.

Walen, S. R. (1985). Rational sexuality. In A. Ellis & M. E. Bernard (Eds.), *Clinical applications of rational-emotive therapy* (pp. 129–152). New York: Plenum.

Walen, S. R., DiGiuseppe, R. A., & Wessler, R. L. (1980). *A practitioner's guide to rational-emotive therapy.* New York: Oxford University Press.

Whitehead, A., & Mathews, A. (1977). Attitude change during behavioural treatment of sexual inadequacy. *British Journal of Social and Clinical Psychology, 16,* 275–281.

Wolpe, J. (1982). *The practice of behavior therapy* (3rd ed.). New York: Pergamon.

Zilbergeld, B. (1978). *Male sexuality: A guide to sexual fulfillment.* Boston: Little, Brown.

Zuckerman, M. (1971). Physiological measures of sexual response in the human. *Psychological Bulletin, 75,* 297–329.

11

Cognitive–Behavioral Family Therapy: Summary and Future Directions

Norman Epstein, Stephen E. Schlesinger, and Windy Dryden

As the preceding chapters demonstrate, cognitive–behavioral concepts and techniques are being applied to the treatment of a wide range of family problems. Although these techniques appear to hold great promise for the future development of the field of family therapy, the realization of their potential hinges on the attention clinicians and researchers give to a number of specific issues: further development of theory, construction and validation of assessment procedures, and refinement of treatment methodologies.

THEORY DEVELOPMENT

In Chapter 1 we proposed a model explicating the roles that particular cognitive and behavioral factors play in family interaction. Whereas this model intuitively makes sense, it is as yet unclear whether we accounted for all of the critical cognitive and behavioral variables that play roles in family functioning. Some of the processes by which certain cognitive and behavioral factors have their impact on family interaction also need clarification.

Three lines of research are necessary to address these issues adequately. The first focuses on investigating whether there are any cognitive and behavioral factors that must be considered other than those included in our model. It is also important to test the causal assumptions of the model (e.g., that family members' cognitions influence their subsequent behaviors toward one another). The second line of research is longitudinal in nature and focuses on identifying the processes by which family interactions develop over time. For example, studies could investigate the possible influences that couples' initial belief systems at the time of marriage have on the subsequent development of family relationship patterns.

The third line of research is concerned with an assumption of our model that family functioning is determined by the individual members' cognitions and behaviors as well as by the family interaction patterns (i.e., that both individual psychological functioning and family dynamics are important). Such research would test the unique contributions of individual and interactional factors in family functioning.

The development of a comprehensive cognitive–behavioral model of family functioning requires data generated from each of these lines of inquiry.

DEVELOPMENT OF ASSESSMENT PROCEDURES

As noted in Chapter 1 and the preceding chapters in Section II, few systematic methods for cognitive–behavioral family assessment have been developed. Development of new assessment methods necessitates a focus on two main areas, the *method* of assessment and the *targets* of assessment efforts.

Methods of Assessment

As described in Chapter 1, there are three major methods of family assessment: self-report questionnaires, clinical interviews, and direct observation of family interaction. Further development is needed with each of these approaches.

For example, new *self-report questionnaires* are needed to assess those cognitions about families described in Chapter 1 for which no instruments currently are available (e.g., family members' expectancies; perceptions that one family member has about the nature of relationships among other members of the family). Development of *interview schedules* will help standardize the cognitive–behavioral assessment of families by helping clinicians focus on the variables necessary for a comprehensive assessment of family interactions. Such schedules would not be intended to reduce the flexibility of clinical assessment. Instead, they would reduce the potential for overlooking important variables during the detailed assessment of a complex family system. Finally, whereas cognitive–behavioral family therapists can continue to draw upon existing behavioral observation techniques for the assessment of families' behavioral deficits and excesses, there is a need for the development of *observational techniques* for assessing cognitive variables in family interactions. Particularly important are techniques for identifying behavioral manifestations of significant cognitions (e.g., spontaneous *in vivo* verbalizations of attributions and expectancies; repetitive behavior patterns), both in the office and during home visits.

REFINEMENT OF TREATMENT METHODS

Because cognitive–behavioral approaches to family therapy were introduced relatively recently, it is important to test their efficacy relative to other family treatment approaches and as applied to a variety of family problems. For example, it is important to know whether cognitive–behavioral family therapy may be the treatment of choice for some family problems but may be less efficacious than alternative treatment approaches for other problems. In the latter case, this involves testing the limits of this treatment approach.

In addition, it is important to evaluate the relative efficacy of the components of a successful cognitive–behavioral intervention package in order to identify the "active ingredients" of treatment. The cognitive–behavioral treatments described in this book include a variety of components (e.g., cognitive restructuring procedures, behavioral skill-building techniques, procedures for increasing rapport with family members), and the maximization of treatment efficacy requires knowledge about the contribution that each component makes to the outcome of therapy. Comparing the effects of cognitive-behavioral family therapy with those of other family therapy approaches and identifying the active treatment components of cognitive–behavioral treatment will help therapists make clinical decisions in a stepwise fashion as treatment progresses.

Investigation of cognitive–behavioral treatment techniques will be facilitated to the extent that they can be operationalized for research purposes. Cognitive therapy for depression has been amenable to empirical tests because its interventions have been specified in treatment manuals and because therapists' cognitive therapy skills can be rated by expert judges. Although the chapters of this book were not intended to be detailed treatment manuals, the authors described procedures of cognitive–behavioral family therapy that appear to be defined sufficiently for systematic observation in research. Similarly, the chapters specified cognitive and behavioral variables that should change as a result of these family interventions, and these could be operationalized for use as treatment outcome measures.

As Leigh Leslie noted in Chapter 2, the degree to which cognitive–behavioral approaches can account for the "emergent properties" of family interaction described by systems theorists appears to be limited by differences in the cognitive–behavioral and systems models. In terms of refining cognitive–behavioral approaches to family therapy, questions remain regarding the degree to which the cognitive–behavioral theoretical model can be expanded to include emergent properties, and whether the cognitive–behavioral model is inadequate as a basis for treating family problems if such a theoretical integration is not possible.

Given that cognitions tend to be viewed as intrapsychic events, one must push the limits of the cognitive–behavioral model in order to generate a concept of a "family cognition" that is different from an individual cognition (e.g., a belief about "proper" behavior) shared by several family members. Is there a cognitive–behavioral analogue to the systems concepts of family interactional "rules" and "metarules" that control group interaction but which differ from the stated beliefs and standards of any single family member? For example, how can the cognitive–behavioral model account for the dynamics in a family where all the members individually express strong beliefs in open communication and family cohesiveness, but where an outside observer easily can see that the family as a group consistently avoids all but superficial discussions of sensitive topics?

On the one hand, one avenue for exploring such themes that might be profitable for cognitive–behavioral family therapists would be to initiate a dialogue with social psychologists who study the formation of shared norms and their impact on social behavior. The goal of such efforts would be to identify forms of cognition that are analogous to the emergent properties described by systems theorists.

On the other hand, it also may be that with further theoretical work the emergent properties of families could be translated ("reduced," in terms of the cognitive–behavioral reductionist model) to existing cognitive–behavioral variables. For example, a "family rule" might consist of a set of interlocking expectancies that family members have developed about probabilities of particular cause–effect patterns in their relationships, based on trial-and-error interaction with each other over a period of time. Members of the family who value open communication but who avoid discussion of sensitive topics may have become alert to subtle cues from one another that particular messages are arousing distress and are likely to produce negative responses from other family members. Consequently, they make almost instantaneous decisions (not necessarily with full awareness) to pursue or not pursue certain lines of conversation. The goal of such analyses of family interaction would be to translate the unstated family "rule" into a map of the expectancies within the individual members *and* the behavioral exchanges among the members that provide the individuals with the cues they use to apply their expectancies and make their decisions about how to behave with one another.

Both of these lines of inquiry seem worth pursuing at this point. However, as interesting and challenging as it may be to try to integrate cognitive–behavioral and systems models of family interaction at a theoretical level, we believe that it is not necessary for cognitive–behavioral family therapy to account for "emergent properties" of families in systems terms in order to be a viable and effective approach to the treatment of family problems.

Another issue related to the foregoing discussion which is apparent in this book concerns the *focus of intervention* in cognitive–behavioral family therapy. Traditionally, cognitive–behavioral therapists who work with individuals have been clear that their focus for treatment is on the dysfunctional cognitions and behavioral excesses and deficits that are implicated centrally in their clients' psychological problems. Where should the major therapeutic focus be in cognitive–behavioral family work? Should therapists target for change the dysfunctional cognitions and behavioral excesses and deficits of each family member, or should there be a greater emphasis on interactions of family members' cognitions and behavioral responses? Clearly, the authors of the chapters in this book vary in the attention that they pay to individual versus interactive phenomena. At this point, we have no empirical evidence concerning the relative efficacy of the two types of intervention, but the cognitive–behavioral model that we presented in Chapter 1 suggests that a family system can be influenced by changes in the cognitions and behaviors of individual members, as well as by changes in interaction sequences among family members. We must wait for results of controlled treatment outcome studies in order to draw more firm conclusions about the most appropriate targets for cognitive–behavioral interventions.

CONCLUSIONS

The preceding chapters suggest that cognitive–behavioral techniques are well suited to family therapy for a variety of major problem areas of clinical concern in family treatment. Indeed, the cognitive–behavioral model of family functioning that we outlined in Chapter 1 comes alive in its application in subsequent chapters. As noted in Chapter 2, at the level of clinical practice, cognitive–behavioral and systems approaches to family treatment can be compatible, and some of the treatment strategies of each approach can be applied in the context of treatment oriented to the other approach. Consequently, it seems advantageous for family clinicians to develop a firm grounding in the theory and practice of both cognitive–behavioral and systems approaches.

A criticism sometimes directed at cognitive–behavioral therapy is that, compared to other approaches, it focuses on cognitions to the exclusion of feelings. Emotion clearly is a crucial part of family life, and an important focus for family change. The chapters in this book demonstrate that cognitive–behavioral approaches to family treatment not only include but also place great value on the emotional experiences of family members.

In the past, many family therapists were not familiar with cognitive–behavioral techniques, particularly because cognitive–behavioral therapy traditionally has been associated with the individual treatment of psychological disorders such as depression and anxiety. We hope that this book has been successful in achieving our goals of describing the current status of cognitive–behavioral approaches to family treatment, providing detailed information about the specific assessment and treatment procedures used in these approaches, and stimulating further interest in clinical practice and research with cognitive–behavioral interventions.

Name Index

Abicoff, H., 185
Ablon, J., 255
Achenback, T.M., 195
Ackerman, N.J., 51
Akiskal, H.S., 292
Alexander, J.F., 5, 8, 9, 107
Allender, J., 225
Allgeier, A.R., 325
Allgeier, E.R., 325
Alvord, J.R., 101
Amish, P.L., 91
Anderson, C.M., 79, 80, 345
Anderson, D., 350
Anderson, J.Z., 153, 154
Anderson, K.E., 184
Anderson, R.E., 53
Annon, J.S., 326
Aponte, H.J., 9, 58–60
Arentewicz, G., 350
Arias, I., 119–122, 124–127, 131, 341
Arnkoff, D., 215
Aron, A.P., 334
Azar, S.T., 103

Baffa, G., 226
Baither, R.C., 255
Baker, L., 58
Bandura, A., 66, 68, 91, 126, 186
Barbach, L., 35, 347
Barling, J., 121, 130, 138
Barlow, D.H., 333–335
Barry, W.A., 21
Bartlett, D., 283
Barton, C., 5, 8, 9, 107
Bass, B.A., 341
Bateson, G., 60
Baucom, D.H., 5, 6, 18–20, 271, 350
Bauer, W., 88

Beach, F.A., 333
Beach, S.R.H., 6, 121, 131, 140
Beamesderfer, A., 298
Beavin, J.H., 54
Beck, A.T., 5–8, 10, 14, 20, 34, 35,
    102, 132, 162, 225, 244, 293, 294,
    298–300, 309
Beck, J.G., 334, 335
Becker, W.C., 101
Becvar, D.S., 52, 54
Becvar, R.J., 52, 54
Bedrosian, R.C., 102, 294, 300, 309
Bell, J.E., 198
Bell, N.W., 198
Bell, W.G., 6, 271
Berenson, D., 255
Berg, P., 342
Berger, M.M., 283
Berger, S.H., 153
Berkowitz, B.P., 40
Berman, C., 35, 172
Bernard, M.E., 42, 185
Bernard, M.L., 89
Berscheid, E., 334
Bertalanffy, L. von, 49–52
Biaggio, M.K., 331
Bienvenu, M.J., 133
Birchler, G.R., 21, 49, 65, 70, 75, 76,
    81
Birkett, P., 225
Birrell, J.H., 90
Birrell, R.G., 90
Blager, F., 90
Blauberg, I.V., 50, 51
Blow, F.C., 220
Blumberg, M.L., 89
Blythe, B.J., 101
Bodin, A.M., 60, 63, 64

Bogaard, L., 186
Bousha, D.M., 88, 89
Bowen, M., 255
Bowlby, J., 231
Boyd, J.L., 5, 279
Brandon, A.D., 134
Braswell, L., 185
Bray, J.H., 153
Breckenridge, J., 225
Broderick, C., 53
Brown, C.H., 193
Brown, H.S., 153
Bryan, L.R., 152
Bryan, S.H., 152
Buckley, W.Q., 50
Bumberry, W., 132
Burgess, R.L., 88, 89
Burgoyne, J., 151
Burns, D., 10, 13, 281, 308, 353
Burton, A., 88
Buttenweiser, R., 89
Byng-Hall, J., 198

Caird, W.K., 347
Calderone, M., 327, 330
Camp, B.W., 185
Caplan, G., 89
Carter, I., 53
Carter, R.D., 133
Catalan, J., 342
Cattell, M.D., 196
Cattell, R.B., 196
Caulfield, C., 88
Chalmers, M., 89
Chamberlain, P., 186
Cherlin, A., 151, 152, 154
Chess, S., 193
Christensen, A., 28
Clingempeel, W.G., 153, 154
Coleman, M., 152
Coleman, R.E., 13
Coleman, S.B., 254
Collins, B.S., 121
Collins, R.L., 119, 124
Collmer, C.W., 87, 90
Conger, R.D., 88, 89, 101
Connors, G.J., 254
Conte, H.R., 337, 339
Cox, M., 152
Cox, R., 152

Crohn, H., 153
Curley, A.D., 121–123, 127, 132

Darling, C.A., 327
Davenport, A.E., 342
Davidson, N., 5
Davis, D.I., 254, 255
Davis, D.M., 339
Davis, P., 255
Davis, S., 255
Davison, G.C., 141
Deffenbacher, J.L., 134
DeGiovanni, I.S., 23
Demm, P.M., 134
Denicola, J., 101
Deschner, J.P., 36, 138
deVisser, L.A.J.M., 21
Dickey, S., 255
Dietrich, K.N., 88
DiGiuseppe, R., 5, 42, 185, 208
Disbrow, M.A., 88
Dishion, T.S., 198
DiStasio, C.A., 255
Dobash, R.E., 119
Dobash, R.P., 119
Doerr, H., 88
Doherty, W.J., 19
Dryden, W., 5, 7, 66, 69
Dubanoski, R.A., 95
Duhe, A.D., 6, 20, 271
Dutton, D.G., 334
D'Zurilla, T.J., 237

Eber, H.J., 196
Edelbrock, C.S., 195
Edwards, A., 339
Egan, K.J., 101
Eidelson, R.J., 20, 301, 341
Ellis, A., 5, 7, 91, 102, 158, 185, 193,
    206, 326, 332, 340, 347, 351, 352,
    357
Elmer, E., 89
Emery, G., 7, 10, 13, 102, 162, 225,
    308, 309
Engel, T., 153
Ensminger, M.E., 193
Epstein, N., 5, 7, 8, 15, 19, 21, 23, 24,
    29, 35–40, 66, 69, 160, 264, 283,
    301, 309, 327, 341

Erbaugh, J., 132, 225
Evans, J.M., 95
Ewald, L., 88
Eyberg, S., 198

Falloon, I.R.H., 5, 21, 22, 24, 26–28, 38, 279
Ferraro, K.J., 130
Feshbach, S., 134
Fillenbaum, G.G., 225
Fincham, F., 6, 7, 19, 20, 133, 140, 160, 271
Fine, J., 339
Fisch, R., 62
Fisher, C., 339
Fishman, H., 303
Fleischman, M.J., 203
Fleming, B., 19, 160
Flitcraft, A.H., 118
Fontana, V.J., 89
Ford, C.S., 333
Forehand, R., 183, 186
Foster, A.L., 341
Fox, S., 13
Fram, D.H., 255
Frank, P.B., 135
Frankel, A.S., 223
Frazier, D., 102
Freud, S., 230
Friedman, D.H., 36, 121, 129, 135, 137, 139
Friedman, J.M., 336
Frodi, A.M., 89
Fulcomer, M., 225

Gagnon, J., 329, 335
Gaines, R.W., 89
Galdston, R., 89
Gallagher, D., 223, 225, 226
Gambrill, E.D., 101
Ganong, L.H., 152
Gardner, R.A., 35
Gdowski, E., 195
Gelles, R.J., 90, 119, 120
George, C., 89
Gil, D.G., 88
Giller, H., 198
Gillick, J.J., 281
Gleberman, L., 128

Glick, R.C., 151
Glynn, T.J., 255
Goldenberg, H., 27, 40
Goldenberg, I., 27, 40
Goldfried, M.R., 141
Goldman, M., 255
Goldstein, D., 122, 134
Gonso, J., 21, 273
Gordon, J.R., 13, 331
Gordon, S.B., 5, 331
Gottman, J., 21, 27, 128, 273
Graziano, A.M., 40
Green, A.H., 89, 90
Green, C., 196
Greenblatt, C.S., 119, 131
Greenspan, S.I., 9
Guerney, B.G., Jr., 38, 177, 273, 275
Guidano, V., 300, 309
Gurland, B.J., 225

Hacker, A., 151
Hagestad, G.O., 220
Haley, J., 9, 99, 100, 184, 303, 319
Hamilton, M., 298
Hammen, C.L., 334
Hanson, R., 88
Harbin, H.T., 198, 255
Harrington, J., 90
Hatch, J.P., 339
Hauck, P.A., 352
Hawton, K., 342
Heiman, J.R., 333, 337, 350
Hendricks, W.J., 283
Hernstein, R.J., 198
Herr, J.H., 226, 241, 245
Hertel, R.K., 21
Hetherington, E.M., 152
Hicks, M.W., 327
Higuchi, A.A., 95
Hill, R., 219
Hindman, M., 283
Hinkle, L.M., 255
Hoffman, H.A., 255
Hoffman-Plotkin, D., 90
Hogan, D.R., 350
Holmes, M.B., 88
Holtzworth-Munroe, A., 6, 19, 271
Hops, H., 21
Horan, J., 209
Horberg, L.K., 264, 276, 277, 281

Hornung, C.A., 130
Houghton, B.D., 135
Huber, J., 123
Hussian, R.A., 226
Hyman, H.K., 243

Ihinger-Tallman, M., 152
Isaacs, M.B., 178

Jackson, D.D., 54, 57, 61, 216, 222
Jackson, D.N., 122, 132
Jackson, E., 23
Jacobson, N.S., 5, 6, 19, 21, 24, 37–40,
    138, 271, 279, 335
Jaffe, P., 137
James, E., 255
James, R.E., Jr., 339
Janis, I.L., 128
Jason, J., 88
Jayne-Lazarus, C., 23
John, R., 128
Johnson, B., 89
Johnson, H.C., 152
Johnson, J.H., 133
Johnson, J.M., 130
Johnson, P., 122, 125, 131
Johnson, S.M., 186
Johnson, V.E., 326, 335, 348, 350
Jones, W.C., 254
Jouriles, E.N., 119, 124, 130, 131, 138
Joyce, M.R., 185
Justice, B., 88
Justice, R., 88

Kalmuss, D., 119, 123
Kanfer, R.F., 94
Kantor, D., 52
Kaplan, H.S., 325, 326, 336, 348
Kaplan, M.G., 88
Kaplan-Mehlman, S., 350
Karacan, I., 339
Kaufman, E., 255, 283
Kaufman, K., 103
Kaufmann, P., 255, 283
Kaya, N., 339
Kazdin, A., 184
Kellam, S.G., 193
Kelley, H.H., 15
Kelly, J.A., 101

Kempe, C., 89
Kendall, P.C., 49, 185
Kent, M.O., 152
Kent, R., 28
Kilburg, R.R., 230
Kimmel, D., 133
King, H.E., 183, 186
Kinsey, A.C., 326
Kirkpatrick, M., 331
Klagsburn, M., 255
Kleban, M.H., 225
Kline, D., 329
Kolodny, S., 326
Kovacs, M., 299, 300
Kuehnel, J., 21
Kuehnel, T., 21
Kuriansky, J., 225

L'Abate, L., 38
Lachar, D., 195
Lahey, B.B., 101
Lamb, M.E., 89
Lansky, M.R., 342
Larrance, D.T., 88
Lawson, A., 255
Lawson, G., 255
Lawton, M.P., 215, 224, 225
Lazarus, A.A., 342
Lebow, J.L., 49
Lederer, W.J., 61
Lehr, W., 82
Lerner, R.M., 65, 67
Lester, D., 225
Lester, G., 5
Levant, R., 56
Levine, E., 102
Levenson, R.W., 128
Levitt, E.E., 184
Lewinsohn, P.M., 244
Liberman, R.P., 21, 272
Light, R., 89
Linn, B.S., 225
Linn, M.W., 225
Liotti, G., 300, 309
Lobitz, G.K., 186
Locke, H.J., 133, 342
Loeber, R., 198
LoPiccolo, J., 337, 338, 340, 349
LoPiccolo, L., 349
Lorber, R., 88

Lynch, M., 89
Lytton, H., 184

MacEwen, K.E., 130
Macksood, M., 339
Mahoney, M.J., 215
Main, M., 89
Mandler, G., 128
Mannino, F.V., 9
Margolin, G., 5, 6, 21, 24, 38–40, 70, 74, 75, 104, 128, 134, 138, 146, 279, 335
Markman, H., 21, 273
Marlatt, G.A., 13, 258
Martin, C.E., 326
Martin, H.P., 90
Masters, W.H., 326, 335, 348, 350
Mathews, A., 342
Mattesich, P., 220
Mazier, H.M., 255
McClure, J.N., 132
McCrady, B.S., 255
McCubbin, H.I., 24
McCullogh, B.C., 130
McGill, C.W., 5, 279
McHenry, S., 38
McKinney, W.T., 292
Meagher, R., 196
Meichenbaum, D., 36, 42, 94, 138
Mendelson, M., 132, 225
Miller, C., 128
Miller, L.C., 195
Miller, P., 255
Miller, W.R., 258
Millon, T., 196
Minuchin, S., 9, 25, 56–59, 67, 70, 303
Mock, J., 132, 225
Money, J., 330
Moore, C., 339
Morse, H.A., 89
Morton, T.L., 88
Moss, M., 225
Munoz, R.F., 244

Navran, L., 133
Neidig, P.H., 36, 121, 122, 129, 135, 137, 139
Nelson, G., 6, 140
Nezu, A., 237

Nies, G., 225
Noel, N.E., 255
Notarius, C., 21, 273
Novaco, R., 36, 102, 138, 208

O'Farrell, T.J., 254, 255
O'Leary, K.D., 6, 19–21, 28, 40, 118–127, 130–138, 140, 271, 341
Oliver, J.M., 132
Olson, D.H., 255
Olweus, D., 183
Overton, W.F., 65, 67

Pagelow, M.D., 123
Paolino, T.J., 255
Parke, R.D., 87, 90
Parkes, C.M., 231
Pasley, K., 152
Patterson, G.R., 21, 22, 40, 41, 101, 177, 183, 184, 186, 188, 198, 203
Patterson, J.M., 24
Pattison, E.M., 255
Peed, S., 186
Peterson, J.S., 255
Piatt, C., 226
Platt, J.J., 279, 343
Polansky, N., 89
Pollock, C., 89
Pomeroy, W.B., 326
Poon, L., 217
Porter, R.B., 196
Pretzer, J.L., 19, 20, 160
Prinz, R., 28
Pruchno, R.A., 220

Quay, H.C., 183

Ramsey, G., 334
Raush, H.L., 21, 22
Ray, R.S., 185
Reese, H.W., 65, 67
Regan, J.M., 254
Reid, J.B., 41, 88, 186
Reidy, T.J., 89
Reiss, D., 67
Reitman, M., 339
Reynolds, N., 128
Riggs, D.S., 120–122
Rigler, D., 122

Ringering, L., 226
Ritterman, M.K., 56
Roberts, C.W., 350
Roberts, E., 329
Robin, A.L., 28
Robinson, E.A., 198
Rochat, R., 88
Rodstein, E., 153
Rohrbeck, C.A., 89, 90
Romney, D.M., 184
Rook, K.S., 334
Roschman, J., 283
Rosenbaum, A., 119, 121–125, 129, 134–137, 139, 146
Rosenberg, D.N., 255
Rosenberg, M., 134
Rosman, B., 58
Rubin, B.R., 193
Rubinstein, D., 345
Rush, A.J., 7, 34, 102, 162, 309
Russell, C.S., 255
Rutter, M., 198

Sackles, J., 209
Sadovsky, V.N., 50
Sager, C.J., 10, 153, 156, 158, 161, 341
Sakheim, D.K., 333–335
Sameroff, A.J., 193
Samios, M., 126
Sanders, N., 272
Sandgrund, A., 89
Sandler, J., 101, 103
Sarason, I.G., 133
Saslow, G., 94
Satir, V., 63
Sayers, S.L., 20
Schachter, J., 140
Schachter, S., 333
Schaie, K.W., 230
Schiavi, R.C., 339
Schlesinger, S.E., 5, 15, 66, 69, 264, 276, 277, 281–283
Schlichter, K., 209
Schmidt, G., 350
Schover, L.R., 337
Schulman, M.A., 119
Scott, S.M., 283
Sears, R.R., 133
Seifer, R., 193
Sharpe, L., 225
Shaw, B.F., 7, 102, 162, 225, 309

Shure, M., 185, 343
Siegel, J.M., 133
Silverstone, B., 243
Simon, R., 225
Simon, W., 335
Smith, J., 53
Smith, M., 275, 276
Smith, R., 193
Smith, S.M., 88
Smith, S.S., 101
Smyer, M.A., 220, 225
Snyder, D.K., 342
Snyder, J.J., 186
Sowder, B., 255
Spanier, G.B., 6
Spinetta, J.J., 122
Spinks, S.H., 21, 65, 75, 76, 81
Spivack, G., 185, 279, 343
Sprenkle, D.H., 255
Stanton, M.D., 255, 283
Stapp, J., 230
Stark, E., 118
Starr, R.H., 88
Steele, B., 89
Steger, J., 356
Steiner, C.M., 255
Steinglass, P., 255
Steinmetz, J., 225
Steinmetz, S.K., 119
Stewart, S., 79, 80
Stierman, K., 220
Stiller, P., 225
Stone, V., 226
Straus, M.A., 119, 120, 129, 130
Stuart, R.B., 21, 23, 25, 40, 74, 279
Sugimoto, T., 130
Swain, M.A., 21
Swanson, L., 331

Taplin, P.S., 88
Tavris, C., 139
Thibault, J.W., 15
Thomas, A., 193
Thomas, E.J., 22, 133
Thompson, L.W., 225, 226
Todd, T.C., 255
Toffler, A., 222
Trexler, L., 225
Turk, D.C., 138
Turkewitz, H., 21, 40, 49, 75, 81, 133
Turner, R.J., 193

Twentyman, C.T., 88–91, 103

Ulbrich, P., 123

VandenBos, G.R., 230
Van der Veen, F., 133
VanDeusen, J.M., 9, 58–60, 283
Visher, E.B., 151–157, 163, 165
Visher, J.S., 151–157, 163, 165
Vivian, D., 130
Vogel, E.F., 198

Wahler, R.G., 183
Walen, S.R., 5, 332, 341
Walker, H.M., 195
Walker, L., 138, 153
Wallace, K.M., 133, 342
Walster, E., 334
Ward, C.H., 132, 225
Watzlawick, P., 54, 57, 61, 62, 70–72, 76
Weakland, J., 57, 62, 226, 241, 245
Wegscheider, S., 255, 265
Weiler, S.J., 337
Weiss, R.L., 21, 100
Weissenberger, J., 34
Weissman, A., 225, 299, 300
Werner, E., 193

Werry, J.S., 183
Wessler, R.A., 7
Wessler, R.L., 5, 7
Wheeler, E.G., 21, 272
White, G.D., 153, 154
Whitehead, A., 342
Williams, A.M., 21
Williams, D., 89
Williams, S.L., 88
Willis, S.L., 230
Wilson, G.T., 134
Wilson, J.Q., 198
Wilson, S., 137
Wincze, J.P., 347
Wolfe, D.A., 101, 103, 135
Wolpe, J., 326
Woods, B., 283

Yoder, P., 186
Young, J.F., 13
Young, L., 88
Youngren, M.A., 244
Yudin, E.G., 50

Zak, L., 137
Zarit, S.H., 230, 241
Zeiss, A.M., 244
Zilbergeld, B., 35, 347
Zuckerman, M., 333

Subject Index

Active listening, 38
Addictions, 13, 42, 254–91
  holistic approaches to, 255
  the "Three R's" of, 282–3.
  See also Substance abuse; *specific addictions*
Addictive families, 254–88
  assertiveness training with, 272, 273–7
  assessment of, 257–66
  attributions of, 259–61, 271–2
  behavior of, 263–6
  case histories of, 281–3
  children in, 267–8
  clinical issues in the treatment of, 283–88
  communication training with, 272–3
  cotherapists used in treatment of, 280
  expectations of, 261–3
  group treatment of, 283
Addicts:
  abstinence for, 285
  coerced treatment for, 285
  self-help groups for, 287
Adolescents, 31–32, 33, 40, 52, 62, 77, 78, 135, 204
  as addicts, 269, 300
  assessment of, 196
  as caretakers, 297
  disturbed behavior of, 201–2, 208
  friction with parents of, 305
  independence needs of, 189
  sexuality of, 330, 334
  in stepfamilies, 155, 160, 164
Adult children, 27
  anger of, 221–2, 227
  of demented parents, 216
  filial duty of, 221, 227
  See also Elderly

Aged. *See* Elderly
Agencies, social. *See* Social agencies
Al-Anon, 106, 287
Alateen, 287
Alatot, 287
Alcoholics, 120, 124, 257
Alcoholics Anonymous (AA), 106, 287
Alzheimer's disease, 216, 236
Alzheimer's Disease and Related Disorders Association, 249
Anger, 19, 107, 108, 221–2, 295
  in addicts, 264
  in adolescents, 155
  in children, 208, 209
  control of, 136, 137, 138
  in parents, 191–2, 206
  and physical aggression, 134
Anxiety, 6, 13, 43, 228–9, 233, 334
Assertiveness, 23–24, 28, 38–39, 122
Automatic thoughts, 13–15, 20, 32–34, 167, 238, 248
Autonomic arousal, 132, 133

Beck Depression Inventory (BDI), 132, 225, 298
Bedwetting, 102
Behavioral experiments, 33–34, 36, 176.
  See also Cognitive-behavioral therapy
A Better Safe than Sorry Book (Gordon & Gordon), 331
Bibliotherapy, 35, 37, 101, 308, 347
Biological parents. *See* Parents, biological
"Blaming the victim," 90
Brainstorming, 141, 178, 264, 345. *See also* Problem solving
"Broken record" technique (Smith), 275

"Catastrophizing," 32, 71, 103

Child abuse, 43, 87–117, 138, 146, 190, 234
  assessment of, 94–107
  behavior modification for, 102
  case studies of, 103–4
  conditions for, 95, 97–98
  defined, 87–88
  and home visits, 111
  legal aspects of, 108–9, 110
  as multiply determined, 90
  and parental misattributions, 95–98
  relaxation techniques and, 102
  reporting of, 110
  and spouse abuse, 135
  therapy for, 109–112
Child Behavior Checklist, 195
Children, 42, 59, 79–80
  adult. *See* Adult children
  and boundaries, 54–55, 57–58
  "burnt," 196
  cognitive systems of, 93
  contracts with, 40–41
  "difficult," 90, 108
  feedback with, 53
  impulsive, 36
  inborn temperaments of, 193–4
  obedience of, 71–72
  permissive attitudes toward, 189–90
  problem behavior of, 26, 39. *See also* Conduct disorder children
  and problem solving, 104–5
  punishment of, 41, 42. *See also* Child abuse
  relations with parents, 35, 137–8
  retaliatory behavior by, 91
  role in family, 24
  socialization of, 55
  in systems-oriented therapy, 75
  See also Adolescents; Infants; Stepchildren
Children's Personality Questionnaire, 196
Chronic illness, 218–19, 243
Cocaine, use of, 256, 262, 272
Cocaine Anonymous, 287
Cognitions, dysfunctional, 172–5. *See also* Perceptions, distortions in
Cognitive-behavioral therapy, 5, 11–12, 29–41, 361–6
  with addictive families, 266–81
  and belief modification, 34–36
  and child abuse, 88–94. *See also* Child abuse
  and conduct disorder children, 183–211
  for counseling schizophrenics, 232
  for crisis situations, 43
  defined, 65–66
  and emotions, 43–44
  and gerontology, 215
  interventions using, 36–38, 90–93, 98–107, 134–5, 207–10, 233–5, 238–9, 241–3, 300–3, 317–23
  with remarried families, 170–9
  and sex therapy, 325–36
  techniques in, 68–74
  theories of, 8–10
Cognitive mediation model:
  for dyads, 15 (chart), 15–16
  for families, 16–43
  for individuals, 10–15
Cognitive restructuring procedures, 30–32
Communication skills, 38–9, 41, 61, 71, 104
  for families, 140, 141–2, 177, 272–3, 310
  in sex therapy, 341
Communications therapy. *See* Interactional family therapy
Comprehensive Assessment and Referral Evaluation (CARE), 225
Comprehensive Drinker Profile (CDP), 258
Conduct disorder children, 183–214
  assessment of, 194–8
  attitudes toward therapy of, 210–11
  behavioral interventions with, 185–6, 202–3
  cognitive deficits of, 208
  cognitive intervention with, 207
  and frustration tolerance, 187–8, 193
  individual therapy for, 184, 199, 219–11
  parents of, 186–93, 205–6
  school problems of, 188, 195–6
Conflict Tactics Scale (CTS), 129–31, 134
Conjoint family therapy, 31–34, 136, 174–5, 179–80, 200, 310
Contracts:
  behavior exchange, 40
  marital, 10
Cotherapy, 135, 180
Counterintuitive interventions, 63–65, 73

Dating, abusive behavior and, 126
Death, 236
  of child, 294
  of parent, 156
  of spouse, 245
Depression, 8, 10, 13, 19, 34, 43, 108,
    124, 125, 127, 132
  in adult children, 238
  assessment of, 298–305
  causal factors in, 292–3
  in children, 190
  and the "cognitive triad," 293
  as concealing problems, 309
  in elderly, 225, 229, 244
  and families, 304, 314, 324
  individual treatment for, 306–7
  self-esteem and, 308
  stress and, 293
Diaries, *See* Log keeping
Divorce, 35, 151, 190
Double Column Technique, for anger, 139
Drug abuse. *See* Substance abuse
Dyadic Adjustment Scale, 6
Dysfunctional Thought Record (DTR),
    225, 244

Elderly:
  assessment of, 223–30
  behavior dysfunction of, 218–22
  brief interventions for, 231
  cognitive deficits of, 217
  families of, 216, 219–20
  housing options for, 222
  services for, 236
  social problems of, 245–6
  socialization of, 245
  therapist's role with, 240–1
  use of language by, 243
Enmeshment, vs. disengagement, 57–58

Families:
  abusive, 90. *See also* Child abuse;
    Spouse abuse
  of addicts. *See* Addictive families
  assessment of, 17–19, 20–21, 26–29
  beliefs of, 17–19
  blaming in, 99–100
  brainstorming in, 35, 37, 41
  coalitions in, 58
  criticism in, 22

decision making by, 235–8
  desensitization techniques for, 104, 105
  of elderly, 215–253
  expectancies in, 18–19
  functional analysis of, 165–6
  intimacy-building exercises for, 178, 179
  organization of, 55–56
  rules in, 61–62, 364
  stress in, 24
  structural modification and, 60
  systems approach to, 60, 80. *See also*
    Systems-oriented therapy
  "trivial" events in, 6
Families Anonymous, 287
*Families: Applications of Social Learning
    Theory to Family Life* (Patterson), 101
Family, nuclear. *See* Nuclear family
Family therapy. *See* Psychotherapy *and
    specific therapies*
Fathers, 55
Feedback loops, 13, 15, 16
Feedback techniques, 39–40, 53–54, 69,
    98, 142, 177, 240, 273
"Fogging" technique (Smith), 276
Functional analysis, 168
Functional family therapy, 8, 11–12

Geropsychologists, 224
Girl Scouts, 107
Grandparents, 153
  of disturbed children, 197
  and remarried families, 162
  See also Elderly
Group therapy, 106, 135–6, 137, 254

Hamilton Rating Scale for Depression, 298
High School Personality Questionnaire, 196
Homeostasis, in families, 64, 67, 79, 81,
    255
"Homework," in family therapies, 106,
    276, 303, 312
Homicide, 146
Hopelessness scale, 225

Incest, 331
Infants, 89–90, 95
Insight, role of, 77
Intellect, effect on treatment of, 41
Interactional family therapy, 60–61,
    62–65, 70, 72, 75

Jealousy, 75, 120, 156
Joining with couples, for sex therapy, 344–5
Joining with families:
  of addicts, 281–3
  in child abuse cases, 107–10
  of depressives, 319–20
  of disturbed children, 198
  of the elderly, 243–50
  in physical aggression cases, 142–4
  of the remarried, 179–81

"Life-event web," 220
Life Experiences Survey (LES), 133
Locke-Wallace Marital Adjustment Scale (MAT), 133, 134, 342
Log keeping, 27, 134, 312, 341
Louisville Behavior Checklist, 195

Marijuana, use of, 260, 269
Marital Communication Inventory, 133
Mass media, and child rearing, 189
Masturbation, 334
Medicare and Medicaid, 250
Metarules, in families, 62–64, 76
Millon Adolescent Personality Inventory, 196
Modeling of behavior, for patient, 37, 39–40, 135, 137
Mothers, 55
MRI, 63–64, 226
Multidimensional Functional Assessment Questionnaire, 225
Multifamily therapy, 283

Naranon, 287
Narcotics Anonymous, 287
National Institute on Alcohol Abuse and Alcoholism, 254
Negative and positive feelings, expression of, 38, 39, 40, 53, 75, 98
Negotiation skill training, 177–8, 344. See also Problem solving
Nocturnal Penile Tumescence (NPT), 339
Nonverbal communication, 274
Nuclear family, 152, 153, 157, 163, 181
Nursing homes, 220, 221, 223, 238

Objectification exercises, 100
Observation procedures, behavioral, 169

Older American Resources and Services (OARS), 225
Overreacting, 71

Parent effectiveness training, 101–2
Parents Anonymous, 106
Parents are Teachers (Becker), 101
Parents:
  abusive, 89. See also Child abuse
  biological, 152, 158, 168, 172, 177
  cognitive intervention with, 204
  death of, 156
  dysfunctional emotions of, 190–2
  expectations of, 95
  frustration tolerance of, 207
  influence of upbringing on, 189
  skill training for, 177, 178, 185
  See also Child abuse; Children; Stepparents
Parents of Learning Disabled Children, 106
Parents Without Partners, 106
Perception, distortions in, 8, 10, 13–15, 16, 21, 30, 93, 107, 140, 301–3, 311–13
Personality Inventory for Children, 195
Personality Research Form, 132
Philadelphia Child Guidance Center, 57
Physical aggression, 21, 22, 90, 91, 137
  behavioral techniques for, 139–40
  cognitive restructuring for, 136, 140
  cotherapy for, 135
  individual therapy for, 144
  legal aspects of, 144–5
  relaxation techniques and, 102, 104, 138, 139
  and self-esteem, 134, 142
  victims of, 143–4
  See also Child abuse; Conduct disorder children; Spouse abuse
Pleasant Events and Unpleasant Events Schedules (Lewinsohn), 228
Positive Feelings Questionnaire (PFQ), 133
Primary Communication Inventory, 133
Problem solving, 25, 28, 38–40, 71, 104, 128, 140
  for addictive families, 265, 279–81
  for children, 197, 209–10
  for the elderly, 229, 234, 235
  for remarried families, 161, 177–8
  in sex therapy, 343–4
Psychodynamic therapies, 9–10, 11–12

Psychosis, 232, 299
Psychotherapies, compared, 11–12 (table)
Psychotherapy, 26, 28, 30
  with children, 199–202
  goals of, 58–59
  for modification of beliefs, 34–36
  and psychoanalysis, 231
  for remarried families, 163–9
  role-playing in, 59. *See also* Modeling of
    behavior
  See also Cognitive-behavioral therapy;
    Conjoint family therapy; Cotherapy;
    Systems-oriented therapy

Rape, 301, 331
Rational-emotive therapy (RET), 7–8, 326,
  340–1, 353, 357
Relabeling, of traits, 9, 135, 139
Relationship Belief Inventory (RBI), 20,
  341, 342
Relationship Enchancement program
  (Guerney), 38, 177, 273, 275
Remarried families, 151–182
  assessment of, 162–70
  beliefs of, 173–4
  bonding in, 153
  communication training for, 177
  dysfunctional attributions in, 159–60
  false beliefs in, 159
  finances and, 156
  forced blending in, 178
  interviewing of, 164 (chart), 164–9
  loyalty conflicts in, 153–4
  statistics on, 151
  stressful issues in, 152–6, 167–8
  time management in, 168, 178
"Report" and "command" concepts, 76
Resistance, approaches to, 79–80
Retirement, 218, 222, 228, 229, 236
Role-playing, 59, 275, 303–4
Rosenberg Self-esteem Scale, 134

Scale for Suicide Ideation, 299
Self-esteem, 6, 19, 122, 134, 308
Self-Evaluation of Life Function Scale
  (SELF), 225
Self-help groups, 249
Sensate Focus, 348, 349
Sex education, 328–9
Sex History Form (SHF), 337–8
Sex therapy, 338–42

A-B-C model for, 355–6
  history of, 325–6
Sexual Attitude Reassessment (SAR), 350
Sexual dysfunction, 35
  assessment of, 336–44
  clinical strategies for, 345–9
  extramarital relations and, 349
  in marriage, 341–2, 346–7, 350–6
  multiaxial system for, 337
  in older adults, 247–8
  treatment of, 325–60
  varieties of, 336–7
Sexual experience loop, 333 (chart)
Sexuality:
  in advertising, 333
  alcohol and, 340
  assertiveness and, 343
  and childhood conditioning, 328
  cognitive nature of, 327
  gender differences in, 333–5
  as secret, 329–31
Single-parent families, 18
Social agencies, 108, 109, 110, 199
Socratic approach, 30, 32, 99–100, 172,
  270, 308, 309
S-O-R model, 66–67
Spouse abuse, 43, 108, 118–50
  and alcohol use, 120, 124
  assessment of, 129–34
  defined, 118–19
  family response to, 123–4, 321–2
  jealousy and, 120
  predictors of, 120, 121–9
  and self-esteem, 122, 134
  statistics on, 119, 126, 130
  and stress, 123, 125, 128
Spouse-Specific Assertiveness Inventory
  (SSAI), 132
Spouses, 5
  aggression by, 6–7
  communication between, 21–23
  dysfunctional emotions in, 7–8
  parental background of, 10
  traits of, 6, 8–9, 19
  See also Parents; Sexual dysfunction;
    Spouse abuse; Stepparents
Stepchildren, 152, 167, 168, 171, 176,
  178
Stepfamilies, 34. *See* Remarried families
Stepfamily Association of America, 181
Stepfathers, 152–3, 164, 166, 168

Stepgrandparents, 153
Stepparents, 152, 168, 305
   differing styles of, 155
   faulty attributions of, 175–6
   inexperience of, 177
   perfectionism of, 158
   role of, 181
Strategic family therapy, 9
Stress inoculation procedures, 108–9
Stress management, 105–6
Structural family therapy, 9, 11–12,
   56–60
Subjective Units of Disturbance Scale
   (SUDS), 353
Substance abuse, 43, 234, 299, 300, 301,
   313. *See also* Addictive families;
   Addicts; *specific substances*
Suicide, 43, 293–4, 296, 299, 306, 307
   ideation regarding, 299, 310, 316
   in physical aggression cases, 146
Suicidal individuals:
   and families, 315–16
   and family triangles, 317
   hospitalization for, 316
   and individual therapy, 318
   and parents, 321
Support systems, 93, 106, 145, 181, 236
Systemic models, of family therapy, 56–65

Systems-oriented therapy, 27, 50–51, 64,
   67–69, 183, 184
   and cognitive-behavioral therapy, 49–83,
   223
   defined, 50–51, 64
   and dyadic analysis, 52
   and feedback, 53–54, 75
   goals of, 52–53
   and insight, 78
   for marital dysfunction, 315
   for older adults, 223
   and social learning, 69

Transactional analysis (TA), 255

University Marital Therapy Clinic (Stony
   Brook), 134
Utopian syndrome, 71

Vaginismus, 326, 337
Verbal Problems Checklist, 133
Videotaping, 33, 37, 169

Walker Behavior Checklist, 195
Wiltwyck School for Boys, 57

You and Your Aging Parent (Silverstone &
   Hyman), 243